THE CAELI

(PRONOUNCED: KAI-LEE)

THE ODYSSEY OF MELAMURI: BOOK ONE

BY BRUCE MULLER & ABRAHAM SHERMAN

TO LEITHIAN

ACKNOWLEDGMENTS

I want to thank so many people who have helped me fulfill this dream. My sweet wife, Teresa, the love of my life, for standing with me and encouraging me all these years. Marija Dial, for taking the time to listen to this story when it was still being formed. Lana Porcello, for helping me with my first edit. Jill Ross, for helping me see the priority of a happy ending. And last but mostly not least, Abraham Sherman, for being my fellow dreamer of "worlds within worlds."

ENDORSEMENTS

"The Caeli" was an amazing adventure that sucked me into the world between its pages. I felt like I was there, inside the book, like I knew the characters! I could feel their emotions and saw what they saw. I recommend this book to anyone who loves a thrilling adventure!

— Jamin (eleven years old)

A spellbinding book with all the ingredients of a great read, "The Caeli" will satisfy even the most discerning reader. Mystery, intrigue, unexpected twists and turns, great character development, and an epic battle between good and evil are all included. I couldn't put "The Caeli" down until I was finished, and then it left me longing for more, as I am sure it will any reader.

— Ruth Marie Hamill
Author of *Kasozi* and *The Christmas Doll*

Bruce Muller and Abraham Sherman have created a very detailed world-view, an interesting mix of true historical events, actual geographical locations, and wild, mysterious, other-worldly powers. All of this is strung into a classic tale of good and evil in conflict. Actually, this is a portrayal of crucial, ultimate, high-level good in contrast to opposing, ultimate powers of evil. As each intriguing new character enters the narrative, the reader is drawn to learn more about what the back story is behind each individual and wonder how he or she is going to fit into this story.

— Dan Lemaire
Author of *Deep T* and *The Second Arrival*

FOREWORD

To those who love to take long journeys to new lands.
Dreams begin when we let our minds wander.
This story has been a dream of mine since I was a youth.

Some call it Atlantis, some Avalon.
Alas, many just dismiss it as an old seafarer's yarn.
But in every tale, there is a truth, a mystery in every myth
And treasures that beckon to the heart of any
Who would come and search them out.

(Translated from the Mysad fragment 1061)

TABLE OF CONTENTS

Prologue 15

Chapter 1. A New Life 19

Chapter 2. Fitting In 33

Chapter 3. Strange Dreams 45

Chapter 4. Lessons in Learning 57

Chapter 5. Wonders in the Night 63

Chapter 6. A Long Story 71

Chapter 7. Growing Pains 79

Chapter 8. Good Words 87

Chapter 9. Redemption 97

Chapter 10. Red Faces and Apologies 103

Chapter 11. A Great Mishap 107

Chapter 12. The Mysenri 115

Chapter 13. Happy Birthday? 119

Chapter 14. The Journey Begins 131

Chapter 15. Mountain Jewel 141

Chapter 16. Vulgladius 149

Chapter 17. The Strangers 159

Chapter 18. A.R.A. *Patagonia* 171

Chapter 19. The Lost Lagoon 185

Chapter 20. The *Musashi* 201

Chapter 21. In the Mountains of Gatún 217

Chapter 22. Two Monks 237

Chapter 23. The *New Day* 253

Chapter 24. Compendium 273

Chapter 25. Fei Yu 279

Chapter 26. The Essence 297

Chapter 27. The Glowing Dark 309

Chapter 28. The Caeli 313

Chapter 29. The Abico Vault 325

Chapter 30. Back Woods 341

Chapter 31. Brumble Berry Serendipity 351

Chapter 32. Western Bound 359

Chapter 33. The Honoo Katana 373

Chapter 34. Sobrante's Point 387

Chapter 35. The Journey Home 403

Epilogue 419

Cast of Characters 422

Glossary 423

The Piaculum 425

About the Authors 428

PROLOGUE

The crimson sky burned! The townsfolk ran, shielding their heads from the fire-fall, calling their children to them as they sought shelter. Some of the islanders chose the protection of underground chambers. Others fled to the shore and their boats, stumbling as they traversed the quaking island.

"Hurry!" the master shouted. He stuffed a scroll into a leather knapsack already brimming with what could not be left behind.

"The tempest is upon us! We must get to the boat!" A mighty, blistering gust of wind blew open the front door, spewing in dust and smoke. The master turned to his rotund, balding servant. "It's too late to save the rest of the gear; we must make haste."

With one deafening roar of "*everyone out!*" the servant relayed the order to the household.

The others, who were dashing through the house gathering books and scrolls, stopped their frenzied search, swung their bags over their shoulders, and headed for the door.

"I'll be right there," the master said without looking back as he dashed into an inner chamber of the house.

He returned to his library, his sanctuary for the last seventy-five years. He staggered over the shaking, heaving floor and darted through the arched entry into the Caeli. After bounding down the spiral stairs two at a time, he stopped before the door he had hoped he would never have to open again.

He placed his hand on the cold, gnarled surface and whispered a tune. The door swung open, and he rushed across the dimly lit room to one of the many round vaults on the opposite wall. His lips moved silently. He stepped aside as the tiny stone portal burst open with a loud bang. He reached inside and took two bulging leather pouches. They clinked heavily on his belt as he ran to rejoin the others. Together they raced toward the harbor, stealing quick glimpses at the island's smoldering mountain.

At the harbor, they crowded onto a thirty-meter, single-masted sailboat. One of the younger men stopped at the pier's edge and began untying the boat's moorings. Just then, several taut-faced men, wearing dark oilskins, came stomping down the pier. "How dare you leave?" they shouted as they approached. "You are in rebellion against the authority of this land!"

The young man untied the final mooring and leaped aboard as the boat drifted away, mere seconds before the angry men reached the pier's end.

"It is too late, my friends!" the master said. "There is no authority in this land any longer. I warned you, and now you will live with the consequences of your actions. Farewell." The wind caught the sail, and they sped out of the harbor.

The men on the dock shouted, the earth's roar muting them.

Fire and burning hail pummeled the island. The master and his household huddled together on the stern of the boat, wordlessly watching the passing of their land. Hot tears rolled down the master's cheeks as he gazed at the magnificent black cliffs fading in the distance.

Then with a mighty jolt that shook the sky, the mountain at the center of the island exploded. As the basalt fractured from the caldera to far beneath sea level, a scalding flash of heat and light burst forth, sending them sprawling to the deck. Jets of lava spewed from the now shattered mountain, arching far out to sea. "To the hold!" the master shouted as the eruption's roar diminished. "The dragon is slain, but her fiery breath still comes!" The first smoking, molten clumps splashed violently into the sea around them.

All but the youngest aboard rushed down into the cabin. The four-year-old boy remained on deck, frozen in wonder.

"Mel!" the master shouted. "Run!" But Mel stood spellbound as a steaming impact wave of seawater surged towards them.

A young man of sixteen years old, last down the steps, stopped, knowing that only he was close enough to help the boy. His attention snapped from Mel to the sky as a huge mass of lava arched toward them. He screamed, turned away from the boy, and scrambled down the steps into the cabin just before a wave of steaming water and a splatter of lava engulfed their boat.

* * *

The rain of lava subsided. The sea calmed. The horizon was devoid of man and boat. A moment passed, and then a craft bobbed to the surface, its sail again catching the wind as though nothing unusual had happened. The sail's fabric was embossed with a scarlet sword, flame protruding from the blade's edges. The hatch flew open, and the panicked master rushed out and grabbed the limp form of the young boy who lay pressed against the railing of the deck.

CHAPTER 1

A NEW LIFE

He awoke face down, the grit of sand between his teeth. His head ached with a deep, guttural rhythm.

"Ow!" he moaned, cupping his brow in his hands. He felt his matted strawberry-blond hair. It was caked with blood, a bandage around a lump on the back of his head.

"What happened?" he groaned, examining his surroundings. He was lying on a rough wool blanket. A folded brown coat with a red stain in its center had served as his pillow before his face had turned to the sand. On either side of him, rock walls rose and formed a cave.

How did I get here? he wondered, his memories elusive.

From his resting place, several shapes of footprints in the sand led out of sight around the corner of the cave mouth. It was impossible to tell how many other people had made the footprints. Several large, wooden, metal-ribbed chests with brass locks appeared to have been dragged into the shelter of the cave. Some were open, their contents jumbled.

He saw the source of his rhythmic migraine crashing against rocks at the cave's mouth. A small sailboat floated in a crystal blue bay just beyond. The footprints closest to the water smoothed gradually with each ocean wave.

He looked at his hands and shirt sleeves, finding them to be those of an eight-year-old. *Who am I?* As he sat up, fresh waves of pain surged in his head. Each heartbeat made his eyes throb.

Wincing, he slowly rose. The sand felt like liquid, rocking back and forth. He balanced himself against a nearby chest and, step by step, made his way to the mouth of the cave. His legs were stiff, as though they had not been used for several days.

The early evening sun hung brightly above the ocean horizon. He squeezed his eyes shut, shading them with his hands. He peered down the beach, hoping for a clue that would help everything make sense.

The broad stretch of sand was rimmed on the inland side by cliffs that rose steeply for several hundred meters. Down the beach, three men huddled around a wooden chest.

Stepping back into the shadow of his sanctuary, he waited, watching. He remembered the blanket and jacket that someone had prepared as his bed. He touched the bandage on his head.

After a moment, he cupped his hands to his mouth. "Hello!" It hurt to shout. When they did not respond, he stepped out from the shadows and shouted louder, waving his hand, "Hello there!"

A tall, broad-shouldered man in the center turned and waved back. "Perfect. You're just in time!" The three of them approached, the tall man resting a hand on his shoulder. "Mel, I'm so glad you're awake. We were getting worried."

The man had neatly groomed grey hair and a short, cropped, silver beard. He wore pressed black trousers and a matching vest with a gold chain dangling from his waist. *Strange clothing for the beach,* Mel thought. His shoes were off, his trousers neatly folded to his knees, and his white silk shirt rolled to his elbows.

Mel squinted as he fought waves of headache. "What happened? Was... was that my name you just said?"

A pudgy, bald man in a bright red and yellow shirt looked at the tall man and raised an eyebrow. Turning to Mel, he said in a thick Scottish brogue, "Come on, Mel, and be serious, boy. You're Mele—" Coughing, he finished, "Melvin Uri."

"I... I am? And who are you?" Mel looked at each of them.

The brow of the rotund Scotsman furrowed deeply with worry as he drew nearer to Mel to examine the boy's wound more closely. "Oh my! The boat's boom must've hit you harder than we thought," the pudgy man said. "I am Oscar Bottoms. This is your father, Telly," he explained, indicating the well-dressed gentleman. Oscar turned towards the young man who was standing in the shadow of Telly. "And here we have Jora Blacksworth, a friend of the family. We've been your shipmates for the past season and have landed here on this northern coast in search of a new life."

"What happened to our old life?" Mel asked, gently touching the back of his scalp.

Oscar again looked to Telly and raised an eyebrow.

"All in good time, son," Telly said as he clasped Mel's shoulder with a loving squeeze. "Tell me, how do you feel?"

Mel looked at the tall man and felt his gaze looking deep into his eyes. Mel shied away from his probing stare. "Like someone hit me over the head with a rock. Why is everything so confusing? Why can't I remember what happened?"

"Could be the result of a concussion, Mel," Oscar chimed in, further examining his head. "I *am* still a doctor, even with most of my instruments left a month's sail away and likely turned to slag. It was a rather unique storm, I would say, that swamped us that day!"

In a flicker of memory, Mel had a sensation of gagging on hot salty water. He shook his head briefly. "Have I been out for a month, Dr. Bottoms?" Mel asked as Oscar pulled back the bandage and looked at Mel's sore scalp.

"No, no, no. This was from standard rough seas three days hence. They say if you don't keep your eye on the boom..." Oscar replaced the bandage. "Now, years ago, that day was somethin'." He stepped back, gesticulating grandly. "The waves were like mountains, and the sky was a thunderin' and a rainin' lava." He spoke rapidly. "It was like we were in the belly of hell itself. We were fortunate to come out with our lives! Why..." Oscar noticed a silencing glare directed at him by Telly. "Well, let's just say you haven't had much luck on boats for the past four years."

Telly turned to Mel and said with a soft, concerned tone, "It's so good that you're all right. We have much to talk about. There are many things to set in order." Telly began counting with his fingers. "We need to get settled. You'll be starting school. There are so many things we need to teach you at home as well. And..." Telly stopped, calmed himself, and took a deep breath. He smiled as though amused by his own anxiety and excitement.

He pointed to the young man with stringy, black hair who was now walking slowly back toward the wooden chest on the beach. "Jora is helping with your tutoring."

Telly cleared his throat, straightened his vest, took out his pocket watch, and checked the time. He closed it with a tight snap. "We must begin right away. I'll leave before dark and find us a place to live. Oscar, why don't you rummage through the trunks and see if you can find something for a freshly cooked meal. Jora..." Telly called gently, but Jora was now further down the beach, etching runes in the sand with a stick. "Jora!" Telly called out. "Why don't you and Mel go look for some firewood? You can help him catch up on some of our adventures?"

Jora continued scribbling in the sand, a crooked grin on his face. "Of course, Master Uri, I'd be happy to help. When do you expect to be back from town?" He dropped his etching stick and walked back toward them.

"By this time tomorrow. Thank you, Jora."

"Master Uri?" Mel questioned his father. "Why did he call you Master? Do we own Jora?"

"No, no, Mel," Oscar said, his puffy cheeks shaking, "it's a term of respect. Jora and I know and honor your father as our elder. It has nothing to do with ownership." He nodded towards Jora, pausing briefly. "Does it, Jora? We are all free men here!"

Jora raised his chin. He pulled a long strand of oily hair away from his eyes and, in a sing-song voice, said, "Free men; 'eye that's what we are." He stepped towards Mel. "Come on, Mel, let's take a walk. I think I saw a pile of driftwood just around the next cliff."

Jora led the way, stepping quickly, his gaze fixed forward.

Mel followed, forced to walk faster than he wished. He looked back down the beach, straining to refresh his memories. Tilting his head to the left curiously, he saw Telly and Oscar easily carrying the huge wooden chest, which had left a deep imprint in the sand.

* * *

When they had stepped around a cliff and were out of sight of the two older men, Jora stopped and glared at Mel. "Can you hurry up?" he barked. "We need to get some firewood, and you're dragging your feet!"

Mel stopped suddenly, surprised. "It's just that I'm... I'm sorry, but I just woke up, and I hurt all over."

"Now, isn't that a shame," Jora chided. "Asleep for days, and now you're just *too* tired to work." He started walking toward a large pile of wood further down the beach.

Mel was not sure if Jora was kidding or if he meant to be hurtful. He decided to walk at arm's length while getting newly reacquainted with this friend of the family.

"How long have I known you, Jora?" Mel asked.

"Your whole life. I was a Vysard apprentice. How long ago was that? Hmmm... about six years now. But then again, you can't remember anything, so what *difference* does it make?"

Mel saw that this young man was almost a foot and a half taller than him and had a strong build. His dark eyes matched his greasy, black hair. He often shook his head in the wind to clear the hair from his face. A twitch in his right shoulder periodically jerked. Mel could sense anger in Jora. He wondered if it was just a dark mood or something more permanent. He was eager to learn what was bothering Jora in the hopes of finding a way to help him. Perhaps he was just exhausted from the long sea journey.

Looking ahead, Mel spied a pile of driftwood at the mouth of a deep cave. "Look, Jora, there's a cave!"

Jora shook his head dismissively and continued trudging through the thick sand towards the driftwood further up the beach.

"Hey, come on, Jora, this pile is closer, and maybe we could explore the cave before we go back." Mel reluctantly increased his pace to a run. He caught up with Jora as they passed the cave mouth. They both stopped and peered into the gaping cold blackness of the cave's open jaws. "What do you think?"

"No!" Jora bit out. "I'm supposed to keep you safe and gather wood. I'm tired of catching the whip for your childish pranks."

Mel looked sideways at him. "Does my... my father whip you?"

"It's just a figure of speech, thumb-sucker."

Mel resisted the urge to settle on his first impression. "Just for a minute. Maybe there's a treasure in there." Something felt familiar. Had he tried to cheer up Jora before?

Jora backed away. "No! No! *No!* I will *not* go with you or lead you there! I detest this stupid assignment, tutoring a whiny little boy. Going everywhere he wants, doing everything he needs. I've paid back what I did and have been punished enough. We will do just as your father said, and nothing more! Is that understood?" He was yelling, pointing his finger at the visibly shaken boy.

"I just thought it might be fun," Mel said apologetically.

"Fun is something we can't afford to have, Mel," Jora said, trying to sound like an adult. "I'm your tutor, and we'll have to work hard and learn how to live among them," he said, gesturing toward the tops of the cliffs.

"What do you mean by 'tutor'?" Mel asked, interrupting Jora's thoughts. "What do you teach me?"

Jora shook his head and spoke to himself sarcastically, "Oh yes! Priority one; answer all his questions." Turning to Mel, he continued, "I have been your tutor since you could talk. I was assigned to train you in all aspects of life. Even simple chores like this are lessons. Even things as stupid as getting firewood," Jora said with a sigh. "We don't have time to get sidetracked. Your father is going to be waiting for us, and I want you to give a good report about this little field trip."

"You said you were an apprentice," Mel noted. "Did you graduate, and now you teach?"

Jora picked a flat stone from the sand and began to turn it on his palm. He chuckled sarcastically. "I was only ever an apprentice. They called me a protégée, *'das wunderkind!'* What a joke!" Jora squeezed the flat stone tightly in his fist and closed his eyes. "Mel, I don't think you'll ever know how close I was to being initiated. I had worked for years. But I got stupid, I guess? That's what they tell me." With a sudden throw, he sent the stone skipping across the water. He and Mel watched as it bounced one...... two..... three.... four... five... six, and then sank. "Speaking of lessons in simple things, it happened kind of like that. One day I was flying along and then plunk into the dark." He turned to Mel and, in his best impression of a teacher's voice, asked, "Now, can you describe what is happening to the stone?"

Mel thought it was a strange question. "Nothing much. It's just sitting on the ocean floor."

Jora said bitterly, "And it'll never *go* anywhere again."

Mel nodded in understanding.

Jora saw a family of porpoises frolicking in the surf near a distant reef. His crooked smile returned to his face. "Let's pretend you're one of those porpoises. That little one on the left there. Your father is teaching you how to catch your food, dance in the waves, and deal with sharks." As he said this, he quickly grabbed Mel around the shoulders and threw him to the sand.

Mel fell with a thud. "Ow! What are you doing?"

Jora continued in a darkly dramatic tone. "And suppose one day you're out swimming with your dad, and a great white shark knocks him aside," he said, pounding his fist into his palm. "And then comes straight towards you!" He jabbed a finger at Mel's face.

Mel thought Jora looked like a cat toying with its food. He was not enjoying this lesson. He was bruised, did not like the tone of Jora's voice, and did not appreciate the emotions stirring in him. But he refused to give in to the fear Jora was trying to provoke. He closed his eyes, composed himself, and asked a question back.

"Where's my father?"

"Knocked senseless," Jora sneered.

"And what about my mother?"

"Long gone, you helpless little sea slug," Jora continued. "And you're next. Lunch! Yum-yum. What do you do *now*?" He approached, his mouth imitating the chomping of a shark, a cold look in his eyes.

In this moment, Mel did not trust his tutor. His heart beat rapidly in anticipation of a fight. His muscles tensed, and he jumped to a crouch, taking a defensive posture that he did not remember learning. Jora reached out to tackle him.

Quicker than Jora could anticipate, Mel leaped and grabbed his tunic, wrapping it around his shoulders and pulling him over backward onto the sand. Mel crouched over him, pressing two fingernails into his temple. "I guess my father taught me well enough to fight off the *sharks*," Mel said angrily and released him.

Jora, surprised at the much smaller boy's ability, stood up and backed away from Mel. He brushed sand from his clothes and laughed defensively. "So he did. So he did, little one. I guess we both learned something new about each other today. Come on, let's grab this firewood and head back. I think your father will be pleased with our little reacquainting session."

Mel, still tense, picked up an armload of driftwood and cautiously began to follow a few paces behind his tutor. "Why are you so angry with me?" he asked.

Jora ignored Mel and said in a low voice, "Let's not tell your dad what happened here. He is a man with a weak heart, after all. I'd hate to burden him with anything that might seem upsetting."

As a raindrop slapped Mel on the cheek, he grumbled, "You didn't answer my question, Jora."

Jora, eager to forget the day's lesson, pretended not to hear.

Mel shook his head. He felt as if he were just awakening from a long, dark dream, one which was fragmented and confusing. And his tutor was not helping. *What kind of life will this be?*

* * *

Telly watched Mel and Jora return along the beach and glanced at the sun setting over the gently curved horizon. He finished eating a tube of salami and a hardtack biscuit. As Jora reached the cave, Telly softly spoke so as not to be overheard by Mel. "How is he?"

"Stronger than I expected," Jora smoothly replied.

Telly sighed with relief. "That is good news." Mel approached, and Telly put an arm around his shoulder and squeezed him tightly. "You are recovering quickly and soon should feel no ill effects. What a brave boy!" Turning to both young men with a bittersweet smile, he nodded respectfully. "Farewell until tomorrow." He slung a knapsack across his back and faced the cliff, surveying the vertical climb ahead. "Now to meet our potential neighbors," he said as he set off across the sand, his enthusiasm thinly veiling his weariness.

* * *

Oscar dug through the chests, searching for cooking supplies.

Jora walked in, his arms full of driftwood.

"How was the wood gathering, fellows?" Oscar asked, still engrossed in his task. "Granted, salt-soaked wood is not the best. It'll be a bit smoky, but it will cook the beans tonight."

Jora dumped his wood in a pile. "Mission accomplished, boss," he grumbled. "The little one has had a hard day and couldn't carry much. He's all bruised and broken, you know."

Mel overheard this and sulked in, regarding Jora with suspicion. He stacked his armload of driftwood neatly and organized the scattered pieces that Jora had dumped.

"Now, we don't need to get testy there, Jora. The lad's just awakened, and he's not all with us yet. It's going to come back to him soon enough. He just needs a little more time to heal."

"Maybe less than you think," Jora muttered.

Oscar turned to Mel. "How are you feeling there, laddie? Did you enjoy getting to know your old tutor again?"

"Oh, it was very interesting," Mel replied, trying to mask his growing sense of insecurity about Jora. He sat down in a corner of the cave, curled his arms around his knees, bowed his head, and listened to the sound of the rain that had begun to pour outside.

* * *

Telly scaled two hundred meters of the rain-slicked, sheer rock cliff in the last radiance of the shrouded sun, his excellent night vision guiding him up the final hundred meters in near pitch-blackness without difficulty. Reaching the coast road, which ducked and weaved along the gently sloped tops of the coastal hills, he turned toward the flickering oil lamps of a town a few kilometers in the distance. All he had available for trade were the gems that he had brought from Martinique. He decided to present himself as a gem merchant from the Caribbean.

The rain stopped as he reached town an hour after sunset. He brushed the last raindrops off his clothes and entered a local pub, the Discovery Inn. He stepped into its smoky, dimly lit interior and looked slowly around. Everyone stopped what they were doing and turned towards him, sizing up this new stranger. Straightening his shoulders, Telly fixed his gaze on the man behind the bar. "Good evening, sir. Would you know where I might procure some lodging?"

"Yea, sure," someone behind Telly blurted out, his voice thickly slurred from liquor. "This 'ere's a great place to stay."

Telly cleared his throat and turned to the man. "I appreciate the suggestion, but this isn't exactly what I am looking for. I was wondering if any housing or farms nearby are for sale."

The inebriated man wore a dark hat pulled over his eyes and smoked a stubby cigar. He coughed as he asked, "Well, who might you be? And what brings you to our little part of the world?"

Telly recited what he had rehearsed while climbing the cliff.

"My name is Telly. I am traveling with my son, Melvin, his friend Jora Blacksworth and my lifelong associate Dr. Oscar Bottoms. We are from the isle of Martinique in the Caribbean, though we have not dwelt there since the eruption four years ago. I am a broker of gems, hoping to find a small coastal village where I might live in peace and make a home."

"Well, don't that beat all, a jew-el merchant," a second, greasy-haired man with a few days beard exclaimed, a wad of chaw bulging in his cheek. "That's what we been missin' round these here parts. We got a lot of need for jew-els, don't we now, Clem?" he asked, looking at the bartender. "I heared you can plop them in the ground and harvest some pert' tasty rubies and such like. Maybe we could take some of his em-er-alds and use 'em to replace our hammerheads."

"Gentlemen, I assure you that though the wares of my trade may find little use in this rural setting, there are many people in the city just up the coast who are well aware of their value. And if I remember correctly, gold and jade are mined sixty-five kilometers south of here. I would be surprised if there were not an appraiser of minerals and gems in this town."

The greasy-haired bar guest replied, "Why, don't you just talk like a fancy gentleman from the old country or sump'in'." He began to laugh at his joke but stopped suddenly, bent over, and hacked a loud series of uncontrollable coughs that came from too many years of tobacco use.

The bartender, a bearded man wearing a black suit with a dirty yellow bow tie, walked around the end of the bar, leaning on a cane. "Take it easy, Jed. This man is a guest in my house." Then, resting against the bar, he lit a well-used black pipe. He took a long draw from it, releasing the smoke slowly. Turning to Telly, he held up his hand, saying, "I must apologize for my rude friend Mr. Malingo here. We're quite a friendly town once you get to know us." He held out his hand in a sign of conciliation. "Name's Clement Smith. You can just call me Clem," he said with a wink. "I'd like to welcome you to our little part of the world."

Telly shook his hand.

"You musta come quite a ways to get here," Clem continued. "Did you go through the Straights or round the Cape? Either way takes nearly a lifetime. If you ever even make it! Which is what you musta done 'cause here you are!" He paused a moment to take another deep draw from his pipe. "I came 'cross with my parents in wagons some fifty years ago. And Jed here, I guess he musta growed here. His folk were here when my parents arrived. I've known him as long as I can remember."

"I'ze here 'for God even showed up, Clem," Jed joked, very pleased with himself. He spat toward the corner and missed the spittoon, leaving a brown splatter on the floor.

Telly patiently listened to Clem's introduction and now politely responded, "Mr. Smith, it is my pleasure to make your acquaintance and that of your friends. I have been traveling, as you said, for quite some time, and I am very tired. If you could in any way assist me, I would be most grateful."

Clem took a seat near where Telly stood at the bar. "Well, come to think of it, the old Mason farm near the cliffs has been abandoned for... let's see..." He squinted and scratched his beard. "Yeah, that place has been available for years now."

"Yeah, the place is *haunted*," Jed said loudly. "Nobody's gonna buy it! It used to be called the slaughter—"

"Now, Jed," Clem interrupted, "that used to be a good farm. It don't matter what's happen in the past. It's got a great view too. Why, you can see clear up the coast from that cliff."

Jed, annoyed at being interrupted, grunted some words that no one could make out and slumped in his chair. Then he said so that all would hear, "It ain't a *clean* place!"

Telly listened intently, watching the expressions of these local men as they spoke of the farm. "I'd love to look at it if I could. Do you know who to contact to see about procuring it?"

"Well, that'd be the county clerk's department," Clem replied. "So your name's Telly? Don't think I caught the last name."

"Uri. It's European. My ancestors came from a land not far from England. I would be more than happy if you could point me in the direction of the county clerk's department."

"In the morning, we'll steer you their way, Mr. Uri," Clem said, beginning to stand. "Where will you be staying tonight?"

"Well, upon expert recommendation, I think I'll stay right here, if you have room."

"Room's all we got. I'll get your things, if'n there's more."

"Thank you, but I'm traveling light," Telly answered. "I would be happy to see my room. Do you require payment in advance?"

"If you wouldn't mind, Mr. Uri. We are simple folk here and like to keep everything on a pay-as-you-go basis."

Telly reached into his knapsack and pulled out a small leather bag. He withdrew one large, green gem and placed it on the bar.

The men's eyes widened, gaping at the glistening stone.

"I'll be... looks like you weren't pullin' our legs. Is that *real*?" Jed asked, leaning over and staring at the stone. His mouth dribbled thick brown goop.

"Quite real, my good sir."

The bartender took the stone and held it to the light. "What am I supposed to do with this pretty little thang?"

"I hope you'll receive it in exchange for my lodging until I can trade for some of the local currency," Telly replied. "I assure you that once another of my gems is appraised and purchased, I will have more than enough to compensate you for your hospitality."

"Well, okay," Clem answered hesitantly. "Just for one night. I'll show you to your room." He put the emerald in his vest pocket, picked a key from a box under his desk, and led Telly towards the back of the tavern.

Jed spat out the last of his chaw, this time hitting the side of the spittoon. He took a long gulp from his mug and, with beer dripping down his beard, spoke to the cigar-smoking man sitting across from him. "You ever seen anyone with a jewel like that? He must have lots more of them thangs where that one come from. If'n they was real at'all."

The other man had had too many beers that evening and sat in a stupor before Jed. He managed a belch and mumbled, "Where'd he say he's from?"

CHAPTER 2

FITTING IN

The next day Telly learned that the name of the little coastal town was Cooperton. Located about two hundred kilometers south of San Francisco, it was named after a pioneer who had owned the land while it was under the authority of Mexico.

Although primarily a farming community, Cooperton also supported a lighthouse crucial for the navigation of California's central coast. For twenty years, the lighthouse had warned mariners of the treacherous rocks of the surrounding stretch of coastline, which had become strewn with the remains of ships that had run aground over the course of several centuries before the lighthouse was installed. The more superstitious townsfolk whispered to each other that the lighthouse was haunted by the souls of those who had lost their lives in the many shipwrecks.

The town itself was a provincial outpost of a forgotten era. The abundance of flowers in every yard lined the streets with living rainbows nearly year-round, thanks to the temperate climate of the region, and supported the town's many apiaries. Cooperton's inhabitants were simple folk who kept busy serving one another's needs and exporting grapes, wine, honey, country jams, and gold and jade trinkets to the larger cities far to the north and south.

Telly found a merchant in town who had served as a mineral and jewel broker in San Francisco and had moved to Cooperton to help facilitate the activity of the nearby Los Burros Mining District. Telly exchanged a second, similarly sized emerald for a considerable amount more than bartender Clem and patron Jed had dared to imagine the night before. Telly settled his bill at the Discovery

Inn with enough currency left over to easily purchase the land. He reclaimed the gem he had provided as collateral, bid Clem farewell, and set off across town.

He followed Clem's directions to the local county clerk's office, where it was confirmed that the Mason farm, which lay just outside of town and had a kilometer of Pacific coastline all to itself, was indeed abandoned. All that was required to take ownership of the property was the payment of back taxes, totaling three hundred dollars. It was a sizable amount for the local farmers, who, due to the farm's reputation, had refrained from the investment. Telly made an appointment with the incredulous clerk to meet the local authorities at the property to complete the sale at three o'clock that afternoon.

Telly returned to the camp in the cave and told the others what had happened. Together they stored their belongings, reloaded the chests onto the boat, sailed around several rocky points jutting from the coastal crags, and moored in a large, sheltered bay.

Harbormaster Timothy "Slim" Jamison loaned them a wagon, reluctantly, after learning where it was to deliver their belongings.

Slim spoke to Oscar, who was busy looking at a long list of items. "Mister, I heard some awful strange stories 'bout' the farm ya'll are movin' to. I'd be real careful if you know what I mean."

Oscar stopped looking at his list and, with a wrinkled forehead, replied, "No, I'm afraid I don't know what you mean, Mr. Jamison. What stories would those be?"

His eyes opened wide. Looking around fearfully, he leaned close and whispered, "That 'ol house is haunted, mister. Used to be a strange family living there that never come to town but once a month. And then they'd send *him* in to git supplies."

Oscar stopped him and said with emphasis, "*Him*?"

"Their oldest boy, I guess, and he was an odd one. He rode their old wagon, never speakin' to no one. He'd slap his list on the merc'tile counter and then just stand there starin' at us all as we walked by. His eyes would be a bulging when the women folk were near, like he'd never seen one 'afore. Soon enough, when we heard he's comin' to town, the ladies'd gather their kids and hide out till he left. Then he'd disappear fer another moon."

"Just sounds like folks who wanted to keep to themselves. Some people are like that," Oscar said, trying to relieve his neighbor's concerns.

"No! It ain't like that a'tall!" Slim spoke a little louder. "It all came to a head one day when the widow McPherson was walkin' home. Most people doubled their pace passing there, with the neighbors' word a' noises in the night and peculiar lights. Willomena McPherson was the daughter of a pioneer. She was as brave a woman as ever was and took her time passin' the farm."

Looking up the road as if something dangerous would be coming, Slim went on, "But this one day she noticed that the gate was broken, and several cows were lying dead just beyond the fence. But they was not just dead; they'd been gutted; their inners pieced together to make some evil sign that filled half a' acre.

"Willow told me later that she had to see what could've done such a terrible thang. She had walked no more than a couple hundred feet when she was overwhelmed with that *smell* that only death can bring." Slim scrunched his nose in disgust.

"Well, she covered her mouth with her apron and pressed on. When she came to the house, the door was already opened. She cried out, but no one was listenin', so walking into the house, she saw something that has haunted her and everyone she's told 'bout it. The inside was barely furnished, but everywhere there were animal parts, and who knows what else that had been slain, all cut and stinking. And blood was wiped everywhere in the house. She told me she felt the presence a' somethin' evil and began to leave but felt urged to check if anyone in the house was left alive."

Slim wiped a bead of nervous sweat from his brow with his shirt sleeve, took a breath, and continued. "She found nothin' and no one. Everybody'd disappeared. She looked around but couldn't tell if any part of the mess was human. She finally left and, despite her age, ran quick to town and told the sheriff."

"What happened then?" Oscar asked, intrigued.

"Well, there was a short investigation, but no one could find any clues as to how or why such a grisly mess was left. After a while, folks tried to forget the inhuman actions that had been done. Since that day, only crazy kids dared go back in that house to see what come to be known as the 'Massacre Farm.' Since then, no local person in his right mind has ever considered buyin' that land."

Oscar folded his arms and looked up. "That is a fascinating story, Mr. Jamison, but I'm sure there is a reasonable explanation for it. Perhaps a bear got to the cows and broke into the house, dragging some of its prey."

"'T'aint likely, Mister Doctor," Slim said, shaking his head. "I'm figurin' we'd just a'soon forgit that bit of our history. The town'll be glad to have a willin' stranger livin' on that farm. Maybe, in time, the terrible memory can be erased when the crops come back again and livestock graze once more in its meadows. I'm sure the local 'thorities were more than happy to git back taxes on the property, seeing that they processed that transaction in record time. Usually takes months ta gets some new land."

"Indeed!" Oscar muttered and went back to loading the wagon. Once all their belongings were accounted for, they bid Slim farewell and traveled to their new abode.

When they arrived at the farm, Telly concluded the land purchase with the county officials, who chose to wait outside the farm's entrance. The old farmhouse was off the seaward side of the country road, behind a battered picket fence and a broken gate that hung by one hinge. After years of mischief at the hands of local boys, the fences and house were badly in need of repair. Most of the windows were broken, and the front steps were missing—the result of a bonfire by six young men who had sought to bolster their reputation by spending an entire night at the old, haunted house.

The new owners stepped inside their home, noticing faded brown stains on the walls. Any substantial remnants of that gruesome day had long since returned to dust or been claimed by local carrion feeders.

Telly looked at the battered, filthy house and took a deep breath. "Well, let's get to work."

Oscar was already picking up loose boards and stacking them neatly on the porch.

Mel's heart was saddened at the sight of the dilapidated shell of a once-grand house. Jora, with a smirk on his face, walked quickly through the rooms, jerking open the drawers and closets.

* * *

One week later, Mel and the others sat in the restored kitchen, discussing the rebuilding of the front porch, when a mighty rumbling resounded from the westward sky. They walked outside and beheld a black tempest bearing down on the coast. The warm afternoon had betrayed the violence of the approaching storm. As they looked out to sea, the gentle winds around them increased to gale force, sending them racing inside to shore up the windows.

Rain and howling wind beat mercilessly on everything within a hundred miles. Roofs were stripped from houses. Barns were set ablaze by lightning strikes. Brush fires in the mountains burned out of control.

The next day, after the storm had passed, Telly and Mel walked to town through the acrid haze caused by the distant, lingering fires. They wished to offer their new neighbors help with any cleanup or repairs they required. Still shaken by the storm and coughing from the thin smoke, the fearful townsfolk hustled out of the way of the newcomers who had just moved onto the "Massacre Farm," curtly declining or ignoring their offers of help. Women hurriedly gathered their children and disappeared behind closed and locked doors. Sensing the fear of their owners, dogs barked at Telly and Mel when they approached.

Mel drew closer to his father. "Why are they doing this?"

"People can be very superstitious," Telly answered. "They don't intend harm, there are just many things they don't understand, and their only defense is to be fearful. In time, when they get to know us better, it'll be different."

After the storm, any townsfolk who had been considering visiting their new neighbors at the farm decided against it.

* * *

The days of work on the house passed quickly, and Telly decided it was time to continue Mel's education. This involved instruction at home and at the local school. Mel's attendance fulfilled one aspect of Telly's intention that each member of the household blend into society and contribute his skills in the coastal community.

Telly made an appointment with the mayor and offered to help establish a community business center to pool ideas for how to better market the town's products. He was told that if the town council agreed to the idea, they would contact him. Oscar offered to assist at the local medical clinic, a one-room examination, operation, and recovery center run by a poorly trained doctor. The town physician was grateful for the offer but declined Oscar's help. The reason was not stated outright, but Oscar knew that he had been turned down due to the locals' fear.

Jora's frequent trips to San Francisco on behalf of his household led to a few of the townsfolk accepting his offer to help facilitate trade. The initial trickle of products entrusted to him grew to a steady stream of goods as more crafters and merchants allowed him to sell their wares and return with their orders.

* * *

Mel stepped through the doors of the one-room Cooperton schoolhouse on his first official day as a student. He saw that all grades met in the same classroom, educated on two different levels. The primary grades of kindergarten through fifth grade met in the front of the room, led by Miss April Higgins. The secondary grades of sixth through twelfth were led by Mrs. Bagroot towards the back. Although Mel was only eight years old, he was far advanced in many subjects and was enrolled in the fourth grade. His father told him that he had always been a good student with an exceptional affinity for language, science, and math.

The first quarter had already begun, and as Mel entered the room, all eyes turned toward him, glaring.

"Allow me to introduce a new student to our class," Miss Higgins said with a cheerful tone. "This is Melvin Uri. He has come a long way to be with us. His family is from the island of Martinique. Does anyone know where that is?"

When no one offered an answer, Miss Higgins addressed the upperclassmen seated in the back of the class. "Would any of you care to guess where the island of Martinique is located?"

No one spoke. They stared nervously at their desks. Finally, one girl around Mel's age meekly raised her hand.

"Yes, Marigold. Do you have a guess as to its location?"

"No ma'am, I don't have a guess," she said quietly.

As the room broke into giggles, Miss Higgins spoke louder, "I'm sorry, Mari, I couldn't hear you."

Mari was sitting up straight in her chair, as always, yet was dwarfed by those sitting in front of her. She had deep reddish-brown eyes and a stack of brown curls that seemed to explode from her head. She said, almost shouting, "No ma'am, I don't have a guess where the island is..."

Before she could go on, Miss Higgins flushed red in the face, snapped a ruler on the table, and shouted "Quiet!" to reign in the growing outbursts of laughter from the students.

"Now see here, Miss Thurman, it is quite unlike you to be sarcastic. And for the rest of you..." She glared at them until they were all silent. When things had settled, she turned her fiery gaze on Marigold and said briskly, "Well, what do you have to say?"

Mari bowed her head and spoke again in her meek little voice. "What I was about to say is that I *know* that the island of Martinique is a French island located in the Caribbean between the Americas, and its eastern shore is on the Atlantic Ocean."

The class was silent with awe, and Miss Higgins' jaw fell open. She cleared her throat. "That is exactly right, Miss Thurman; forgive my correction. I should have known better of you." She turned to the rest of the class and said emphatically, "This child is in third grade, and she knows her geography better than all of you. Perhaps you should read your books as carefully as she does."

Mel took a seat, thankful that the pain of his introduction had been lessened by the class's attention to Mari. He wanted more than anything to fit in, to be invisible, to prevent people from looking at him strangely, and to avoid giving them any reason to ask questions he was not willing or able to answer.

Later that day, Mel was working in his math book when Miss Higgins came to a stop beside his desk. "Mel, I know that you are new here, but we are all required to begin at the beginning of our books. Math is a progressive discipline. You can't know what's ahead until you've walked through the steps to get there. I'm afraid you'll have to begin on the first page like the rest of the children."

Mel looked at her, blinking. "I think I've done all these problems before, Miss Higgins. They all seem to come so easily."

Miss Higgins scratched her head and narrowed her eyes. Lowering her voice, she asked, "Well, have you done this work before or not?"

Mel realized that he had nearly revealed his memory loss and quickly responded, "I'm sure I've covered these lessons, Miss Higgins. Can you test me?"

She chuckled good-naturedly. "This is the first time a child has ever asked me to test him, but very well." Then, thinking she could easily humble this young man, she had him turn to a place far back in the book. "You have five minutes to finish this problem."

Mel smiled and began working.

Miss Higgins went about her task of helping each student with his work and exactly five minutes later came back to Mel's desk. "Well, it's time. Let's see how you've done."

Mel held up his finger, concentrating deeply.

Miss Higgins tapped her foot. He finally put down his pencil and handed her the math book. She rolled her eyes, thinking that Mel was trying to bluff his way out of a foolish boast. But when her eyes focused on the page, she saw that he had accomplished each step with exact detail and excellent penmanship. She blinked several times and then spoke softly. "Mr. Uri, you have indeed done these problems before. In all my years of teaching, I have never seen such excellent work by so young of a student. Education must have been excellent in French schools."

Mel smiled and asked, "Did you check the other side?"

* * *

The Uri household joined the Cooperton Baptist Church, where Mel was introduced to more of the local children and overheard them recounting the community legends. Often, the churchgoers and their children would gossip about one another rather than pay attention to the Bible lesson. It was here that he first heard of what had taken place years before at his new home.

As was the church's custom, the children received separate instruction before the family worship service. On one Sunday, Mel was seated, as usual, at the back.

While they waited for the Sunday school teacher to arrive, one of the local boys, Bobby Simcox, who had a reputation for being rowdy, began recounting a story he had told many times before. He ignored the fact that Mel, the new member of the Sunday school class, was now an occupant of the "Massacre Farm" as he began to boast, "Yep, me an' my brother Billy stayed all night once at the ol' farm. We couldn't been there more than an hour when we first heard them sounds."

The other kids' eyes widened. As they huddled together on the narrow wooden bench, one trembling little girl asked, "What sounds, Bobby?"

Beaming from the attention, Bobby stood and began to pace.

His brother Billy moved to the back of the class, glanced shyly over to where Mel was sitting, and turned away in embarrassment.

Bobby continued. "The screams, the howls! The sound a' them dying still echoin'. It pert near caused us to run 'way. But we didn't. We stuck it out all night. And it didn't get no better. As a matter of fact, we think we saw some of them walkin' round, crying out fer justice."

The kids cowered closer. One of them turned and noticed Billy hunched over in the back of the room, trying to be invisible.

"Is that so, Billy? Did it happen like Bobby said?"

Billy's face flushed beet red. He turned toward the wall and mumbled, "If he says so."

"What did you see and hear, Billy?" the youngster asked again.

"I don't like to talk 'bout it. Let's get to studyin' the Bible."

At that moment, the teacher entered and nodded to Billy. "Amen to that. Everyone, please bring out your Bibles."

Bobby's morbid story was the first time Mel heard one of the horrific tales that the locals loved to tell. He went home frightened.

* * *

After noticing Mel's unnerved condition and finding out what had happened, Telly attempted to lift his spirits. "Don't believe those old stories. They're just the chattering of frightened people who are trying to share their fears with others, thinking it will help them feel less afraid or less alone." Telly held onto his son. "Nothing of that sort will ever happen as long as I'm around."

This comforted Mel, though, in the following days, he awoke at times with the fear that his father had disappeared. In such moments, he felt the hot breath of dark spirits stalking him. This immobilized him with fear. His father was nowhere near, and it was up to Mel to face these demons. He could almost smell the bloodlust in his foes. He would hide under his covers and try to think of beautiful things to take away his fear. He thought of birds singing and the moon setting on the ocean. But then the fear would rise within him again. He would get up and run frantically through the house, looking into all the rooms. Having left the shelter of his bed, he became exposed to the spirit world, and the demons began to swoop on him. The faster he ran, the closer they came. But for some reason, none of them was ever able to sink its fangs into him. It was like they were toying with him, as a cat toys with a mouse.

Finally, he would wake enough to realize where he was. Then he would find his father's room. He would lay panting on the floor at the foot of his bed, huddling under whatever covers had fallen to the floor. He wondered how he always awoke the next morning tucked in his bed. Ultimately, peace came when he remembered his father's comforting words.

CHAPTER 3

STRANGE DREAMS

One day, Mel watched as Jora milled fresh, locally logged redwood that had been delivered by wagon. As Jora operated the bandsaw, Mel noticed that it was like the ones at the mill in town except for its power source. The Cooperton mill ran on steam-driven belts fueled by wood. The blades of the Uri mill ran much faster and with little noise, except when wood was being cut. Mel could find no steam generator, and in the place where exhaust smoke usually vented, there was only steam.

"What does this run on?" Mel asked incredulously.

"Don't we want to know everything?" Jora replied snidely. "Just know that it works and keep your mouth shut. If you see someone coming up the path, give a yell, and we'll turn on the simulators that make it look like the ones in town." Jora went back to work, visibly intending to ignore any further questions.

* * *

Mel watched from atop the cliffs as his father walked on the beach below, toying with a strange-looking surveyor's scope. The distance obscured many details, but it appeared that his father was examining the cliff as if planning to build something. After an hour of watching him study the precipice, Mel was distracted by a majestic California condor soaring overhead. When he looked back down at the beach, his father was gone. He peered along the stretch of sand, confused. It was high tide, and there was no way off the beach except to climb or to take the beached boat they kept in the neighboring inlet. Yet his father had disappeared. When he thought to go looking for him, he turned and there his father was standing next to him at the top of the bluff.

"How did you get up here so fast?" Mel spouted.

"All in good time, Mel. There is much left to learn before you can know these things. But you are asking excellent questions."

Mel quickly grabbed the opportunity to ask, "What was that tool you were using on the beach?"

"Dreams, son, I was playing with my dreams."

* * *

Mel kept quiet and to himself at the Cooperton school and did not acquire friends easily. One spring day, just after he turned nine, he got on the wrong side of a local bully.

Tiff Benson, a seventh grader, stomped over to where Mel was talking with a female schoolmate. "Whadda ya think you're doing?" Tiff sneered as he shoved Mel. "This here's my sister. I don't want your kind messin' with her mind."

Mel was startled and stepped back. "I'm sorry, I don't understand. What do you mean, messing with her mind?"

"You know what I mean, cowpie!" Tiff bellowed. "You and your weird dad. Who knows what goofy stuff you're doing at the ol' Slaughterhouse. We hear all kinds of strange noises, and we're sure it's 'causa some sorta demon worship goin' on at your place!"

"What're you talking about?" Mel queried. "We don't do anything like that! And who is this 'we' who said so?"

"Don't matter, pig breath! We know it's true, and I don't want you messin' with my sister!" Without warning, Tiff hit Mel directly in the stomach, knocking all the wind out of him and sending him crumpling to the ground. Tiff jumped on top of him, swinging both arms in a flurry.

Mel groaned and, taking hit after hit, began to lose consciousness. As he faded, flashes of light sparked in his head, and a clear vision appeared to him.

Mel was playing in the yard of a large house on a sea cliff. The sky was a tumultuous, roiling dark mass. An electrical storm crackled in the nearby mountains. He heard voices shouting—angry voices directed towards the house. Men were brandishing axes and hammers and raising torches to the sky in defiance.

He could see his father inside the house, standing at the window. The fireplace was lit, shadows flickering against the wall. Someone stepped to his side, putting an arm around his shoulder. It was a woman, and she was shaking. He drew her away from the window by both of her arms, hugged her protectively, and stepped out of sight.

The angry, protesting voices rose in tone and volume. Then one of the men threw a piece of basalt toward the house and shattered a window. Another projectile followed, and finally, a torch flew through one of the broken panes and ignited the room on fire.

The skies above split and roared with flashing bolts of energy. Laughter and screams mixed with an insane chant that repeated over and over again. It rang in his ears, filling him with dread. Frozen with panic, he felt trapped in a no man's land between the screaming crowd and the now burning house.

Then the earth began to tremble, and the mob let out a shout. The people scattered as massive flaming hailstones fell from the sky. A figure ran towards him from the house, her head covered by her hands, weaving back and forth through the blazing barrage. Seemingly pummeled by smoldering streaks of light, she ran towards him, arms held out, screaming something he could not understand. And then he felt safe, lifted away from the tormented island. He felt arms around him and smelled burning flesh.

* * *

Mel woke in the school office, Miss Higgins leaning over him. When she was sure he was breathing smoothly, she put him in her carriage and drove him out to the Uri farm. She rang the bell at the front gate. After several minutes, a tall male figure approached.

"I'm, um, terribly sorry," she stammered. "There was a minor incident at the school, and I needed to bring your son home."

Telly looked at his bruised son and sighed deeply, his forehead wrinkling. He looked directly into Miss Higgins' eyes and asked sternly, "Who did this?"

She answered, a little fearfully, "Well, I, er, I, ummm, really am not at liberty to divulge that inform—"

"What was the cause then?" Telly interrupted more sternly.

"I'm not, not, I'm not sure..." She lied. "There was a problem on the playground and then a fight. I'm not sure who started it, but your son came out the worse. I am so terribly sorry." She looked at the damaged child and covered her face with her hands, nearly crying. "This will never happen again."

"I'm sure it won't, Miss Higgins. Thank you for bringing him."

"If... if there is anything I can do," she said hesitantly. "This was all a terrible misunderstanding, I'm sure."

"I'm sure it was," Telly said softly. He lifted Mel out of the seat and looked at his son's bloodied face. He closed the gate and carried Mel toward the house.

"I hope I'll be seeing Melvin tomorrow, sir. I hope that things will get back to normal soon as can be." She cried out after his retreating frame.

Telly thought to himself, *Things **are** back to normal.*

* * *

Later that evening, after Oscar tended Mel's injuries, Telly warned that retaliation would not be an act of good character and then treated Mel to homemade sugar balls with vanilla cream filling.

"Do we worship demons?" Mel asked after taking a few bites.

"Is that what they said to you?" Telly asked compassionately.

"Yeah, and that 'noises' come from our farm," Mel said.

His father sighed deeply. "Fear is an infectious disease, Mel. It causes people to imagine monsters where there are none. When people don't understand, they tend to speculate. The noises they heard came from our tools and machines that are different from their own. I wish that we could invite the whole town to our farm and show them that there is nothing to fear, but they would not understand our technology and would become even more afraid of us. We are not of this land, Mel. Our ways are distinct, and the less we can reveal, the better."

"Then why am I even going to school? Wouldn't it be better if I just stayed home and learned from you?"

"No. That would bring too much attention to us. They would send their authorities out to investigate. The people of this land are motivated by fear and appetite. Try to make friends with them, but don't become like them. They want things they shouldn't have and lash out at those who don't join them in the pursuit. It is best to live among them and be an example of a peaceful lifestyle. Go on and finish your treats. This day and its troubles will pass." After Mel finished eating, Telly gave his son a loving hug and pointed him towards his bedroom.

Mel went to bed with a sore body and an encouraged heart. The terrible things Tiff had said still lingered in his mind, though their ugly edge now felt dulled.

He was confused by the vision he had seen during his beating at school and resolved to ask his father about it in the morning.

* * *

That night, Mel had another dream.

The howling wind screamed incessantly, blowing sand into the air. The full moon was cold and far away, casting a ghostly grey light. He had been here for years and yet had just arrived. He looked at his hands, recognizing himself. He put them to his face and felt a cold, tingling sensation. He squinted to prevent the swirling sand from blinding him. His head reeled in a confused delirium, trying to understand why he was in this place that felt both new and familiar.

Then a figure appeared who resembled a twelfth-century monk, wearing a hooded black frock that hid his face. The Monk spoke to him in low, whisper-

ing tones. Despite the roaring wind, he could hear every syllable of the Monk's gentle voice inside his head. But he did not understand what was being said. It was as if the Monk were speaking nonsense, mumbling phrases from an obsolete language. He strained to see the Monk's face but could not peer around the enshrouding frock.

They walked forward through the sandstorm, amid a landscape of seemingly endless sand dunes rippling into the distance. He "must" have seen this vista before. He felt that this vision was a recurrence with a purpose, like a lump of dough being folded into itself. Again and again, he had come to listen to this stranger in this desert place beyond the world. He looked up to find the moon, but there was only light coming from the other side of a thin but living membrane. He held his hands to his ears to silence the screaming sirens of the whistling wind, but they did not diminish. The Monk's voice remained clear and calming, speaking in tones that a parent would use with a young child. Mel did not feel afraid.

They were walking, yet their position was fixed. He was aware yet felt that he was in a daze. His head was bursting with confusion, but he felt an inner peace that he was supposed to be here, that he was about to learn something that would change his life.

The wind increased its fury. The cacophony of the storm rose to a fevered pitch, and the voice inside his head began to shout above the rage of the storm. The surface of the desert began to tremble, and as had seemingly happened a hundred times before...

Mel woke, sitting up straight in his bed and gasping for breath, sweat pouring down his face. The vision began to slip away. He tried to hold onto its sensations and remember its details as he scrambled for his notepad and pen and began to write. His forehead furrowed in a painful squint as he grasped at memories that were evaporating like the morning dew. As Mel frantically wrote by the moonlight streaming through his window, the silence of the night was broken only by the cry of an owl as it swooped upon the mouse that was frantically fleeing from its talons.

* * *

In the morning, Telly found Mel's bedroom vacant. He called for him in the house and across the farm, to no avail.

Hours later, Mel walked into the kitchen, tired, bleary-eyed, and still bruised from the beating he received from Tiff. Telly asked, "Where did you go this morning, Mel? I was concerned."

"I woke too early and couldn't get back to sleep. I went up to the top of the hill to watch the sunrise," Mel responded with a sigh. His face brightened. "It was amazing! The clouds spread the light out in a hundred red beams. It was quiet enough that I could hear my blood moving through my ears." He sat at the table and gently rested his sore head in his hands, tilting it sideways.

Telly smiled at Mel's appreciation of a beautiful moment and then stopped and looked directly at his weary son. "You've been dreaming again?" he asked.

Mel simply nodded.

Telly responded, frowning, "I wish you would drink that herbal tea I mixed for you before you go to bed. These dreams are draining you of your vitality."

"Dad," Mel exclaimed plaintively, "there's something about them. They're *so* real. When I wake up, I wonder if this is just the dream and that's the real world." Mel paused, and his face was overtaken by a troubled expression. "When I was at the hill, I heard a woman singing, but there was no one there. It was her voice. It had to be." Mel fell silent, his eyes looking at the rough wood grain of the old kitchen table. He was desperate to remember, pushing his mind to pierce through a thick fog. "Tell me again of my mother," Mel said in defeat, not looking up. "I can't see her face. I can remember what it felt like to be around her, but even that is fading."

Telly again recognized the weariness and pain in his son that the two of them had shared for the past five years. He walked over and sat next to him, wrapping his large arm around his shoulders.

"As you know, she was named after her great grandmother Eleanor, or Ella, as we call her, which means 'God is my light.' In due time you will see how wonderful that name is! Your mother loved you very much, Mel. She used to take you up on a hill like ours when you were first born. She would sing to you as the sun rose. I can remember her twirling around, holding you over her head, laughing, and making silly sounds to you. You and your mother were always together. I know how you must miss her."

Mel laid his hands flat on the table. "I can't *remember* her."

"I am sorry that she was taken from you when you needed her most," Telly said, his own sadness welling up.

"Why did she die, Dad?" Mel asked with a little edge to his voice. "You still haven't told me. You said there would come a day when you'd explain it. Will that be soon?"

"Soon, son," Telly said in a comforting, low voice as he patted Mel's back. "Soon."

"Dad, yesterday when Tiff was pounding on me, I saw something. It wasn't a dream. It was like... like it was really happening, or it was a memory. I was somewhere else, and I was a little kid again!"

Telly, in his usual manner, got himself a fresh cup of tea and sat across from his son. "Tell me all about it."

Mel related the whole vision of the house, the angry mob, and the island barraged by fire. "Did this happen?" Mel asked his father. "Or do you think it's about something happening now?"

Telly had stopped drinking his tea when he began to hear the details of Mel's vision. He was silent for several moments. "'Soon' has come," he said in a calm voice.

Rising, he led Mel out onto the front porch, where they took seats overlooking the ripe wheat stalks swaying in the fields nearby.

Telly lit his pipe and began to speak. "Mel, this is a memory. You described word for word the circumstances of the day your mother was taken from us, and yet you were just four years old. How you could remember this in such detail astounds me." He gazed out over their property, a distant look in his eyes. "We were living in our château on the eastern sea cliffs of Martinique. It was a property very much like this farm, though the house was much larger. Our view extended for miles, north and south. We could see the sunrise from nearly every room. I remember the way her auburn hair would catch the morning light and shine like filaments of gold." He paused, swallowing hard. "I loved your mother and wanted the best for her. I made our house strong enough to withstand any hurricane that would sweep over our island, yet it was a place tender enough for her to raise her roses and jasmine and to raise you, my son."

Telly stopped speaking for a moment and wiped his eyes, focusing on the planks of the porch. When he had composed himself, he turned to Mel and saw his wife's eyes looking back at him. His heart felt constricted, and he hesitated, but he knew he needed to continue. "From that home, I fulfilled my duties as the leader of the Vysards for many years. Wherever we may go, I will continue to serve as the 'Gatekeeper.'"

Mel leaned forward expectantly. "That first day, on the beach, Jora mentioned that he was almost a Vysard."

Telly's brow furrowed. "Did he? Hmmm..." he said while stroking his beard. He took a deep breath and again turned his attention to Mel. "A Vysard is a keeper of knowledge, like a librarian in this country. He keeps the historical records of his people. When someone needs to know a fact or needs to learn to do something, they go to a Vysard. He researches the topic and gathers the related documents to help address their need."

"You mean like Mrs. Smyth?"

Telly thought of the pudgy woman with thick glasses who worked at the local library. She always dressed like she was going to a Sunday picnic. Even inside the library, she would wear outlandish, gregarious hats lavishly adorned with a potpourri of fruit and birds. Telly smiled at this thought. "The difference between the responsibilities of Mrs. Smyth and those of a Vysard depends on what is done with the information." Telly saw that Mel was confused. "Mrs. Smyth may know where to find a certain book you are seeking. Some of them she has read. A Vysard is not only required to know all the documents that he dispenses, but it's also incumbent upon him to be able to do something with that knowledge. For instance, if you wanted to know about mining or astronomy, you might ask for a book on the subject, but can the librarian tell the inquirer from personal experience about every aspect of mining procedure or name every constellation in the night sky? That, and much more, is what's required of a Vysard."

Mel shook his head in incredulity. "To know something from personal experience on every subject would take forever!"

Telly smiled and took another puff on his pipe. "It does take a long time. There are a great many subjects, yet there is a limit to the number any one Vysard must master. The Gatekeeper develops a command of select topics and a passing knowledge of every subject but delegates other areas of expertise among a small circle of trusted Vysards, who, themselves, delegate the knowledge of everyday matters to others whom they trust. Within the network composed of the Gatekeeper, the Vysards, and their helpers, is someone with extensive personal experience on every topic."

"What have you learned the most about, Dad?"

"I have focused on the responsibility that passed to me to keep our ancestors' technological records. There were others in our community in Martinique who resented my responsibility. They felt that I was hoarding the knowledge of our ancestors, that I alone was preventing them from using the knowledge to increase their prosperity. They knew I would strictly adhere to the rules that were passed down to each Gatekeeper."

Telly took a deep breath and looked Mel square in the eyes. "Mel, there are records of innovations that our forefathers developed millennia ago that have been sealed away because of their incredible power and the danger they could pose were they to fall into the wrong hands. It is my duty to keep the scrolls secure, and I have done this faithfully."

A pained expression crossed Telly's face. "One day, many of the younger men on Martinique demanded that I turn over the scrolls and allow them to discover for themselves if the reward of the technology was worth the risk. I refused. Some of the more inquisitive and forceful men broke into our home while I was on an expedition with your mother. They forced my lifelong friend Oscar to tell them under threat of your death where the records were kept. They thought they would begin by responsibly using only one of the old inventions to mine for minerals and gems and thus display that they could be trusted with the rest.

"Something went terribly wrong, and by the time I returned, they had set off a chain of events that caused the local dormant volcano to awaken. This began a firestorm that burned many fields and orchards and homes. The very men who had caused this disaster blamed me for withholding the information that could've helped them control the tools.

"You were in the yard watching the mountain when the mob arrived. They demanded that I produce the remedy to quench the results of their foolishness. As they tried to burn our house, I relented and went to explain how the firestorm could be calmed.

"As I was describing the solution, the volcano let loose another salvo of molten earth, much more powerful than the earlier firestorm. A spray of lava began to fall all around the house. Somehow, miraculously, you were not hit. Your mother saw you and ran to your rescue. Oscar was in the backyard watching for intruders when he heard you scream just as a mass of volcanic liquid must have hit your mother and taken her life." Telly stopped, unable to go further without choking up. "By the time Oscar got to the front, you were being carried by Jora, who had pulled you to safety away from your mother's body. We found her nearby. She had passed and was burned beyond recognition, but miraculously, you escaped unharmed." He stopped trying to hold back his tears and let them fall freely. Mel joined him and, after a moment, put his hand on his father's sleeve.

Telly was comforted by the presence of his young son, whose life had been purchased at the price of his mother's. He continued, "During the week when the mountain rested, before we were forced to flee the island, we buried her on the same hill where she used to dance with you at sunrise. She loved that spot so much." He stared off into the distance, past the meadow and out to sea, puffing on his pipe that had long since burned out.

Mel had many more questions but realized that now was not the time to ask them. He hugged his father as they both wept, the pain of love and loss flowing through them like a cleansing flood.

CHAPTER 4

LESSONS IN LEARNING

Five years passed quickly as Mel continued to study both at school and at home. Mrs. Bagroot, who taught the older students at Cooperton School, was regularly confronted with the fact that Mel was much more advanced than others his age. She did not know what to do with him. At fourteen years old, he was ready to study subjects that she had never taught to her eighteen-year-olds. Soon after he became her student, she began simply supplying him with books. She allowed him to teach himself, though she insisted that he sit with his age group. The children around him thought he was trying to show off and teased that he did not really understand the books he "pretended" to read. To Mrs. Bagroot's relief, Mel never asked her any questions, as many of the subjects he was studying were beyond her understanding. If something stumped Mel, he would wait till after school to ask Oscar or his father.

Mel discovered that Oscar Bottoms was a "doctor" of many subjects who loved to be asked for advice. He had the bad habit of pontification and on occasion, would talk on and on about a subject. Mel could tell that he was about to wax eloquent when he began with the phrase, "Eye' laddie, when I was young..."

Aside from his studies, Mel also participated in a regimen of physical training. It began with morning exercise, which included running for several miles and gymnastics before school. After school, Mel would sprint home to begin his afternoon lessons. These included training in swordsmanship and a variety of martial arts. Telly knew several leading martial arts teachers from Japan and, though ocean travel was costly and extremely slow, had hired them to instruct himself and his students in Martinique.

Jora loved sword training and was highly skilled. He and Mel practiced with broadswords rather than the thin rapiers common to fencing. Jora's size and strength gave him an advantage over Mel, whose objective in each lesson was to prolong the time before Jora would disarm him and inflict a punishing strike with the flat of his blade. Jora began each day's sword training with the phrase, "Today, I'm gonna teach you a lesson." He seemed to relish the sessions of "bash my backside," as Mel came to think of them.

Over the years of sword training, from the time when Mel was eight years old to when he was fourteen, he had grown stronger and had forced Jora to use increasing energy to maintain mastery.

Finally, there came a moment when Mel not only avoided being disarmed but also turned the tables on his teacher. Mel stood over his disarmed foe, remembering his humiliation at Jora's hands. His heart pounded from the thrill of this long-awaited victory. The opportunity was before him to repay Jora for the years of taunting defeat, but then he remembered his father's words about not becoming like his enemies. He picked up both of their swords and carefully placed them back into the case on the wall.

From that moment forward, Jora refused further sword training with Mel. At night, Mel often heard him sparring frantically on his own.

* * *

One of Mel's favorite activities was rock climbing with his father. Each time, they put on their hobnail boots and climbing clothes and special gloves with exposed fingertips, which allowed them to grasp the smallest of outcroppings, and made their way by boat to the cliff-enclosed beach.

The first time they approached the base of the huge granite precipice, Mel took one look up and subconsciously began to step back toward their boat.

Telly's brow furrowed, then he offered his son an encouraging smile. "Mel, you will do fine. You received rock climbing training in Martinique from the time you were first able to cling to a rock wall, and that training continued during our four years of travel."

"I wish I could remember how brave I was then," Mel responded, trying to make light of his fear, even as his eyes grew large at the challenge before him.

"Your body will remember."

Telly started Mel on an easy route to show him that he was more capable than he thought. After Mel accomplished several small goals, Telly chose harder and steeper climbs. This continued for hours, Mel's father guiding him up the steep cliff. Eventually, Telly chose a few of the cliff's most difficult routes, and Mel approached and ascended the rock face without fear or doubt about his ability to safely accomplish the climb. Invigorated by the adventure and camaraderie, they climbed that day until sunset.

After sitting and resting together while watching the crimson orb sink into the vast expanse of the Pacific Ocean, Telly rubbed his hands together. "Now, the climb will be more interesting."

Mel tilted his head in puzzlement.

"The blind climb," Telly said as the dark blanket of night began to enfold them, devoid even of the light of the moon.

"The what?" Mel inquired.

"We climb by instinct, approaching each hold one at a time. We won't try to see the whole route but will instead take each step based upon the feel of the last. This may seem frightening at first, but I assure you that you've accomplished more difficult climbs under worse conditions than we have now. See, the stars are shining, giving us a hint of light. You need only open your eyes wide and use your peripheral vision to see all that lies before you. Let's give it a try, shall we?" Telly jumped to his feet and began climbing quickly out of sight. A minute later, Telly called out from the dark rock face above. "This way!"

Mel put his hands on the lowest holds, took a deep breath, and began the blind climb. He climbed slowly at first, gaining confidence one hold at a time. With his attention focused solely on the challenge at hand, a half hour of slow, deliberate climbing seemed to pass in a dozen minutes. As Mel neared the crest of the cliff, he heard his father's encouraging voice.

"Two more moves, and you'll reach my hand!" Telly cried out in excitement and pride.

Moments later, Mel finished the climb and was pulled to the clifftop by his father's strong hands. The moon had just risen and was showering its silver light on them from over the peaks of the coastal mountains to the east. Its sudden illumination spilled onto the beach far below. Mel was astounded at his accomplishment.

"Nothing is impossible to those who have been trained and who are careful with their steps, Mel."

Mel's smile was big and bright, even in the dim light of the moon. "Thank you. I never would've chosen on my own to do that."

"Life is one continual expression of joy to those who are not paralyzed by a fear of failure. Just remember how you didn't want to step out at first. Most of our greatest challenges seem overwhelming at the start, but when we take one step at a time, it's all quite simple in the end."

* * *

Mel and Telly spent most evenings together in the Uri household study at the end of the hall, digging through its many bookshelves and sitting at a small table near the home's second fireplace to discuss philosophy, religion, and forms of government.

Telly did not attempt to hide ideas from his son. He did not want Mel to simply mimic his beliefs. He explained the many views on a topic and trusted in Mel's ability to discern for himself what had merit and what pandered to the vanity of man.

Mel loved these discussions. Occasionally they left the study and walked out to the edge of the cliff, a favorite habit during the warm and clear summer evenings. There they watched the moon and stars slowly descend into the gentle kelp-filled swells of the ocean, listening as the waves lapped softly against the shore below.

On these nights, it was only a matter of time before one or the other of them remarked on the crafted nature of reality and the amazing cycles of life. They discussed the depths of eternity and the existence and character of the Creator, who, by His incredible imagination, had so carefully designed every aspect of the world.

Many times, Mel lay back with his hands behind his head and tried to breathe in the depth of what he was beholding in the night sky. He stretched his mind and tried to wrap his thoughts around the size of the universe and the importance of his place within it.

On several occasions, Telly warned his son of a danger inherent in the wondrous creation. "We must be careful that we're not misled by the marvels we take in through our senses, Mel. The Greeks had a word for what you are observing. It's called Gaia, or the 'spirit' of this world. Indeed, she is incredibly beautiful, but she is transitory. What you see is a passing form. Neither you nor I nor any human being can stop the progress of events. We should learn to enjoy the beauties of the moment but not let them lure us into thinking that they can meet all our needs. There are many in this world who, rather than simply acknowledging and enjoying God's workmanship, choose to worship and trust in the creation rather than the Creator."

These were Mel's favorite moments, and he hoped they would last forever. He listened to his father's warnings and tried to store them in his heart.

He did not know how drastically things would one day change in his world on the cliff overlooking the vast ocean.

CHAPTER 5

WONDERS IN THE NIGHT

One stormy evening not long after Mel turned fifteen, the Uri household finished dinner, Oscar told one of his many stories, and Mel reluctantly went to bed. The wind slapped incessantly against the sides of the house. Telly stopped by Mel's room and said that he needed to attend to some important matters before turning in for the night. During storms, Telly often became active on the types of projects that were best masked by the sounds of thunder and howling winds.

Mel had been asleep for several hours when he was awakened by deep vibrations emanating from beneath the house. *Woomp sheee… Woomp sheee.* Mel looked towards the ocean and saw flashes of color pulsing in the cloudy night sky. But this was not from the storm. Curiosity overcame him, and he crept out of his bedroom.

He passed Oscar's room and watched as he turned over, grunting several unintelligible words. Mel thought, *Everything that man does is loud!* Continuing, he found his father's room empty.

He cautiously opened the front door, remembering the irritating *screech* it let out when opened. Once outside and into soft grass, which muffled his footsteps, Mel broke into a slow jog, careful not to twist his ankles on the uneven ground.

He neared a hill by the cliff. Sporadic flashes of color emanated at intervals from just over the rise. He slowly edged forward, ducking even lower during the outbursts of light.

As Mel peered over the top of the hill, his heart suddenly filled with wonder. There, just shy of the cliff's edge, stood his father, bathed in light that was streaming from a shallow, open pit in the soil. Mel watched as Telly crouched, opened a small box, raised his hand over his head, and placed something into a depression in a wall of the pit. He stepped back and shielded his eyes just before fresh sparks of gold and green erupted, casting a giant shadow of him over the field. As the light faded, Mel saw that the pit had grown five meters wider but no deeper, the soil blown to the side in a heap, leaving the bedrock exposed. After Telly repeated this process several times, he stepped down into a now thirty-meter-diameter pit, the top half of his body still visible above ground.

Mel crept along the top of the hill to the point closest above the pit. He could now observe his father in detail.

Telly, standing on the bedrock, held a tool similar in appearance to a trowel and waved it in wide, sweeping arcs. The rock melted away like wax before a soldering iron, leaving behind a black molten mass. Telly formed this into shapes that rapidly cooled and became as hard and smooth as onyx. In this way, he crafted a subterranean structure, sculpting rooms and arched doorways down into the earth like an artist shapes a statue. At places near the cliff, he thinned the walls till they were transparent.

Mel circled around the excavation to a place where he could see the outer cliff wall and discovered that the places where windows had been created still appeared from the outside to be undisturbed rock surfaces. He crept to the edge of the pit and continued to watch. He was tempted to run and shout to his father, but he did not know if he would get in trouble for observing this.

Down through hundreds of meters of rock, Telly carved his castle. At times he used short, chopping movements to create stairs, window seats, and bookcases. As he descended ever-lower, Mel ventured after him at a distance, not daring to interrupt.

Finally, when Mel estimated that his father was thirty meters below sea level, Telly turned and carved a passageway out towards the ocean. After being gone for several minutes, he appeared again. He turned a corner and stood in anticipation. A low, muffled *woompaa* sounded, accompanied by a brilliant burst of orange light. A violent rush of air escaped from the passageway, up through the many levels of the sculpted structure, and out the top of the pit like hot air venting from a factory's chimney. Mel pressed himself flat against the wall as the air streamed past. He wanted desperately to run to his father, but fear kept him back.

After Telly again disappeared down the passage, Mel's curiosity drew him to carefully follow. He glanced back up the way he had come and saw the magnificent structure his father had crafted in one night. Turning again to the way ahead, he came to the passageway's entrance and stepped inside.

The room was a massive, transparent, perfectly shaped dome on the ocean floor, ten meters high and half a hundred meters in circumference. He looked up and immediately experienced intense vertigo. The sun was just rising, sending tangerine and turquoise light filtering through the web of the sea above. In the center of this massive, inside-out fish tank stood his father, gazing in rapt wonder at the aquatic vista surrounding him.

Mel sat on the smooth, black floor to regain his balance. He saw in his father someone he had never seen before. He wondered what his father would do if he knew he was spying on him.

Just then, Telly looked at his son sitting on the floor with both hands flat against its smooth surface, trying to balance himself. An immense grin came over his face. "Perfect! You're just in time! Come here; there's something I want to show you."

Mel tried to stand, but with the swaying sea above him, he lost his balance a second time and tumbled to the ground.

His father laughed gently. "It takes a few minutes to get used to it. Look at the ground and walk towards me. Once you're here, you can hold onto me."

Once again, Mel stood, this time fixing his eyes on the black floor. This method was helpful but still challenging, as the floor's sheen reflected everything above with shadowed clarity. As he moved, his father also stepped towards him, and soon he was held secure by strong, tender hands. Mel looked again and was enthralled by the fish of all shapes, sizes, and colors. Above them, two huge humpback whales swam in tandem.

"Look at this world, Mel! Twice as much of the Earth is covered by this than by the world of dirt and hard gravity. Down here, there is no fighting over land ownership, no need for courts to contest rights, no wars, and no lack for any of the citizens. This is the world as God made it, free and bounteous."

Mel, still clinging to his father's shoulder, looked around, captivated by the living beauty surrounding them.

"Here is what I wanted you to see," Telly said like he was giving a Christmas present. He grasped Mel's shoulders and turned him to face the coast, just in time to see the sky explode in a burst of light as the sun rose fully. The room was enveloped in an aquatic kaleidoscope of colors and shadows. The whales danced in the sunrise over their heads.

Mel, nearly speechless, looked at this room and back toward the stairway of rooms that led to the clifftop. Without fear of rebuke, he asked his father, "Who *are* you?"

Telly simply smiled.

* * *

Telly escorted Mel back up the winding stairs to the surface. The cool night air was quickly giving way to the warmth of dawn and its accompanying scent of seaweed. Mel watched as his father used his trowel-like tool to build a trapdoor entrance to the onyx pit. After a few applications of light-producing explosives set into the mounded soil and directed toward the pit, there remained no indication above ground of the massive structure beneath. Telly and Mel used shovels to smooth the surface of the soil.

"Tomorrow, we will sow some rye here for the goats to feed on," Telly explained.

Once home, Telly took Mel to the hall closet and, pushing aside several coats, knocked three times, then twice more, and whistled a few notes of a tune that they both knew. The back of the closet swung open noiselessly, revealing a dark, narrow, downward stairway made of the same material as the underground structure.

"This is the entrance to our Caeli," his father explained reverently. "One day, you will go through here and down to a floor that I have yet to build, far below the observation room, for your initiation at the vaults."

Mel was so tired that he barely understood what his father said. "My initiation? And... What's a Caeli?"

"All in good time, son. Now to bed. It's been a long night," his father said while seeing him to his bedroom.

After being up most of the night, Mel was emotionally drained. He flopped onto his bed and almost immediately fell into a deep sleep. He dreamt of multicolored, flashing fireworks and fish that swam through the air.

* * *

Hours later, Mel woke and wandered into the kitchen, rubbing his bleary eyes. "What time is it?" he asked huskily.

"It's almost time for lunch, laddie," Oscar replied. "I tried to wake you for hours, but you lay there like a log wedged in a beaver's dam. Today, after your math course, I need to tell you how to straighten out your sleep patterns." He took a deep breath, preparing to further chastise Mel.

"I know, Oscar," Mel said with a playful scowl. "I didn't sleep too well."

"That's only part of it. Sometimes you sleepwalk or cry out, and I wonder where you're going."

"Where I'm going?" Mel asked hesitantly, suspecting that he knew of the previous night's escapade.

Oscar stared off at nothing. "Some say their dreams take them

67

into the other world. It's a place that's here and now, yet more than here and now. If you catch my meaning." Oscar returned from the depths of his thoughts. "Another time, I'll tell you more about it. This day is already unusual enough."

Mel tensed. "Have you talked to my father?"

"He headed south after breakfast. Said he was off to prepare a new project. And this morning, Jora set out for San Francisco."

"Do you know when my father will be back?"

"Sorry, laddie, I don't. But he left a note for you."

Oscar fumbled through his pockets. After taking out four pens, a dozen entangled paperclips, and three other crumpled notes, he finally produced a piece of yellow paper and handed it to Mel. "I should've remembered to give you this right away." Oscar lumbered over to the cabinet, selected a large jar of jam, and began to slather it onto several slices of buttered bread.

Mel picked up the note, which read:

Mel,

It's almost time for you to begin your final apprenticeship. I have gone to make preparations on your behalf. I hope to return soon, but only after everything is seen to.

If I am delayed, Oscar knows what to do. He is incredibly wise, Mel. Don't let your familiarity with him cause you to miss who he really is. I am deeply in his debt. For you to master the next level of your training, you must study under Oscar. Please pay him the utmost respect and attention.

Jora can help you, but only to a point. One day, your lessons will require you to go on alone. All Vysards must face the greatest lessons of the Caeli for themselves. Vysards or not, all those of the Image will come face to face with the Essence of Life on their own. I can prepare the way, Oscar can train you, Jora can keep you sharp and fit via your exercises, but you must face Him alone.

With all my love,
Telemai

Though he had many questions about the content of the note, he was particularly confused by his father's signature. "Telemai?" Mel exclaimed aloud.

Oscar nearly choked on his buttered, jam-covered bread. He washed it down with a half-pint of orange juice from the glass he held in his other hand.

"Is that my father's real name?"

Oscar quickly swallowed the last of his lunch. "Telemai? Where did you hear that name?"

"It's here in the note. It's how he signed it," Mel said, holding up the piece of paper. "Didn't you read it?"

"No, I don't read other people's mail. Nosiness is a dangerous habit. Been the ruin of many a good person."

"Why have I never heard him use this name?" Mel insisted.

"Well... well, that is a deep subject, Master Mel," Oscar said while stroking the whiskers on his chin. "Yes, well, there's no getting around it. This changes everything. I didn't think it would come to this so soon, but there you have it. Gone to prepare for a new project, indeed! You'd think I'd get more of a warning," Oscar grumbled good-naturedly.

"Oscar?" Mel asked anxiously. "This changes what?"

Oscar suddenly became very sober and looked into Mel's eyes with a piercing, blue gaze. "There are many things I must tell you." Putting his arm around Mel's shoulder, he began leading him toward the living room. "I hope you have a couple of hours on your hands. This is going to be a long story."

CHAPTER 6

A LONG STORY

Mel stepped back into the kitchen, grabbed a chunk of sourdough bread, a wedge of goat cheese, and a tall glass of orange juice, and followed Oscar into the living room.

Oscar settled into the large rocking chair. He took out his pipe and lit a pouch of rum-soaked tobacco. Mel sat in his chair, apprehensive over what he was about to hear.

Oscar began his story. "As you know, we came from the Island of Martinique. Our little colony migrated from the British Isles some six hundred years before Columbus sailed."

"Six hundred years?" Mel balked. "The history books would—"

Oscar lifted his pipe and answered firmly, "The history books don't tell you anything that the writers don't want them to. I imagine those 'history' books don't mention that the Vikings populated North America five hundred years before Columbus."

Mel nodded, gripped his armrests, and sat ready to listen.

"As I was saying, we came to Martinique from the British Isles, but there are a few more details to where we came from before that. Mel, our people are some of the last survivors of a civilization that thrived on an island chain in the Mid-Atlantic, nearer to the British Isles than anywhere else. To their citizens, the isles were called Delemni. According to Plato, they sank into the ocean thousands of years before he wrote of them."

Mel could not make sense of this according to his understanding of history and leaned forward to interrupt.

Oscar raised his hand. "There's a lot more to be said, boy. Delemni was far advanced in all sciences. Much of the world was still living as warring clans, while we lived in peace on our islands. We had hot and cold running water and smooth, paved streets. Our buildings were sheathed in precious metals as common to us as brick and mortar were to the Hittites. You've heard of the use of electricity in San Francisco and other cities? Well, millennia ago, we had something stronger."

Oscar leaned forward, wonder writ large across his face. "We harnessed the power of magma, laddie," he said seriously, his bushy grey eyebrows furrowing together. "The life force of the planet. We harvested the treasures of the earth, powered our cities, and created weapons the rest of humanity couldn't imagine. To access this energy, we had to burrow deep into the earth's core. This was a fine course of action if taken carefully because, like our bodies, the earth has ways of mending itself. But the desire for power and the glitter of gems took over the hearts of our people and led them to dig too quickly. They couldn't get more as fast as they wished. That's when the critical point was reached, and once the line was crossed, it was irreversible.

"The end came quickly. There'd been warnings that the earth was unstable—tremors in the mountains, minor tsunamis here and there. The great mountain of Poseidon, where Atlas, our first king, resided, was hissing and spouting. They should have heeded the warnings and known the end was near. But no, like our people have done many times since, our ancestors did not stop."

Mel sat forward in his chair, his jaw clenched. "Then what?"

"Why, then the earth had had enough of the foolish prying and said, 'No more.' The whole Atlantic ridge sank in one night!" Oscar explained with a look of horror. "The shame of it was that not just the greedy ones perished. Thousands upon thousands of innocent people were lost because of a few who couldn't control themselves! The bridge to Britannia was broken and submerged. The work of generations melted, and our nation was shattered.

"A few escaped. Your own ancestor, Natu Fian, the first Gatekeeper and counselor to Atlas himself, was one who heeded the earth's warnings and fled before the disaster. Those who escaped moved to all parts of the world and started their lives over. Natu Fian, considered one of the 'Old Ones,' had taken with him the ancient scrolls. He created a hidden Caeli, the one we call the Grand Delemni Caeli, and vowed to never again allow open access to the old knowledge. He made his son swear to serve as guardian of the scrolls should he die, and thus the tradition of the Gatekeeper entered your family line.

"Whenever your forefathers settled in a new place, they created hidden chambers and sealed in vaults the portion of the records they were carrying with them. Not your ordinary vaults, mind you. Only those who had mastered the strictest disciplines could enter the caves and open the vaults. And then, only by permission of the Gatekeeper."

Oscar stood up from the rocking chair and paced back and forth. "It happened again, everywhere they went. Things would be fine, and then someone would begin to misuse the knowledge. That's what occurred in Martinique. I watched it happen! They *would not* listen to your father. They said they were 'in control' and that they could handle the power," he began to mock.

Oscar checked his attitude and turned to Mel, whose mind was reeling. "Your father knew what was coming, and he warned them. After the incident when your mother was taken, they relented, and Mt. Peleé calmed itself. But a mere week later, they forgot how close they had come to complete disaster and delved in again. They dug faster than ever, obsessed with gathering power, like their ancestors before them. Your father pleaded with them until the last moment, and then we were forced to flee. We took our boat and the scrolls we most needed and escaped the island, you by the skin of your teeth. For the next four years, we visited the eastern shores of the Americas, hiked over the isthmus to Panama City, near where they're building the canal, bought a new boat, and spent a while in Japan before settling here. Now the time has come. I must begin to train you in our other ways."

Made breathless by the mountain of revelation that had just been imparted to him, Mel sank back in his chair. "Well, that explains why our household is different, doesn't it?"

Oscar smiled. "Aye, that it does."

The strange phenomena that Mel had witnessed the night before, and the day's several mentions of a new level of training, had provoked his imagination and led to one especially alarming speculation. "Oscar?" Mel asked hesitantly, as if seeking permission to raise a difficult subject. "Last night, I was awakened by some strange noises and went out to investigate. I saw my father near the cliff. He was digging... no, *crafting* an entire subterranean building, using forces I could not understand. Was it wizardry?"

Oscar raised an eyebrow. "Oh, he did, did he? I suppose that explains why we're having this conversation today. You know, I'm beginning to wonder if I'm the last person to hear about things around here."

"Oscar!" Mel implored.

"Oh, right. No, it's not wizardry, but science, lad. It's part of the technology our ancestors developed long ago. Your father is a Vysard, a 'wise one,' not a wizard. A Vysard is a servant, a guardian, and a caretaker of the creatures of the earth. He has been fully trained in his craft and has passed the final stages of discipleship. His aim is not to exercise power over others but to bring peace, and he must be ready to stop evil in its tracks when necessary. Your father is one of the greatest Vysards this world has ever known, and you will be too, young Melamuri."

"Melamuri?" Mel asked in surprise.

"That's your Delemnite name, Mel. Actually, it's Melek 'al Uri. Which translated means 'King of Heaven.'"

"King of what?"

Oscar smiled and patted Mel on the head. "Not the celestial 'heaven,' just the island of your ancestors. It was named Uri, from the word ouranos, which you already know means heaven. Uri was the chief island in the Delemni chain. And don't let the word 'King' go to your head. Just because you descend from a line of earthly kings doesn't make you one. You must have the character of a king before you ever have a crown on your head. Nobility isn't just something you're born into; it's who you become by your decisions. Take your father, for example, as humble a man as you'll ever meet. Yet you'd hardly believe he's heir to the throne of Delemni and Gatekeeper of our peoples' knowledge, now, would you?"

Mel mouthed the word "Gatekeeper." "He told me a little about it years ago, that it was like a librarian."

Oscar snickered. "A librarian, he said?"

Mel frowned. "He said we'd talk more about it later, but we never did!"

"Him informing you of his Delemnite name was my sign that 'later' had come. And here we are, talking about it. A bit more 'later' than you would've liked, I suppose. Telemai Uri is your father's whole name. It means the 'completion of heaven.' Like his ancestors, your father was trained to complete the work Natu Fian started millennia ago."

Mel was amazed. "Why tell me now? I'm finally old enough?"

"I wish that were the only reason. Your father didn't say as much, but I suspect he decided it was time for you to begin the apprenticeship of the vaults because of the increasing activity of the Strangers." Beads of sweat had begun to trickle down Oscar's face. He nervously wiped them away with his sleeve.

"You asked about wizardry," Oscar continued. "There are wizards in this world, but they call upon dark spiritual powers as the source for their abilities. We do not speak of them often, and when we do, it is always with the hope that we won't fall prey to the same enticements. They would have us use our knowledge to serve ourselves rather than others. Such men were among the first ancestors of another, less benevolent group that escaped Delemni, and they continue amongst them to this day. We call this group the 'Strangers.' They are loud, violent, and empty people who can never have enough power. We do not usually speak of them as Delemnites but rather as people of Xenos, the home of the Strangers—more of a place of poisoned beliefs than an actual land. Troublemakers they are, to put it lightly. It was a touch of their spirit that stirred up the others in Martinique. Recently, they have been stepping up their efforts to track your father, as they did with his forefathers. And they will seek you."

"What do they want from him?" Mel asked hesitantly.

"The same thing they wanted in Martinique, but far greater. If they manage to invade all the Caelis around the world, they will use what they find to trace the location of the Grand Delemni Caeli itself, which still houses the bulk of our people's knowledge, including all of the most precious secrets. Once there, they would steal its contents and become the masters of this planet."

"My father can stop them, can't he?"

Oscar's face grew pale. "Not on his own. He will need all of our people who are still faithful to Delemni and their sworn allies from among the other nations, not of our kin. We will need many more of these allies, but we can't go enlisting just anyone. We have always been careful to hide our way of life. If we, who were raised with this knowledge, can be corrupted by it so easily, then those who are not of Delemni, who have lived in relative poverty and powerlessness, would fall even more quickly. We have a name for the people of other nations—Terrans, or 'people of the land'—but there is no essential difference between us. We are all the race of Man. All created equal in the image of the Creator."

Mel sat still for a moment, trying to process all that he was learning. A nagging thought turned his look of awe into one of confusion. "I can't remember learning all of this before, but it feels like I must have. Years ago, my father told me about my mother and the troubles in Martinique, but more of it than that seems familiar. I knew these things when I was little, didn't I?" Mel said as more of a statement than a question.

"Most of it. What was appropriate for your age."

Mel shook his head. "It's been seven years since we arrived in

Cooperton. Since my injury. What if hearing this sooner could have helped restore my memories?"

Oscar nodded with understanding and replied in a calm, low voice, "Before you woke up, your father and I discussed how things might go. We hoped for the best, but if you woke and had trouble remembering, he wanted you to have a chance to begin again, to live like a normal person, free from the pressures of our people. Free from the hate that had been directed at our household. You would go to the local school, make friends, and have a normal childhood. We would tell you just enough to provide you a gradual reawakening to the things of your former life. It was harder than we imagined. At times we felt we weren't being honest. It broke your father's heart to see how you'd been harmed in the accident with the swinging boom of the boat. But he trusted that eventually, you would recover all that you had lost."

Mel had grown increasingly uneasy as Oscar spoke. He slouched forward, resting his head in his hands. "Recover all that I lost? It's like I was born on the Cooperton beach when I was eight! I don't know what'll come back and what's gone. I can barely remember the day my mother died! And I was purposely not helped?" Mel's face contorted in confusion and anger.

"It was a chance for a simpler life for you, so we took it, knowing that one day the whole truth would be revealed. When we didn't tell you everything there was to say, or when an answer was withheld, it was meant for your good. If we erred in this, we'll answer to Him for it." Oscar paused, fighting back emotion. "We're sorry, Mel. Sorry about your mother. Sorry about your memories. Sorry that us being different makes it hard for you to make friends."

Mel looked into Oscar's gentle, apologetic eyes. His confusion and anger melted into grief. "I'm sorry for being angry and doubting you and my father," Mel said, leaning forward and surprising Oscar with a hug.

"It's all right, laddie. We've all been through it together. And that's how we'll stay, whatever the future holds."

Secure in the hug of his father's best friend, a man whom he regarded as a dear uncle, Mel found the courage to be vulnerable. "How am I supposed to train the way he wants when I can't remember the first half of my life?" he asked fearfully. "Why would he want a broken student?"

Oscar smiled with compassion and reassurance and patted Mel on the back. "He did not doubt the plan to keep training you, not for one moment. As you continue along your path, more will come back. You've already surprised us with how fast you've recovered. You still have, in your inner being, all the training that was fed into you as a child. You are a storehouse of knowledge and skills."

Filled with a mixture of emotions, Mel sat again in his chair and looked at his hands. He knew that Oscar was right. Everything he was saying fit with his experiences. During the past seven years, he had wondered why he was more attuned than his classmates to the world around him. His knowledge and behavior had continually surprised him.

Oscar, not often given to moments of silence, laid down his pipe, leaned forward, gently placed his hands on Mel's shoulders, and looked deeply into his eyes. "Because of your lineage, you will feel like a foreigner in this world, but it also gives you a chance to be a leader of men. You are called to do your duty to your father and his purposes. You must be prepared and equipped to oppose the intrusions of the Strangers. They will always be at work somewhere. It's on you, laddie, that your father has placed his expectations. *You* are his most important work and are to be the next Gatekeeper. It's *you* he's molding to change the world."

CHAPTER 7

GROWING PAINS

Mel hoped each day for his father's return. At times he imagined his voice calling from outside the house. Yet every time he ran out to greet him, he met only silence. Three weeks after the conversation with Oscar, Jora returned from San Francisco, smugger than ever about the success of his trade business.

At school, Mel explained that his father had gone away on business. He enjoyed school, despite his class's pace of study being too slow for him. The math his grade was learning was embarrassingly simple compared to what he was studying in the advanced books that Mrs. Bagroot supplied to him, which, in turn, was simpler than what Oscar was teaching him at home. During class time, Mel found relief in solving problems easily when much of the rest of his world was in emotional upheaval.

Two of his most adamant opponents were his former Sunday school companions, Bobby and Billy Simcox. They were twins and, like pack hunters, attacked when they were together. They often shoved Mel back and forth, insulting his "snobby" ways.

Mel was intensely concerned with avoiding attention, as he had been instructed to try to blend in, so he chose to allow undeserved insults and aggression to be sent his way without retaliation. He could simply talk himself out of most situations. The Simcox twins were amused at both his accent and his wit.

One afternoon at the playground, after Mel had spent most of his time at school worrying himself that his father would never return, a gang of boys gathered to taunt him. The Simcox twins got caught up in the frenzy. As the boys gathered to enjoy their "sport,"

Mel was having difficulty holding his emotions in check.

"Where's daddy, boy?" they mocked, mimicking his accent. "Gone away again. Oh, too bad." They knocked his books out of his hands and punched him in the arm.

Mel saw that the girls were watching from a distance. Between shoves, he noticed Marigold Thurman regarding the boys with disdain. In the years since Mel had met her on his very first day of school, she had grown into an attractive young woman, short of stature, with more curls than ever. "Why don't you leave him alone, you big bullies?" she shouted. "He's only from another country; what's wrong with that?"

Some of the boys left the fray with Mel and turned to Marigold. "Oh, is he your boyfriend now, Mari?" they taunted her. "Can't stick up for himself, so he needs a *girl* to defend him." They pushed her into the circle with Mel.

"Mel and Mari, how sweet the sound," one of them mocked, his hand over his heart. "I think you two belong together."

Someone crouched behind Mel while two others pushed him, sending him flailing backward. Getting up, he saw two boys shoving Mari. He squinted, focusing on his surroundings. His body tensed, blood flowing to his muscles. Everything slowed, and the nearby boys became statues. He sensed his distance from each of them and felt their vulnerabilities.

Before he could stop himself, he pounced. He grabbed the boys who had shoved Mari and spun them, swiftly sending them sprawling away. He crouched and, spinning on his hand, swept the legs out from under those who had pushed him. They tumbled like trees in a tornado. He sprang to his feet and, with touches on the back of the neck, knocked two unconscious.

Mari backed quickly away from the scuffle in awe, stepping toward the other girls, who stared in astonishment at the spectacle unfolding before them. As Mari approached, they withdrew from her and dispersed as though she would bring the danger of the moment upon them. Mari stood at the edge of the playground, alone and confused, and watched Mel.

Mel now came to Billy and Bobby Simcox, who had stopped motionless in their tracks. Mouths agape, hands held out defensively, they stepped back and shouted in unison, "Noooo!"

Mel saw the fear in their eyes and followed their gaze to the groaning boys strewn across the playground. He had brought attention to himself and felt ashamed. "I'm sorry, I'm so sorry," he said humbly, hanging his head and walking away quickly.

Mari let out a tense breath and walked away in a different direction, toward her home. As she went, she glanced around, looking for her friends, who were nowhere to be seen.

Bobby and Billy, awestruck, watched Mel depart. They looked at each other and, without saying a word, started after him. When they had almost caught up, Bobby called out, "Mel, slow down; we need to talk to you."

"Why? Didn't you see what I just did?" Mel protested. "I could have killed you."

"We had it coming. We pushed you a little too hard, and we want to say sorry," Billy said.

No, you don't realize what just happened. I really could've killed you. I have abused my training. I have shamed my teachers and myself. "Please leave me alone." Mel increased his pace to a run as he continued toward home, berating himself as he ran. *How could I have lost control like that?*

"Mel!" Bobby ran after him, yelling excitedly at his retreating back. "What you did back there was stand up for yourself. It was fantastic! We've never seen anyone move as fast as you did. We've just got to learn how you did it. Could you show us?"

"No!" Mel shouted back emphatically. "I will not teach you how to hurt others." He easily outdistanced the panting Simcox twins, who were forced to stop and hold their sides in exhaustion.

* * *

The Simcox twins reached home excited.

"Who would've thought that little Melvin Uri could pull off moves like that? He was like a madman! I've never seen anyone, not even Garth Malingo, move that fast! Did you see the look on Paul Weathers' face? I thought he was going to pee his pants," Billy said. They doubled over in laughter.

Still trying to catch his breath from their run, Bobby added, "And... and Mari, she didn't know if she should run or hug the guy. Wow, wait till we tell Garth about this. He'll think we're just pullin' his leg."

A frown came over Billy's face. "Wait, Bobby, I'm not sure telling Garth would be the best idea."

"Why not?" Bobby asked, still giggling to himself.

"Because Garth is the meanest guy in town. He'd want to fight him. He would smear Mel all over the schoolyard. I don't care how fast he is; if Garth got a hold of him, he would break his face."

"Hmmm, I'm not so sure about that," Bobby replied. "I think there's more to Mel than meets the eye."

"Maybe he just got lucky or somethin'. Would you want to have someone go tell Garth that you were some great street fighter? He'd come gunning for you faster than a hornet after its nest is knocked down. I just don't think it would be a good idea."

"Are you going soft, Billy?" Bobby punched him in the arm. "Mel looked like he can handle himself if he gets mad enough. Maybe we ought to make sure Mari's there just in case Mel needs a little motivation?" Bobby guffawed.

"I don't think that's funny. And I ain't gonna tell Garth nothing about what happened today."

Bobby smirked. "You think he won't find out? Why he probably already knows. Something like this is going to spread like wildfire. I bet Garth's already on his way to the Uri farm."

A look of alarm came over Billy, and he ran out the door. "Bobby, I gotta go. I just remembered something I gotta do."

Bobby went to the door and stuck his head out, calling after his brother. "It ain't none of our business, Billy. Let it be!" But Billy was already far down the road, dust kicking up behind him.

* * *

Billy arrived at the Uri farm out of breath and sweating. He leaped over the picket fence, ran to the house, and pounded on the door. "Mel! Mel! I gotta tell you something! Mel!"

The door opened after a moment, and Oscar looked at the flush-faced young man. "And what brings you here in such a huff, laddie? What's all this hollering about?"

"I gotta talk to Mel, sir!" Billy gasped. "It's 'portant!"

"Aye, that it must be, to put you in such a tizzy. Well, master Mel is not in the house at the moment. You'll have to check the lookout. That seems to be the place he's favoring lately."

"And where would that be, sir?" Billy asked, looking anxious.

Oscar pointed toward a big tree near the cliff overlooking the coast. Billy immediately took off running.

"Ahh, youth!" Oscar said to himself, "To be able to run like that again." He took the last bite of a fresh-baked muffin he had been eating when Billy had knocked on the door. Musing, he said, "Of course, I never cared for running in the first place." He closed the door and walked toward the kitchen, the vision of another muffin filling his mind.

* * *

Billy saw Mel from a distance. He seemed to be sleeping, and yet, as he got closer, he saw that Mel's eyes were open, a faraway expression on his face.

Billy slowed and approached cautiously. "Mel, you all right?"

Mel seemed to be emerging from a daze as he focused on Billy. "Oh yeah, I'm okay. What are you doing here?"

"I come to tell you you're gonna be in big trouble!" he stated quickly. "If you ain't already."

"In big trouble? With whom?" Mel asked.

"Be warned; Garth Malingo is gonna come lookin' for ya."

"Garth?" Mel questioned. "What in the world would a gorilla like Garth want with me?"

Billy looked at the ground and nervously stammered, "He's the biggest goon in town. He has never lost a fight and hasn't had a person in town that could challenge him in years. He doesn't like it when anyone gets a reputation for being a fighter. Once he hears of it, the first thing he does is come lookin' for 'em so he can put 'em in their place."

"Well, I don't plan to challenge him. I'm not a fighter. I don't like what happened today. It's so... so... barbaric. He doesn't have anything to worry about with me."

Billy sighed and looked with concern at Mel. "No, that's not the way it works with Garth. When news of what happened gets out, he'll come lookin'. Why, I remember what he did to Donny Fletcher two years ago, when Donny got angry at Dawson Smith and beat him up. Donny was walkin' tall for a coupla days. But when Garth found out about it, he went gunnin' for him. Donny said he didn't want to fight, but Garth started pushin' him 'round, and soon enough, he got mad and took a swing at him."

"I am not going to take a swing at Garth Malingo; he's older than I am and twice as big. Why would he feel threatened by me?"

Billy looked at Mel with a serious glare. "Garth broke both his arms." Billy let that sink in for a moment. "Donny was younger than Garth, smaller, but that don't seem to matter with him."

"Garth broke Donny's arms because he beat *someone else* up?" Mel asked, shaking his head.

"Garth is 'bout as sick as they come," Billy replied. "The only one that's sicker, they say, is his dad. He's got to be the meanest cuss this side of the mountains. And he raised his boy to be just like him."

"Well, what do you think I should do?" Mel asked.

"I don't know, maybe get a gun or somethin'."

"Get a gun! Are you crazy?" Mel blurted out. "To protect myself from someone I've never even spoken to? In case he gets mad about something that happened between people who go to a school he no longer attends?"

Billy stared in shock at Mel's ignorance of Garth's reputation. Then he raised his hands and backed away. "You can't say you weren't warned. If Garth comes here later, nothin'll be on my conscience. I'll leave you to your thinkin' or whatever it was you were doing." Billy turned and walked back towards the road.

Mel sat thinking about the scenario that Billy had just described. He looked toward the road and, still seeing Billy's head bobbing in the unique manner of the Simcox twins, yelled out to him. "Hey, Billy! Thanks for the warning."

Billy turned and waved goodbye. "I'd wish you good luck, but you're gonna' need more than that."

CHAPTER 8

GOOD WORDS

Nothing unusual happened at the Uri farm in the hours after Billy's visit. Garth did not make an appearance, but his menace grew in Mel's mind. As dusk fell and Mel began thinking seriously about how he would defend himself against the new threat of Garth Malingo, he heard a familiar whistle from the direction of the road.

"Dad's home!" Mel yelled out to no one and sprang to his feet. He ran around the house and met his father as he walked in through the front gate. He flung his arms around him, holding him tight in a long hug.

"Oh, my! To what do I owe this burst of affection?" Telly asked jocularly, bittersweet emotion misting his eyes.

"I was afraid you weren't coming back."

"Now, why would you think that?" Telly asked consolingly. "You are my priority. At times, serious matters must be seen to. I am sorry that they take me away for so long, but if it is my path, I will always come back."

A pained expression crossed Mel's face. "What if someday you don't?"

"Then, on that day, you will have the strength to bear it. But why worry about days that may or may not come? Today has a way of giving us plenty to think about, doesn't it? I'm here now and glad to be home. I'm tired and hungry and looking forward to a nice, long bath and one of Oscar's famous meals."

"Yeah, like the fatback and beans we ate every night while you were gone?" Mel jested, wrapping his arm around his father as they walked toward the house.

* * *

The Uri household sat down to the first dinner that they had had together in several months. They ate barbecue chicken, potato salad, and a dessert of lemon meringue pie. After the plates were cleared, Mel helped Oscar set the table for after-dinner herbal tea and sat down next to his father, hoping to have their first substantial conversation since his return. Telly picked up his large cup of steaming tea, blew across its gold-leaf rim, and took a sip. Mel had an idea that brought a grin to his face. "Melek 'al Uri, huh? What a mouthful!"

Telly gave a sudden, deep belly laugh, spraying out his tea and nearly falling out of his chair. "Not the most difficult Delemnite name by any means! I gather Oscar told you a certain, particularly long story?"

Mel smiled brightly.

Oscar raised an eyebrow. "Aye, and thanks for the warning."

Telly doubled over again, pounding his hand on the table in laughter and rattling the tea accouterments. "Home is where the 'wise guys' are, as they say. You lot are reminding me of two rather eccentric, dear friends of mine who help me with some important work. I hope to introduce you to them someday, Mel."

"I know who you mean," Oscar said with a smile. "Some of our oldest friends." He and Telly shared a fit of laughter.

Jora rolled his eyes, embarrassed by their jovial spirit.

"Cooperton isn't the same without you, dad," Mel said, suddenly serious. "Today sure gave me plenty to think about."

Telly noticed the concern on his son's face and focused a thoughtful gaze on him. "What is it?"

Mel paused, reflecting on Billy's warning. "If someone with a bad reputation threatened to hurt you, how would you respond? I mean, what measures would be okay to take to defend yourself?"

"Did someone threaten to hurt you, Mel?"

"Well, no, not exactly," Mel answered, suddenly having second thoughts about bringing up the day's events.

"What is the problem then?" Telly asked.

Mel reluctantly recited the account of the playground brawl. He told of Billy Simcox's warnings about Garth Malingo.

When he was finished, Jora spoke with some incredulity. "You fought eight guys at one time? Are you sure you didn't imagine it?"

"Jora, I saw this young man, Billy, today," Oscar rebutted. "He looked more than a wee bit scared. Said he had to talk with young Master Mel here. I was feeling that there was something amiss."

"Oscar, get serious!" Jora rebuked. "Mel's not a fighter. He was probably running away, and they all fell down laughing."

"Jora," Telly interrupted sternly, "there are many reasons to believe that Mel is telling the truth. I met Garth's father, and he is just as Billy Simcox described. I don't think it's beyond his son to commit this kind of mischief." Turning to Mel, he asked, "What do you think, Mel? Do you believe that this Garth fellow will come looking for you?"

"I'm not sure, but if half of what Billy said is true, I don't want to get on the wrong side of his fists."

"Why not just carry a Sazo?" Jora asked with a twisted grin.

"Jora!" Telly's voice roared as he slapped his hand on the wooden table. "We will not speak of this."

"Sazo?" Mel inquired. "What's that?"

"Mel," Telly replied, "there are many things that we must not discuss until it is time. Jora was out of line in mentioning this. Please trust that we do not keep anything from you that you need to know. You'll learn of the Sazo one day. Just know that it's something to use only when absolutely necessary." Turning to Jora, he said in a stern whisper, "We will discuss this later."

Jora sulked out of the kitchen; his arms folded defiantly.

In the Uri household, Mel had become accustomed to there being issues that were forbidden to discuss. The dark past and the evils active in the world, which Oscar had since described to Mel, bothered Telly, and at times he simply stopped the conversation. Mel had often tried to pry into what was so bad about certain subjects, but his father had always stood fast and refused to speak of them. Despite Mel recently learning of his family's lineage, the mention of a Sazo had again provoked Telly's concern. Mel could always tell when the discussion was over simply by the way Telly pronounced his name.

"Mel," Telly said with gentle strength, "in answer to your earlier question, there will always be threats, and occasionally we must defend ourselves. But always seek peace first. Then, if all else fails, you can and should protect yourself."

"How?" Mel asked sincerely.

"First, 'how' to seek peace, then 'how' to protect yourself," Telly replied.

The plan for Mel to avoid confrontation with Garth and what to do if this attempt failed took the rest of the evening to establish.

* * *

The next day there was an excited buzz in the schoolyard when Mel arrived. Kids stared at him as he passed, gathering in small groups and whispering to each other. When Mel happened to step close to one crowd or another, they would back away as if association with him would somehow cause them harm. When he stepped inside and approached his book box, he found a black skull and crossbones mobile hanging above it.

Mel was first to take his seat, as usual. When the rest of the class filed in, they all sat as far away from him as possible. He surmised that they were acting in fear of Garth. He did not look forward to the confrontation, despite the preparations he and his father had discussed the night before. He felt alone and abandoned by his schoolmates.

Mel wondered how Mari would behave toward him today. She was almost always late and, true to form, had yet to arrive for class.

She often lost track of time. Mari was one of the most popular girls at school. She knew all her classmates and was admired by many. Her actions the day before were puzzling to Mel. She had risked her popularity by siding with him, a not-so-popular boy whom many regarded as "different." She had stood up for him and endured rejection for perhaps the first time in her life.

Mel smiled as she entered the classroom. When she saw him and made eye contact, Mel quickly looked away, concerned that her aligning with him would again cause her trouble. He could not bear the thought of another incident like what had happened the day before.

Much to Mel's surprise, Mari sat directly behind him. There was a rush of murmurs throughout the room. As Mrs. Bagroot tapped her desk to bring the class to attention, Mari placed a note in Mel's back pocket. The note stayed there, feeling like a hot iron, until the end of class.

As soon as the bell sounded, Mel ran to the one-stall bathroom, closed the door, and took out the note. It read: "GO HOME ANOTHER WAY TODAY!" That was all. It could only mean that Garth was planning an ambush.

Mel stepped outside and saw that everyone had dispersed. He began walking home, still deciding whether to flee or to face Garth.

He came to a place where an alternate route home diverged from the main road, and he stopped in his tracks. There was no one else in sight. He had experienced rejection before and knew that having the word "coward" added to the litany of abuse aimed at him would only feel like more of the same. The trouble with Garth was unlikely to end if it were avoided this day. Mel knew that this was a moment when he needed to decide what kind of person he would be.

He took a deep breath and continued along his usual path towards home. He rounded the corner, approaching the bridge outside of town, and was amazed at what he saw. There, on the hills surrounding the bridge, on each side of the creek, was the entire student body of the Cooperton school. Mel was reminded of a coliseum of spectators waiting for the gladiators to join in battle.

Garth was there, on the bridge, like Goliath waiting for David, pounding his fist into his palm.

Mel stopped and surveyed the area. There was no turning back. For the honor of himself and his father, he had to face this brute. He continued towards the bridge, noticing that the gang that had attacked him the day before had secured front-row seats, their faces rabid with anticipation. He saw Billy and Bobby Simcox. Billy was shaking his head from side to side while Bobby nodded. And he saw Mari, towards the back of the crowd, looking terrified.

Mel stopped at his end of the bridge and called out, "Hey Garth, are you sure you want to do this? I'm not a threat to you. There are no problems between you and me. Let's just talk for a few minutes; I'm sure there's a way to work this out." Sweat was beginning to roll down the small of Mel's back.

"Dar ain't nuttin' we need ta work out," Garth grunted. "Dis here is 'bout someone who thinks he's sumtin' special. I'm here ta teach you some mannas." He stepped to the center of the bridge with thudding footsteps that resounded across the creek. The gang of boys yelled out, cheering him on.

Mel saw that this was not going as hoped. Garth was being spurred on by the crowd. Mel remembered Donny Fletcher's broken arms and wondered if the damage that Garth could inflict would ever heal and be normal again. Still, he stepped forward, planning to attempt to reason with Garth once more.

"I understand that you are, what, two years older than me? You look like you're at least nine inches taller than I am and at least one hundred pounds heavier. Who is going to think more of you because you beat up a little kid like me?"

"I dun't know what you're talkin' 'bout. All I see is a kid that's too big fer his britches and needs some 'umbling."

"Have you ever been 'umbled, Garth? Anyone ever beat on you?" Mel asked, watching Garth wince when he said it.

"That ain't none of your business, boy, and you shut your mouth." He stepped forward, slowly moving across the bridge.

"I'm not going to stop talking because you order me to, Garth. Neither one of us is stupid, so why should we fight like animals?"

"Sho' yo' stupid. Yo' stupid cause you're messin' with my friends and my town. Now I'm gonna teach you how not to talk so stupid never 'gain."

Mel stood his ground, speaking quickly as Garth lumbered forward. "Garth, I'm not messing with your friends. You don't have any, not real ones. All your so-called friends keep on your good side because they're afraid you'll get mad and beat them up. I live outside of town and don't care to claim any reputation here." Just then, Garth came close enough to strike. Mel quickly ducked as his log-sized fist swooshed overhead. He darted behind the giant, stepping back several paces.

"You don't need to do this, Garth. You are by far the stronger fighter. I yield to you. You are the victor," Mel pleaded.

Garth stepped side to side, trying to get ahold of a very elusive Mel. Garth began to pant and mumbled under his breath, "You don't need to do nothin'. I'm cleaning up the mess. I won't let you down. I'll stop this foolish boy for ya." He shook his head to clear the fog in his mind caused by the unexpected exertion.

Mel noticed Garth talking to himself and wondered if there was not something more to his anger than met the eye. As he maneuvered around him, keeping just out of reach of his deadly arms, he decided to go to the next phase that his father had discussed with him the night before. He allowed Garth to grab him and instantly regretted doing so. His arms constricted like a python, and Mel's shoulders were squeezed beyond anything he had felt before. Still, he allowed himself to be drawn towards Garth's mammoth bulk and prepared to carefully use his free hand.

He reached around Garth's neck and pressed behind his ear with all his might in one sudden movement. Garth's neck felt like a tree trunk. There was so much muscle shielding him that Mel wondered if he had miscalculated. Then, with a spastic convulsion, Garth fell to his knees, his eyes bulging and his tongue hanging from his mouth. He was fully conscious but paralyzed.

A groan went up from the bloodthirsty spectators. Their champion had fallen. They shouted, "Get up, Garth, don't let this little foreigner best you. Get up and fight!" When he failed to respond, some began to jeer, "You gonna let this little twit bewitch you? When your old man finds out, he's gonna tan yo hide."

The *Kyusho Jitsu* pressure-point strike had left Garth frozen in position, with Mel still entangled in his grip.

Mel watched as Garth's eyes watered at the mention of his father's wrath. "You aren't a loser. You have more worth than what this crowd or your father sees. And you're still the toughest guy in town," Mel reassured him. Though Garth had not yet regained his ability to speak, he looked pleadingly at Mel, begging for mercy.

Mel chose to enact the final phase of his plan. He let out a tremendous, painful yell, broke from Garth's grip, and ran away across the bridge and down the road. Garth's cheering supporters turned quickly to heave their taunts at Mel's retreating back.

Garth, on his knees and stunned, slowly regained his mobility. He could not understand what had just happened. He had never doubted that he would beat this kid. He had done everything just like he always had, and then it was like he was hit by a lightning bolt. He had lost sensation and control of his arms and legs after Mel had struck him just *once* behind the ear. Now, several minutes later, he was just beginning to recover.

Something had happened that he had never experienced before. It was not that he had been defeated, though this was the first time that he could remember that happening. It was that someone had shown him *mercy*. The last words that Mel had spoken were not words that people usually said to a beaten foe. Mel's words had affirmed who he was. When the other kids had yelled threats about what his father would do when he found out what had happened, a part of him had hoped that Mel would finish the job. There was still a good chance his father would figure out that he had lost the fight, even though Mel had acted hurt and had run away screaming.

At least they think I won! Garth thought as he slowly got up to greet his cheering admirers. His head hurt. His ego was bruised. And he was confused about the behavior of Mel, who had not shown any fear. He was glad that it looked like he had come out the victor. But deep down, he knew that the full account of the fight would get to his dad.

* * *

When Mel neared home, he saw Jora peering out of the living room window, wearing his crooked grin, apparently eager for the opportunity to gloat over Mel's wounds. He and Telly met Mel as he stepped through the front door.

His father asked, "How did things go?"

"About like you said. I tried to reason with him, but he wouldn't listen. Then he came at me, and I let him catch me. Boy, I thought that would be a lot easier than it was, but I used that move you taught me last night." Mel reenacted the posture he had been in and how he had struck. "For a second there, I didn't know if that move would fell an elephant like Garth. But then he was totally paralyzed, with me trapped inside! I had to wait until his muscles could move again just to get myself out of his grip. Then I pretended to be hurt and ran off as you told me. I made it look like he was the winner, dad! I hope it worked, for his sake."

"It's only our ego that must win, in most fights, Mel," Telly said, rubbing his chin. "Many more victories are won by befriending our enemies, when we can, than by vanquishing them. Now, let's put this behind us and return to our work." Telly smiled proudly at Mel while affectionately ruffling his hair, then turned and entered his study.

CHAPTER 9

REDEMPTION

The next morning, as the Uri household was eating breakfast, the front door suddenly resounded with loud pounding. Shouts from outside signaled a visit from a very agitated neighbor.

"I thought this might happen. Come, let's greet our guests," Telly said as he put down his steaming cup of black tea and walked calmly towards the shuddering wooden portal. The door had an eye-level, barred hatch that could be opened to allow those inside to see out. There, filling the full frame of the hatch, was the grizzled face of Jed Malingo.

"How nice to see you again, Mr. Malingo," Telly said politely.

Upon opening the door, the massive bulk of Garth's dad filled the entryway. Telly could see Garth cowering in the background, his face bearing the marks of a recent beating. Jed stormed into the house with pounding footsteps and stood with arms crossed. His face was flushed red, the veins in his neck bulging. His muscular arms flexed convulsively as he began his tirade.

"What'd you do to my boy? Yesterday 'e came home actin' tough, but I seen he was a whipped puppy. Had trouble movin' at first, and his head was all mixed up. And then I hear'd from another boy's pa 'bout some magic move your boy made on him that put some kind of hex on 'em. I always figured that you folks here were strange. But now I know it's some kind of black arts or sumthin'."

"Mr. Malingo," Telly began, "it's a pleasure to have you in our home. We were just eating breakfast. Would you care to join us?"

Garth's eyes widened, his nose already having caught the aroma of fried bacon and toast. "I'm starved, Pa, couldn't—"

Jed turned and backhanded Garth across the face. "You shud-dup, boy! This is all 'cause of your bumbling!"

Garth retreated, his head bent and his eyes wincing from the sting of his father's hand.

Telly looked at Garth's quivering form and spoke to Jed with authority, "Sir, that was completely uncalled for. Garth has sought only to win your approval. He did not fail you yesterday."

Jed snapped, "That ain't none of your business, so just keep yo' 'pinions to yerself. Now I want to know what your son did to my boy, so's I can unhex him."

Telly, arms calmly at his sides, sized up Jed, who was now toying with something in his coat pocket. Telly tried to discern how long Jed could be appeased before his temper would blow.

"Your son," Telly explained, "approached my son yesterday at the bridge to quote, 'Teach him some manners.' He assaulted Mel in front of a crowd and apparently came out the winner."

"He didn't come out no winner! Yo' boy did something that sucked the spirit right outta him. Some kinda magic to best us, that's for sho'. We ain't never been bested, and especially not by some baby-faced foreigner!"

Telly replied, "I assure you there was no magic involved. It was a pressure-point strike that causes temporary paralysis, a simple self-defense move that we learned from a Japanese teacher."

"I shoulda figured as much! More foreign mumbo jumbo. We shoulda never let any of you people come into this country. It's the likes of you gonna cause the ruin 'a all 'a us."

"I believe Malingo is of Spanish descent," Telly replied. "Aren't we all of at least some foreign roots in this land?"

Flustered, Jed bellowed, "Don't change the stinkin' subject! That don't explain why Garth is so beat down."

Garth interrupted, "Pa, he done beat me, fair and square, and that's the plain truth."

Jed raised his hand again, and Garth jumped out of range. Jed's lip sneered. "What do you know about truth, you stupid clod of mud? You barely know how to tie your shoes by yourself. The truth is that no Malingo ever was a loser. You didn't lose that fight! You lost your nerve! And you stained *our* name!"

Telly watched Garth with compassion as every word that his father said hurt him visibly. "The only thing Garth lost in that fight yesterday was the lie that he was invincible, that he needed to use intimidation to gather friends, and that he was worthless unless he was feared. The reason why Garth is so downtrodden has been evident since you first entered this house. It is you who is beating him; it is your callous opinion of his potential and your own poisoned words that have cursed his self-image and led him to slump before you."

"That's enough, you stinkin' warlock!" Jed screamed as he stepped back, pulled a revolver from his pocket, and fired it twice point-blank at Telly's chest.

* * *

The sound of the rounds firing and the smoke that billowed out of the barrel masked the counteractions that Telly had taken a split-second earlier. From a small tube hidden under his shirtsleeve, he had launched two tiny projectiles of his own. There were two sounds, like a sledgehammer hitting an anvil as the bullets came to an abrupt halt. Jed let out a terrible scream, dropped his gun, and grasped his hands together in pain. Pain turning to rage, he lunged forward and swung his fist at Telly. In mid-stride, with all his might behind his outstretched arm, his hand hit with agonizing force against the invisible wall that had stopped the bullets. Meeting the unexpected barrier, Jed lost his balance and fell forward, splitting his lips against a hardwood chair as he tumbled to the floor. When he rose to his knees, a frantic look covered his face as he held his pain-wracked hands to his throat, apparently unable to speak.

Garth quickly wrapped a handkerchief around his father's gun and put it in his pocket. Jed's bleeding lips agape and his eyes full of brokenness and bewilderment, Garth grabbed him and dragged him from the house. The Malingos turned and stumbled along the path towards the road, Garth supporting his limping father.

* * *

Mel blinked with astonishment. The end of the Malingos' visit had transpired so quickly and had been so unprecedented in his experience that he did not trust his perception of what had occurred. After a few moments, he gathered his wits. "What just happened?" he exclaimed.

Telly, relieved by the way the confrontation had ended, sighed deeply and asked, "Shall we finish breakfast?" He turned and walked back into the kitchen, followed eagerly by Mel. Oscar and Jora kept watching through the front windows until the Malingos were out of sight.

"Dad! Tell me! What happened? Mr. Malingo just shot at you! He was too close to miss! Why aren't you dead?"

"Mel, please have a seat and finish your breakfast. I'll explain it all to you in a minute."

Mel obediently sat and ate and kept his peace while his father took a few bites of now cold toast and sipped the last of his lukewarm tea.

Shortly, Telly looked up from his plate. "Do you remember me correcting Jora about mentioning a Sazo?"

"Yes," Mel said with curiosity.

"A Sazo," Telly said, "despite sounding like an Italian dessert, is a weapon. The word is an acronym for *saevio arma zelus oppugno*. As you know from your Latin, it means 'the unquenchable war flame.' It was developed ages ago by our ancestors to serve a variety of purposes. The pellet projectiles are liquid hydrogen orbs encased in magnetic fields. The device has many settings. What you witnessed were two of its mildest uses."

Holding a small cylinder with several buttons on one end, Telly continued, "This is the Sazo projector, which fires the pellets.

These are triggers that tell the Sazo what to do. If I push this one," he said, pointing to a blue button, "it tells the pellets to launch to a prescribed distance and emit a close to absolute zero temperature burst. Thus Mr. Malingo's distress in trying to rid himself of his frozen gun. Unfortunately, he was inhaling when it opened, and his voice may never return. He has experienced the equivalent of frostbite to his lungs and the front side of his body. He'll be howling tomorrow and will have a rather unsettling appearance for quite some time."

"What about the bullets?" Mel persisted. "I saw the gun go off, so why weren't you hurt?"

"That," his father explained, "is one of the other functions. If you push this," he said, pointing to a green button, "it creates a brief magnetic field, which was what halted the bullets, and proved the worse for his fist."

Jora stepped into the kitchen, having heard Telly's last statement. "See! Mel should've taken one to the fight!"

"Jora," Telly responded, "this technology is not to be used in public or by the inexperienced. In the past, the Sazo has caused fear among the Terrans, and they've driven our people from their lands. For this and other reasons, it became a bane of our forefathers. One must use it wisely, or it will affect the way he views himself. Mr. Malingo's choice to bring a similar tool was part of what emboldened him to act foolishly today. I hoped for a peaceful resolution but did not consider it beyond him to seek violent retaliation. Though it was a risk, I'm confident this non-lethal use of the Sazo will not be broadcast to the community."

Jora sneered with doubt. "If you don't think this is going to get around, you're kidding yourself. Jed will be telling everyone within a hundred miles that we used 'black magic' on him."

"I disagree, Jora. Of all the wounds he received, the one to his pride was the most severe. Physically, he might never be able to speak again, and he doesn't know how to read or write. I believe we are safe."

CHAPTER 10

RED FACES AND APOLOGIES

For several days Mel expected a reaction from the locals. But his father had calculated correctly. Jed had become mute, and Garth had stayed home to tend to his dad's injuries. There was quite a stir over Jed's injured appearance when he finally left his house and showed up at the bar several nights after the incident. He looked like a lobster in the process of molting, with his skin healing and his ruby-red eyes bulging. His wounded expression betrayed broken pride. He was able to communicate only through gestures, which led the locals to believe he had become a bit "touched in the head."

Behind his back, the local men agreed that Jed must have gotten too drunk, fallen into his fireplace, and swallowed hot coals in the process. This theory got a hearty chuckle from the local boys when their fathers recounted Jed's misfortune. When Garth was asked about what had happened to his father, he shrugged and mumbled, "I dunno."

* * *

At school, the boys teased Mel daily about his humiliation at the bridge. They mocked his retreat by running across the schoolyard, screaming, and waving their arms above their heads. Mel ignored this, knowing that eventually, the fight would be chalked up to just another victory by Garth, and his classmates would move on to the next new, convenient target for mockery. He took comfort in knowing that his ruse during the fight had succeeded in saving Garth from humiliation in the eyes of his peers.

* * *

Mari Thurman had a different impression than the others of what had transpired that day. She had kept her eyes fixed on Mel rather than whooping it up for Garth like the rest of the kids. She had seen that the crushing power of Garth's massive arms had put considerable strain on Mel, but he had remained completely calm. She had seen when Garth had tumbled helplessly to his knees and Mel had talked to him while still trapped in his grasp. Why Mel had run off confounded her, but she knew it was not because he was afraid.

To her disappointment, her schoolmates had continued to reject her since the day of the playground brawl when she had aligned herself with the "little Euro-brat," as they called him. They now kept her at arm's length, as if her foolishness would spread to them. "Ewww!" they said while shuddering as they gathered in circles to giggle and gossip about her, preferably when she was near enough to see and hear them. "How could she fall for such a loser?" they jibed.

Mari was hurt by this treatment from her friends but did not let them define her self-image. *I didn't fall for Mel,* she reasoned to herself. *I just saw him being treated terribly and felt compelled to do something.* In response to this compassion, those who valued popularity over character had made sure that Mari became a social outcast. She discovered the day she stood up for Mel that the loyalty of her friends was fragile.

She had noticed on occasion how Mel looked at her with sympathy when he realized that she was being mistreated.

* * *

One afternoon, Mel was walking home and saw Mari sitting by herself at the creek near the bridge. For days he had wanted to speak to her, and he knew this was his opportunity. He summoned his courage and approached her. "Hey, Mari," he said sheepishly.

She looked up. Seeing that it was him, she smiled, and her eyes brightened. "Hey, Mel," she replied, looking straight at him, "whatcha doin'?"

Averting his eyes, he kicked the ground with one foot. "I just wanted to say I'm sorry," he said and turned to leave.

"Sorry for what?" she quickly asked.

Mel slowly turned around while still backing toward the path. "I'm sorry I've caused you so much grief. Your life was easy before that day at the playground. I'm sorry about your friends and that you have to spend so much time alone now," Mel said, occasionally glancing up to see how she was responding.

Mari looked steadfastly at Mel, not averting her gaze. She leaned back and, with a calm laugh, said, "My best friends are still with me. They don't care who's popular."

"But all your schoolmates won't even talk to you anymore, except to mock you," Mel replied.

"I don't mean them. They're as fickle as a gooseberry cobbler. One minute they love you and are as sweet as can be; the next, they turn on you and go sour. My true friends are still with me."

Mel stopped backing up and looked straight into her big, brown eyes. "I don't understand."

Mari grinned playfully. "Come on, Mel, you know the same friends I do. I've seen you sitting alone too. Out there on the cliff, staring out at the ocean. You were singing as you watched the birds swoop by on the breeze. I watched as you followed that squirrel for an hour as she circled around that old oak tree in your yard. She stopped and squirrel-talked to you, and you talked right back to her," she said with a laugh.

Mel flushed red with embarrassment. He had no idea that Mari had been watching him. He stammered, a little defensively, "Was that... right to be sneaking around watching me and never letting me know?"

"Oh, I wasn't sneakin'. I was right there in front of you in your yard the whole time." She looked at him inquisitively, as if she were trying to see past his outward appearance. "Mel, every morning before school, I get up early to milk our family's cows and collect the eggs. Chances are, that's the only kind of life I'll ever have. Now, here you are, one of the smartest people I've ever known. You understand things that most folks can't, and who knows what you'll do with your life, but even you don't see everything that's right in front of you," Mari finished cryptically.

Mel realized that this was what Oscar meant when he talked about "no-nonsense" gals. He stood frozen with befuddlement.

She continued, "Your old friends are the same ones I've ignored these years as I've tried to please all those silly girls."

Mel realized that both he and Mari now knew the pain of others withholding approval and had learned that their joy must never depend on anyone else's opinions of them. For the first time, he felt understood by someone from outside of his own household. Mari had caught his attention from his first day at the Cooperton School seven years before, and now he felt that she was becoming his first true friend. But that long-sought word did not seem like enough to describe this girl. A sudden thought made him smile. "Well, at least you don't have any *proof* I was singing to birds and chasing squirrels."

Her eyes narrowed playfully. "Oh, Mrs. Rose McFluffy could definitely serve as a witness," she said, imitating the running movement of a squirrel with her hand.

"Hmmm, then I'm forced to plead guilty," Mel said with a laugh. "I'll see you tomorrow, Mari." He turned back toward the path leading home.

"See you then!" she replied as they each waved goodbye.

When Mel was almost out of sight, he turned and yelled out, "The witness's name is *Mr.* Timothy Thumin."

She yelled back, "Sounds a lot like Thurman to me, Mel!"

CHAPTER 11

A GREAT MISHAP

As Mel returned home from school, his father was waiting for him at the gate of their farm. He was dressed to go on another journey. As Mel approached, he could see that his father's eyes were worried. "Is something wrong?" Mel inquired, his heart noticeably beating. He hoped that he was not about to hear bad news, which he had learned had a way of telegraphing itself before he heard what was going on.

"Nothing is wrong, *now*," his father said.

Mel wondered at his inflection of the word "now." "Where are you going?"

"I've heard a rumor that I must investigate. I don't know how long I'll be gone. But don't worry about me; I'll be back."

"Back from where?" Mel queried.

"The way these things usually work is I go to the source of the rumor and follow it from there."

"What did you hear?" Mel asked, leaning his books against the old, weathered gate post.

"Mel, I can't say right now. I don't wish to set you up for unmet expectations or anxiety. Trust that when I get definitive information, you'll be the first to know. I will be keeping track of you. Some great challenges will be upon you quite soon. I have the utmost confidence that you will overcome any obstacle that comes your way. No matter how difficult and discouraging circumstances may seem, you will find a way through them. The life you will discover on the other side is worth it, forever." He hugged his son, kissed him on the forehead, and started walking down the road, a long, white staff in his hand.

Mel had a sinking feeling that his father had meant for their farewell to be more than a word of encouragement before a temporary parting. Mel had so many unanswered questions and felt a strong urge to run after his father and beg him to let him come along. But he stood and watched the retreating back of his father, tears gathering in his eyes, and spontaneously cried out, "I love you!"

Telly turned and smiled, his eyes full of love and weeping. "And I love you!"

And then he was gone around a curve of the road.

* * *

Weeks passed with no word, and Mel began to experience a heavy sensation in his heart. Telly had gone away several times before but had always quickly sent word concerning why he was delayed and how long it would be before he returned. Mel's foreboding mood at times wrinkled his forehead and caused the old wound on his head to throb.

After Telly had been gone for two months, still with no word, Oscar began to share Mel's concern and decided he would go looking. He hoped to find him in Cambria, a town that was to be Telly's first destination. He packed a month's worth of food into the wagon, though he said the trip would only take a few days. He lined the wagon seat with soft cushions, placed a large chest full of his most colorful clothes in the back, and set off down the southern road that wound its way through the coastal mountains.

* * *

One evening, after a long day of work on the Uri farm, Mel stepped into his father's study, which had been moved to a cliffside room on a middle floor of the Caeli. It was to this room that his father had often retreated. Mel peered slowly around at the sculpted shelves packed with hundreds of books that had been collected from around the world.

Half of the room protruded from the cliffside, appearing from the outside to be a granite outcropping. Inside, Telly had skillfully fashioned this protrusion to have five transparent sides. The floor looked to the rocks below, the ceiling to the skies above. A side door opened onto a small, disguised balcony. Mel and his father had often sat there for hours, reading or watching the pelicans glide past.

This evening, Mel was there to search for any clue concerning his father's quest. Telly had given Mel full access to his study, noting, "The things you shouldn't yet see, I'll put where you can't find them." Like a cat in a new house, he proceeded to investigate everything. He turned over random objects on shelves, looking under each one. He opened the desk drawers and carefully pulled out the items, looked at them, and then placed them back exactly as they were. Mel's knack for remembering how things fit together, cultivated through practice with Oscar's puzzles, served him well on this occasion.

Finally, after exhausting every option short of pulling out every single one of his father's books, he looked to the ceiling and asked, "Where are you? Why do I feel so uneasy?" His father had taught him to be discerning and to listen closely to that still, small voice that had so often warned him of possible danger.

He took a seat in the overstuffed chair in front of the huge transparent side of the room overlooking the ocean and pulled his knees up to his chin. His father would not have approved of him putting his feet on the chair without taking off his shoes, but Mel was so preoccupied that he did not even think of it.

Just then, the door to the study opened, and Oscar burst in, panting with exertion. It was the first time Mel had seen him since his departure to search for Telly six weeks before. "Mel!" he huffed, catching his breath. "Your father has had a great mishap!"

Mel jumped to his feet, partly from the news and partly from being startled out of his deep concentration. "What... what did you say? A what?"

"A mishap!" Oscar groaned. "An anomaly of standard safety. An... an accident, I'm afraid!"

"What kind of accident? Is he all right? Where is he now?" Mel spit his questions out in rapid-fire.

"Well," Oscar said with an apologetic whine, "I... well, we... oh, I don't know! He simply disappeared."

"He what?" Mel snapped.

Oscar was in a fog of exhaustion from his travels but knew that Mel needed to hear the full account. "I'll start at the beginning. I tracked your father to the eastern foothills of the Sierra Nevada, near a mining town called Bodie. He looked fit as a fiddle when I met him and was happy to see me. I told him you'd become quite concerned for him, and he said that things would be difficult for you, but you'd be all right. He was expecting some information from someone he was to meet. When we got to the predetermined place, well..." Oscar began to drift off in his thoughts. "Mmm... in the tumult, I lost track of him, and there was so much confusion and things stirring so rapidly, and the sounds were all around us. And, well, I just don't know what happened." He hung his head and clasped his hands around the back of his neck.

Mel took a deep breath. "Oscar," he said in a soft voice, "if you would please tell me exactly what transpired."

Oscar sensed the safety of the study and the concern in the heart of young Mel. He calmed his nerves and began again. "We'd just passed Sonora after coming over the pass from Bodie. We reached the meeting place about sunset, and the skies were filling with clouds, turned purple by the evening light. Sonora has an extraordinary history. Did you know that out of that one hill, they extracted three hundred tons of g—"

"Oscar, you were telling me what happened!"

"Oh, right," Oscar said, clearing his throat. "We had just rounded the bend of the river, and there, dancing on the water, was a whole flock of Mysenri!" His eyes bulged as he said the name.

Mel's brow furrowed in puzzlement. "A flock of what?"

"A herd, or a flock, or maybe you have to call them a bevy? At any rate, they were Mysenri, water sprites, spirits, fairies, elf people, or some such thing. I... I have never seen them before, just heard stories about them. They are very unpredictable. And they are not too keen on us clumsy folk."

Mel was becoming irritated, wanting Oscar to get to the point, but his curiosity was piqued. "I've never heard of such creatures."

"Of course not," Oscar replied. "They avoid us like the plague, with us making all the racket that we do and upsetting the peace in the forest. They can hear us from miles away and make themselves scarce when we're close. You may have seen them without knowing it. They can look like a flock of butterflies or dragonflies."

Mel asked, "Why haven't they been written about? In my education, I haven't come across any scientific records."

Oscar laughed. "But you have, laddie, and you didn't know it. There've been hundreds of books written about them. Don't you remember the stories in *Fairies in the Hinterland*?"

"Those were just fairy tales, made up to entertain children."

"Fairy tales indeed! Do you think that every word in the local newspaper is the truth? There's often more fiction in reports of current events than in the *Grimm's Fairy Tales*, boy. Every good child's story has an element of truth to it. How would they go about teaching us moral lessons if the foundation wasn't at least partly true? There's another world out there, and you know it. Far more than just what our five senses can tell us. There are a hundred dimensions we can't see with our eyes, but does that mean they aren't there? No, it's just that we can't see them yet."

"Yet?"

"There's a time and a place for everything, lad. Once in a while, we are chosen to catch a glimpse."

Not yet fully convinced, Mel nonetheless decided to play along. "What happened after you saw them?"

"They began to swarm your father. You know, I've heard that people have the nasty habit of disappearing when they show up. Your father didn't seem surprised at all; it was as if he were expecting them and had been looking for them for some time. I'd thought we would be meeting a regular person. You know, your father is very mysterious. He makes plans and does things that very few people ever find out about. He's just like that, so veiled."

"What happened then?" Mel asked more firmly.

"Well, there they were, seemingly thousands of them, dancing like fireflies on the river. I thought I was seeing things, with the sun setting and the colors and the sound of the river roaring in my ears. I'm not all that stable around running water anyway, with my vertigo, you know."

Mel had crossed his arms and was beginning to tap his foot.

"Where was I? Oh yes, the singing! That's what convinced me. The sound of their wings fluttering sounded like a choir of monks chanting a Celtic hymn. It was beautiful. But then something happened because they went into a frenzy and began to swirl around like a swarm of bees, Telly right in the middle of them. He was a veritable statue of peace. At first, I thought he was talking to them, but he wasn't talking, he was singing along with them! Then he seemed to tell them something important because they swarmed even more excitedly, expanding out, then coming together again in a tight pack. Their song got louder and louder, and they were hovering around your father when suddenly..." Oscar stopped, staring as if looking far away.

"And then what, Oscar? What happened then?"

"He spoke through the singing and the raging of the river. 'Tell Mel. He'll know what to do when it's time.' And then I turned to fetch my notepad, and when I looked back, he'd disappeared! Gone! And all the Mysenri with him. It was so strange."

"Tell me what? Was that everything he said?" Mel implored.

"Just those exact words," Oscar said apologetically. "I'm so sorry, Mel, but I don't understand it myself."

Mel thought, *What am I supposed to do now?* It was three months until his sixteenth birthday when his father was supposed to take him to the deepest level of the Caeli to open the Abico vault, the first of the eight forbidden chambers. He had been told that from these vaults, he would learn the most crucial lessons of his life. His father had mentioned a pivotal decision that Mel would have to make. How could he go forward now? And exactly what had happened to his father?

Mel was so full of questions that he could barely maintain his composure. He looked at Oscar's disheveled, distraught face and realized he was in a similar condition. "Oscar, please forgive me. You've had a long, confusing journey and did the best that anyone could hope. You must be exhausted and hungry. I baked some fresh sesame seed cakes and left them in the kitchen. You're welcome to them."

Oscar, hearing the mention of food, recovered his wits and walked to the door. He paused and looked back. "I'm sorry, young Master Mel." He stepped out of sight up the Caeli stairway.

Mel was alone again. He searched his inner being for something that would tell him where his father had gone. He sat in the deep, cushioned chair and longed for his father's voice to fill the study as it had many times before.

"Mysenri?" Mel mused. "Where have I heard that before?"

He looked at his father's bookshelves and then arose and began to examine the library. The books were organized by genre; the academic books together, with philosophy and science placed alphabetically in separate subsections. At last, Mel found the section labeled "The Unseen World," and just where it was supposed to be, the book *Fairies and other Elusive Creatures.*

CHAPTER 12

THE MYSENRI

Mel immediately opened the book to the chapter on fairies.

Fairies are misunderstood and highly underestimated.
The Mysenri, as they call themselves, are multi-clan creatures. They populate the sparsely inhabited areas of the
world, dwelling in places that retain the stillness of nature.
Some clans live near wooded streams, others in the desert, and still others dwell in the mountains. Each clan has
unique powers associated with its environs.

They are an old race of beings and are not to be trifled
with. When humans draw too near, the Mysenri typically seek to blend into their surroundings. Occasionally,
when a person lumbers upon them during their afternoon rest, they may be startled, awaken abruptly, and become agitated. It is rumored that, upon occasion, persons
who trespass their territory are never heard from again,
though these accounts have yet to be confirmed.

Standing at the bookshelf, Mel realized that the large book was
beginning to feel heavy. The chapter was fascinating but quite long,
so he settled back into his cushioned chair and continued reading.

Despite their diminutive size, the Mysenri are a fierce
people. They have been known to rally in overwhelming
swarms to drive away hostile intruders. Their tiny weapons, which consist primarily of arrows and knives, are

typically coated with a potent venom, a single dart being capable of rendering unconscious the largest of mammals. Folk tales assert that they can cast spells to confuse their enemies. It is said that they use singing to lull intruders into states of euphoria—a distraction that allows them to then blend safely into their surroundings once again.

As elusive creatures, they do not deliberately reveal their presence to anyone unless they so choose. They are very selective when deciding who will receive this honor, and to this date, no definitive pattern has been observed. If a flock of Mysenri is encountered, it is recommended that the individual remain calm and not run from them, as this can convey the impression of a threat and result in incapacitation, perhaps indefinitely.

There are thought to be seven major clans of Mysenri living throughout the world. Their territories are defined either by natural borders or through agreements between the reigning clan chieftains. They speak individual clan dialects but also share a common language that allows them to communicate between groups. They speak many human languages and are also capable of communicating with humans through telepathy and elaborate songs that bypass the language-based cerebral processes. These songs are said to enable the individual to perceive pictures in the air that convey considerable information with few words.

The clan of Mysenri whose territory encompasses North America is perhaps the best understood. This group is led by an exceptionally fierce chieftain named Gwyneth and includes as many as two hundred thousand who are loyal to her leadership. She has been known to respond to intruders and to seek out communication with select persons for her own purposes, as occurred in a famous incident in the 1600s.

The interaction was recorded in the notes of the honorable explorer Colonel Clifton Wetherby. In 1642, along the way to China, Colonel Wetherby stopped on the west coast of North America to resupply his vessel. It was there that he encountered the diminutive, yet powerful Gwyneth, who warned him that a great evil spirit was about to descend upon China and provoke the Ming army to destroy the Kaifeng seawall. Due to delay caused by storms in the Pacific Ocean that year, the warning to the people of Kaifeng was not received in time, and over 300,000 persons drowned in a single violent act. Colonel Wetherby's account was not the first time in history that men had reported being warned of impending disasters by "angels" or other messengers of various physical sizes who bore little resemblance to human emissaries.

The Mysenri lifespan is thought to be long by human standards. Their ages have never been definitively determined, but records of the same Mysenri individuals have been discovered over one thousand years apart.

No exhaustive analysis of the Mysenri has been found, nor does one appear to be forthcoming. It is supposed that whoever encounters them, if they are permitted to leave, is put under an oath or a spell that prevents the disclosure of any more information than the Mysenri allow.

Mel set the book down, sensing his fears fading away. He knew that the Mysenri would have contacted his father only for a good reason. If he had received a message like the one given to Colonel Wetherby, which would require him to travel across the world, it could be a long while before he arrived back home.

Mel breathed a sigh of relief and resignation, accepting that his father would not be there for his sixteenth birthday. If Oscar's newly unsettled state of mind persisted, he would not be able to fulfill his role in the trip to the Abico vault on the forbidden level of the

Caeli. Perhaps Jora would be Mel's best hope for assistance. He had always been involved before when Mel had gone through a transition in his training.

He again opened the huge book, to the chapter entitled "Mer People and the Giant Squid," and began to read.

CHAPTER 13

HAPPY BIRTHDAY?

The day dawned in crimson glory. The sounds of birds chirping in the trees mingled with a warm morning breeze. The sun rose in a sky awash with orange and purple towers of cumulus clouds stretching from the coastal mountains to the distant ocean horizon.

A ray of sun fell across Mel's face, waking him and causing him to squint. He rubbed his eyes and stretched his arms in a wide arc. Suddenly he remembered what day it was!

He shot out of bed and pulled on his trousers, brown wool sweater, and shoes. At the window, he paused to stand in the warm morning light. Closing his eyes, he breathed deeply and let the sun touch his face and glow red through the curtains of his eyelids.

He recalled Mari's smile from that day by the creek when they had first felt that they understood each other. In the six months since then, they had met along the path between town and the Uri farm many times to talk of everything under the sun and to explore the redwood canyons surrounding Cooperton in search of natural wonders. They had found salamanders in the mud under decayed logs, tasted the touch of nectar from the base of sticky monkey flower blossoms, jumped across rushing creeks, clambered along fallen trees, and encountered the occasional rattlesnake. They had spoken of everything except his household's Delemnite heritage, a subject that Mel knew had the potential to change things between them—a risk he was not yet willing to take.

Stepping into the kitchen for breakfast, he found a note on the table. He sat and ate as he read. The note was from Oscar and announced that he had left early that morning on another search for

Telly. He trusted that Mel and Jora would keep busy with the new lessons. Mel put down the note, disappointed that Oscar would not be there for his big day but encouraged by Oscar's confidence that he and Jora could handle the proceedings. Mel had watched for three months as Oscar had grown increasingly anxious in his desire to find and help his missing best friend.

After finishing his meal, Mel's heart nearly burst with anticipation as he raced to his tutor's room. "Jora! Today's the day! It's time to get up!" Mel eagerly shouted.

"Oh, go away; it's too early," Jora groaned as he drew his covers over his head, rolled over in his bed, and pulled his pillow around his ears.

"No, Jora! Today's my birthday! Today's the day I get my next lesson! The one on the forbidden level!" Mel said, eyes wide open and his voice filled with excitement. "After all this time, I finally get to open the Abico vault."

His father had described the lessons that he would learn in the secret vaults on the lowest level of the Caeli as a rite of passage, saying, "Mel, the Abico is the first of many tests that will challenge your attitudes and motivations. Your ability to responsibly handle the power that comes through knowledge is not determined by what you know or what you can do, but by *who you are*."

The memory of these words stirred Mel's zeal. "We need to get going." He pulled the covers off Jora with one sweep.

"You little mud sucker," Jora seethed, lashing out at Mel, who easily avoided his sleepy lunge. "Get out of here before I give you a lesson you'll remember for a month."

"Come on; you said you were looking forward to this."

Jora regained his covers and wrapped them around himself, surrounding his face as if with the hood of a cloak. *Today is the day, all right. And I definitely have been looking forward to this.* He sat up slowly and cleared his throat. "Sorry about that, Mel; I'm just not a morning person."

"It's okay," Mel conceded gently, still brimming with eagerness.

"How soon will you be ready?"

"Soon," Jora replied. "I just need some privacy for a moment."

"I'll meet you at the entrance."

As Mel closed the door, Jora's countenance darkened, and he jumped up quickly and began throwing things out of his closet as he searched for something he had concealed in the mess.

* * *

The Grand Door to the forbidden level of the Caeli was across from the entrance to the underwater observation room. Before now, only Telly or Oscar had opened this door to retrieve scrolls.

Mel paced in the hall in front of the Grand Door, clutching the key, which he had found where he and his father had placed it months before. Mel realized now that his father had anticipated that he might not be there on this most important of days. *Why else would he have been so careful to show me where he kept the key? How did he know that he could trust me to not go alone?*

Jora arrived, his hair disheveled and his shirt untucked, as usual. "Do you have it? Let me see!" Jora demanded. "You knew where it was all along, didn't you? And hid it from me. I bet you've snuck down here many times, haven't you?" Jora accused, his voice dripping with bitterness.

"No, I haven't," Mel said, stepping back and clutching the key. "That wouldn't have been right. You've heard the warnings. The vaults are only for those who are fully prepared."

"Oh yeah, I forgot," Jora sneered. "And all this time, it was *you* who was being prepared while I endured your struggles with the lessons. Come on; we must continue your training, mustn't we?"

"Jora, this is a special day for me," Mel implored, his sense of delight beginning to give way to apprehension.

Jora sensed Mel's concern. "You're right. I'm just grumpy in the morning. It'll pass." He reached out and squeezed Mel's shoulder in a brotherly gesture, noticing that he was tense.

They each took a lantern off a nearby shelf. Mel began to unlock the huge wooden door. Jora shifted anxiously from one foot to the other, ready to pounce, his breath producing wisps of condensation around his face. "Can't you hurry up?" he insisted.

Mel paused briefly. "They say that patience is a virtue."

When the lock finally clicked open, Jora pushed his way past and barked, "I think I've had just about enough of your little proverbs." He ran ahead, disappearing down the spiral staircase that descended just inside the doorway.

Mel withdrew the key and followed quickly after him.

The flickering, swaying lamplight, and the dripping of water on the walls, along with the steam-like condensation that billowed out of their mouths as their breath labored in their haste, lent a surreal air to the experience. Something in Jora's pace caused a warning in Mel's heart. He could not identify the source of his concern, but his premonition was unmistakable. Mel's heart began to beat faster. He had an acute case of the jitters and began to shake.

The slick onyx walls and damp stone stairs reminded Mel of the night he had watched his father sculpt the Caeli. He felt that he should have been walking slowly down these stairs with his father, speaking in reverent tones of what was ahead, not descending recklessly to keep up with Jora, his disgruntled tutor. Mel had long awaited this day, but his father's absence and Jora's impatience made this journey feel cold and dark. The echoing sounds of his and Jora's hurried footsteps clopping down the staircase only reminded Mel of how this day, which had begun with great joy, was now ringing hollow.

They finally reached the bottom of the stairs, their ears feeling the increased air pressure of this lowest level of the Caeli. They came to a circular landing and approached a door that looked as old and solid as the mountains themselves. Four-inch wide metal bands crisscrossed the hardwood. In its exact center was a large, triangular keyhole surrounded by an elaborate brass encasement.

Jora snatched Mel's key. He tried it in the lock, to no effect. He cursed. "Was there another key that you forgot?"

"This is the only one that he showed me. Perhaps if I tried?" Mel placed his lantern on the floor and reached for the key.

"Don't touch that!" Jora screamed as he pushed Mel away. But Mel had already grasped the key and held it as he fell onto the landing. Jora jumped towards him, trying to wrestle the key away.

Mel curled himself into a tight ball as he yelled, "What is wrong with you, Jora? Stop!"

Jora realized that he was not going to be able to untangle Mel's arms and legs, so he relaxed his grip and stepped back. "Oh, Mel, you can never take a joke. Always too serious. Come on, try your best. Let's see what you can do."

Mel stayed in his defensive posture as Jora backed away. Then he slowly rose to his feet, cautiously walked to the door, and placed the key in the lock. He turned it first left, then right, then left twice again, as he had been instructed by his father. The lock clicked, and he turned the knob, pushing the huge door gently forward. It swung open easily as if the hinges had been oiled the day before.

Mel picked up his lantern and held it out into the newly opened chamber, revealing only bare floor as far as he could see. With their lanterns at arm's length, they stepped forward. They were in an immense, arched cave lined with hundreds of safe-like compartments on two opposing walls. Rolling ladders on each side allowed access to the several rows above eye level. Most of the compartments seemed to have been opened. In the lower rows at the back of the cave, the vaults were undisturbed.

"Wow!" Mel exclaimed, his eyes widening as he took a deep breath. "This place is huge! And look at all these compartments. Is this where my lessons have been stored?"

"The more recent ones, yes," Jora said. "I learned most of these lessons when I was your father's apprentice. I had such great love for the ancient crafts. I was so zealous until..." Jora stood with his teeth clenched and his forehead furrowed. "Until... until..." He seemed to be losing himself in his memories, then said quickly,

"Until Telemai chose me to be your tutor. He wanted the best teacher for his son."

Jora stepped in front of Mel and walked quickly toward the undisturbed vaults in the far corner of the cave.

"Jora, what are you doing? I'm the one that must open the Abico vault. You know what my father said, 'You can't go on until you've learned the last lesson, and then you must go on alone.'"

Jora stopped in front of the unopened vaults and turned to face Mel. He rose to his full height, a dark look upon his face. "For years, I have endured your sniveling, 'my father said this, my father said that.'" He spoke with increasing vehemence. "Fourteen years ago, I was ready to open the Abico. I was destined to be a great Vysard. It was I who warned your father of the rebellion that was arising against him. It was I who saved your miserable hide on the dark day of the mountain. It was I who gave of my life and breath these many years so that you could attain the privilege of coming here today. Without me, you wouldn't be here. And now I am going to prove that I was always worthy of the next step."

"Jora, don't do this. We don't know what—"

"It was your miserable father," Jora sneered, "that bound me to you. If it had not been for him, I would have had access to this lesson long ago. He allowed his judgment to be warped by my one stupid mistake. Simply curious, that's all I was. I didn't want to steal the secrets of the old ones. I just wanted to hear how their meetings were conducted. I crawled up in a tree overlooking the fire circle and I just listened. That's all; I just listened." His eyes began to water as he stopped and cleared his throat.

Mel backed toward the doorway. "I... I don't understand."

"No! You don't, and you never will, you son of a snail! You are just like your father. Obsessed with the *right way*!" Jora mocked. "Well, now I'm going to show you, and the ghost of your father, that I was treated unjustly, I was judged wrongly. I was ready, and I am still! And I will not be denied what is rightfully mine. Your father was wrong, *wrong*!" Jora screamed as he reached out to the handle of the first unopened vault. And then, speaking to an unseen presence, he shouted, "Telemai! I hope you see what a mistake you made by denying me *my destiny*!" He pulled a Sazo from beneath his cloak and aimed it at Mel while he reached out with his other hand and turned the handle on the vault.

A brilliant flash of light burst forth with a deafening "*whoomp.*" Blinding flashes of blazing magnetic rays engulfed Jora's body. He was blown across the room, a shattered remnant of flesh and bone.

The first concussive wave pushed Mel through the doorway, where the partially closed wooden door protected him from the explosive rays. Rock bits and bone particles stuck into the door.

"Jora!" Mel shouted in anguish. He noticed a wound in his side. He saw a bone protruding from his chest. He thought it was one of his own ribs, but upon closer inspection, he saw that it had pierced him from outside of his clothing and must have come from Jora. Mel reached and, with an agonizing tug, removed the bone fragment from his side. The open wound bled profusely. Mel held a hand tightly to it to stop the flow.

Stunned, Mel got up slowly and walked across the debris-strewn floor. He looked in pity and horror at Jora's distorted remains. His heart sank when he saw the vault that had been disemboweled. Small fragments of a scroll and what looked like pieces of a small bag still burned within it. The full scope of the disaster dawned on him. Jora had lost his life in a foolish act, and Mel's future had been derailed.

The Abico vault's defense mechanism had annihilated its contents, yet the next seven vaults remained unscathed. Mel did not know what lesson the Abico had contained and understood that if he tried to go on to the next vault without first learning from the Abico, he would share Jora's fate. Mel glanced again at Jora's remains. "What am I to do?" Mel asked aloud of the empty room.

With his head hung low, his clothes torn by debris, and the smells of sulfur and blood hanging around him, Mel hobbled out of the chamber, pulling the door after him on its silent hinges and withdrawing its key. Still holding his hand tightly to his wounded side, he ascended the stone steps for what seemed like an eternity.

As Mel stumbled into the kitchen looking for supplies to dress his wound, he saw the note on the kitchen table that Oscar had written. It seemed like days had passed since he had read it. His whole world had been turned upside down, and now, for the first time, he was alone in the Uri home.

Mel sighed, a tear running on his cheek as he said to himself sarcastically, "Happy birthday, Mel."

* * *

It was raining outside, the lightning splitting the skies like forked daggers. Mel relived his traumatic experience with each new thunderous volley. He wandered around the house, eating little and reading none. He did not know what to do or where to go. He feared that if he told Mari what had transpired, she would view him and his family as monsters and feel a responsibility to report them to the authorities.

No one came to visit the farmhouse. No news came in the post. The silence of the home left Mel even more despondent. He walked past the secret entrance to the Caeli but could not bring himself to retrace his steps to the spiral stair and face the mess in the chamber of vaults.

On the third day, Mel decided that he would have to go and clean the room. He prepared a grave behind the house, out of sight of anyone who might wander by on the road or come to visit. After gathering the necessary equipment and supplies, he entered the Caeli and slowly descended toward the level of the observation room and the first grand door, remembering the excitement he had felt just three days earlier. He paused at the door, shuddering at the memory of the first cold touches of that day. He took a lantern and continued past the door and down the spiral stair, his current task born of grim necessity.

He reached the landing and the inner door, which he had left ajar in his stunned retreat. He raised his lantern to look just inside the entrance. The room appeared unchanged. He slowly stepped in, waiting for the expected acrid smells to assault his nostrils, and was surprised to smell nothing. He looked fearfully into the corner where the remains of Jora had landed, and, to his amazement, the body was gone! He ran over to the spot and looked in every direction. He wondered if he was mistaken about where the body had been thrown by the blast. He crouched and looked at the ground closely. Debris was everywhere, including faint traces of blood, but there was no Jora. In disbelief, he lifted his shirt to check the wound that had been caused by the fragment of bone. The wound was still there and was healing well. But what had happened to Jora's remains?

Perplexed, Mel sat, resting his back against the cold, smooth stone of the chamber's wall. Taking a deep breath, he tried to still his mind, hoping that a moment of focus would enable him to discern any clue that he might have missed. Across from him was the shattered vault where his ill-fated lesson had been stored. He noticed a faint hum coming from within the cavity where the Abico vault had been.

He walked over to the cavity, cautiously peering within. The hum grew distinctly louder as he drew nearer. Hesitantly, Mel carefully reached inside and cleared out some debris. A faint, purple light beamed through the dust. He sprang back, nearly tripping and falling on rubble. Slowly, he again reached into the cavity and cleared away debris, finding the end of a buried tube.

Mel's heart skipped as he wondered if this could be a surviving copy of the next scroll. He quickly dug deeper, freeing the tube. Stepping back with the tube in hand, he saw that it was encased in a magnetic field that must have shielded it from the blast. It felt like glass to the touch. He surmised that this technology was similar to the Sazo pellets. He estimated that the glowing cylinder was about twenty-five by one and a half centimeters. The purple light flickered in synchronization with the hum of the magnetic field's vibration. The tube appeared to contain a rolled parchment. He turned it over, trying to open it.

Exasperated after nearly a half-hour of trying to open it, he put it down. He glanced around the room, wondering what else he might discover. He looked at the remaining unopened vaults and despairingly mused upon what wonders they would have revealed had his studies not met such a tragic interruption.

Mel shook himself, vowing that he would never again allow that dark spirit of hopelessness to attach to him. He turned back to the glowing tube he had placed on the floor. Picking it up, he noticed that its radiance had not changed, yet the hum of its vibration had become markedly louder. He closed his eyes and tried to imagine what his father would do in this situation.

To his surprise, the tube grew warmer. He dared not open his eyes as its glow was becoming intensely bright, illuminating the inside of his closed eyes with scarlet patterns. Its heat intensified, and its sound grew louder, becoming like the piercing scream of a train whistle splitting the air. Mel wanted to release the tube. His hands were close to burning. His ears hurt from the wail.

Then, suddenly, it stopped. The tube became silent, its light went out, the magnetic field dissolved, and Mel found his tensed hands crushing the now unprotected parchment. His muscles ached, his ears rang, and sweat was streaming from his brow. His clutching hands had nearly torn the parchment in half. He began to carefully unroll it under the light of his lantern.

Rather than finding the all-capital title of a lesson scroll, Mel discovered that it was a personal letter written to him! It read:

HAPPY BIRTHDAY?

My dear son, Mel,

If you are reading this, then the Abico vault has been breached. Its loss presents you with several difficulties.

As you know, the eight chambers that contain the last lessons of a Vysard's initiation have been designed to open safely only when the individual possesses the emotional resonance gained by learning the preceding lesson. The seals of each vault are set to fully destroy its contents in the event of a breach, thus preventing access to the knowledge by anyone who has not had the necessary training, but more importantly, by anyone who does not have the necessary maturity to responsibly handle the knowledge. Any attempt to skip to another vault would activate its built-in security measures and cause a catastrophic effect like what occurred with the Abico. The greater the emotional misalignment, the greater the repelling force of the vault.

Because these last lessons must be personally experienced and not simply intellectually conveyed, I could not teach you what this lesson contained even were I there. Mel, I am deeply sorry that you will not be able to learn the lesson of the Abico and thus gain the ability to proceed to the Piaculum vault if you remain in Cooperton.

You must take a journey to discover what the continuance of your training demands of you. This will require you to search for clues that will be perceived only as you venture forth. You may have to travel great distances and may find great treasure, but do not get distracted.

You must take companions, as you will not be able to accomplish this alone. But know that you will be alone when you face the final trials. Be discerning when accepting others into your party. Your companions will shape your character, so beware of false friends. Those who would join you will seek you out. You must never speak of your quest; never share the goal of your journey, except with those who would protect your secret with their lives.

You must set out immediately, as the breach of the Abico has initiated a time-sensitive sequence intended to reduce the risk of future attempts to exploit the seven remaining vaults in this Caeli. If you have not overcome the present obstacle within three months, the Piaculum vault will automatically self-destruct, and so forth.

Seek an old friend of mine named Armando Lucia at South Fork. He has transportation waiting. Tell him that you are the son of Telemai Uri.

You may need to take some of the gems for major purchases. Those who receive you as you travel will offer you the rest of the provisions you will need.

Trust in the silent voice that guides you to your destiny.

With all my confidence,
Your loving father

Mel finished reading the letter and was hit by a cold wave of panic. *How will I know where to go after South Fork? I have only three months to find the answer, and I've already wasted three days at the house!* He took one last look around the disheveled room, sighed deeply, and locked the door on his way out.

CHAPTER 14

THE JOURNEY BEGINS

Mel refilled the empty grave he had prepared for Jora and began gathering what he would need for his journey. He tied his sleeping gear to the bottom of a knapsack containing clothing, a compass, a knife, a box of "Thermion" fire-starting kits, and a bag of Sazo pellets with their projector. He searched the kitchen for food that would last on his travels. He packed sweet flatbread, strips of jerky, bags of grape juice, and a variety of dried fruit. He filled two canteens at the farm's freshwater spring and tied them to the sides of the knapsack where they could be easily accessed.

Taking one last look at the remaining equipment and supplies around the house and knowing that his knapsack was already full, his heart groaned for the convenience that would be lost while he was on his travels. He knew that for a journey of unknown duration, it was important to travel light. He was consoled by his father's words that others would offer him provision along the way.

Mel left a note for Oscar, telling him of Jora, of the letter from Telly, and the beginning of his great quest. He pulled his knapsack on and left the house. He paused in the yard and stared at the closed door of the house he had lived in for the past eight years. "I wonder how long this will take?" he asked himself aloud as he turned and headed along the path to the road.

Mel's destination was to the south, away from town, yet he turned toward Cooperton, intending to speak with a certain someone before setting out in earnest.

* * *

Passing through Cooperton, he saw the smoke from chimneys fluttering upward in the stillness of the late morning air. Shadows lingered around the buildings, and the streets were nearly deserted. He felt lonelier in town than he had when he was by himself at the Uri farm. He had lived here for years and still felt like an outsider. He had no friends except for Mari. Most of the attention he had received from his peers had come in the form of ridicule. Despite these painful memories, Mel knew that such treatment had been the price for his family to live safely away from their real enemies.

He was excited about his journey. Would there be dangers? Would he be able to recognize his objective when it appeared? Would Mari want to accompany him? Would her family allow it? So many questions filled his thoughts, bringing confusion and doubts. He decided to take his mind off the uncertainties by singing a song. The ode comforted him and renewed his spirits.

As he walked toward the Thurman home, he watched as billowing cumulus clouds gathered on the horizon like an ancient army in full grandeur, aligned, ready for battle, shields set in a row, brilliant shafts of light streaming through them, forming a golden crown of spears atop the azure skies. Walking from one side of the road to the other, he followed the shafts of light illuminating a puzzle of earth and leaves.

Mel's heart beat faster as the oaks of the Cooperton road gave way to the willows marking the border of the Thurman farm. He could hear their animals calling excitedly from the back pens. Someone was taking care of feeding time. Mel saw the front of their house and Mari's flower garden just off their entry path.

He halted, his shoulders slumping. The family's two wagons were nowhere in sight. This could only mean that they had gone out of town. The whinny of a horse again brought his attention to the backyard. A glint of hope returned to his eyes as he broke into a run, hopped a fence, and rounded the side of their house.

A wheelbarrow had been pulled alongside the horse corral, and beside it stood Billy Simcox, throwing flakes of oat hay and alfalfa over the fence to the Thurman's three broodmares, each accompanied by its foal. He turned suddenly, startled by the sound of Mel's rapidly approaching footsteps.

Mel tried not to look disappointed. "Billy, what're you doing here?"

Billy breathed a sigh of relief and rolled his eyes good-naturedly. He hooked buckets of grain to metal hoops on the fenceposts alongside the hay as he spoke. "You know, Mel, last time I checked, it was me 'at had permissin to be on the Thurman farm."

"Where are they?" Mel asked impatiently.

"What's got a bee in your bonnet? If you're hopin' to visit your favorite cheerleader," he said with a friendly, teasing wink, "then I wish I had better news."

"Is she all right?" Mel asked fearfully.

"It ain't like that. They gone a few days 'go with their wares to San Francisco, made a family trip of it. I'm to keep an eye on the place and see after their animals for a few weeks."

"A few weeks?" Mel asked in exasperation.

"Sure! They're gonna pay me," Billy explained with a satisfied smile. "You want me to tell Mari anythin' when she gets back?"

Mel had many things he wished he could tell Mari right then. Many things he had wanted to ask and adventures he had wanted to share with her. In his mind, his quest had met its first great setback. He would have to leave town without anyone he knew and trusted. He realized that a long moment had passed, and Billy was staring at him, expecting a reply. "Please tell her I've had to go on a journey of my own, for a few months." Pulling his thoughts away from self-pity, he suddenly remembered a need he had forgotten in his haste to leave town. "Oh, and Billy, everyone at my place has left town for one reason or another. I'm hoping Oscar will be back soon, but do you think you could please look after our place and our animals like you are for the Thurmans?"

"Sure thing, Mel. Dollar a week?"

Mel smiled at Billy's entrepreneurial spirit. "Sounds fine. When you see Oscar, let him know the terms, and I'm sure he will compensate you right away. And thank you, Billy." They shook hands, and Mel waved goodbye as he walked back toward the road.

* * *

Mel hoped he could sneak by the Malingos' house without being seen. To his chagrin, Garth was sitting on the front porch in an old rocking chair. "Hey, Mel!" Garth shouted. "Whatcha doin'?"

Mel did not know where he stood with Garth and replied evasively, "Oh, just going for a hike."

"You look like your goin' on a pretty *long* hike!"

"Just to South Fork," Mel replied, hoping he could keep moving without becoming entangled in conversation.

"He's gone," Garth said abruptly.

Mel stopped, fearing that Garth knew his father had disappeared. "Who's gone?"

"Pops," Garth said nonchalantly, "sayin' he had to recover from what happened over at yer house. 'Coursen, that's what I think he said, him a gruntin' and makin' signs with his hands. I think he gone to his Ma's house. I'm pretty sure he gone a little loco too."

"Well, may it work out for the best," Mel said superficially, again walking away down the road.

Garth stood and boomed out, "Yes! It's real nice already! And all causa you."

Not knowing if he was being sarcastic, Mel stopped and braced himself for another conflict as Garth continued speaking and walking toward him.

"It's nice not havin' your ears boxed every time you mess up, not havin' ta work your hands to the bone every day your dad drinks himself stupid. I woulda never had the guts to tell him to his face, but I hated that man even if'n he was my dad. I been set free by you'n yer dad, and I'm in yer debt." Then, as if he thought of a brilliant idea, he said, "And now I got nothin' ta do, so how's about me taggin' along with you fer a spell."

Mel was taken aback by this sudden turn. He did not know what to say. He finally found his tongue and managed, "Uh, I don't think that's the best..."

"There ain't no but 'bout it. Wherever you're a' goin', I'm a' goin' too. I just gotta learn how you did that trick on the bridge, the one that turned my legs ta jelly. I ain't never seen nothin' like it a'fore. I ain't needed for nothin' 'round here no mo.'"

Garth wheeled his huge girth around quickly and ran into the house. After some rustling and banging, he emerged carrying a small gunny sack and a bag that looked like it held a kitchen's worth of provisions. "I'm ready; let's git."

Mel's forehead wrinkled as he suspected this might be an awful idea. He did not even know this lumbering giant. His only interaction with him had been recent and unpleasant. He did not know if Garth might eventually revert to his old, violent self.

Then he remembered his father's letter, the part that spoke of how his traveling companions would find him. He looked at the intimidating frame of this overgrown, adolescent tree trunk and wondered if this was going to be one strange odyssey.

"Okay, Garth," Mel surrendered, "let's go. Though, to be honest, I'm not sure I know exactly how to get to South Fork."

"You're in luck, seein' as I know every 'nook and cranny from here to 'tuther side of the Sierras," Garth said, as eager as a Great Dane puppy being taken on a long-overdue walk.

Mel smiled at his new companion's bravado. "Well then, I would be much obliged if you would guide us."

"Ooh," Garth said, struck by a sudden thought, "not just me. Lemme get my 'orse." He went around back and reappeared leading an old, broken, mule-looking, mud-caked hag of a mare with one blind eye.

Mel groaned audibly. "You call that a horse?"

Garth replied unashamedly, "Yep, and a stronger, more loyal friend can't be found. My pa won her in a poker game 'bout five years ago. She's a mite less ornery without him beatin' her like he done. Mind you, she's a bit skittish o' strangers. Her name's Bob!" He glowed with pride over his hunched, distended-bellied beast.

"*Her* name is Bob?" Mel questioned, muffling a chuckle as he looked at the unsightly animal.

"Bob is a whole mess better'n 'Puke Fer Brains.' That's what my pa used ta call 'er." He began mimicking how his father used to ridicule the horse. "'Tell that useless puke fer brains mule to do this or that,' he'd holler, and then he'd haul off'n whallop her or me, whichever was closer. But I never thought she's useless; she's been good ta us. And she's got uncanny skill goin' through the mountains, 'specially at night. Ain't she a beaut?"

Mel took a long look. "To be honest with you, Garth, she's only got one eye. And she's a muddy mess. Look at her."

"Well, bein' purty is somethin' on the inside, I heared. As fer her eye, one day, she didn't want to pull a tree that was blockin' my Pa's view of the mountains. He told me ta 'get out thar an make her move, or I'm gonna kill 'er.' I went out and helped her, and the tree fell the wrong way and crushed his chicken pen. So's he comes stormin' out a'cussin' and hits her with a poker still red hot from the fire, right in the eye. It done gone blind, and that's why it's all white. And then he starts a beatin' on me again, screamin', 'You big, ugly, stupid kid, I hate you, I hate you, *I hate you!*'"

By this time, Garth had leaned his head back and was shouting into the air. Mel realized that it was not just Garth's father who was yelling. It was Garth who was yelling back at his father. His eyes got a crazed look in them, and he put his hands over his face.

Mel walked cautiously over and put his hand on Garth's immense shoulder.

Garth immediately began sobbing uncontrollably. He gulped between sobs, just able to say, "It was you. You, Mel, that's the first ta tell me I weren't worthless."

Surprised, Mel asked, "Me? When?"

"On the bridge, don't ya remember? You was tellin' me I weren't no loser, that I had somethin' a worth inside. You were the first person in my whole life who didn't think I was a big, stupid puppet." He burst out in a fresh volley of sobs and leaned his bulk over onto Mel's small frame, which could barely hold him. As Bob the horse bent and nuzzled Garth's neck, Mel saw in her face a genuine love for her tormented master.

* * *

Mel and Garth camped on the side of the road that night. Garth snored like a thunderstorm. Mel found only fitful sleep and had recurring visions of Garth standing over him with his hands lifted and threatening.

* * *

The singing of birds woke Mel at dawn. Soft waves of warmth and moisture rose off the grass. Bob was chewing voraciously on sweet clover by the side of the road, Garth nowhere to be seen. Bees searching for their morning nectar buzzed gently among the flowers. Clouds floated lazily overhead, visible between the gaps in the redwoods. *A fine morning for an adventure*, Mel mused.

He watched carefully as Bob walked and sniffed around for a fresh tuft of sweet grass. A sudden thought led him to get up and begin foraging through the brush. After finding a clump of the greenish-yellow plant he was looking for, he took a handful of regular grass, combined it with the plant, and offered it to Bob. She gladly ate it from his hand and continued with her foraging.

Garth returned to camp as Mel fed Bob. "See, Mel, she's a great friend when ya get ta know 'er," Garth reassured him.

"Yeah, Bob is a fine animal," Mel replied. "Say, does she always favor her left side when grazing?"

"Seems like it, nowadays. How come, do ya think?"

Mel watched Bob lazily munch on the clover. "It has to be her eye. There might be something we can do to help her."

"Wow, you're right! She's keepin' her good eye forward," Garth said, scratching his head. "Dunno what's to help, though."

Mel began gathering some more of the greenish-yellow plant, carefully pulling up the roots with it.

"Hey, that taint good fer nuthin'. It's 'skunk weed.' Ain't a critter fer a hundered miles thad eat that."

"Oh, you might be surprised," Mel said with a sly smile. "This 'skunk weed,' as you call it, is a unique plant that I learned about in herbology class."

"Whassat?" Garth said, rubbing his belly. "Whatchacology?"

"Herbology," Mel said, wondering how long this conversation would last. "It's the study of plants and how they can help fix medical issues."

"And what's she got that a plant could fix?" Garth said with a puzzled look on his face.

Mel gave Bob another handful of grass and skunk weed. "Eating this plant helps sharpen eyesight. It has even been known to cure a type of blindness. I figure, since we have nothing to lose, we can feed it to Bob and see if it might make it easier for her to find food and to see in general."

Garth became defensive and said with a slight growl, "How long we got to feed her this stuff? What if'n it don't work? It won't make her sick or nothin', will it?" He began to pat her long brown and white muzzle, touching the dark red star-shaped pattern between her eyes.

"No, I assure you that it will only be good for her. You should try it too. I have been eating this root for most of my life, and I have excellent eyesight."

Garth grunted, "Thar ain't no way I'd ever be caught eatin' skunk weed. If word 'a that ever got out, I could never show my face proud again."

"Garth," Mel said in a pleading tone, "with the way you squint at things in the distance and the headaches you've told me about, you might be surprised what this little herb could do for you. And

I don't think that 'showing your face proud' ever got you anything of real benefit anyway. Maybe it'd be easier if you stopped calling it 'skunk weed.'"

Garth's brow furrowed. "You wouldn't tell no one I done ate it would you? I suffered 'nuff 'barrassment a'ready."

"If anyone asks, I'll just call it what I know it as."

"Whassat?" Garth said, one eyelid slanted up.

"In Latin, this herb is 'caecus curatio,' or 'Blind Cure.'"

Garth sighed in resignation, took a handful of clover and herbs, put it in his mouth, and said, while chewing, "This gotta be one of the dumbest thangs I ever done."

Mel smiled while taking a handful for himself. "Garth, one of the dumbest things we do is not taking good advice and not taking risks. Give this a few days, and then tell me how dumb you feel."

"Humph," Garth grunted while Bob nuzzled him under his chin. The three of them stood close together, taking their herbs for the day, looking like a group of cows chewing their cud.

CHAPTER 15

MOUNTAIN JEWEL

In the late afternoon, Mel and Garth rounded a bend in the road and beheld South Fork, a small, provincial ranching community forty kilometers south of Cooperton. Here, the coastal mountains retreated inland, leaving several thousand acres of rare flatland gently sloping down to a precipitous seaward edge. A sinuous central creek watered lush pastures and tumbled in a thin waterfall thirty meters directly into the crashing surf. A patchwork of fence lines and a smattering of clay tile roofs stretched to the south. In the distance, Mel could see that the flatland tapered off as the mountains again crept forward and dove directly into the ocean, cut only by the steam shovel and dynamite-hewn coastal road.

A chatty local man who Mel approached on the edge of town enthusiastically told the newcomers about his community, seemingly in the spirit of convincing any would-be landowners. He described how the postman arrived once a month and delivered mail to homes that had been there since long before the Spanish colonization. The neighbors knew each other by name. The grocer was familiar with his customers' favorite brands and would pull them without needing to be asked.

Mel mentioned Armando Lucia, whom the local man described as a blacksmith who raised horses and owned a livery stable across town. He came from a family of horsemen who had traveled from Spain many generations earlier. Mel and Garth thanked the man and continued through town, a half hour later finding the threshold of a stable with "La Caballeriza de Armando Lucia" painted on it in faded, cracked letters.

As Mel and Garth approached the weathered archway, Garth looked out across the barns and corrals of the stable. "I'm guessin' we're here to get a 'orse? 'Cause Bob don't need no mo' care," he asserted with affectionate bluster. Bob caught the scents of the stable and nodded her head with excitement, pulling forward on her halter.

"It was recommended that I pay Señor Lucia a visit. He's an old friend of my father."

A handsome Spanish man with a deep tan and neatly combed silver hair tied in a ponytail approached, glancing over Bob with the look of a discerning professional. He greeted the two young men with a nod. "Hello," he said in a precise tone with only a hint of a Spanish accent. "How may my establishment be of assistance to you two gentlemen? Armando Lucia at your service." He gave a quick bow and clicked his heels together.

Garth was surprised by Armando's well-mannered flourish. "Gentlemen?" he asked, smiling.

"Ah, yes," Armando responded. "Though you may be young and looking somewhat road-weary, I always expect the best of anyone who crosses my path. I have found that expecting the best usually brings it out."

"Well, I never...," Garth mumbled in astonishment.

Mel stepped forward and put out his hand. "It is a pleasure to meet you, Señor Lucia. I am Melvin Uri, son of Telemai Uri. This is my friend, Garth Malingo. My father seemed to indicate you would be expecting me."

Armando took his hand, a slight tremor in his own, and said in a respectful tone, bowing once again, "Melek 'al Uri. Anticipating, not merely expecting, sir."

Mel was startled to hear his full name. He suspected there was more to this "old friend" than he had been told.

"Mel, whatchamawhosit?" Garth interjected, perplexed.

"I'll explain later, Garth," Mel reassured him with a smile.

"I gather that your father is elsewhere," Armando surmised.

Hesitant to discuss his father with a recent acquaintance, Mel responded, "He said that you were keeping something for me."

Bittersweet sadness touched Armando's countenance, as at the thought of an impending parting, and he looked at the young, dirty faces of Mel and Garth. "You have traveled some distance. Please forgive my rudeness. Would you care to freshen up and join me for dinner? My wife and four daughters are visiting my sister-in-law across town for the weekend, so I must apologize in advance for the meager fare that I am able to cook. Then I will show you what your father had me set aside for you."

Mel nodded his assent.

Armando turned to take care of Bob and stopped suddenly, looking intently at her. He took her drooping chin gently and brushed some mud away from the markings on her forehead. He gasped and shouted, "Mons Candeo!" and embraced the neck of the startled beast. "Where did you find her?"

Garth immediately became defensive. "I didn't find her 'tall. My pa won her fer an squer in a poker match."

Ignoring Garth's reply, Armando kept questioning, "What has happened to her eye? And that dreadful sag in her back, what have you been using her for? Pulling trees?"

Garth felt a rush of guilt over the condition of Bob and stammered, "Sorry 'bout her eye. My pa got mad and..." Garth stopped and asked, "Hey, what's this? You act like you know Bob, and what was that funny name you cal't her?"

"*Bob*?" Armando shouted indignantly. He straightened himself to his full height, nearly ten centimeters taller than the already hulking Garth. He said with authority, "Mons Candeo may have been won in a poker match, but before that, she was stolen! She was six months old when she was taken from my barn, five years ago. Her name means 'Mountain Jewel,' for the star marking on her forehead. She was my finest filly, the product of ten generations of selective breeding. She was the pinnacle of what I have been working for all my life, and you have the common gall to call her *Bob*?"

"Well, it's better 'an what Pa used to call 'er, Pu—"

Mel interrupted, "I am sure Garth had nothing to do with her theft, Señor Lucia. His father was abusive to Bo..., excuse me, Mons Candeo. If it were not for the kindness of Garth, she would probably be dead."

Armando bowed to Garth and apologized, "I am sorry, my young sir. I was startled to find her after so many years. I am afraid I lost my temper. Please forgive me."

Garth was not used to being vouched for and was certainly not accustomed to having others, especially older, distinguished gentlemen, apologize to him. He stared at Bob and mumbled, "S'okay." Then, mourning her poor condition, he turned his face away. "Yeah, we used 'er to pull trees. I'm... I'm sorry."

Armando looked at Garth with compassion and put a comforting hand on his shoulder. "All is well; Mons Candeo is home!" he stated excitedly. "We shall clean her and recover her once-glorious beauty before you set out. Come, let us eat. Here is my stableman to care for her. What a day of rejoicing this is!" With a sweep of his arms, he pointed towards the house. "This way, sirs! Please, follow me!" Garth handed Bob's reigns to the stableman, and Armando marched the two young men through a jasmine archway and across a cobblestone courtyard to the house.

* * *

At dinner, they listened to Armando talk of his life as an equestrian. He told them of how his forefathers had come to America many years before Columbus and how they had been secluded in this small community for centuries before Spain colonized California.

Garth did not know his history well enough to dispute Armando's claims, and Mel kept silent, deciding to listen carefully to information that was being revealed so candidly to such new acquaintances. The two young men responded occasionally and hungrily shoveled food into their mouths as Armando spoke.

After ample portions of mountain veal, candied yams, and apple pie, Armando pushed back from the table. "It is time!"

He led them across an inner courtyard of the hacienda, past a horseshoe-shaped fountain, and through a double-door gate. The idyllic pastures and corrals beyond were bathed in the pink and orange hues of the setting sun. Armando stopped at the gate of a corral and said with pride, "There have been only two horses in the past century that could be considered among the Earth's finest workmanship. I give you one of these, Campitor, the warhorse."

He flung open the gate. With the sun setting, a glare was in their eyes, forcing them to squint to see the huge, black horse that barreled like a locomotive out of the corral and into the pasture. In the cool evening air, his excited breath poured forth in plumes of condensation like smoke billowing from a fire. Campitor reared up on his hind legs and pawed at the sky triumphantly.

Garth shaded his eyes with his hand. "Wow! I ain't never!"

From the far side of the pasture, a golden-colored horse joined Campitor, and they ran side by side at breakneck speed across the pasture.

As Garth watched this second horse against the glare of the sunset, his head tilted to the side, and his brow furrowed. He shook his head skeptically. "Nuh-uh." The horses rounded a curve and were no longer in front of the sun, which allowed them to be plainly seen. Garth's eyes went wide, and his hand covered his mouth in astonishment. "Bob? I'll be!" Bob had been washed and brushed and now glistened with oil and sweat as she kept pace with the fiery, black stallion.

Armando watched the horses with admiration and affection. "Both Campitor and Candeo are a cross of Andalusian and Thoroughbred and are an unmatched blend of intelligence and speed. They are fast *and* fierce. Candeo is the fastest I have ever seen. At five months, she could outdistance a prime two-year-old. Campitor has the strength of a draft horse and the dexterity of a dressage mount," Armando boasted. "Though not related, they are bonded by an affection that few can understand. They were separated at six months old, and yet they act as if they have never been apart. Be careful with Campitor, as he is not fully broken."

Mel watched the huge black horse with a fascination he had never experienced with any animal. He walked steadily toward the now stomping stallion, approaching him as if he were being called by the horse, not looking to either side, not hearing those who were yelling for him to stay clear.

As Mel neared the frothing stallion, Campitor calmed and allowed Mel to touch his muzzle. The horse inhaled deeply and exhaled warm breath onto Mel's hand. Mel slowly embraced Campitor's massive neck, which the horse accepted. Mel found himself speaking words that he could not remember learning. "*Soluto tantus campitor! Sis comodo supplex furor equito?*" or, as he heard in his mind, "Greetings, great warhorse! If you are willing, please kneel to permit me to enjoy a ride."

Campitor bowed, lowering his knees to the ground. Mel had never ridden without a saddle but automatically grabbed the horse's long, silver-tipped mane and pulled himself up. Campitor stood to his full height and began strutting around the pasture in perfect ease.

"Oh my!" Armando gushed. "In all my years, I have never witnessed such instant camaraderie. This horse has resisted my best trainers, and yet you speak to him, and he obeys. Your father was right when he said that Campitor would know you."

Garth felt emboldened by Mel's triumph and approached Campitor. The horse nodded rapidly in irritation, warding off Garth's attempts to touch him as he stepped away. Garth backed up, holding his hands in the air. "Whoa thar! I didn't want ta hurt ya. I'ze just want ta be your friend too."

Mel leaned forward and spoke into Campitor's ear. He calmed and stood still for Garth to touch him. Garth was hesitant to reach out his hand a second time. The horse sensed his reluctance and pushed his nose towards him. Garth patted Campitor gently between the eyes.

"Whall, that is some special talkin' you makin' in that 'orse's ear. Do you reckon you could teach me that too?"

Mel dismounted and shook his head. "I'm not even sure what I said. I knew the meaning in my mind, but I don't remember learning the words. I don't understand any of this." Mel turned to Armando. "Señor Lucia, can you explain what just happened?"

"Campitor and Candeo are unique and not easily explained. It seems that she has restored to him a sense of peace that he could find nowhere else. Your moment with him showed the mind and heart of an Andalusian, but I also saw the bond of a warhorse with its master. Yet another sign that he is the greatest warhorse ever beheld by men."

Mel looked puzzled. "What makes him a warhorse?"

"The instincts of a battle steed have been unmatched in him from the start," Armando said proudly. "Horses are the greatest fighters on this planet. They thrive in the heat of battle. They ignite at the smell of blood. They are empowered by the sounds and even the pain of a fight. And Campitor is the most fearless that has ever walked the Earth. The fact that he has resisted my training regimen, and has let few approach him, shows the fortitude of his will. Now that he has Candeo by his side, he will be invincible."

Mel did not know what would come of this reunion of two such great creatures. All he could think of was that he had many mysteries yet to investigate and no more time to spare.

"Thank you, sir, for showing us this fine horse," Mel said. "Garth and I are on a quest and will need to be leaving at the earliest opportunity."

"Of course, Master Uri," Armando said while bowing. "Forgive my manners. You must be tired after the day's walk and are welcome to rest here until morning. Please let me offer you sleeping quarters."

Mel agreed, and Armando guided them to a long row of one-story stucco rooms with red tile adorning the walls to shoulder height. He ushered them into a room lit by a blue kerosene lamp and then departed, bidding them goodnight. There were two beds, each with a large, dark wood frame and four thick spiral columns leading to a canopy above.

Garth stared at the bed that was to be his. "Ooowee," he said in awe. "I ain't never been on a bed like that a'fore. Don't seem right to just flop on down."

Mel smiled at the luxury that was so new to Garth. "Well, I'm exhausted and fully intend to 'just flop on down,'" Mel said, playfully mimicking Garth.

"You makin' fun—a—me?" Garth asked with a frown.

"Yeah," Mel replied, "I am." He threw a huge feather pillow at the scowling giant.

"Hey, watchit!" Garth said defensively, easily batting it away.

Mel laughed. "I was just playing."

"You was?" Garth tentatively asked. "Huh. My pa wasn't much for that when I was growin' up. But I 'spose there's no harm in it." He launched the pillow back at Mel with surprising force.

"Exactly!" Mel realized that leaving Cooperton meant that Garth's life, like his own, was changing in good ways. "Garth, chances are, South Fork is just the beginning of this journey. I think we're going to find an exciting world out there, with new friends. And you won't have to fight to prove anything to them."

Garth leaned back on his feather pillow and sighed deeply. "Wow! Hey Mel! You know what I was thinking? We oughta change Bob's name. You got any ideas?" Without waiting for Mel's reply, Garth continued, "I like the Mons Candeo thang that he named her, but people gonna call her Candy. She's too strong a 'orse ta be called Candy. What'd he say that meant anyway?"

Mel remembered and responded, "Mountain Jewel."

"Yeah, Mountain Jewel," Garth said, letting the words roll around in his mouth like a buttercream sweet. "We could call her 'Mountain' or 'Jewel' or, hey, I got it! We could call her 'MJ'!"

Mel groaned, rolled over, and pulled his pillow over his ears as Garth jabbered to himself about the horses and their journey.

CHAPTER 16

VULGLADIUS

Mel awoke the next morning to the sounds of horses playing frantically in the courtyard. The stomping of shod hooves on cobblestone echoed through the building with what seemed like the force of an entire herd. Mel peered, sleepy-eyed, out at Campitor and Mons Candeo and watched their morning frolic.

Garth stumbled out of bed. "I don't think I've slept that good n'all my born days. Can barely git up. Say, what's that noise?"

"It's the horses. They're playing!"

"Well, I wish they'd play a little quieter. I coulda slept all day. What time is it anyway?"

Mel looked at a clock on the wall, impatience suddenly gripping him. "It's time to go."

"Where we goin' now?" Garth yawned.

"I'm not sure, but we need to get moving. We'll eat and then hit the road," Mel said while organizing his backpack.

"Mmm, I can smell the bacon sizzling." Garth wandered out into the hall, following his nose.

Mel heard Armando call to his stable hands from the kitchen. "*Tire el vagón alrededor al frente, rápidamente!*" Armando was speaking Spanish, yet Mel could understand every word. "Pull the wagon around to the front, quickly!" Mel wondered at his unexpected familiarity with Spanish. *Was this part of the training I received as a child?*

* * *

After a breakfast of blueberry muffins, eggs, and bacon, they stood to leave. "Thanks much, Señor Lutcia," Garth managed, practicing his social graces. "Hope ta' visit again, someday."

Armando stepped out into the morning sun, followed by Mel. Garth stayed to gather breakfast leftovers for the road.

Outside the gate of the hacienda was a four-meter-long wagon with seating for two and a storage compartment at the front end of the bed. It was being pulled by Campitor and Candeo, who were settling into their new, padded chest harnesses.

"What's this?" Mel inquired.

"Your coach," Armando answered.

He has transportation waiting, Mel remembered from his father's letter. "My coach?" Mel asked. "But it's just a wagon."

"Yes," Armando replied, "to our eyes and the eyes of others. But it must be special, as your father made it himself. He told me to hide it till you came." Armando leaned over and spoke in Mel's ear in a near whisper. "It was made for a very special journey." Armando rested a hand on the side of the wagon and said aloud, "I hauled it into my barn and covered it until now. I did not know how long it would be before you came for it, but your father paid me well to keep it and to care for Campitor. I am sad to see him leave, but this day was destined to come."

"Campitor?" Mel asked with a quickening of his breath. "Does Campitor come with this?"

"Of course, Master Uri!" Armando said in disbelief. "I thought that Señor Uri would have prepared you for this. Yesterday I was convinced that he had when you took command of Campitor."

Mel shook his head. "I don't understand what happened yesterday. And what of Mons Candeo? She was yours."

"Perhaps I could demand to keep her, but she no longer thinks of herself as mine, and in Campitor, she has found her lifemate," Armando said with a hint of sadness. "She is happier now than ever before. I could not bear to separate them after they were apart for so long. And it is good for Campitor to watch and learn from her. She helps to calm him. Despite being treated poorly for most of her life, she is very cooperative. I was not able to put the harness on Campitor's shoulders until he saw that she willingly submitted to hers. No, she must go with you. I do not know where you are going, but I suspect it might be a long journey, and Campitor's strength, tempered by Mons Candeo's humility, will serve you well. The two go together.

"But please, do not remove Campitor's shoulder harness. It is light and will not burden him in the least, and your father's strictest orders were that once it was put on, it was never to be removed for any reason."

Mel examined Campitor's padded leather carriage harness and discovered a red gem embedded in its breastplate. He surmised that this unusual component would somehow prove to be the rationale for his father's strange command. "Thank you, Señor Lucia, for the many ways you've helped."

Armando nodded. "*De nada*. It is my pleasure."

Garth stumbled out onto the veranda, eating a huge muffin, his pockets bulging with other treats. Seeing the wagon and horses harnessed together, he shouted, "Mel, this gonna be *ours*? Hot spit, Bob, ain't they got you gussied up? Oh... sorry, Señor, I meant ta say, Mountain Jewel."

Armando winced. "Whatever she'll respond to is what you should call her. But remember her dignity and her breeding. Please try not to let it be a name that is below her station."

"Señor Lutcia, I'll call her sometin' that'll make ya proud."

"I'm sure you will, Señor Malingo," Armando said with a smile. "Señor Uri, your coach has food for several weeks, cooking tools, and blankets. You will not be in need for some time."

Mel climbed up and took the reins, and Garth sat next to him.

Armando continued, "You may want to check the compartment in the bed of the wagon. It is locked, but I assume that you will know how to open it. I now leave you with blessings from House Lucia. I hope to see you when you return." He waved at them as they pulled away down the dirt driveway.

Out of sight of the house, Mel pulled the horses to a stop as they reached the end of the driveway.

"Uh, where ta now, boss?" Garth asked.

Mel sat quietly for a moment. "I don't know."

The horses began to grow restless.

Mel continued, "Thank you, Garth, for coming along. I won't be able to do this without help, without friends. There's a lot I'll need to figure out as I go, and I don't know where this will end."

"No problem. Just great to git 'way from Coop'ton."

Mel smiled at his friend's simple enjoyment of the adventure.

Campitor stomped the ground, and, unbidden, he and Candeo turned in unison and started off down the southward road. "Apparently, we go south," Mel observed matter-of-factly.

Garth laughed. "Sounds fine, ain't been that way as much."

On each side of the road were tall cherry trees in full bloom that gently showered the two adventurers with a light pink snowfall of petals as they set out, guided only by an instinct of the horses.

* * *

They traveled for hours before stopping to let the horses loose to graze and drink from a mountain creek. Mel and Garth snacked on the provisions in the wagon and, when it was time to leave, whistled for the horses to return. There was no response. Minutes later, they discovered them in a small mud hole near the creek. Campitor and Candeo were rolling on their backs, flinging mud onto each other. Campitor still wore his shoulder harness, the red gem now covered with mud.

"Oh man," Garth lamented, "they'ze losing all that purty work the stable men heaped on 'em back at Lutcia's. It'll take hours ta get 'em all gussied up again."

Mel watched their behavior for a moment. "No, I think they know what's best for them. This'll make them look more like common horses, less tempting to horse thieves."

"It'd be pert' stupid person who'd tackle wi' them horses, that's for sure."

"Yes, I would pity the man who would try to steal either of them. But this way, there will be one less reason for anyone to try."

Garth nodded his head towards the wagon and said, "Well, ya ever gonna check it?"

"Check it? Check what?"

"The box back there," Garth said, rolling his eyes.

"Oh, the storage compartment. I completely forgot. Let's see if we can open it."

Mel and Garth moved some of the supplies that were covering the plain wooden storage compartment, which was built into the bed of the wagon. It was completely sealed and lacked any apparent lock or latches. Garth pulled out a long knife and tried to find a crack in its lid. A low hum came from the surface of the box as he searched in vain for a place to begin prying.

The sound brought cold fear to Mel's heart, and he quickly but gently reached out and steered Garth's arm away from the compartment. "That's good thinking, Garth, but I don't know if a knife can open this. Stand back for a minute and let me see what I can do." Garth complied.

As soon as Mel touched the compartment, the steady hum changed to a pulsating sound, and writing appeared on the upper surface with lettering like that that Mel had seen on the vaults in the Caeli. He closed his eyes and concentrated on the tonal frequency of the sound. He tried to duplicate it with his voice, humming in unison with it, but nothing happened. He tried once more, singing, but with the same result. A thought came to him. "Garth, could you please come here for a minute."

"Whasis 'bout, Mel? All that hummin' and stuff. You know how strange this looks?"

"S.M.R., Garth."

Garth stared blankly.

"Sonic-magnetic resonance is the key. The box is magnetically locked and will only open to the proper tones. It's like tumblers in a lock. The right tune will turn them. Come and help... you'll see."

Garth climbed back into the wagon and kneeled next to Mel.

"This lock is more complicated than others like it that I've opened. It might need more than one note to work. Try humming this," and he demonstrated a vocal note for Garth to emulate.

"Uh," Garth said reluctantly, "I ain't the sangin' type thar, Mel. I don't think I can do it."

"Come on, Garth. I'm not asking you to sing. Just hum a little. Please try. I can't get this open without you."

"Okay, I'll try." Garth glanced around to make sure no one was watching and turned back to the box with a pained expression.

Together they began to hum, taking deep breaths and letting out a series of tones. But nothing happened.

Garth looked dizzy from sustaining his low note and said, panting, "I'm not sure if it's likin' my sangin thar, Mel." His eyes opened wide in a moment of revelation. "Wait!" Garth shouted. "If you git ta say what comes naturally to you, why can't I just do what comes naturally ta me?"

"Oh, whatever, Garth," Mel said in slight frustration. "Are you ready?" With that, Mel raised his hands and began to let out a low, growling tone. "Come on, Garth, I need your help!"

Finally, Garth let out a deafening "holler," and, as his breath was almost expended, there was a loud *snap* from the compartment, and its lid shifted slightly.

"Holy San Fran!" Garth yelled.

Mel smiled. "Let's see what's under this lid."

The lid, which had been impossible to budge, was now as light as a feather, and they easily tilted it up on its interior hinges and leaned it back against the wagon seats. Inside the outer, plain box was a second box, much older in appearance, made of thick mahogany and about one meter long and thirty centimeters wide.

Mel reverently reached out to touch it. The box sprang open, releasing a hiss of pressurized air. They were immediately bathed in a shimmering, multi-prismed light. A cold vapor rose from the box. When it cleared, they beheld the ivory-handled and diamond-encrusted hilt of a broadsword in a plain brown leather scabbard. The word *Vulgladius* was inscribed on the handle.

Mel did not touch the sword. He studied it carefully, noticing every detail.

Garth, enthralled by the sword's beauty, could not restrain himself and reached out to touch it.

Out of the corner of his eye, Mel saw Garth's hand about to grasp the sword. "Garth, *stop!*" But he was too late, and a blinding flash of light burst forth from the sword, throwing Garth backward like he had been kicked by a mule and knocking Mel flat in the bed of the wagon. Garth landed on the ground nearby with a thud. Mel sprang up and turned toward him. "Are you all right?"

Garth groaned and rubbed his sore rump. "What happened?"

Mel scrambled down and knelt next to him, giving him a hug.

Garth pushed him away. "Hey, hold on thar."

Mel stood back with a smile. "I'm just glad you're all right!" His expression changed to one of concern. "Garth," he said somberly, "you can never touch that sword. It could've killed you."

"I dunno what's goin' on here," Garth said with suspicion, "but I got kicked clean on my rear by a sword? I know swords ain't nothin' ta mess with, but how could it kill me just sittin' in its box?"

Garth's mishap had brought the secret of the sword to the fore. Mel decided to be honest without offering any unnecessary information. "Do you remember what I said about S.M.R.?" Garth nodded, squinting to remember. Mel continued, "The same forces that kept that lid shut are active in this sword. Except here, when the person is not in tune with the sword's magnetic field, he is repelled." Mel, remembering Jora's destruction, spoke slowly, "I've seen this happen before, and the results were disastrous."

"Like what?" Garth asked innocently, getting back to his feet. "Like gettin' kicked by a 'orse?"

"My tutor tried to open a vault that he shouldn't have, and it was like he was holding an exploding stick of dynamite."

"Gowannn!" Garth said as if Mel were kidding. "That cain't happen. It just knocked me down."

Mel pulled up his shirt and showed Garth the still-healing wound in his side. "This is where a fragment of bone struck me. It broke two of my ribs as well."

"I ain't never heard of nothin' so crazy a'fore." Garth walked cautiously to the side of the wagon and peered at the sword's shimmering hilt. "What's them funny letters on its handle thar?"

Mel looked at the sword, in awe of its latent power, and explained, "It's two words made into one. *Vulcan* was the fire god of the ancient Romans, and *gladius* is the Latin word for sword. Put together, they mean 'Fire Sword.'"

Garth stared at the hilt. "It's bright, but I don't see no fire."

Mel did not know what further capabilities the sword might have but saw no point in keeping them secret from Garth, as he would almost certainly witness any moments when Mel would have to use the sword during the quest.

"Let's take a closer look," Mel said, leaning over Vulgladius. He lifted the sword from its box and held it, noticing how incredibly light it felt despite its length and breadth. He drew it from its scabbard slowly. Once fully free, the blade started humming, and a flame began burning and crackling within it.

Garth backed away in awe. "Ooh, I see it now."

Mel placed the scabbard in the bed of the wagon and stepped away to a safe distance. He held the sword with both hands and slowly swung it back and forth. It pulled towards whatever direction he moved it, as though sensing his intent. He walked over to a pile of sticks and made a gentle chop. The sword sliced easily through the sticks, igniting them. He drew Vulgladius back, and Garth rushed forward, stomping out the flames.

Mel glanced at their surroundings and got a new idea. He walked over to a boulder on the side of the road, drew the sword back, and, in a flicker of movement, sliced at the boulder. For several seconds nothing happened, but then a section of the boulder slid loose, and an inch of the rock on either side of the cut melted like wax onto the ground. Mel quickly stepped back from the molten dribbles.

Seeing the melting edges of the rock, Garth cried out, "Whoa, whoa, what *is that thang?*"

Mel took the scabbard from the bed of the wagon to sheathe Vulgladius. Just before the sword reached the scabbard, the flame disappeared, and the blade quieted. Mel placed the sheathed sword back into its mahogany box and closed its lid.

He noticed the corner of a piece of parchment protruding from under Vulgladius' box. He withdrew the parchment and saw that it was a map, though none of the words or places on it were familiar to him. He rolled it and put it in his coat pocket.

He and Garth closed the storage compartment's lid, which snapped into place and once again would not move.

They reattached the horses to the wagon, and Mel took the reins. He looked at Garth, who was still sweating from the experience. "Garth, we can never speak of this publicly. Vulgladius is part of an ancient and very secret technology. My father knew we may need it at some point on this journey, but until that day, let's forget it exists."

Garth was stunned by the way Mel was taking this whole event in stride. "That's gonna take some doin' ta forget what I just saw. But all right."

Mel sighed. "Thank you, Garth." He flicked the reins, and they continued their journey down the quiet, tree-lined road, the air carrying the scents of heather and molten rock. As they went, Mel pulled the map from his pocket and studied it. Despite his best efforts, he could not recognize the names, and the landmasses remained unfamiliar. But there was something itching in the back of Mel's mind, a question he decided to investigate at the first library they could find along their southward route.

CHAPTER 17

THE STRANGERS

The next day, in the early afternoon, Mel and Garth pulled into the sleepy trading town of Cayucos, which was nestled against the region's rolling, grassy coastal hills. The town was home to about four hundred persons, its buildings interspersed with live oak trees. There were four saloons, a barbershop, a post office, and a courthouse adjacent to the town square. The town's patch of land sloped gently to a broad, sandy beach, where a nearly 300-meter pier reached out into deep water.

Mel stopped the wagon beside the front yard of a man working in his garden. "Hello there!" Mel called out. "We're looking for a library. If there's one nearby, we'd greatly appreciate directions."

"The library?" the man asked, raising his eyebrow. "What in the world would two young men be wantin' in a library on a day like this? Oh! You ain't lookin' for the Injun girl there, are you? Well, forget about it. That girl's 'bout as interested in boys as my hog is bacon."

"Where might we find it, sir?" Mel asked politely.

The man eyed them for a minute. Mel became aware of the afternoon heat and the flies buzzing about their heads. Finally, the man continued, "For the library, ya go to the end of this block, turn left, and it's just past the mercantile."

"Thanks much," Garth said, tipping his finger to his head as they pulled away down the street.

They passed the old courthouse and turned as directed, seeing the mercantile and then the library. The small, white clapboard shack appeared to have been converted from a one-room schoolhouse in years past. Mel wondered if this was where most of the inhabitants of Cayucos had received their primary education.

They parked the wagon, hitched the horses, and stepped into the small room. Glancing around, they were amazed at how many books the building held. Books were piled everywhere, stacked high, and overflowed off every shelf.

"How we gonna find anythang in here, Mel?" Garth groaned.

Just then, a red-haired, green-eyed, pig-tailed girl, about fifteen years old, poked her head out from behind a huge stack of books and asked, "Can I help you?"

Mel was startled by the freckled girl and responded, "Yes! We are looking for maps of Mexico and Central America."

The redhead blushed at the presence of two boys about her age in her library. "I'm sorry. I forgot to introduce myself. I'm Polly Logan, the librarian. I've read almost all these books, and I'm especially fond of maps. We have a very old map of those areas, which has been rather popular with out-of-towners recently."

She walked directly to a shelf and withdrew a large leatherbound book. "This was found up the coast in an old, abandoned lighthouse. It looks to have been drawn in the sixteenth or seventeenth century, presumably as an exploration chronicle. But it could be much older. Why do you need to look at maps?"

Mel hesitated at this question.

Garth, sensing the awkward silence, jumped in. "We'ze just a coupla treasure-crazed kids, hopin' there's gold to be found there."

Mel turned, his eyes bulging at Garth's poetic surge. "Let's just call it research," Mel said, trying to balance Garth's theatrics.

Polly squinted in doubt. "Well, bring it over here to the light," she said, clearing a handful of books off a desk by the window. "Sorry, but we are pretty tight for space. Since this is the only library in the county, we get all the books that folks don't want."

Mel placed the book on the desk. "Thank you, Miss Logan."

"Please! Call me Polly!"

Mel smiled at the glint in her shining green eyes. "Polly it is."

He opened the dusty cover. The pages revealed a world he had never seen but that was instinctively familiar. The maps bore notations in several languages, all of which Mel understood immediately. He began pointing at symbols and codes on the page. He explained much of this to Garth, who was dumbfounded that Mel could read something that appeared so cryptic.

Polly overheard much of the conversation and stepped over to them. "Excuse me, whoever you are! Where did you say you're from? I've been looking at these maps for years and have only discovered that most of them are written in long-dead languages. How is it that you know them?"

Mel balked and cleared his throat. "My name is Mel, and this is Garth, and we haven't said where we are from. And I don't intend to answer further." Mel knew his act was unconvincing but had seen that false bravado could, at times, quench questions.

Not so with Polly Logan. She walked right up to Mel and stood her ground. She noticed that she was almost as tall as him, which emboldened her further. But, remembering what her aunt had taught her, that gentleness can go a long way, she softened her tone. "I'm not trying to steal your *treasure*." She took a long, sarcastic look at Garth, who turned away. "I just love to learn, and nobody has passed this way in years who could help me with these maps." She leaned close, looking over his shoulder at the book.

Mel felt a little uncomfortable, feeling her breath and smelling the scent of honeysuckle on her hair. He pointed at a coastline depicted on the map. "These markings explain the currents. And these numbers are the soundings."

Polly pointed to the legend in the upper right-hand corner. "What's this word here?"

Mel examined the word, **ζενοιδσ**, recognizing it as old Greek. After a moment of disbelief and a flicker of fear, he replied, "*Xenoids*. It means 'strangers.'" Careful to sound as casual as possible, Mel continued, "My guess is that the persons who composed these maps either were from a place called Xenos or they identified the land they were surveying as 'strange' and its inhabitants as 'strangers.'"

Polly gasped and stepped back, covering her mouth with her pale, freckled hand.

"What's wrong?" Mel asked, startled by her reaction.

Polly swallowed and looked like she had seen a ghost. "Just last week, there were two men in the mercantile who spoke with a strange accent. When the shopkeeper asked them where they were from, one of them showed a crooked smile and answered 'Xenos.' The other one made signs to stop talking. When they were asked where that was, they simply packed their things and left. It got the whole town talking about how more newcomers have been passing through recently. They tend to keep to themselves, so we try not to ask too many questions. The same two men came here yesterday."

"Did they ask about these maps?" Mel inquired.

Polly nodded her head.

"Can I take this, please? It's important," Mel pleaded as he turned the pages, searching for one map in particular.

Polly stood firm, her hands on her hips. "I am sorry, but I cannot let this book out of this building for any reason. It's in the reference section of the library, and no one can check it out. I would be quite remiss in my duties if I were to—"

Garth was shaking his head and finally exclaimed, "Mel, what's goin' on?"

Mel found the page he was looking for and spun towards Garth. "We have to make a copy of this map, quickly, and then get out of here. We may be in danger. Polly, can you do us a big favor and not tell anyone that we were looking at this book?"

Polly was flustered at being interrupted. "Okay, 'Mel' and 'Garth,' you two can't agree on why you even want the map. And now you're saying you could be in danger? *Who are you guys?*"

Mel answered quickly, breathing anxiously between sentences. "I'm just a kid looking for answers. And this map is a clue. It would be safest for us to leave as soon as possible."

Garth found a blank sheet of paper and a pencil and handed them to Mel. His hand whirled around the page like that of a professional artist drawing a sketch, and in just a few minutes, he had duplicated the map almost to the last detail. He stepped back and double-checked.

Polly's eyes opened wide in amazement. She had never witnessed such a feat of duplication.

Garth leaned back against a desk and grinned. "Every day, he does somethin' I ain't never seen a'fore. It's gotten that if he didn't do somethin' odd, I'd start thinkin' somethin's wrong."

Mel pocketed his copy of the map and, with the help of Garth's muscles, hid the map book under a large pile of oversized encyclopedias. Mel turned once more to Polly. "Please, if you could keep this a secret, I would be most grateful."

Polly nodded in agreement.

Mel climbed into the bed of the wagon beside the storage compartment and paused, glancing around to see if anyone in town was watching them. Although it had taken Garth to open it the first time, he knew he would have to learn to open it on his own in case a moment arose when he needed Vulgladius. He touched the lid, searching through his memories of his training for a key to opening this compartment by himself. To his surprise, the lid suddenly unlocked. He deduced that its first use had retuned the mechanism to provide him and Garth with ready access. From his coat pocket, he took the parchment map and his paper duplication of the page of the map book and laid them beside each other in the wagon's compartment. His breath quickened. The landmasses matched. Leaving the maps within, he closed the compartment's lid, which again snapped into place.

Polly energetically waved them goodbye as they pulled away, and smiled as they quickly and subtly returned the gesture. This had been the most excitement she had ever had at the library, and she hoped she would see these two young men again someday.

Garth looked over at Mel. "Which way we 'eaded?"

Mel, focused forward, said in a hasty tone, "South, far south."

* * *

They spoke little as they went. Mel glanced in every direction to ensure that they were not being followed.

They had traveled about an hour when Garth leaned back and put a hand to his stomach. "Gettin' hungry." He jumped in the back and rummaged through the food that Armando had sent with them. "Hey, Mel, yon some grub?"

"No thanks. We need distance between us and that town."

"I don't see what's the big deal. I mean, who cares if some of them 'strangers' was snoopin' 'round town. What's to say they're after us?"

Mel, realizing that Garth was in for the long haul, thought it might be good to share a little more of what their quest might involve. "Garth, do you remember how I said I'm not from around here?"

Garth nodded and grunted, "'At's whacha said," Garth smiled at himself. "But yo' funny way o' talkin' had gave it 'way 'afore."

Mel continued, "My father said that we came from a place that was destroyed by some very powerful people. The same kind of people that Polly saw in that town."

"Whaddaya mean destroyed?" Garth asked skeptically.

"I mean they made our island explode!"

"No way!" Garth coughed. "How could some'un git a whole island ta blow up?"

Mel furrowed his eyebrows and explained, "They didn't destroy the whole island. They caused the volcano that was near the inhabited side to erupt and bury our city."

"How could they do that?"

Mel sighed in exasperation. "It's difficult to explain. It happened, and I was told to stay away from them."

"Well, anyone comes lookin' for a fight, we'll make 'em wish they 'adn't." Garth finished eating and returned to his seat.

Mel noted the growing dimness under the boughs of the live oaks along the road. "It's going to be night soon. Time to make camp, somewhere off the road."

Mel guided the horses into a grove of trees atop a hill. The location provided them with cover and a place to watch the road in both directions. To minimize their exposure, they decided not to cook anything and instead snacked on some dried fish and crackers, Garth devouring them as though he had not eaten in hours. There was no moon as darkness fell, the surrounding landscape lit solely by the light of the stars.

They were about to go to sleep when they heard a twig snap not far from their camp. Garth immediately tensed, ready for a fight. Mel motioned with his hand for him to keep still. They sat motionless, hearing nothing but their own breathing and the beating of their hearts. Then in the starlight, a shadowy figure appeared. The silhouetted form was taking deep but silent breaths from recent exertion. It seemed to look directly at them and moved forward with sure but silent steps. Mel was ready to strike, his awareness sharpened by the tension. As the figure approached close enough to hear their breathing, Mel sprang forth quickly and tackled the intruder with a loud thump. Garth followed, joining the scuffle.

"Ow! Wait! It's me! Polly!" she exclaimed, breathing strenuously.

Mel let go. "Polly? What are you doing here?"

"Can you get this horse off of me?" she asked, gasping in discomfort, as Garth had sat on her to subdue her with his weight.

Garth quickly stood and grumbled, "I ain't no 'orse!"

After brushing herself off, she caught her breath and snapped at Garth, "You weigh about as much!" And turning to Mel, she continued, "I was thinking about what you said, and after you left, I noticed that some men over at the saloon were watching you, and headed out right after, keeping back and out of sight. I nearly died just from running through the woods to get around them and reach you first, but I had to come and warn you that you're being followed."

"How many was there?" Garth asked very seriously.

"'*Were* there,' Garth," Polly corrected him.

Garth frowned.

Polly stood with her hands on her hips and glared at Garth. "There *were* three that I saw leave together. If another didn't go and round up more. Considering the way you greeted me, it looks like you're expecting trouble. You're not running from the law, are you?"

"No, we are not. And I apologize if I hurt you," Mel said.

"I'm alright. I've been knocked down before. Not many people could move so fast I couldn't evade it." Polly glanced back down the road. "You should break camp. Those men were not far behind me, and if they have any luck, they'll find you too."

"Hey, how *did* ya find us? We thought we was bein' real tricky comin' here," Garth said.

"'*Were* being tricky,' Garth," Polly protested. "Honestly, why can't people speak their own language?"

"'Old your 'orses there, little girl—" Garth began to correct her.

"Sorry, Garth," Mel interrupted, "but I think Polly is right."

"'Bout my Anglish?" Garth pouted.

"No, about us moving on. It probably wasn't a wise decision to stop here. Let's pack up and hit the road."

Polly helped them gather their bedding and belongings back into the wagon. She wondered who these adventurous boys were, exactly, and what might be in store for them. "Hey! Can I come?" she blurted out.

"What?" Garth and Mel asked in unison. Mel continued, "Out of the question, Polly. We are in danger, as you pointed out. And we have little room or provision—"

"Garth asked me a question," Polly interrupted. "'How did I find you?' I've been tracking most of my life, taught by my aunt, who is an Esselen Indian. As for provisions, I can forage better than most people can shop. I can find food and water where ants can't. Besides, I have no reason to stay here. There are several regulars at the library who will inevitably squabble over who gets to take charge once they notice I've gone."

"What 'bout yer kin?" Garth questioned.

Polly winced at his pronunciation. A somber moment later, she sighed. "My parents died of consumption when I was six. My adoptive aunt and uncle found me starving in our home and raised me after that. Last year I moved out of their house and into the little room behind the library. I'm on my own now."

"Well, what 'bout yer friends back in town?" Garth asked.

"I have no friends in that town. That's why I wanted to be the librarian so I could spend more time with 'Tom Sawyer' and 'Huck Finn.' My only friends are trapped in books." She grew silent, and then with tears flowing on her flushed, freckled cheeks, she whispered, "I won't be any trouble. *Please*!" she pleaded.

"I still don't think it would be a good idea," Mel responded, standing his ground.

Just then, a ball of light streaked from between trees a hundred meters back in the direction of town, passed just over their heads with a whooshing crackle, and burst into flames in the woods behind them.

"Time to go!" Mel shouted. "Polly, run the other way. Steer clear of us, and you'll be all right." Mel and Garth jumped into the wagon and began to move.

Polly scrambled into the back, crouched among the boxes of provisions, and stated resolutely, "I'm not staying here to find out if those guys will be nice to me. I'm going with you."

Mel called out to Campitor and Candeo, and they began to gallop down the opposite side of the hill. Passing through the nearly complete darkness under the forest canopy, the horses instinctively avoided the many trees on the hillside.

There was shouting behind them as their pursuers cleared the top of the hill. Glancing back, they could see that there were seven of them, riding in a full frenzy after them.

Polly was having second thoughts about joining Mel and Garth. Their wagon would not be able to outpace horses bearing single riders. They would be overtaken before they even reached the river. And if they made it to the river, the wagon's wheels would bog down in the hip-deep water. Her heart sank. She could hear the hoofbeats and frothing breath of pursuing horses as they closed the distance. She wished she had stayed home this night. What would her aunt and uncle say if they heard that her body was discovered with two unknown boys an hour outside of town?

The wagon reached the southward road, and to Polly's astonishment, Campitor and Candeo broke into a full gallop that made their previous ferocious pace seem like a canter. The wagon gained speed in a way that felt to her as though it were being drawn by an unseen force beyond the abilities of any team of horses. The faster the wagon went, the smoother the ride became. *This little wagon should be coming apart right about now,* she thought. Somehow, they were not only keeping ahead of their pursuers but nearly imperceptibly opening the distance between them.

Then she heard the river roaring ahead, and her heart sank again. *Oh well, it was an exciting ending to a very short chapter of life.* As they approached the river, she yelled out to warn Mel and Garth, but they continued unfazed, staring forward. Polly braced for a catastrophic impact as the horses continued at a full gallop towards the thundering river.

A war cry arose behind them. Their pursuers knew that the wagon could not possibly survive this. They slacked their pace, waiting for their quarry to be swept downstream.

As Campitor and Candeo's strength drove their hooves through the rushing water, something inexplicable happened. The wagon did not submerge but instead glided above the surface like a flat rock in mid-skip. Even as they were halfway across, and should have run out of momentum, still they continued surging forward at full speed. The wheels were not moving. There was no wake behind them. The wagon was floating above the water. The horses kept galloping.

The pursuers stopped at the riverbank, glaring and shouting. If even the river could not slow the wagon, they knew they would never catch their prey.

When the wagon reached the far bank, the horses did not let up but kept on at a full gallop for another hour. By the time they slowed, they looked as if they were barely winded. Sweat glistened off their coats in the starlight. They now proudly cantered together like two prize horses that had just won a race.

Mel and Garth glanced into the back of the wagon and saw Polly sleeping peacefully on their blankets. Mel was concerned that this hapless young girl had intruded on his plans. He was considering whether they were already too far from her home to drop her off. He estimated that they were now fifty kilometers from Cayucos. He suspected that the hostile gang of seven men would likely be keeping an eye on her home for some time.

"Well, we's stuck wit her, huh?" Garth grunted in disapproval.

Mel looked at Polly's fiery red hair and her petite features and then back at Garth's huge, bulging features and said, "'*We're* stuck *with* her,' is what I think Polly would say."

"Yeh, whatever," Garth said. "I'm starved; what we got ta eat?"

Mel rolled his eyes. Leaning back, he scanned the night sky, chose a constellation by which to confirm their direction, and continued to guide the horses southward.

CHAPTER 18

A.R.A. *PATAGONIA*

The dawn came too soon for Polly. She awoke startled and confused to find herself in the back of a moving wagon. Then she remembered the events of the previous day and felt a wave of excitement mixed with trepidation.

On the other side of a storage box and crammed against the side of the wagon was the massive form of Garth, snoring like a sawmill, the empty paper wrappers of four whole wheat muffins strewn around him.

Mel heard Polly stirring. He thought it strange that she had slept through Garth's cacophony of snores.

"Mel," Polly said while gently touching his arm, "I think I was a little pushy in wanting you to take me along."

"Good morning, Polly," he responded. "Do you make a habit of jumping into moving wagons being chased by people armed with plasmatic orb projectors?"

"With what?" Polly asked, looking sleepy-eyed as she took the seat next to Mel.

"Never mind."

They sat next to each other in silence for several minutes, each thinking about how to break the ice.

Polly nervously twirled her red curls with her fingers as she wondered if she had made a big mistake by joining these reckless young men. The night before, she had been sure she was going to die, but instead, it had become the most exciting night of her life. Now she was miles away from her boring but safe routine back in Cayucos. She was thrilled to be on an actual adventure. This was not some fantasy in a book.

Finally, Mel spoke. "You mentioned that your parents died when you were six?"

Polly was confused that Mel could be so snide one moment and then show compassion the next. She did not know how to answer right away.

Mel turned to face her, noticing how the sunlight sparkled in her eyes like two large emeralds set in speckled gold. She reminded him of another girl he knew who had curly hair.

Polly looked away wistfully. "I can barely remember them. I was very young. Their illness was not uncommon to people who took the pass close to wintertime. It finally got the better of them months later as we lived on the coast. They were Paul and Molly. They wanted to combine their names, so they called me Polly. I wish I had known them longer. Sometimes I get the feeling that they are somewhere nearby. Maybe not in this world, but somewhere. I can't explain it. Does that sound crazy to you?"

Mel suppressed a feeling of sorrow that was welling up in him. He kept silent, struggling with painful memories of his own.

Polly saw his eyes water, pools of tears gathering on his lower eyelids. "I'm not the only one with a story like that, am I?" she asked, already having guessed the answer.

Mel wiped a tear from his cheek, swallowed hard, and said in a choked voice, "My mom died when I was young. My father disappeared several months ago. I'm not sure if he's still alive."

"And now you're off looking for him?"

"Not exactly. I'm following instructions he left for me."

Polly nodded, deciding not to pry further about the journey just yet. "Were you old enough to remember your mom?"

Mel breathed deeply and answered, "I was four. I get little glimpses now and then. My father raised me and told me what she was like. She had long, auburn hair that I can almost smell sometimes. Jasmine, I think. I see her in dreams, always smiling."

"It's like that for me too!" Polly exclaimed. "I can still remember my dad's hands. They were large and calloused. Sometimes, when I'm afraid, I can still feel his arms around me."

They sat side by side for an hour, reminiscing about their families and chatting about books and their interests back home. When Mel mentioned his best friend, Mari, Polly lit up with joy. "Marigold Thurman from Cooperton? I met her a few months ago! Her family came to Cayucos to trade, and she stayed at the library for hours!"

"That sounds like Mari," Mel said with a big smile.

Polly remembered the old map that Mel had been so excited about and asked, "Where are we going, anyway?"

"Well..." Mel stalled. He saw Polly's anxious stare. "Polly, I tried to discourage you from coming with us, so please understand I didn't want to put you through any inconvenience..."

Polly raised an eyebrow at Mel's awkward politicking. "Perhaps I should rephrase my question. *Where are we going?*" she asked loudly, suddenly serious.

"Gatún," Mel blurted, hoping to preempt further outbursts.

"Gatún?" Polly wondered. "I don't remember a town in California named Gatún. Is it in southern California?"

"No," Mel stated flatly, not wanting to look her in the eye.

"Gatún? That's a Spanish word!" She thought out loud. "Is it in Mexico? Oh, I've always dreamed of going to Mexico!"

"No, it's not in Mexico either," Mel answered.

"Judging by the sun, it's clear we're going south. But *where?*" Polly asked, tapping her foot.

"Panama," Mel responded quickly and with finality.

"Panama?" Polly mused, not believing it at first. "Panama, the *country?*" she said, irritation growing in her voice.

Mel realized that Polly was not going to be satisfied with a simple answer, so he clarified, "Gatún is along the new canal. Is it sounding familiar?"

Polly sat stunned, then suddenly stood. "*Panama!*" she yelled, waking Garth with her cry. "Are you *crazy?*"

Mel tried to remain calm. "I know it sounds preposterously far, but it's where I must go."

Garth leaned his sleepy head forward and asked, "What's all the ruckus 'bout?"

Polly, grappling with the concept of such a huge journey, snapped out, "Do you have any idea where you're going, Garth?"

"Nope," he answered, squinting in the sunlight. "Should I?"

"I should hope so! According to Mel, we are about to travel nearly to South America. Oh, and by the way," she said, turning to Mel, whose head was hunched between his shoulders like a puppy that had just chewed his master's shoes, "what exactly are we going to do there?"

Though Mel valued his brand-new friendship with Polly, he was becoming concerned that her attitude might hurt the morale of their group. He also did not want to give away the secrets of his quest. He stopped the wagon, sat up straight, and looked directly into Polly's eyes. "Polly, I appreciate that you warned us about those men who followed us from Cayucos. It was brave of you to take that risk. If you're having second thoughts and want to find a way back home, I will understand."

Garth looked at Polly, who seemed on the verge of tears, and asked, "What's wrong?"

Polly turned her watering eyes toward Garth and whispered, "He doesn't want me to go." She turned back to Mel. "I'm sorry, you're right. I did jump aboard; I did want to go. It's just that we're going so *far*! I haven't been out of my county in the last six years. The distance was way more than anything I expected. Please accept my apology. I will stop being nosey."

Mel raised his eyebrows as if to say, "And?"

"And bossy," Polly finished with a sigh. "Let's do whatever it takes to follow your dad's instructions."

Garth sat scratching his head and rubbing the sleep out of his eyes. "Would y'all sort thangs out a little softer? I need s'more sleep." He rolled over and pulled a blanket over his head.

* * *

With Polly now committed to their group, Mel decided to discreetly explain more of the personal history that made the journey necessary. He was careful to describe the unique elements of his heritage in the general terms of "training" required to take over his father's responsibilities as the guardian of the records of a forgotten nation, the name of which he did not share with Polly at this time.

It took hours for him to describe to her what had happened to him and his family from the early days in Martinique onward. She sat still, enthralled by his account and intrigued by the phenomena surrounding his memory loss. She listened with a chill as he told her of the Strangers, some of whom had threatened their lives the night before. If she had not seen the plasmatic orb and ridden in the wagon that could hover across water, she would have assumed that his mentions of extraordinary inventions and volcanic eruptions were an embellishment. True to her word, she was polite and non-confrontational in her inquiries. Finally, his account reached the point where their paths had intersected in Cayucos, which led to him explaining why they were headed to Gatún.

"The old map in the library matched the one on the parchment your dad left for you?" Polly asked, fascinated.

"Exactly, and the one in the library showed much more of the region. The words and symbols were in the same language. I compared the shapes and, sure enough, the landmass was Panama, with my father's map marking a specific location in the mountains near Gatún. Somehow, the Strangers are figuring this out. They might already know what I'm supposed to find there."

Polly tried to sound positive as she asked, "Won't it take months to get to Panama on this wagon?"

"I've been considering our options. If we take a ship from Los Angles, it should be just a few weeks from there to Panama."

"What about the wagon and the horses, not to mention the cost of booking passage?"

Mel reached behind them into a box and pulled out a small bag. "I think these will take care of any expenses."

Polly took the bag and looked inside. Glimmers of green and red sparkled from the handful of gems. Her eyes grew wide. "Are these real?" she asked.

"Yes. Completely real. My father was a gem broker of sorts," Mel evasively replied. "I think that just one of these will pay for our horses and the wagon to be transported."

"I should think so!" Polly exclaimed.

* * *

Three days later, they reached the mountains overlooking the San Fernando Valley. They could see the harbor of Los Angles in the distance. Mel hoped to reach town the next day and exchange some of the gems for cash, then quickly find a ship and book passage to Panama City. With ten days already having passed of the ninety days before he had to be back in Cooperton to open the Piaculum vault, and still not having left California, Mel began to wonder if any form of transportation could get him to his objective and enable a return journey in time. Travel was already bound to account for more than half of the window of time. The unknowns of what would be required in Panama would be the decisive factor.

That evening, after Garth and Polly had retired for the night, Mel went to the wagon and opened the storage compartment. He took Vulgladius out and walked several hundred yards away into the high desert to practice swordplay. He slashed at a cactus, again witnessing the cutting and burning power of the sword. He wondered if he would ever have to use this deadly tool.

On a hilltop not far away, Polly sat hidden in the dark. As she had been drifting off to sleep, she had heard *whoosh, whoosh, whoosh* in the distance and had followed Mel. She watched the crimson arcs appearing in the pitch blackness. Some of the things he had told her on the road had hinted at profound mysteries, but nothing had prepared her for seeing this weapon in action. She saw the sword shine brighter as Mel wielded it with greater intensity, swinging rapidly and precisely at the air and objects near him. At times, the blade became so bright that it illuminated his face and arms.

Polly did not move during the nearly two hours that Mel performed his exercises. As he put Vulgladius back in its scabbard, the light of the sword extinguished. Polly, suddenly aware of Mel's return to camp, quickly and silently scampered back ahead of him, just in time to crawl under her blanket. Mel crept back into camp, returned Vulgladius to the sealed compartment, and slipped under his bedding without a sound. Polly peeked out from under her blanket and saw Mel lying there, settled and breathing steadily, as though nothing unusual had happened that evening.

* * *

For Mel, it became another night of stepping into "the other world," as Oscar had put it.

A buzzing sound swirled around Mel's head. He opened one eye to behold the interior of a dark cave, dimly lit from the cave's narrow mouth. A damaged boat lay in pieces nearby. Mel's head throbbed in pain. Holding the back of his neck to control the intense ache, he tried to remember what had caused this calamity.

"Maybe we ran aground?" he wondered. "But where are the others? Surely I'm not the only one who survived." His eyes darted about the cave, and there, among the wreckage, he saw two legs protruding. With a gasp, he said, "Oh no! Oh no!" He reached the heap of rubble and began pulling boards and iron bands off the body.

At last, he rolled the body over and gasped. It was himself!

* * *

The next morning, before dawn, Mel woke before the others and went to a ledge of the bluff where they were camped. He was greatly shaken by the dark dream. All he knew was that the vision foretold his death in a sailing accident. He sat dazed as the dawn broke, the sun slowly warming his face.

The others soon woke. The three friends together stowed their gear, readied the horses and wagon, and set off down the road toward the city in the distance.

* * *

Mel found a jewelry merchant on San Pedro's unpaved main street who bought several of the stones for a fair price.

They went to the port and booked tickets to Panama City on a clipper flying the Argentine flag. The vessel had been christened the A.R.A. (Armada de la República Argentina) *Patagonia*, and, true to its country of origin, the entire crew spoke Spanish. Mel discovered that the hint of his familiarity with Spanish, which he had experienced while visiting Armando in South Fork, was only a small part of his near fluency with the language. He found that he knew the unique Castilian accents, which were common in Argentina, and quickly made friends with many of the crewmen.

Despite the uniquely effective suspension of Mel's wagon, Polly and Garth were delighted to be done traveling by road. The three friends were shown to a bunk room on the third level. They put the horses and wagon in the hold, where they shared stalls with several horses that were to be sold to the gauchos on the pampas of Argentina. The *Patagonia* set sail on the evening's tide.

* * *

The sailing conditions were ideal during the first week. Each day the ship made approximately three hundred kilometers of progress southeast toward the fifty-kilometer-mile wide isthmus linking North and South America, which was their destination, and which was to be the first port of call along the *Patagonia*'s voyage. Mel and the others spent most of their time on deck, enjoying the fresh ocean air and interacting with the crew. Polly and Garth practiced phrases in Spanish and began asking simple questions on their own. The three friends wandered around the huge ship, gazing out on the endless blue of the Pacific Ocean.

Eight days into the journey, dark, ominous clouds invaded the horizon. The captain announced that it was hurricane season and that their course required that they sail near the storm that was brewing. He instructed the guests to stay in their cabins until the *Patagonia* emerged on the other side of the tempest.

About two hours into the rough seas, Garth became concerned for the welfare of the horses. The three friends decided they should go together to the hold. They clung to each other as they were tossed from one side of the stairs and corridors to the other as the massive ship plowed through the heaving seas.

When they opened the hatch to the exposed deck, they were horrified at what was happening all around them. The wind was powerful, blowing at over seventy knots and taking with it any objects that were not strapped down. There were mountains of water looming over the ship. The swells crashed and subsided as quickly as they appeared, casting waterfalls over the deck. Polly screamed at the sight of the raging seas surrounding them.

"It's all right; we can wait for a lull," Mel reassured her. The three of them locked arms and, several minutes later, ran the distance to the hatch leading down to the hold. Their hearts were in their throats as they made the soggy, slippery sprint. They entered and shut the portal, heaving a collective sigh of relief.

Descending the stairs, they came to a large, dimly lit room that smelled of hay and oil. One kerosene lantern at the opposite end of the room swayed back and forth. The horses, secure in padded canvas slings, were noticeably agitated from the motion of the ship, stomping their feet, snorting, and staring with wide-open eyes. As the three young people staggered towards the stables, Garth suddenly gripped Mel and Polly's shoulders.

"Wait!" he whispered urgently. "There's men at the wagon. Looks like theyz'e tryin' to break into the storage 'partment."

They crouched low, cloaked in the dimness of the hold, and crept closer, the sounds of their movement lost in the noise of the storm. Two men were in the bed of the wagon, prying at the compartment lid with crowbars, and a third man was behind the wagon in the shadows.

"Whaddaya wanna do?" Garth whispered.

Mel surveyed the situation and felt impelled to confront it openly. Without answering Garth, he stood and stepped forward.

"Hey! What are you doing?" Mel demanded in Spanish.

The men were at first startled by the voice from the darkness and jumped, metal rods poised defensively. The third man disappeared into the shadows behind the wagon.

"We were told that there may be some contraband in this wagon," a man with a scar on his cheek replied in English. "We're just doing our job. Who are you?" he demanded.

Mel stepped into the direct light of the kerosene lamp and announced in English, "I happen to be the owner of this wagon. It does not contain any illegal substance, nor are you authorized to police this ship."

"Now, how could you know that?" the scar-faced man snarled, emboldened by the realization that he was being confronted by a young man.

Mel, unfazed by the man's arrogance, replied, "You're not part of the crew. Who are you?"

"Well, aren't we the clever one," the other man in the wagon said while stepping down to the floor of the hold. He was larger than the scar-faced man and had a sneering upper lip. "We've been paid to get the map with your destination marked on it, boy. You've got some kind of spell on this box, and we need it open. Why don't you just come over here and help us out before we have to put some hurt on you."

Mel stood his ground. "No, I don't think that's going to happen. Please leave, or I will call the captain and have you forcibly removed."

Polly screamed as the third man had snuck around and found her hiding in the shadows and was now enfolding her.

"Well, well, what do we have here? Looks like another church mouse, Bill. Maybe we need to squeeze the little one and see if the bigger one squeaks." Polly screamed and thrashed about like a cat being held up by its tail.

Mel's heart was suddenly filled with indecision.

Out of nowhere, Garth came running like a bull bent on goring a matador. Full force, he hit the man who was holding Polly, knocking him down and freeing Polly, who scrambled out of the way. Bill and the scar-faced man jumped on Garth and strained to pin him as he kicked and squirmed ferociously. Once he was sufficiently restrained, Bill scrambled after Polly and grabbed her by her ponytail, jerking her to her feet. Garth screamed at the top of his lungs for them to let Polly go.

"That is enough, *children*," Bill said, dragging Polly to the wagon. "You will get the map for me now, or else I'm going to have to see how brave this little girl really is." He took his crowbar and held it forcefully against her stomach. Polly winced in pain and looked pleadingly at Mel.

Garth saw that they were hurting Polly and looked to Mel. The expression on Mel's face made Garth immediately stop resisting. "Oh, you shouldn't a gone and done that."

The men holding Garth smiled as their friend inflicted pain on Polly. The scar-faced man looked at Garth. "And what can any of you do about it?" he asked and laughed cruelly.

Like a bat darting from its cave, Mel flew at Bill. He kicked the crowbar out of his hand, simultaneously striking the side of his neck like a lightning bolt. Bill tumbled instantly to the ground, moaning and grasping his neck.

Taking advantage of his captors' surprise, Garth broke loose and proceeded to pound the face of the nearest man. Meanwhile,

Mel caught the scar-faced man with a rotating scissor kick to his feet that sent him toppling to the deck. Mel drew his elbow up and hit him in the solar plexus. This knocked the wind out of him, and he began gasping for breath.

He pushed a finger that felt like a hot poker into Bill's neck. "Who sent you? And why are you looking for a map?"

Bill was just regaining his sense of balance. He sat and looked in astonishment at this young man who had just soundly beaten what was one of the toughest gangs on the west coast. He stared at the hand that was close to his throat and figured that this young kid likely had more surprises that he did not want to find out about. "I... I... don't know who hired us. It was a dark, smoky bar in Long Beach, and a guy with a hood and gloves said he had to get something from a couple of kids on this ship. We thought it was a prank. But he paid us half of the cash up front. Said we'd get the other half when we brought him the map."

"Did he say why he needed the map? And where you were to deliver it?" Mel demanded.

"No, no, he didn't say nothin' 'bout why he wanted it. Just told us he'd meet us in a bar in Panama City called The Lost Lagoon. That's all I know. We're not gonna push this any further. Why don't you guys just forget this ever happened?" He spoke while trying to get to his feet. As he reached back, supposedly to push himself off the deck, he swung around with a pistol in his hand.

With a newfound superiority, he motioned Mel toward the wagon. "Now, if you don't want yourself or your friends hurt, I suggest you open that chest."

Mel resigned himself and jumped into the wagon. He opened the compartment easily, withdrew the parchment map, and quickly closed the lid, which again snapped into place. He handed the map to Bill.

"Hey, hold on there!" the scar-faced man shouted, still gasping to regain his breath. "How do we know there isn't something in there worth more than this map?"

Bill squinted, greed stirring in his heart, and frowned. "I wish we had the time, Millard, but the brunt of the storm has passed, and we've got to finish this job." Pointing the gun at the three youths, he motioned them towards the stairs.

Garth tensed. Mel put a hand on his arm, communicating for him to wait. Polly's gaze sank to the floor, and she began to whimper. Mel took her hand with a reassuring squeeze and led the others as they complied with Bill and climbed the stairs. They opened the door and stepped out onto the storm-thrashed deck.

In the screaming wind, Bill had to shout to be heard. He ordered the youths to follow him. The three of them clung to each other to avoid being swept overboard. Bill lined them up at the railing and raised his gun.

Mel moved his right hand, pretending to point in fear at the rising gun. Suddenly, a blinding light erupted in front of him, and the three men were caught in a wave of heat. Simultaneously, a huge swell crested over the deck and swept them all off their feet. Garth grabbed a dangling rope as Mel and Polly held onto him like abalones on a rock. The three men washed by them, flailing their arms and grasping for something solid as they went over the railing and out into the sea.

The three drenched youths coughed and sputtered. They clawed back onto their feet on the slippery deck and, in a daze, crossed to the door leading to their cabin.

When they were safely behind their locked door, Garth let out a war whoop. Polly gave him a big hug. They turned and saw Mel sitting and heaving with emotion.

"Are you hurt, Mel?" Polly asked, stepping to his side.

Mel breathed in gasps as he thought about the nightmare they had just experienced. He finally calmed enough to choke out, "I think I killed them."

Polly was puzzled. "Mel, they got blinded by lightning. And then a wave swept them off the deck. You didn't do anything to make that happen."

"You can do some strange thangs," Garth chimed in, "but you didn't send no hurricane."

Mel shook his head, grappling with his actions. "I didn't have to use the Sazo on full power. They must've died from it before they could've drowned."

"What? Use the what-o?" Garth asked in confusion.

"You've seen it before, when my father used it."

Recognition and memory flashed in Garth's eyes, and his face was suddenly pale and pained. "Yeah, I seen it all right."

"That earlier instance was one of the lowest settings."

Garth nodded solemnly. His face was suddenly grim and resolute. "If'n ya did, they got what they asked fer. They was gonna kill us, that's for sho'."

Polly was at a loss. "What's this all about? What's a Sazo?"

Mel did not have the emotional energy to explain to Polly about the Sazo and how he had worn it under his shirtsleeve in case something like this were to happen. "It's one of the secrets I mentioned on the road. I'd like to tell you more about it in the morning if that's okay."

"Of course," Polly said supportively, many questions still swirling in her mind.

Mel lay in his bunk and closed his eyes. His friends were safe. Now he began to wonder how he was going to explain to the ship's captain why there were suddenly three fewer passengers aboard.

Garth pursed his mouth and raised an eyebrow. "Was what was on that map real 'portant?"

"Why?" Polly asked.

"'Cause their boss was holdin' it when they went overboard."

CHAPTER 19

THE LOST LAGOON

Early the next morning, Mel spoke with Jorge Ascensión, the captain of the *Patagonia*. He was an older, bearded man with weathered brown skin. Speaking to him in Spanish, Mel fully recounted the events of the night before. The captain did not pry into the significance of the map and expressed surprise at the harrowing account up to the point of the events on deck when he began to nod.

"Señor, I was watching from the bridge last night," Captain Ascensión revealed. "I saw these men that you speak of and what happened to them. They were not members of my crew, I assure you, and were not on the manifest. I saw them preparing to kill you, but I was too late to stop them, I'm afraid. I drew my pistol and was stepping onto the deck to intervene when you were saved by that miracle of lightning. It was justice that they were swept from my deck."

Mel was astonished that the captain had observed their predicament and greatly relieved that he regarded him and his friends as innocent. The secret of the Sazo had been narrowly preserved. From the higher vantage point of the bridge, the captain could easily have seen that the flash of light came from the deck and not from the sky. In his rush to come to their aid, he must not have seen the origin of the light.

Mel thanked the captain and descended to the deck, where Garth and Polly were reclining in hammocks and basking in the warm sun of the now calm weather to relax after the previous night's ordeal. Mel reclined in the hammock beside them. "The captain saw everything on deck and thinks it was lightning! I wish that were the case."

"What's to question, Mel?" Polly said. "We all saw it. You seem bent on taking the blame for the deaths of those goons."

Mel leaned close and spoke in low tones. "Polly, you asked me about the Sazo. It's a gun of sorts, a projectile weapon that uses temporary magnetic fields and extreme cold or heat to subdue or... kill opponents." He subtly showed her and Garth a glimpse of the projector attached to his wrist under his shirtsleeve.

Polly's eyes went wide, and she looked at Mel with a new, bittersweet respect. She did not want him to continue being weighed down by an undue burden. "Garth is right, you know. They picked the fight."

Mel let out a deep sigh of resignation and nodded in agreement. "It could have ended very differently. I'm just thankful we're safe."

Garth groaned. "Well, I guess we oughtta just head back once we can. Seein' as how we won't know where we're goin'." He grimaced at the thought of having to return home.

Mel pulled a rolled sheet of paper from his pocket and handed it to Garth. As he began to unroll it, Polly exclaimed, "The map from your father! I thought it washed overboard last night!"

"It did," Mel answered. "I redrew it this morning."

Garth beamed with pride and relief. "See!" he said to Polly, who had a concerned look on her face. "I tolt you he does somethin' like this every day! Hoowee!" He turned back to Mel. "Does this mean we don't hafta go back?"

Mel nodded, then paused. "But before we go any further, I want to say that I'm sorry I got both of you into all this trouble. This really is between me and the Strangers. We're fortunate we weren't killed last night."

Polly, who had been shaking her head in disbelief, looked at Mel like he had just escaped from an insane asylum. "You don't expect us to go traipsing around the jungles of Panama following a map that you just drew, do you?" she inquired.

"Yes, I do. This map is identical to the one that washed overboard, though I would have rather just kept the original. When I see something, I remember."

Polly wrinkled her nose and looked to Garth. "Is he serious?" Garth smiled and tilted his head in a "well, yeah" gesture. She turned back to Mel. "It's a huge risk. What if you missed some important detail? We could get lost and die."

"Even without the map, I doubt we'd get lost. With your tracking skills and Garth's ability to find his way around the mountains, we'd at least get back to Panama City." Mel pointed at a red mark on the map. "Right here is where we are to go."

Polly heaved a sigh. "You know, if I hadn't seen you draw the first map, hadn't ridden in a wagon that hovers over water, and hadn't watched you use a fire sword and a lightning gun..."

Mel rolled his eyes and smiled good-naturedly, then suddenly stared somberly at her. "Wait, you watched me use a fire sword?"

"That night in the hills," Polly explained.

Mel's eyebrow rose. "I guess I wasn't as covert as I'd thought."

"I know I shouldn't have," Polly said apologetically. "The sound of it woke me up. It was like nothing I'd ever seen. So beautiful shining in the dark. Speaking of which, what keeps it from burning through its sheath or through the wagon?"

Mel considered his response carefully. He and Garth and Polly had faced death together and likely had a long future ahead of adventures and shared adversity. The two others were trusting him to guide the journey and keep them safe. He decided it was time to reveal a little more about the technology that he possessed. He glanced around the deck and made sure that all the crew members were out of earshot. He was aware that a few of them understood some English, and after the events of the night before, he did not want to be overheard.

"Vulgladius, the fire sword," Mel said softly, "is a little like a lantern, an encased flame. In this instance, it's a plasmatic flame encased in a magnetic field that has been fine-tuned to give the sword its shape and edge. When it contacts an object, the field shifts, exposing the core, which is burning at nearly 3000 degrees Celsius.

Whatever has been touched is first cut and then melted or burnt. When the sword is not in use, the magnetic field perfectly encases the core."

Garth's eyes were now closed, his breath coming in deep and regular snores.

Mel smiled. "I don't know; maybe we should figure out how to use a magnetic field to hold back the power of Garth's nose."

Polly laughed. She became lost in thought, marveling at the concept of a sword-shaped magnetic field containing a source of heat as hot as a volcano, yet which fit safely into a thin leather sheath. "How has this stayed hidden so long?"

Mel remembered his father's warnings about disclosing too much information to others. Despite Polly's fiery temperament and outspoken manners, he could tell that she had an honest heart, and he somehow knew that he could trust her. For the next hour, he told her much more of what he had left out during their previous conversations in the wagon.

At the conclusion, Polly's mouth was agape. "You said before that your dad kept the records of a lost civilization, but Atlantis? And your ancestors are from there? I thought it was just a myth."

Mel stared out across the Pacific Ocean, imagining the ruins of a wondrous world under waters like those surrounding the *Patagonia*. Palatial homes now inhabited by fish and crustaceans. Ancient laboratories overgrown with coral. Roadways turned into forests of kelp. He wished that the islands of Delemni could be raised again but knew this was only a dream. A catastrophic breach of the Earth's crust had been healed at a great cost that could not be undone.

"It wasn't always a myth," he said wistfully. "It's best that it now be regarded as one and that secrets like Vulgladius and the Sazo stay hidden. We've seen the evil that can come from great power being held by people who aren't ready or who aren't responsible."

Polly asked, "You're talking about the Strangers who chased us and hired Bill's gang, aren't you?"

Mel nodded soberly. "They're likely from one of the scattered tribes of Delemni and are trying to gain access to the Grand Caelis." Mel and Polly became quietly contemplative and reclined in their hammocks, watching the horizon beyond the ship's rail.

* * *

The ship sailed for several days within sight of the coast. Mel stood at the rail, reflecting on his quest and occasionally discerning details along the rocky shore. He shook his head, dispelling doubts about the unknowns that awaited them in Panama.

Polly stepped to the rail near Mel. "What's the plan for when we get to the city?"

"First, Garth and I will take a quick look around The Lost Lagoon, where the map was to be delivered, to see if we can learn anything more about the people following us. Then we'll all head into the mountains."

"Only you and Garth will take a quick look?"

Mel looked at her sideways. "Or you could go alone, and we'll stay with the horses."

Polly gave Mel a sarcastic pout. "I see how it is."

* * *

The *Patagonia* docked in the Balboa district of Panama City at dusk several days later. Polly decided to busy herself grooming the horses in the ship's hold. Captain Ascensión assured Mel that no one would disturb her.

A thick fog wet the piers and caused the streetlamps on the shore and along the avenues to glow like blurred orbs. The occasional clanking of shop doors opening and closing and the clip-clop of passing horses' hooves on cobblestone resounded in the moist evening air.

The Lost Lagoon was a seedy bar in the city's old quarter, two miles away from the harbor. Here, the roads were not maintained, and whole sections of the original stone were missing, either taken as souvenirs or carted away to help strengthen another road. The area stank of rotten cabbage.

As Mel and Garth approached the decrepit wooden building that housed the bar, they noticed the additional smells of musk and mushrooms. They cautiously pushed open the splintered wooden door, which looked like it had not been painted since before either of them was born.

Garth was the first to step into the smoky room. This bar brought back all the old memories of going into many similar places to find his inebriated father and drag him back home. The first time he had entered a place like this, it had been like encountering a den of roaches. Each bar's odors of sweet rum and sweat were nearly identical.

Mel followed closely after Garth and approached the bartender, an older man with a grizzled beard, enormous nose, and a face nearly as red as a beet. He looked seventy years old, but Mel suspected he was only in his forties.

"Excuse me?" Mel asked in Spanish. "Have you seen any strangers recently that look American?"

The bartender responded in English in a gnarled accent. "Yeah, lots of them, mate. New canal workers mainly. Yer looks like a couple of yanks yourselves. If'n ye could, I'd much appreciate it if ye could speak in English. I ain't yet got the knack with Spanish, 'avin just shipped in. Ye here for the canal?"

Mel took a seat, glanced at Garth with an "I don't trust him" look, and then turned back to the bartender. "We're just passing through and looking for other American visitors in town."

The bartender emitted a low, guttural laugh that concluded in a fit of spastic coughing. He finally choked out, "Ye won't be findin' any tourists in the likes of this place, mate. I'd say try over on The Limey's side of town."

Out of the corner of his eye, Mel saw movement at a shadowed table at the far end of the bar. A singularly strange man wearing a hood and gloves stood and headed out the back door. Three others stood up from the same table and went out the front.

Mel touched Garth's arm. "Time to go, Jerry."

Garth turned with a "Whadu jus call me" look on his face and saw Mel wink. "Okay, Sam, I guess we been lookin' on the wrong side a' town."

Mel turned to the bartender. "Do you have a water closet?"

The bartender pointed at a nearby door. "Only if'n ye dare."

Mel tugged on Garth's sleeve, and they stepped through the indicated door and locked it. The small room was filled with a repugnant stench.

"Woowee!" Garth exclaimed, holding his nose. "What're we doin' in here anyways?"

"Looking for another way out. The guys that hired the gang we encountered on the *Patagonia* have set ambushes at the front and back doors."

Garth's eyes went wide, then filled with grim resolve. "Ya remember why ya brought me along, right?"

"We're not looking for a fight. I suspect they're armed, and I don't want to repeat what happened on the ship."

"They think yer dumb enough ta have the map on ya?"

"I don't know what the goons are thinking, but their boss in the hood and gloves likely plans to get the map at any cost. We should have ignored this place and just gone into the mountains. Here, help me get this window open. This is where we'll be leaving The Lost Lagoon."

Garth gave Mel a boost up. "They're gonna keep followin' us, ya know."

"Most likely, but that doesn't mean anyone has to die tonight." Mel opened the interior shutters only to see that the opening was also barred shut. Garth moaned, "Whaddu we gonna do now?"

"Just keep me here for a minute. I've got an idea!" He took several Sazo pellets from his pocket and crammed them into cracks in the wall at the base of the bars. "Now, get back." Mel carefully pointed the Sazo at the bars and pressed it, setting off the freezing pellets. The bars silently took on a shade of grayish white. Garth again boosted him up, and he gave the bars a sharp tap. They fell apart like they had been made of powder encased in a thin layer of ice.

Mel and Garth quickly helped each other through the window and into the night-shrouded alley beside the bar. They peered around the back corner of the building and saw a group of men watching the door. Turning the opposite direction, they followed the wall to the front of the building and stopped at the corner. Not three meters away from them were the men Mel had watched exit the bar. They had since been joined by several others and the hooded man, who was giving orders too low to be overheard.

Mel quickly scanned his surroundings. He saw a door in the building across the alley. Motioning for Garth to follow, he crossed the alley and tried the door. It gave a barely perceptible groan, much too loud in Mel's estimation, and then swung open. After entering and carefully locking the latch behind them, they crept through the dark house, every step eliciting creaks from the floorboards. They reached the front room and edged to a window facing the street. They could see the mob still waiting outside The Lost Lagoon.

Garth saw that they were outnumbered. He had always enjoyed charging like an enraged bull into a knock-down fight, but their current situation gave him pause. He whispered to Mel, "They'z crazy mad, lookin' like a pack 'a wolves already smellin' blood. And the way they'z swingin' thar pistols 'round, I'm thinkin' it'd just make their night to go an' shoot us all up."

The men were becoming impatient. Through the slightly open window, Mel could hear as they began to make loud, intoxicated boastings. "Let's go get 'em, Neco. There's only two of 'em. And they're just kids! Why're we waitin' out here?"

"Not yet," Neco growled his retort, his face hidden deep within his hood. "The small one is dangerous."

Hearing himself mentioned, Mel instinctively shrank against the wall and slid to the floor, as out of sight as possible. There was little doubt now that this man Neco was a Stranger who knew who Mel was and who wished to thwart or exploit his quest.

Creaking sounded from the ceiling above them. Garth grabbed Mel's arm. "There's somebody comin' from upstairs!" They crept quickly across complaining floorboards to a shadowed corner.

The scantly illuminated bearer of a low-held lantern steadily descended the stairs to floor level. Here the light was raised and revealed its holder, a young Asian man. He turned and peered into the shadows past the lantern's reach, speaking in English with a Japanese accent at a low volume so as not to be overheard from outside. "It is no business of mine why you hide from those men, but I ask that you please leave and not bring trouble to my home."

Mel heard the inflections of his accent and surmised that he was from a province in the south of Japan. "My deepest apologies," Mel responded in fluent Japanese. "I did not mean to involve you in my trouble. Please, we are as anxious as you are that we leave this house, but we find ourselves surrounded."

The Asian man stared in disbelief and continued in English, "Are you from Kyushu?"

"No," Mel said and stepped into the light, followed by Garth. "We are Americans."

"*Indeed*," he exclaimed doubtfully. "How do you know my dialect? There are only three thousand of us left in our province, the rest killed by the government."

Mel shook his head. "I have no time to explain. Is there another way out of this house?"

"Are you from Japan?" he asked in a tone of command. "There are many in my homeland who would see me dead."

"My friend, I am no assassin. Currently, we are the ones fleeing for our lives. Can you help us?"

The Asian man saw that Mel and Garth were young and that they were the prey of a violent mob. He decided for the moment to rest his suspicions unless they gave him reason to do otherwise.

"Quickly! This way!" he said and led them to a large room with a hand-woven Oriental rug in the center of the floor. "Hurry, we must roll the rug." As he and Mel worked together, quickly and carefully rolling the rug aside, a trap door was uncovered beneath it. The Asian man raised the door and leaned it aside, revealing a ladder leading down into a tunnel dug deep under the house.

Mel shook his head. "What if those men come here looking for us? They would see this and easily follow."

"My sister is watching from the shadows and will make every-thing as it was. Please, if you would follow me." After the three of them had descended, he led them with quick strides through a long tunnel.

"This tunnel, and others, were built at a time when there was a large Chinese population responsible for laundry labor. The workers were not allowed in town, not allowed to walk on the same streets as the Europeans. They lived in camps outside of the city. When the laundry was to be washed, it was left at the house we just came from."

Mel interjected, "How did a Japanese man come to live in a Chinese community? Weren't you concerned the Europeans would notice the difference?"

"The Europeans consider it beneath their dignity to look us in the eye. If they did, they would likely think, as they do elsewhere, that we all look the same. The Chinese community has welcomed us and kept our secret."

"Whydda people think y'all look the same?" Garth questioned, following closely after the two others.

The Asian man smiled, amused by Garth's innocence. "It is because of our similar skin tone and the shapes of our eyes."

Mel related to this man's experience of being treated as an out-sider after the prejudice he had faced in Cooperton.

The Asian man continued, "Ever since my people came to the Americas, we have been put to work doing menial tasks like laun-dry, mining, or building railroads. But that suits our purposes just fine." He sounded like he was smiling.

"You don't mind doin' them thangs?" Garth asked skeptically.

"We are very private people. Our customs are quite different from those of the Europeans. And we are patient, willing to wait for the right opportunities."

"What'd those be?" Garth queried, intrigued.

"We were a flourishing civilization when the Saxons were still dwelling in caves. When Alexander was trying to conquer the world, we were studying algebra and inventing gunpowder. The time will come when the silent Asian will rise out of his ghetto and teach in colleges and run the world's factories."

They reached the abrupt end of the tunnel. After climbing an old ladder, they passed through another trap door and stepped into a darkened room that had the musky scent of incense.

"This," the Asian man announced, "is my real home." He lit a second, larger lantern that brightly illuminated the room. The house was sparsely decorated with dark hardwood furniture that sat low to the floor. Two walls were draped in tapestries. A third wall was covered by an elaborate silk painting of a snow-capped mountain landscape with cascading waterfalls and a small Japanese town. Thin paper shoji screens separated the main room from the contiguous rooms.

"Wow!" Garth marveled.

Mel turned to the man and bowed, saying in Japanese, "May I ask your name, so we may honor you as you deserve?"

The young man listened in wonder. He was not accustomed to seeing a Westerner show such respect.

In the brightness of the room, Mel could now see that their host was in his late teens. In the colorful light reflected from the tapestries and the painting, Mel saw that the young man stood nearly as tall as Garth yet was much slenderer. He had a long, braided ponytail, a thin goatee, and stern but kind facial features.

"My name is Meiji Rei. I am the eldest son of Meiji Chiba, who is a prince of the southern island of Kyushu and lives in the town of

Arao. You may call me Rei. I was educated by my province's best scholars. My father wanted me to be familiar with the way of the western man, so he enrolled me in an American missionary school, where I learned to speak your language and became acquainted with your culture. My sister and I are living here in anonymity, hidden in the guise of working-class Asians."

"Holy mackerel!" Garth blurted out. "You're a prince! I ain't never met a prince a'fore." Garth clumsily bowed.

"I am merely the son of my father. *He* is the prince. Royalty in Japan is not something you automatically acquire. It must be earned. If you are to be a leader, men must first follow you. Too many of the 'lords' in our nation are following the way of violence, evoking fealty through threats, and depending on loyalty birthed from fear. My father is not this way, and because he resisted those in leadership and made political enemies, he has been labeled a traitor. I fear for his life. He secretly sent me and my sister here, where we are to wait for word as to when we can return." His face became distinctly saddened in the flickering lamplight.

Garth glanced through a partially open paper door into an adjoining room and saw a glass case that held two pearl-handled swords of different lengths. "Wow!" gawked Garth as he walked into the other room and stopped next to the case, followed by Mel and Rei. "Look at that! Is it a trophy or somethin'?"

"No," Rei said in a low voice. "These are Musashi swords and were the property of the greatest swordsman Japan has ever known. My father gave them to me to remind me of our history. They are over three hundred years old."

"Woowee! That *is* old. But they don't look it. How ya keep 'em all shiny like that?"

"Samurai care for their swords the way others care for their horses or even their children. To a samurai, his sword is his life."

"Sammy who?" Garth inquired.

Mel spoke. "The samurai are a caste of Japanese warriors whose duty is to protect their master. These swords are among the most precious items on Earth. Musashi swords have been made by master craftsmen who use technologies that have been kept secret for thousands of years. This class of weapons is considered sacred by many of the Japanese people."

Rei was incredulous at Mel's explanation. "How is it that one so young knows so much about Japanese culture?"

Garth smiled. "Mel here knows all kindsa stuff! Why he's even got a sword hims—"

"Garth! Not now!" Turning to Rei, Mel bowed again. "Please forgive me for being so impolite. Let me introduce myself and my friend to you. My name is Melvin Uri, of Cooperton, California. This is my neighbor, Garth Malingo. Our friend Polly Logan is tending to our horses aboard the docked ship we took from California. I wish that I were able to explain how I learned many of the things I know. An accident years ago robbed me of my memories of early childhood. The things I learned during my first eight years only come back to me when I need them. I was told that during that time, our household lived in Japan for a while."

"I am sorry to hear of your accident, Uri-san," Rei said as he politely bowed. "May you someday find complete healing." He turned his attention back to the swords in the case. "My father did not acquire these swords because he is a prince. He is a master craftsman of the kind that you described, who was entrusted with the oldest secrets of forging the swords of the samurai. Ever since the samurai were disbanded forty years ago, he has had to make his swords in secret. His political enemies are loyal to Emperor Meiji, and when they discovered that he was still manufacturing the swords, they used it as an excuse to put him in prison for years. When he was released, he returned to our town and began farming. While living this humble life, he covertly trained me in the ways of the samurai and passed to me the secrets of the old sword-making techniques. It was when he discovered that he was being set up for further accusations and imprisonment that he sent me and my sister away and gave us these two swords, not just as a reminder, but also so they would be kept safe."

"Is your family related to the emperor, having the same surname?" Mel asked.

Rei looked startled. "This is a very personal, family matter, not to be discussed casually. Suffice it to say, my father deserves the name more than the emperor."

Mel sensed a growing kinship with Rei and could relate to his personal history of being descended from royalty, with its many immense responsibilities, and living as a foreigner far from his homeland. He found it remarkable that two individuals from opposite ends of the Earth shared a common struggle. He spoke to Rei in his native tongue. "We share the same blood struggle, the same mandate to protect something we hold dear and to fulfill responsibilities that have been entrusted to us. I, too, am separated from my father and am seeking to obey his last request. If it is possible, and you are willing, I would be honored if you would accompany us to our objective in the mountains of Gatún."

Hearing his language spoken with fluency and respect by a Westerner provoked in Rei a high regard for these boys on the run from a violent mob. "I gladly offer you my assistance," he said in Japanese, with a respectful bow. "What do you expect to find at your destination?" he asked in English.

"Answers, and perhaps knowledge of my father's location."

"Gatún is but sixty kilometers north of us. Using the canal, we should be able to reach it in a day, maybe two."

Garth smiled. "Yer comin' with us? Don't that beat all!"

Rei grinned ever so slightly.

"He is," Mel reassured Garth, gratefulness filling him with a swell of emotion. He addressed Rei again. "The men outside The Lost Lagoon will keep following us. Other groups have tried to kill us twice in the past several weeks. We won't be able to pass through the canal undetected. They'll see us, and there may be a very unfortunate confrontation."

"Yes, this presents a great challenge," Rei responded, deep in thought. "But there may be a way. Consider this young samurai at your service."

Just then, a young Asian woman entered the room, carrying a longbow. She was just over a meter and a half tall, with long, straight, black hair. She was dressed in a traditional kimono of white and scarlet silk, with an obi belt tied around her waist. She bowed to the three young men and then whispered in Rei's ear.

"Gentlemen, this is my younger sister, Meiji Mihoshi. She is a fierce warrior and a faithful friend."

Garth laughed at the petite girl, who seemed to be barely in her teenage years. "Fierce warrior? J'you just say them thangs so guys won't try 'n get sweet with her?"

Swish... Thuwunk. Twice, the air beside Garth's head was fanned, his face framed by two arrows impaled in the wall.

Garth's eyes widened.

"Do not underestimate Mihoshi," Rei said calmly. "She is a master at *Kyudo*, Japanese archery, and at moving unseen. Though she is quiet, when she wishes to communicate, she can be most persuasive."

Garth, red in the face, watched as the small, silk-frocked girl put away her bow. He said apologetically, "Sorry there, Miss Mihoshi. I seemta forgot my manners." He bowed awkwardly.

Rei continued, "Mihoshi has informed me that the men outside The Lost Lagoon have scattered and are searching throughout the city. She says that if you are in need of her skills, she is also available to help."

CHAPTER 20

THE *MUSASHI*

After several hours Mihoshi returned with word that the men had dispersed from the area between the house and the docks. She assured the others that they could pass safely if they were careful. Rei took the sheathed Musashi swords from their case and tied them to his back. After glancing along the streets of his neighborhood, he led the others back to the *Patagonia*. They climbed the gangplank and descended to the hold.

Polly was using a body brush to groom Candeo. Garth playfully snuck behind her and picked her up. She let out a scream that was quickly muffled by one of Garth's big hands. She dropped her brush and kicked and squirmed like a captured wildcat. Finally, her elbow found Garth's abdomen. He let her go and hunched over in pain.

"Ow, Polly! Whatdya haffa go do that fer?" Garth moaned.

Polly vented her outrage. "What were you thinking? I've been feeding the horses and worrying my brains out over what could've happened to you guys. I imagined all kinds of horrible things. Then you grab me like that and act surprised that I'm upset?"

"Wow, Polly! You was worried 'bout us?" Garth gave her a weird smile, still wincing from her well-placed elbow strike.

"*No!*" Polly answered, catching herself. "I was worried about myself! I was worried that I would be stuck in the middle of Panama. I didn't even go to the galley for dinner because I was *alone!*" She noticed Mel and the two new persons who were with him, immediately calming. "Oh, hi, Mel. Who's this?"

Rei turned to Mel and said with a smile, "You were right, my friend, she is like a firecracker."

Polly turned a shade of red. "Like a *what?*"

Mel grimaced slightly. "Polly, this is our new friend Rei and his sister Mihoshi. They are going to help us get to Gatún."

"Hello, Rei and Mihoshi. I'm sorry," she said, "it's just that my playful friend caught me rather off guard."

"No need to apologize, Miss Logan," Rei responded. "I thought that you acquitted yourself rather well. I consider it an honor to be in the presence of such aggressive allies." He reached out, took her hand, and bowed respectfully, followed by Mihoshi.

Polly hastily bowed in return, then picked up the body brush and continued grooming Candeo.

Rei looked over the horses with awe and then turned to Mel. "These must be your steeds. What beautiful beasts they are!"

"Beasts?" Garth protested. "Campy and MJ ain't no beasts. They's a cross 'a top breeds."

"Please do not misunderstand me, Garth. I meant no disrespect. I have seen none finer, and I was raised with horses."

Mel stepped forward and scratched Campitor's neck. "They're called Campitor and Mons Candeo, in addition to Garth's nicknames for them."

"Yes, proper names for both." Rei walked to Campitor and spoke softly to him while stroking his muzzle. "'Charger,'" he said, interpreting Campitor's name. "That describes what he loves to do in battle." And then, turning to Candeo, he said, "And this one certainly is the Jewel of the Mountain. Do I notice that she has trouble seeing from one eye?"

"Trouble seein'?" Garth huffed. "She's all blind in that eye."

"On the contrary, sir," Rei said. "I see life within it. Observe." He flicked his finger towards Candeo's eye, eliciting a blink.

Garth stepped to her side, his eyes moistening. "MJ, MJ, you can see! Mel, is it them plants we been feedin' her?"

"I believe so, Garth," Mel answered. "And I bet your headaches have been less severe too. With a lot of love and help from friends, it's amazing what can be done for a person or an animal who has been crippled by adversity."

Garth felt his forehead. "Ya know, you're right! I ain't got no headache fer days now, and yesterday I was lookin' at the horizon and a sure as sassafras I could see it clearer than ever a'fore."

"*Euphrasia officinalis*," Rei said to Mel.

"Yes," Mel replied, "mixed with cassia seeds and bilberry fruit. I've read that it can restore eyesight. Do you know herbology?"

"Yes, it is one of the disciplines of our culture. We were using herbs for medical cures before Thebes was built. My ancestors came from one of the early dynasties of China. We owe much of our heritage and medical knowledge to our cousins across the East China Sea. Though I would love to speak at length of our history, I fear that we cannot tarry. We must plan our course of action and set out, or we may be discovered."

Garth was still stroking Candeo's muzzle, saying, "You can see. I'm so sorry fer what my pa did to ya, MJ." Candeo responded affectionately, nuzzling Garth.

The five companions gathered close together around the map and, over the following hour, devised their strategy. They would leave the *Patagonia* aboard Rei's small ship, the *Musashi*, and make the transit of the Culebra Cut section of the canal. Once in the Lago Gatún, they would land on the northeast shore, pack their supplies, and proceed by wagon the rest of the way.

After finalizing the plan, Rei slipped undetected away from the *Patagonia*, promising to meet them at the appointed time.

Mel's heart grew heavier as he felt the responsibility of having drawn two more people into the uncertainty of his quest.

* * *

At four o'clock in the morning, Captain Ascensión had his crewmen open the seaward side door of the cargo hold to prepare for a discreet transfer of the horses and wagon.

The four anxious adventurers sighed with relief when Mel discerned a wooden ship of the *Musashi*'s description approaching through the fog. Being a midsized Chinese junk, it would be just large enough to effectively transport them and their gear. Its hold, though much smaller than that of the *Patagonia*, had a side door of its own and could accommodate the wagon and horses.

Less than a minute after the *Musashi* appeared, Rei brought it alongside and threw a mooring line to Mel. Rei rushed belowdecks, opened the *Musashi*'s side door, and waved for the *Patagonia*'s crew to lower the cargo planks. "We must hurry!" he implored his companions. Mihoshi assisted with the transfer of gear and, despite her diminutive size, skillfully handled several cumbersome armloads. Mel caught her eye once, and she quickly looked away and returned to the task of moving supplies. The horses and wagon were transferred, along with provisions that Mel had purchased from the captain.

In a matter of minutes, they were ready to depart. Mel thanked Captain Ascensión and boarded the *Musashi*.

They pulled quietly out into the harbor without having attracted any unwanted attention. Eager to leave the vicinity before sunrise, they set sail immediately. Though their departure had gone smoothly, it had taken more time than originally planned.

Once they were underway, Polly had the opportunity to be more fully introduced to Mihoshi. She discovered that the petite girl's name meant "beautiful star" and sensed that it suited her perfectly, with her hair that flowed to the small of her slim back, her delicate facial features, and her feminine but surprisingly strong hands and feet. Mel, Garth, and Polly had never seen such an embodiment of innocence and humility.

Exhausted by a sleepless night of events in Panama City and their preparations at the harbor, Garth, Polly, and Mihoshi soon went belowdecks and fell fast asleep in their cabins.

Mel chose to stand watch with Rei on the deck and frequently looked back throughout the morning. The silence, broken only by waves slapping against the hull, helped Mel to relax as much as possible while remaining vigilant. The morning wind blew softly, filling the sails and revealing to Mel a picture sown into them of a fire-breathing dragon standing on a flaming sword impaled in a mountain of bones. "What does the design on the sail represent?" Mel asked Rei in a whisper.

Rei, pulled from his enchantment with the sea, looked up slowly and said in an equally hushed tone, "This is the sign of the 'Protector of the Spirit of Fire.' It is my namesake."

"What is the meaning of the bones?" Mel inquired.

"Those are the remains of my ancestors who died defending the craft that I now must carry on to the next generation. They are a reminder that I did not acquire this privilege by my own skill but by the efforts of those who have gone before me. I imagine that the quest that you are on is like my own. If you are willing, I will enjoy hearing more of it, as we now share a common path."

Mel knew that he owed Rei a great debt. Rei had saved his and Garth's lives and was now risking his own safety by helping them. Mel sensed that he was a man of honor and could be trusted. He began by asking a question. "Have you ever heard of Delemni?"

When Rei responded that he had not, Mel told Rei the story that his father and Oscar had told him. Half an hour later, Mel finished recounting the essentials of the history of his people and the relevant details of the past eight years of his life. He looked at Rei, who was silently reflecting on what he had learned. Finally, Rei spoke with wonder in his voice. "I thought it was just a fable!"

"Which part? Or all of it?" Mel asked with a gentle laugh.

"The *Kuki*, or what you call the Caeli, has been recorded in our myths. I did not expect to learn that they were true. The world that you describe is thought to have been utterly lost."

* * *

Less than an hour after setting sail from Panama City, they entered the Pacific side of the soon to be officially opened Panama Canal. Weeks before, Rei had heard from canal workers in the city that the wardens were allowing passage to select vessels willing to pay a high fee to participate in preliminary test runs of the canal. Mel paid the fee and was informed by the canal wardens that it would take two and a half days to reach the Atlantic Ocean. Ropes were attached to the prow of the *Musashi* and hooked to a team of mules who pulled the vessel forward through the looming metal entrance into the first set of elevating locks.

* * *

The landscape on either side of the canal rolled by at a lazy pace. The thick, humid jungle teemed with colorful birds dancing through the air, gorging themselves on a feast of tropical bugs. The occasional cry of a monkey shrieked through the muggy silence.

Polly and Garth emerged on deck, rubbing sleep from their eyes. She took a seat at the railing, dangling her feet over the side.

"Hey there!" Garth greeted the two other young men wearily. "Y'all been up all day?"

"Most of it," Mel replied. "Did you get enough sleep?"

Garth smirked. "I ain't never get 'nough sleep! I prolly could sleep all the way ta where we's goin'. I don't think that there's such a thang as too much of sleepin' nor eatin'."

Rei looked at the mountain of a young man. "Puppies and old men need their sleep."

Garth stood upright in indignation. "Who ya callin' a puppy, old man?"

"My friend, it is just a proverb from my country."

"I'll tell you," Garth said crankily, "in my country, we don't take a hankerin' to folks insultin' us first thang in the mornin'."

"Please accept my apology. How may I amend my breach of cultural etiquette?" Rei asked calmly.

Garth frowned. "I got no idea what ya just said, so I ain't so shore ya didn't insult me again!"

Rei suppressed a lighthearted smile at Garth's ignorance. An idea occurred to him of how to resolve the tension between them and establish an order of respect in their group. "I suggest we settle this like gentlemen," Rei said and disappeared into the hold.

Garth looked over at Mel. "How'm I sposed to know how a gentleman settles thangs?"

After a few moments, Rei reappeared on the deck, his hands full of protective padding and two bamboo sticks. He handed one set to Garth and began putting on his own.

"Kendo," Rei announced, "is how we practice for war. It is every bit as exhausting as a real battle, yet no one dies. It is also an excellent way for friends to settle issues with one another."

"I ain't got no problems with ya, Rei," Garth said apologetically. "I just don't always git what you're talkin' 'bout. Sometimes I can get my tail feathers ruffled by just 'bout anybody."

"What a curious reservoir of analogies you possess, Garth," Rei said as he finished attaching his kendo armor. He pulled on his helmet, assumed a battle-ready stance, and pounded the deck with his bamboo sword.

Garth put his kendo armor aside. "I don't want ta fight ya, Rei. I could hurt ya. I mean, I'm almost twice your weight and..."

Whack! Rei's bamboo sword hit the back of Garth's leg.

"Hey! Ow! Rei, what was that fer? I ain't got no beef with ya. Come on; I don't wanna hafta woop on ya. I mean, ya saved my life last night, and we should be..."

Whack! A sharp blow resounded on Garth's other leg.

Garth got red in the face and began mumbling to himself. "Why, now you gone and done it. I guess I'm gonna hafta wipe this deck with your long, black ponytail." As he pulled the gear on, he realized that he knew nothing about this kind of fighting and decided instead that he would rely on what he knew best. He threw the gear down and charged Rei with the kendo stick raised.

Rei deftly sidestepped his attack and pummeled him with several swift, stinging blows to his backside. Garth tumbled into the rail and quickly got back up, swinging back.

Rei pivoted, using Garth's weight and momentum against him. *Whack!* Rei's bamboo stick struck Garth in the stomach as he raced by. He stumbled, hit his head on the mast pole, and fell to the deck with a thud.

"I would advise you to put on the gear, my friend. This could be a long session," Rei said in a menacing tone.

"How long we gonna do this?" Garth asked, already exhausted in the sweltering heat.

"As long as it takes for you to learn not to lose your temper when someone says something that you do not understand. You are too easily offended. If you cannot restrain yourself from flying into a rage when a *friend* jokes with you, what will you do when someone who wishes you ill attempts to provoke you to violence?"

"Okay, okay, I gitit. I'm sorry for losin' it. I just ain't as smart as some folks. Makes me want ta start poundin' on whoever's makin' me feel bad."

Rei took off his helmet and gloves and reached down, pulling Garth to his feet. Rei looked directly into his eyes and said with compassion, "Garth, do not let others define who you are. You were made unique. The symbiotic design of creation would not be complete without your existence. You are neither smarter nor less intelligent than God made you. Find your identity, and you will realize your purpose."

Garth did not understand all the words that Rei had spoken, but in his heart, he knew what was being said. He realized that this young Japanese man was not only an excellent warrior but was also a great teacher. Garth knew he would learn much from him if he could just keep his own mouth shut. Not knowing the correct words to use to express his respect for Rei, he bowed and said, "Thank you for the lesson!" Pausing for effect, he added with emphasis, "*Captain* Rei."

* * *

Mel and Polly had watched this confrontation. As much as Mel had wanted to rush in and help Garth, he had known it would be a valuable lesson. When Mel saw Garth's humble response and the respect he had gained for Rei, he was grateful that he had stayed out of it.

Polly, on the other hand, had been disgusted at first by what had seemed to her to be a ridiculous display of male bonding. She had not been sure how the conflict would turn out. She had grown fond of Garth with his overgrown, puppyish ways. And she had not wanted him to hurt Rei, who was the object of a new fascination for her. He was different from any other young man she had ever met. He was reserved, quiet, and mature. His physique seemed thin and almost frail as she compared him with the massive build and brute strength of Garth. Watching how Rei had taught this lesson had caused her admiration for him to heighten. He had not only shown skill and courage against the raging attacks of Garth but had also shown compassion and wisdom in speaking with him. She felt drawn as if by a magnet to learn more about Rei.

An hour after Garth's kendo lesson, they entered the last of the elevating locks. Mihoshi joined the others on deck, and they sat together and watched the huge gates, chain barriers, and pump mechanisms that worked together to provide safe across-land transport of vessels from one ocean to the other.

After they passed the lock and began sailing along the Culebra Cut section of the canal, Polly approached Mel, who was watching several monkeys swing effortlessly through the trees. "How long do you think it'll be before we have to head back to California?"

Mel's lazy smile turned into a puzzled expression. "*Have to* head back? I don't know exactly what will happen or how long things will take at the location marked on the map, but I hope we can fulfill our purposes there and start the return journey as soon as possible."

Polly stared past the rail. "That's too bad."

Mel smiled bittersweetly, guessing what was on her mind. "I'm enjoying the company of our new friends too, but Panama City is their home."

"If we can avoid the Strangers, couldn't we stay for a week?"

Mel shook his head. "This has always been a two-way journey with no time to spare."

Polly let out an angry sigh and walked away. She sat by herself against the cabin top, turning her back to Mel.

Garth walked over to Mel and sat. "You guys havin' a spat?"

Mel turned back to the jungle. "I reminded her of something she already knew, and she got moody and walked away in a huff."

"I hear ya, Mel. I ain't never been 'round girls much. I always had lots ta do at the shop, fixin' it up an' stuff."

Mel remembered the dilapidated shack next to Garth's house, which he had mentioned was his "shop," and marveled that he had spent any time at all "fixin' it up."

Garth gazed over at Polly's flame-red hair. "But ya gotta admit, she shore is purty."

Mel was taken aback by this suggestion about a girl that he considered to be just a friend. "I've been focused on keeping us alive and haven't had much time to think about it." Noticing Garth's confident smile, Mel interjected playfully, "You're right, though. She's a stunner! Her eyes are quite pretty in the morning light, and her face practically glows when catching the sunset. But I've noticed that she seems to have taken to Rei. She hangs on his every word and bats her eyes when he looks her way."

Garth snorted. "I ain't noticed nothin'. Ya really think she takes a hankerin' to him?"

Mel laughed and punched Garth's solid shoulder. "Sounds like someone needs to do a little talking himself with the lady."

Garth stared at the deck and heaved a sigh. "I ain't the talkin' type, an' she's all smart an' stuff. Why she says more words in one hour than all the words I know. I feel like a fool talkin' ta her."

Mel smiled gently at this insight into Garth's self-image. He put a hand on his forearm. "Well, I guess you'll have to find a way to talk without words then, won't you?"

Stymied at Mel's meaning, Garth walked the opposite direction from Polly, shaking his head and mumbling beneath his breath.

* * *

Early the next day, as they continued sailing slowly along the Culebra Cut, Polly sat sullenly staring ahead. Their safe passage thus far was not enough to cheer her. She was mulling over the pain she felt at Mel's seeming lack of understanding toward her. How could he not see that her interest in Rei was just one aspect of wanting to stretch this adventure out for as long as possible? This was the first time in her life that she had felt truly alive! The others in the group all seemed anxious to get the adventure over with. Depression settled over her. She drew her legs up close and buried her head between her knees, her eyes closed.

Polly did not hear Mihoshi approach and sit next to her.

"Polly?" Mihoshi asked. When she did not respond, Mihoshi continued, "Do clouds cover the sun forever?"

Polly heard the analogy and seethed within, thinking, *Of course not!* "What's your point, Mihoshi?" she asked curtly.

"Is there not always hope?"

"What does hope have to do with anything?" Polly bit back.

"Hope lights the dark and shelters us amidst adversity."

"What adversity? Mel is completing his mission; you and your brother will be going back to Panama City to wait for your dad. Garth will probably go back to Cooperton to become the local blacksmith. Why not have hope? Everything is *just peachy*!"

"You did not include yourself in your observations."

"No, I guess I didn't," Polly said.

"Are there not also many good things in store for Polly?"

Polly was tiring of this discourse. "No, there are not!" she replied heatedly. "All of you will be going on with your lives. I've never had much of a life to return to or carry on. All I had was being locked up in a small-town library. For the past few years, I've lived through characters in books. When I read, I'm not lonely anymore. I go along with great men and women on their adventures. I hate finishing a book because I lose my friends.

"Before Mel and that lumbering ox of a boy Garth came along, I didn't know if I could go on with my life. The people on this ship are the only real friends I've ever known, and I don't want to think about what things will be like after this ends. No, Mihoshi, there isn't always hope for Polly Logan."

Mihoshi was surprised at the depth of despair in this girl who had seemed so vivacious when she met her. She paused to compose her thoughts, not wanting to tread clumsily upon a fragile heart. Finally, she said softly, "I have known you for little more than a day and have been inspired by your intelligence and energy. Surely the people at home will come to value you as a friend."

Polly, who was feeling empowered by speaking openly of her pain, simply said, "Yeah, if they didn't think I was plain ugly and didn't hate me because they think I'm part Injun."

Mihoshi smiled subtly and sensed that Polly was getting closer to what was really bothering her. "I don't think you're ugly, Polly. You are beautiful."

Polly shook her head in disbelief. "Then how come all the guys used to mock me, calling me 'red skin with hair on fire'?"

Mihoshi giggled at this word picture. "Boys mock mysteries to keep them at a distance. You, Polly Logan, are beautiful first because you love deeply and are committed to your friends. As for your red hair, I see it as the rarest gift. In all my life, I have never seen another person with such radiance. I see your hair as a reflection of your soul. It is fiery and passionate. Right or wrong, you put your whole heart into whatever you do. That is a rare character trait in a world of timid people."

Polly wrinkled her face in a painful grimace and said through clenched teeth, "Then I'd rather be timid! This 'passionate mystery' was going to *kill* herself! I was so tired of being alone, so sick of the pain."

"But you did not follow through because of the grief it would have caused others."

"Whose grief? I didn't have any friends. My only kin were my aunt and uncle, and they were too busy to even notice me."

"You didn't do it because of us."

"You? I didn't even know you yet."

"Are you certain? There are times when the eyes of our spirit are given a glimpse of the sun waiting above the clouds."

"How could you know anything about 'the eyes of my spirit'?" Polly asked, her aggressive demeanor faltering as tears began to stream down her cheek.

"They are the same as mine. I find no joy in living in hiding, separated from my father while he is in danger on the other side of Earth's largest ocean. Hope is a prophetic insight given to show us the possibilities of the future. The sun still shines above our circumstances. All storms will pass. The hope of many adventures is dormant in your spirit, and it may be that the rain of adversity is required to awaken that hope."

Polly relaxed at Mihoshi's calming voice and gentle imagery. "I'll still have to go back to being alone at the Cayucos library."

Mihoshi took Polly's right hand in both of her own. "Perhaps your life has many chapters yet to be written. There is a proverb that says, 'We can never go back, only forward.'" Mihoshi smiled comfortingly at Polly, stood, and joined her brother, who was folding his clothes and packing them into a knapsack.

Polly looked out over the prow of the *Musashi* at the gently winding channel ahead of them. The melodious song of the inland jungle rang vividly in her ears as she enjoyed the morning sun.

* * *

Several hundred mosquito bites later, they left the Culebra Cut and entered the expansive beauty of Lago Gatún. Thirty kilometers remained between them and the point where they had decided they would anchor and continue the journey on land.

After the previous day's lesson in humility, Garth and Polly followed Rei around the *Musashi* like sheep following a shepherd. Rei spoke in a soothing way, often quoting people who had died hundreds or thousands of years before. Polly found herself drawn to his confident presentations. Garth stayed close to Rei not only because he was amazed by his leadership and maturity, but also to keep an eye on the interaction between him and Polly.

After sailing for more than a day through the narrow, noisy channel, the center of the lake was relatively quiet, the calm broken only occasionally by distant animal cries from shore. Mel took a turn at the ship's wheel and found it peaceful to steer the vessel over the smooth water and thread its path between the many islets of the lake. While in this dreamy state, he suddenly realized that someone was standing close by.

"Do you have a question, Mihoshi-san?" Mel asked without turning his head.

Mihoshi, embarrassed at being discovered, was tempted to disappear below deck. Curiosity drew her forward. "My brother says you are of the lost tribe of the *Ou Shotou*," she explained.

Mel's eyes opened wide in surprise. He hesitated to respond. "Pardon me?"

"The *Ou Shotou* is a fable about sunken islands that we were told as children to scare us into obedience."

"And how would it do that?" Mel inquired.

"According to the fable, at one time, there was a great city that was perpetually illuminated, where fruits and vegetables grew wild. The people there mined the earth for treasures. It is said that some willful men brought darkness to that pleasant land. They dug too deeply and opened the secret lair of a fire demon, who was so angry at being disturbed that he lashed out and destroyed their land."

Mel listened intently as she spoke. Her words provoked memories of showers of flame descending around him, a house on fire, and his mother running and then shielding his body with her own. He drifted in thought, standing still and expressionless.

"Mel-san," she tugged at his arm, "what do you see?"

"Huh?" he asked, startled out of his daydream. He waved a swarm of insects away from his head. "Memories. Old memories of things that happened to me, and I imagine happened to others too many times before."

Mihoshi nodded. "I heard stories of strange men who lived on the island of Krakatau. For many years, they dwelt in the shadow of a massive volcano. One day, word began to spread throughout the Indonesian Islands that jewels and precious metals were being exported from Krakatau. It was very strange, as it was such a small island whose primary export was bananas. Then, thirty years ago, the island exploded, and much of it sank beneath the sea. The eruption was heard five thousand kilometers away and caused tsunamis that killed over thirty-six thousand people. It is a familiar pattern, as you know perhaps better than anyone."

Mel's mind again reeled. Fire fell from the sky into the ocean. Huge waves frothed and raced toward him. He closed his eyes and heard Jora scream as he fled to safety and left Mel at the mercy of the sky and sea.

Mihoshi continued, "Many lives have been lost, and many will be saved."

CHAPTER 21

IN THE MOUNTAINS OF GATÚN

They reached the northeast shore of Lago Gatún and dropped anchor beside a protruding sandbar. Mel struggled to hold the stomping and snorting Campitor and Candeo back as Rei and Garth opened the side door and positioned the ship's cargo planks to create a path down onto the beach. The moment the path was ready, Mel released the horses, and they galloped exuberantly down the planks and out onto the open shore.

The five friends together rolled the wagon onto the beach and then sat in the shade and enjoyed a restful lunch of cheese and fresh-squeezed juice from guavas that grew beside the lake. Garth and Polly helped Rei unload food stores from the lower cabin. Mel and Mihoshi packed the provisions into the wagon.

They had just finished covering the goods with a tarpaulin to protect against the always possible sudden downpours of the Panamanian climate when the horses suddenly stopped their play, and an eerie, inexplicable silence settled over the surrounding area, broken only by the cry of a harpy eagle. The horses trotted back and stood next to the wagon. Mel took this earlier than planned opportunity to finish their preparations for departure by hitching the wagon to the horses. The air was still except for an intermittent, gentle breeze that brushed the beach with a silky-smooth warmth.

Rei sensed something amiss in the lingering silence and raised a spyglass. He scanned the terrain and the lake for signs of movement and gasped! A schooner with three masts was approaching swiftly across the still water, its sails slack.

"This is most unusual!" Rei announced. "How can a sailing ship speed through the water when there is no wind?"

"What?" Garth asked, startled. He stared out at the lake in the indicated direction. "Ain't no one can do that 'cept with steam engines, and I don't see no smoke followin' 'em."

Polly stepped next to Mel and grabbed his arm. "It's them. Isn't it?"

Mel stared at the approaching ship, now visible to the unaided eye. His expression shifted to one of grim determination. "Yes. I'm afraid it is. We must move swiftly." He shouted to Rei, "I would advise you to depart immediately. I don't think they'll follow you. They're looking for me."

"My friend, you know better than that, the mind of a samurai." Rei ran to the *Musashi* and ducked into his cabin. Moments later, with his swords already on his back, he emerged with Mihoshi's bow and arrows. He threw the bow and quiver of arrows swiftly to his sister, who snatched them from the air and donned them in one fluid movement. Mel looked at his two new friends with a concerned, pained frown.

"We will fight," Rei said with a guttural, warlike snarl. "We will not let these 'Strangers' attack you without coming to your defense. These men are called *Piku Oni*, or 'cowardly ogres,' though in truth, they are not fit to be called men. They prey upon the helpless and imagine themselves to be great warriors!"

"I can't ask you to join this quest," Mel pleaded. "These enemies are led by a man of my nation. He knows who I am and wants what I am seeking and will stop at nothing. Please do not stand with us. Flee while you still have the chance."

"We will not run as mice from a fox. We have trained all our lives for combat, and we *will* stand with you, Mel-san. If necessary, we will fall with you."

Polly suddenly pointed in alarm at the approaching vessel. "Everyone down!" she screamed out. A huge, flaming, tangerine-colored ball of energy rushed toward them across the water. Just as they were lying prone on the beach, it slammed into the side of the *Musashi* with a deafening concussive *thump*, immediately engulfing the ship in flame.

Rei watched as burning particles fell around them, an amused but angry grin on his face. "Well, that settles it. We shall be traveling together. And I *will* meet these bandits, and we shall see who prevails."

Mel grabbed the horses' reins and ran toward the ship. "This way!" he shouted to the others.

Polly could not believe her eyes. "What? 'This way' *toward* the fire?"

Mel shouted back, "You see any better cover?"

Polly let out a frustrated grunt and raced after the others. The friends gathered at the water's edge, the burning wreck of the *Musashi* between them and the approaching vessel.

Rei looked across the lake around the edge of the blaze. "Mihoshi, please return their gesture but do not aim to kill, yet. Let us put fear in the hunter." He handed her his spyglass.

She peered through it and handed it back. "The ship's wheel as they near the islet?"

"An excellent choice."

Mel shook his head. "They're still at four hundred meters. No bow can shoot that far, let alone hit a mark. Shouldn't we save the arrows until they're closer?"

Rei was focusing intently on the lake and did not respond. His hand suddenly went up in warning. "Another comes!" A moment later, a second earsplitting impact shook the *Musashi* and enraged its flames.

"Won't be too many more 'a those 'til we're hidin' behind nothin'!" Garth shouted.

Rei looked intensely at his sister. "Mihoshi, it is time."

Mihoshi fearlessly stepped out from behind the cover of their burning ship, kneeled, nocked an arrow, and stood, taking aim. Her breathing slowed to a stop, and she loosed the arrow, which seemed to disappear into the open sky. She repeated this process two more times in rapid succession and stepped back into cover.

Rei raised his spyglass. Through it, he could see Neco and his men gathered at the ship's wheel, looking toward shore through spyglasses of their own. Neco was aiming a second device with his other hand. A moment later, Mihoshi's first arrow lodged in the deck just feet in front of them and her second arrow sank into the bulkhead behind them. Her third arrow pierced and split one of the eight handles of the ship's wheel. Neco and the others jumped back in surprise and ran out of sight. The helmsman flinched as he fled, leaving the wheel spinning and unmanned. Rei laughed and lowered his spyglass. "At least their pride is wounded." He rested a congratulatory hand on his sister's shoulder. She breathed deeply, her mouth moving with a silent prayer.

Mel cautiously peered around the flames, straining to see the approaching ship, and then looked at Rei skeptically. "You can't be serious." Then, to Mihoshi, "No offense."

"None taken, Mel-san," she said, suppressing a smile.

Mel reached for the spyglass to confirm that the arrows had found their mark. Rei drew the spyglass back, shaking his head, and pointed at the ship to redirect Mel's gaze. Those on shore watched in awe as the distant vessel veered haphazardly from its previous course and crashed into one of the many islets in the lake.

"They are slowed, but only for a moment," Mihoshi explained.

Mel's jaw dropped. "It was no accident that we met you in Panama City, was it?" he asked.

"Are such meetings ever accidents?" Mihoshi replied coyly.

Mel bowed respectfully and then turned to the whole group. "Let's get moving!" he shouted, ushering them toward the wagon.

Polly, Garth, and Mihoshi climbed into the bed of the wagon as Rei and Mel took the front seats. Mel shook the reins, and the wagon leaped forward, Campitor and Candeo pulling the heavy load with little effort into an open field that led away from the lake and into the foothills.

Polly held Mihoshi as the wagon thundered across the field and up a small rise. At the summit, they could see a range of ominous mountains not far ahead of them. Mel pulled back on the reins, stopping the wagon.

"The mountains of Gatún," Rei observed. "For years, the canal builders have told of fierce tribes here who protect blood-sworn secrets. They also say there are no wagon roads through these mountains, which may make our crossing impossible."

Mel looked back at the lake and the three-masted ship, which had freed itself from the islet and was returning to its original course. It was moving more slowly and was listing. It appeared to sit increasingly low in the water as it neared the shore in the vicinity of the still-burning *Musashi*. Mel returned his focus to the mountains. "Nevertheless, it's where we must go." He shouted "Hyah!" and the horses again pulled the wagon forward with surprising speed.

"MJ can get us through," Garth boasted.

Polly looked surprised. "Garth, I know her eye is getting better, but she can still hardly see out of it. And these are mountains she's never been in before. She won't even know the scents that could help her find her way. I'm not sure we should trust her to decide our route."

Garth smiled confidently. "You just wait. I seen MJ in mountains we ain't never been in 'afore. She found her way on a moonless night, back when she was all blind in that eye. It's like she's got an extra sense or somethin'. She's surefooted as a mountain goat and stronger'n three mules. She'll get us over all right, you'll see!"

* * *

They reached the base of the mountains in less than an hour and pulled the horses to a stop at the mouths of two canyons that diverged ahead of them. Each member of the party scrutinized the two paths to discern which would provide the best route over the mountains. Polly quickly reached a conclusion but bit her tongue while Mel and Rei discussed the options. Several minutes later, a decision still had not been made, and Candeo began to nod her head toward the right and whinny, pulling gently against the stock-still Campitor and the wagon's brakes. Polly watched Candeo with an amused smile of resignation and spoke. "The canyon on the right looks best to me."

"Why is that, Polly?" Rei questioned, doubting that she had any real expertise in choosing a route. "Why not the path next to the stream?"

Polly assumed her librarian demeanor and continued. "We are in the driest time of year for this region, and the stream path still has running water in it, which means that even though it is flat and wide here, it will become steep and narrow up there where the water runs down gorges that have been carved deeply by a constant flow," she said while pointing up to where the mountains were hidden in clouds. She turned and pointed to her preferred path. "That path is a dry bed of comparable size, which means that it was formed more by seasonal runoffs, which have a much higher volume of water and tend to create wide rather than deep gullies with fewer obstructions at the higher elevations."

"Did you read this in books?" Rei asked dubiously.

Polly's face was resolute. "My aunt is a full-blooded Esselen Indian. We used to go on hikes, and she would teach me."

Rei nodded apologetically. "I stand corrected, Polly Logan. I am convinced. What do you think, Mel-san?"

Mel turned to Polly, who wore a "don't push me on this" expression. He turned the wagon toward the dry gully.

* * *

Hours later, they crested what appeared to Mel to be the first of three ridges that they would need to cross to reach the other side of the range. The terrain had changed from the thick underbrush of the lower jungle to a barren landscape of rocky slopes and boulders. Mel stopped the wagon at the top of the narrow pass and looked back down the route they had taken. "I wonder if our pursuers will choose the same path."

"They'd have to be blind not to," Polly commented. "We've left enough sign for even the most novice of trackers to follow."

"Or they might know a quicker way," Garth ventured fearfully. "They mighta split up an' is waitin' for us on t'uther side."

"Perhaps," Mel admitted, "but we shouldn't let speculation get the better of us. One thing I know is that we can't lead them all the way to the location marked on the map. This little pass is the best natural bottleneck yet along our route. We need to prepare while we still have time."

* * *

The team climbed out of the wagon and studied the surrounding terrain for half an hour, discussing contingency plans as they went. Finally, Garth spoke about what had been in the back of his mind since the start of the strategy session. "Mel, what about Vulgladius and that shootermajig? Shouldn't we plan on them first?"

Rei turned to Mel. "What is he speaking of?"

Mel considered for a moment if he should explain the two pieces of technology to the new members of the group but instead simply went to the storage compartment in the bed of the wagon. He moved several pieces of cargo aside and opened the lid. He grabbed the pouch of Sazo pellets and attached the projector to his arm, then pulled out the sheathed sword and fastened it to his belt.

"These," Mel explained, "are tools my father left for me. He warned me sternly to never reveal them to non-Delemnites, but we are about to stand together in a physical confrontation. I will take the lesser risk of making you aware of them."

Rei's curiosity was piqued. "I understand the use of a sword. But marbles? Have you been trained to use them in combat?"

Mel shrugged and stated meekly, "I've used the Sazo twice to save my life. And Vulgladius is not a common sword, as you will see. I've never used it in battle but have had plenty of practice. I was trained by my father and by another gifted swordsman, my tutor, Jora Blacksworth."

"Practice is not the same as a battle, my friend," Rei said. "In the heat of the battle, your emotions can play tricks on you and cloud your abilities. I suggest that we follow my lead when the fighting begins. Though I am young also, I have been trained as a samurai warrior all my life and have had several opportunities to put that training to use."

Mel knew that his experience in battle could not match Rei's and realized that his friend could be the answer to something that had been troubling him. "Rei, I am grateful for your expertise. It may be exactly what we need to keep me from having to use the unique capabilities of these tools. If I'm forced to use them, it will result in many of Neco's men losing their lives, and I want us to spare them all if we can." Mel bowed to Rei in genuine respect. "I will follow your lead."

The somber look of wonder on Rei's face revealed the even higher esteem with which he now regarded Mel, as well as the weight of the responsibility of leading their group in non-lethal combat. Rei was reminded of the alluring noble character of his father, which had shone brightly during those portions of Rei's training that had focused on non-lethal methods. To the young samurai, this fight would now, more than ever, reflect his family's honor. "Very well, Uri-san," Rei responded, bowing in return. "This is my proposal...," Rei began and proceeded to explain his strategy in detail.

Several minutes into his descriptions, Polly frowned and shook her head. "I disagree!"

The rest of the group had been fully engrossed in Rei's plan and felt as if they had been slapped in the face. Rei politely asked, "With which point and on what basis do you disagree, Polly?" The others fidgeted, expecting Polly to retract her case so Rei could continue describing his plan.

Instead, Polly went on, speaking quickly. "You are focusing our resources too narrowly. Sun Tzu wrote, 'When you have few resources, spread them out and draw the enemy to yourself. Once the enemy is scattered, you can use your gifts to defeat your overconfident foe.'"

Rei bowed. "You have read *The Art of War*. Your observation is excellent, Polly," Rei remarked, surprising the others. "What do you propose?"

Polly quickly went around the group, asking each person to describe his or her strength, and then deferred to Rei. "Now you know what abilities are at your disposal to place in the most effective positions. We will do as you say."

Rei nodded, turned to the group, and laid out a new strategy.

* * *

As the sun set, the evening fireflies appeared, flittering throughout the canyon. After the friends finished their initial preparations at the location chosen for the battle, Campitor and Candeo and the cart were taken a half mile beyond the pass, and the horses were set free to graze on the area's sparse vegetation.

The young people returned to the pass and split into two groups. Upon Polly's advice, they doubled back along the canyon's edges to the chosen location so their returning tracks would not be detected. They took their positions on either side of the ravine and waited. Rei, Garth, and Polly were on one side of the canyon, while Mel and Mihoshi were on the other. The gentle light of the fireflies bore no premonition of the life and death struggle that was to come. Polly shook with anticipation. She had not imagined that her adventures would include this.

After waiting for what felt like an eternity, the steady footsteps of men ascending the canyon arrived much too soon. Polly counted eleven men in modern clothing, plus two Panamanian men who constantly darted from one side of the canyon to the other, looking for any sign of movement. Several loud, bearded men led the main group, followed by the hooded man, Neco. Following him were the rest of the men, with a wagon at the tail end of the caravan.

Once the men had passed and the scouts had been narrowly avoided, Rei signaled to Mel by releasing a handful of captured fireflies. Rei quietly descended into the canyon and followed the men, shadowing their wagon. He climbed aboard silently and, with one swift movement, knocked the driver unconscious.

* * *

Rei darted to the south as quickly as a rabbit. The three closest men shouted and took off in pursuit. He rounded a rock outcropping where Mihoshi was hiding in wait. He signaled to her and disappeared into a recess of the boulders. Mihoshi kicked a rock down the hill and screamed loudly while scrambling up the slope, pretending to struggle with the climb. In the darkness, the pursuing men did not perceive that their quarry had changed. They yelled in anger and followed Mihoshi. Once out of their eyesight, she scampered deftly up the escarpment.

Mel watched with concern as Mihoshi was pursued by the three armed and angry men. Once he saw how quickly she scrambled over the rocks, he knew that she would be able to stay out of harm's way.

Mel remained where he was, his eye on his primary opponent, Neco, whose hooded cloak resembled that of a monk. This appearance, coupled with Neco's malevolence, struck Mel as profoundly ironic. He wondered if Neco were not, in fact, a fallen figure who once had been a genuine monk. Whoever Neco was, Mel hoped that he might yet turn from the ways of the Strangers.

At that moment, on the opposite side of the canyon, Polly dislodged a strategically placed rock, starting a rockslide that separated the two groups of men who had remained in the canyon. The two

Panamanian guides, sensing a battle that was not their own, immediately abandoned the others, disappearing into the night. Neco
glanced toward the canyon's edges and then turned and distanced
himself from the unfolding conflict, walking quickly up the canyon.

Mel followed Neco, maintaining just enough distance to avoid
being detected.

* * *

A group of five men climbed toward the source of the rockslide.
Garth let them pass where he was hidden and then followed them,
drawing close enough to hear the curses seething under their breath.
Finally, within arm's reach, Garth grabbed two of the men by their
heads and pulled them together swiftly. With a sound like two watermelons being dropped, the men were instantly knocked unconscious. The remaining three spun around in disbelief.

"I thought we were chasin' kids!" one said, looking at the be-
hemoth form of Garth, who had just incapacitated two men with a
single move.

"Who cares?" another replied. "There's still three of us. No
one's gonna best me, however big he is. Let's git 'im!" The three
men rushed Garth together.

Garth stood his ground like an oak tree, not moving a muscle
until they were almost upon him. Then, with a speed they did not
expect, Garth grabbed one of the men by the neck and spun him
under his massive arm. The iron fist of his free hand connected
with the nose of the second attacker, sending him sprawling back,
holding his broken and bleeding nose. The remaining man stopped
and pulled out a knife. Garth quickly punched the man pinned
under his arm, dropping his limp form to the ground with a thud.
Now, with both hands free, Garth rose to his full height. "My pa
used ta come at me with one of them when he was drunk. I don't
think you'll be stickin' anyone tonight, mister."

The man rushed Garth, who grabbed his hand and bent it back, causing the knife to fall and clatter down the rock slope. The attacker's forward momentum, combined with Garth's unyielding grip, caused his wrist to break, and he fell to the ground screaming. He and the man with the broken nose scurried away from Garth, left the three others who were unconscious, and fled as fast as they could back down the canyon.

* * *

Rei watched as the last two men who had yet to join the fight left the canyon in the direction of Mihoshi and her pursuers. He stepped out and shouted until they turned toward him, and then he sprinted and leaped away across the tops of boulders, leading the two men in the opposite direction of Mihoshi. They followed at ground level, and after a minute of darting amongst the boulders in pursuit of the elusive Rei, they became disoriented and stopped. Rei crouched atop a nearby boulder, watching them carefully.

"You sure we should be in here, Ben?" one man asked, his eyes glancing around in the shadowy light. He drew his pistol and spat nervously on the ground. "We got tricked into here."

"Carl, will you shut up?" Ben snapped. "We're just chasin' one of 'em for cryin' out loud. How dangerous could he be? If they had guns, they'da shot at us already." Ben drew his pistol and stepped around the nearest boulder, Carl close behind.

Rei watched the two men approach. Ben held his gun at the ready, his breath laboring from the exertion of the chase. His eyes were black with fear. When he was near to where Rei was perched, he stopped and rested for a moment, bending over to catch his breath. Rei pounced like a panther, swooping on Ben with a swift hand chop to the back of his exposed neck. He went down like a sack of potatoes, his flinch reflex causing his gun to fire into the dirt. Carl quickly raised his pistol and began firing in Rei's direction. The bullets ricocheted harmlessly short as Rei retreated among the boulders.

* * *

Garth followed Mihoshi's trail. After a much-belabored climb over the same rocks that Mihoshi had easily scaled, he found her sitting on the crest of the hill.

"What happened to the guys that followed ya?" Garth asked.

"They seem to have fallen asleep," she said, pointing to a pile of unconscious bodies off to one side.

Garth's eyes bulged in astonishment. "Howdya do that?"

"Deep breaths," she explained. "Climbing this hill caused them to breathe deeply. I simply exposed them to the contents of one of these." She held up what looked like a small vial of perfume and mimed throwing it to the ground near the men.

"Well, I'll be a pig's ear," Garth chuckled.

Pistol fire erupted among the boulders a hundred meters away. "It is Rei!" Mihoshi leaped to her feet and ran towards the sound.

* * *

Polly had waited with a supply of stones ready to throw and had watched breathlessly as Garth fought the five men. She had feared that his reassurances earlier in the evening about being an accomplished fighter had largely been bluster. At first, seeing how many opponents he faced, she had regretted her promise to stay back from the scuffle.

Now, as she approached Garth's three still-unconscious foes, she felt equal parts relief and consternation, knowing she would never hear the end of it. She also noticed a more subtle sense of peace and safety regarding Garth, which had followed his triumph and which she had not known could ever be so strongly focused on one person.

As she reached the unconscious men, she watched for any sign of them beginning to stir and kept an eye on her surroundings in case the two injured men returned. She discovered a length of rope in the knapsack of one of the men, which she guessed they had brought along to bind whoever had started the rockslide. She knew that if it had not been for Garth's courageous disregard for his own safety, it would have been her who got tied up. Quickly making use of knots that her aunt had taught her, she bound the men securely in a group and used their bandanas to tie gags in their mouths. Moments later, they began to regain consciousness, groaning from the beating that Garth had given them.

Polly ran to the wagon, where she found another length of rope and similarly bound and gagged the driver. The two bedraggled and scared horses hitched to the wagon of Neco's men looked at Polly with plaintive eyes. She hurriedly unhitched their harnesses, and they ran free back down the canyon.

Having bound all the men in the vicinity, Polly took another length of rope from the wagon, climbed back up the hill near the rockslide, and waited nervously at the pre-appointed place. Moments later, she heard gunshots and ran toward the source of the sound, ready to help her friends in whatever way she could.

* * *

Rei led Carl in a circuitous chase away from the canyon. The moon had risen, and its light cast long, strange shadows across the rock-littered landscape.

Carl rounded a corner and spotted Rei's silhouette thirty feet in front of him, apparently hunched over with fatigue. "Time to teach you a lesson." He fired multiple times, unloading his pistol into the bent form. Out of bullets, he stepped forward to view the results of his work, only to see that he had wasted his ammunition firing at a shadow cast onto the surface of a boulder. Rei stepped out and faced Carl, revealing his intentional ruse. Carl threw down his gun and drew the infantry officer's sword that hung from his belt. "Lesson ain't over."

"This is the fight I was hoping for," Rei responded menacingly.

Carl slowly approached and circled the calm, young samurai who appeared to be in no hurry to draw his sword, attempting to turn him so his back would be against a boulder. He raised his sword, feigning an overhead attack, then shifted to a lunge pointed at Rei's chest. Rei quickly stepped aside, letting Carl stumble forward against a boulder.

Rei drew his katana from over his shoulder. "You are mistaken in thinking that *I* am the student of this lesson."

Carl's eyes burned red with anger, and he rushed at Rei, slashing viciously. Rei parried each stroke, the clang of metal against metal echoing across the broken terrain. Carl attacked Rei repeatedly, only to be met by his seemingly effortless defense.

By this time, the gunshots and sounds of swordplay had drawn Mihoshi, Garth, and Polly. They watched from up the slope as the opponents moved among the boulders. Mihoshi dared not fire an arrow to disable Carl for fear of hitting Rei, and neither Garth nor Polly was equipped to help against a swordsman. To their relief, it did not appear that Rei needed help.

Garth was amazed at the calm, deliberate moves Rei was making to avoid being cut. The friends watched in hushed anxiety as Rei allowed Carl to tire himself out completely. Seeing that his opponent was exhausted, Rei pricked Carl's hand, and his sword fell away. He followed this with a rounding kick that spun Carl's head around, felling him to the ground.

Mihoshi called out her brother's name in concern and congratulation and ran toward him. As Rei turned to meet his friends, who were descending the hill, Carl revived on the ground behind him and pulled a gun from his boot, aiming it at Rei's back.

A stone whooshed past Rei's ear and smacked into Carl's face, knocking him senseless. The stone was followed immediately by an arrow from Mihoshi's bow that would have hit Carl between the eyes had the rock not struck him first. Rei kicked the small pistol from Carl's hand.

Garth and Mihoshi spun around to see Polly standing there, a scared look on her face.

"Wow!" Polly said, panting from a rush of adrenaline. "It's been years since I did something like that!"

Garth walked over and gave her a bear hug. "Woowee, sister, you got a wicked fastball there. I'm glad I ain't never been on the wrong end 'a one 'a yer pitches."

Rei approached Polly and bowed. "Thank you, Polly. I owe you my life."

Just as Polly was about to respond, a hideous screech echoed from further up the mountainside. As the three others hurried toward the sound, Polly quickly stooped and bound and gagged the unconscious Carl. Rei, just before passing from view, turned and shouted toward Polly while pointing toward another area of the boulders. "Polly, there is another 'asleep' among the boulders!" Polly waved in acknowledgment and headed in the indicated direction.

* * *

Mel followed Neco from a distance as he strode steadily away from the fighting in the canyon. After the robed man crossed a ridge and descended out of view, Mel cautiously approached the crest and peered over. Neco stood a hundred meters away in the middle of a small valley. He had turned to face Mel and was swinging a flaming sword of his own in circles over his head and on either side of his body, flickers of the sword's light briefly illuminating him and the flat ground around him. Attracted by the heat and light, fireflies began to swarm in the small valley.

Neco's face was completely hidden by his hood, but Mel did not need to see his expression to recognize that his demeanor was that of a madman. He emitted dark, otherworldly moans and cries that pierced the still night air. Mel, his sword not yet drawn, approached him slowly, fully conscious of the challenge that was being issued.

As Mel drew nearer, he noted that Neco's sword bore more than a passing resemblance to Vulgladius. The two weapons were, to all appearances, identical. This, and the plasmatic orb projector that Neco had used to destroy the *Musashi*, confirmed Mel's suspicion that his menacing opponent was of Delemnite origins. Mel wondered if this dark monk might know where his father was.

When Mel had approached within twenty meters, Neco activated a device on his belt. A forty-meter-wide translucent red dome appeared, centered on him, and crackled and sparked with electromagnetic energy. Its edge shifted across the ground with Neco's slightest movements, igniting the sparse foliage.

"Now, there is no escape," Neco hissed.

Mel ignored the swirling sword and the red dome and remained focused on the shadow under Neco's hood. "I am Melek 'al Uri, son of Telemai Uri and heir to the throne of Delemni," Mel stated in a loud, fearless voice. "What was your name before you became Neco, 'the slayer'?"

"Silence, *boy*!" Neco screamed with the varying intonations of a dozen simultaneous voices. He brought his swirling sword to an abrupt halt, plunging it into the stone of the valley floor. The ground shook, a thunderous rumble resounding across the landscape. A molten puddle formed around the weapon. "We will not be questioned by one such as you! We know well who you are, son of failure, though you have *never* known us!"

Mel put his hand to the hilt of Vulgladius. "I know that a man of Xenos could not touch a sword of the Vysards unless he had first wielded it as a friend of Delemni." Mel stretched his empty hands out to the sides in a gesture of vulnerability and supplication. "I speak now past the multitude of Neco to that man of my people. Neco's triumph over you brings only tragedy and slavery. Do not allow your weapon to remain a token of defeat. Do not continue to bear it for the corruption and deaths of those it was made to protect. Who would have gained, ultimately, if the attempts to kill me and my friends these past weeks had succeeded? Man of Delemni, will you return to life and freedom?"

Neco laughed. "*Attempts* to kill?" he asked with a whining sneer. He shook his head, his voice regaining its smooth, threatening tone. "Do you not know that we could have destroyed you many times over? Your death is a small thing we will trifle with if we must. We seek first what you also are seeking."

"And what would that be?" Mel asked warily.

"The truth!" he shouted. "We seek the knowledge of the ancients! We and you seek the same answers to questions that most men would never dare to ask."

"Save your flattery. I do indeed seek answers, but only to the questions my father has given me to pursue."

Neco pulled his sword out of the ground, the plasmatic blade glowing red with his anger. "Then you are a bigger fool than your father was. He possessed all the power and knowledge yet refused to use it. He was a weak-willed, sniveling slug of a man who disgraced our noble race by his sheer cowardice."

Mel sensed Neco's impending strike. As if in slow motion, Mel pulled Vulgladius from its scabbard and met its counterpart mid-air in the first of a flurry of movements. As the swords swung and collided in cuts and parries, a hail of exploding, plasmatic sparks sprayed out onto the ground, melting small puddles in the stone. Every attacking movement from Neco was intended to kill, while Mel sought only to disable his opponent.

Mel drew back in preparation for his own attack. Neco leaned toward him like a bird of prey and let out an inhuman, earsplitting screech that echoed through the mountains.

Mel advanced and made a low, sweeping slice. Neco jumped over the blade and responded with an overhead attack. Mel rolled to the side, and Neco's flaming blade bit into the ground, cleaving and melting the stone. The sounds of their conflict echoed like a thunderstorm in the small valley, a short distance from where Mel's friends were also fighting for their lives.

Hit after hit was blocked or parried as Mel and Neco attacked and defended in intermittent cycles. Though Mel was much smaller than his opponent, he was quicker at maneuvering to avoid attacks. Time after time, Mel repositioned himself and countered, only to meet an impenetrable defense.

After fifteen minutes of non-stop aggression, both Mel and Neco were showing signs of fatigue. In a last burst of ferocious energy, Neco roared in anger and swung his sword in a circling slice intended to decapitate Mel. Mel ducked and countered with a slash that severed his opponent's left arm above the elbow. Neco hissed angrily while backpedaling away from where his sleeved and gloved arm lay on the ground. The remainder of his upper arm was hidden in the folds of his robe.

As Neco retreated, the edge of the dome rapidly approached Mel, who followed his foe to avoid the burning red barrier.

Mel saw no apparent bleeding from Neco's upper arm, which he knew could be explained by the fire sword having cauterized the wound, but he was aghast that Neco showed no signs of pain.

CHAPTER 22

TWO MONKS

Mel's team reached the ridgetop and peered into the small valley. In the dim light, they could see Mel and Neco, whose left arm lay severed on the ground. Surrounding them was the massive electromagnetic field. Mihoshi nocked an arrow and let it fly at Neco, only to see it disintegrate against the red barrier.

"By all that is sacred, what is this magic that encircles them?" Rei whispered to the others.

The team stealthily descended toward the combatants, stopping behind a boulder on the valley floor. They could only watch and pray for their friend as the battle progressed.

A minute later, Polly appeared at the ridgetop and began to make her way down toward the boulder. As she went, she suddenly turned and glanced at the nearby hills, hearing a steadily growing sound that echoed like a heartbeat of metal on stone. She saw what looked like a phantom approaching swiftly across the landscape. She continued into the small valley and joined the others behind the boulder.

* * *

"Enough of these courtyard calisthenics," Neco shouted and stood his ground, his voice seething with anger. "It is time to ensure that you will no longer share in the knowledge of our ancestors." Neco sheathed his sword and, from beneath his right sleeve, unveiled a weapon that resembled an overgrown Sazo. Mel recognized it as a plasmatic orb projector and discerned from the way that Neco was

237

holding it that he was setting it to the maximum.

In the moment before Neco could fire the weapon, Mel weighed his diminishing options. Neco could retreat too quickly for a sword attack to stop him. Mel knew that a Sazo could neither overcome nor directly defend against the larger weapon, but he sheathed his sword and readied his Sazo, nonetheless.

Neco leveled his weapon at Mel and fired while backpedaling.

As the ball of flame *whooshed* across the short distance between them, Mel dove diagonally forward while activating the Sazo. A seemingly diminutive blue shield flashed before him, deflecting the plasmatic orb, which dissolved against the red dome. Neco hissed and continued firing. With each shot, Mel's evasive moves and deflecting actions became less effective as Neco's aim narrowed in on him. The few attacking pellets that Mel managed to fire were easily blocked by red, shielding shots from Neco.

Neco began to cackle as he fired, knowing that his victory was imminent. With just one more shot required to hit his target, a sudden sound like a bellowing train whistle behind him caused him to spin around and fire reflexively at the new threat. The hurried shot went wide of its fearsome target.

There, with half of his body within the dome, was Campitor, rising on his hind legs, whinnying, and snorting. The gem on his harness glowed, emitting a spherical, blue magnetic field around his body that repelled the red dome. A bevy of lightning bugs swirled within the blue sphere. He instantly began a fearless gallop, his one goal to trample the mad monk who threatened his master. When Campitor passed within the dome, the blue sphere faded away.

Neco, with nearly imperceptible quickness, adjusted the device on his belt. The red dome disappeared and reformed as a two-meter-wide sphere around him, its only opening moving as he aimed his orb projector. With this opening pointed away from Mel, he was invulnerable to the several Sazo pellets Mel projected directly at him, which were absorbed by the red shield.

"No, Campitor! Get away from here!" Mel shouted as he shifted his Sazo to deflect the shots Neco fired at the horse.

Neco chuckled malevolently. "Yessss," he hissed. "First, you shall witness the demise of your 'mighty' steed."

The fireflies swirled around Campitor as he charged forward. His breath billowed and trailed behind him like the steam from a locomotive. His body was covered in sweat from his approach across the mountainside, foam dripping from his muzzle.

"*Abolesco abominor*!" Neco cried, or as Mel understood it, "Die, hated one!"

"No! Campitor!" Mel shouted, knowing he would not be able to deflect Neco's next shot.

Neco's weapon propelled a huge ball of plasmatic flame directly at Campitor, which instantly engulfed the horse. The monk turned to gloat at Mel, lowering his orb projector and creating a complete red sphere around himself. Neco was unaware that the ball of plasma continued to roll on directly towards him.

Neco laughed maniacally, unable to tell that the look on Mel's face was not anguish but astonishment. Neco turned at the last second and shrieked as the mass of destruction passed through his shield and consumed him in an unmerciful fury of flame.

The crackling ball of plasma continued beyond Neco and halted a mere meter from Mel, singeing his clothes. Inexplicably, the inferno vanished, leaving Campitor standing alone and unharmed. The swirl of fireflies flickered out and disappeared.

Mel ran to the horse and embraced his neck. "Campitor," Mel whispered, "thank you, my courageous friend. I don't know how you survived that blast." Mel saw that Campitor's formerly red harness gem was now glowing with an icy blue hue. He reached to touch it and instinctively pulled back from its burning hot surface.

* * *

Mel's friends ran to his side, their faces full of surprise. Polly rushed to him and hugged him with all her might, tears running down her cheeks. Mel was at first stunned by this intensity of affection, then patted her on the back comfortingly.

"Danged if I ever seen anythin' like that," Garth said, stroking Campitor's mane. "It's a plumb miracle ya both ain't bar-b-cued!"

Rei approached Campitor with an analytic gaze. "I must agree with Garth. I never imagined I would behold such a conflict nor witness the miracle that preserved this horse."

Mel looked at each of his four friends, marveling that they appeared unscathed after a fight with eleven men on rough terrain. "One of many miracles we've seen tonight. Are all of Neco's men..." He trailed off, hesitant to hear the details of the resolution of the fight. His eyes scanned the ridgeline between the valley and the canyon.

"Alive?" Mihoshi asked. "Yes. They were protected tonight."

"Well, mostly alive," Polly specified. "There were two guys who got away who will be remembering Garth less-than-fondly for a couple of months," she said proudly.

Garth smiled awkwardly, not sure whether to feel accomplished or embarrassed.

"And another," Rei added, "who will have a headache thanks to Polly Logan," he said while bowing respectfully to her.

Polly's face flushed red with a sudden wave of self-consciousness. "The nine who are still around will have to roll their way back to Panama City."

Mel shook his head. "We can't leave them bound and gagged in the mountains, at the mercy of wild animals and the elements. We are still a ways from the spot marked on the map, and I don't know how long things will take once we get there."

"Rei and I will escort them back to the shore and signal the canal zone police, who may already have been drawn by the smoke of the *Musashi*. Then we will rejoin you," Mihoshi stated.

Rei nodded in agreement.

"Hmmm," Polly interjected. "I hope that plan doesn't depend on using their cart to move them. I may or may not have set their horses loose," she explained with a half-smile, half-grimace.

Mel chuckled at her evasive confession. "We can hitch their wagon to the back of ours and pull them to the shore. We'll lose one day at most, which I will allow if it'll save their lives. Campitor and Candeo can handle the load, especially since the route is almost all downhill." He pointed to Campitor's glowing harness. "I suspect that his miracle tonight was due in part to the gem on his harness. See how it pulsates with his breath. A mechanism in the harness must have reacted to his zeal and activated the gem, protecting him from the shield and the plasmatic orb."

"Indeed," Rei said, tugging at his goatee. "Your ancestors' science is more advanced than I could have imagined. If only your father had provided you with your own gem to wear."

"I'm not sure it would work with a human being. I doubt that any person could rival this creature's raw fervor."

"I dunno," Garth interjected, "Neco had one 'a them too."

"Yes," Mel acknowledged, "a weaker one, dependent on the same dark powers that animated him." Mel heaved a deep sigh. "Unfortunately, he was one of many fallen children of Delemni."

Mihoshi put her hand on Mel's arm. "Where is the monk?" she asked soberly.

"I reckon he's a piece 'a burnt toast 'round here somewhere," Garth boasted on Mel's behalf. Garth glanced around and saw no remains anywhere in sight. "He musta gone and got all burnt t'up. Only way I can figur' it."

"Even his bones?" Mihoshi ventured as she carefully examined the ground where Neco had fallen. She retraced the course of the fight and picked up a two-foot-long object wrapped in tattered cloth. "A short, intense flame could have burnt away all soft tissues, but his bones should have remained. It is curious that the only thing left behind is this mechanical arm."

"What?" Mel gasped.

"The arm you severed from his body is a mechanical device, made to look and function as though it were real." Mihoshi held out the cloth-wrapped limb.

Mel took the arm and examined it, finding a dense array of wires, gears, and metal tendons. In shock, he slipped the arm into his knapsack and took off running toward the canyon.

* * *

The young people discovered loose lengths of rope on the ground where each of the men had been bound during the fight. The men's wagon sat abandoned. Tracks in the patches of vegetation indicated that they had made a hasty retreat down the canyon.

With occasional glances behind them, Mel and his friends led Campitor to where they had left Candeo and their wagon. They re-hitched the horses and continued a kilometer further into the mountains toward their goal. Rounding a curve, they came upon a cave where they decided they would hide the horses and wagon and take refuge for the rest of the night. At the back of the cave, they made a small campfire and sat close together around it to allow its smoke to thin the cloud of insects that buzzed insistently around their heads. Mihoshi chose a sheltered vantage point outside to keep watch in case Neco's men resumed their pursuit.

The friends gazed across the flickering firelight, exchanging few words. Occasionally Polly shuddered, remembering the horrendous events that had taken place just hours before. Mel held the mechanical arm on his lap and examined it closely, a somber look on his face.

Finally, Garth spoke. "Mel, I ain't gettin' why yer bothered 'n all, seein' as ya just beat the guy 'at's been trackin' us for weeks."

Mel, who had been deep in thought, looked up. "Did I? Was he defeated, or was he just an automaton?"

"A what?" Polly asked.

"An automaton," Mel explained, "is like a real person. It speaks and appears authentic but is just a machine."

Rei looked at the mechanical arm. "Or it may be a portion of a prosthesis. If Neco were only a machine, could he have used a sword of the type you wield?"

"I used to think I knew what the Strangers were capable of, but it's becoming clear that they innovate continually." Mel turned his gaze to the fire. "Perhaps they've found a way that a person's emotional imprint can be transferred to a machine, but that would still require a fallen Delemnite behind the puppet." He looked again at the mechanical arm. "Whether this is part of an automaton or is a prosthesis makes little difference. If the Strangers already know how to build marvels like this, I fear to think of what they would do were they to gain access to even greater knowledge. They would certainly build more entities like Neco, and worse."

The others were silent after hearing Mel's conjecture and glanced nervously at one another.

Mel continued. "The quest we are on is more than a personal need of mine to discover who I am to become. The entire world may be in jeopardy if the information in question is not safeguarded and controlled. We must hasten our journey."

Garth sat upright. "I figure that means 'hurry up,' but I sure do wish we knew what we was hurryin' up to get ourselves into."

Mel nodded. "I know what you mean. I'm not even sure whether the mark on the map will be the end of the journey."

Mel looked at the horses where they stood, chewing on grasses that had been gathered from outside the cave. The night air undulated with millions of jungle insects. Fireflies darted about, creating living patterns on the black canvas of the cave's mouth.

An unfamiliar woman's voice spoke from beyond the firelight. "Follow the light to the *new day*."

* * *

The small band of weary warriors quickly jumped to their feet and took cover behind outcroppings of the cave wall. Mel and Rei drew their weapons while Polly gathered a handful of stones, and Garth lifted a tree limb from the pile of firewood to use as a club. Rei feared for his sister, knowing that only a dire circumstance could have prevented her from apprising them of newcomers.

The seemingly disembodied woman's voice began singing a potent melody that overcame the friends with a sense of calm. Each of them relaxed, stowed their weapons, and sat back in their places by the fire. Mel knew instantly who was coming.

A group of fireflies entered the cave in unison and approached. As they drew near, it became clear that they were not insects but tiny persons with gossamer wings. They flew gracefully into the encircling firelight and settled onto the pile of firewood. Their bows and swords reflected the campfire's dancing flames.

Mihoshi appeared from the shadows of the cave's mouth and sat next to her brother. "Mysenri!" she whispered in wonder.

Garth and Polly were speechless, unable to believe their eyes.

Mel stood and bowed. "Welcome," he said reverently in their language. "How may we serve the lords of the forests?"

A buzz of excitement stirred among the Mysenri. The voice from beyond the firelight spoke again, now in the same strange language that Mel had spoken. "Long has it been since we have had a new human with whom to speak in our native tongue. We knew this would be true of the son of Telemai but find it delightful nonetheless." A diminutive, fierce-looking female, clothed in a forest green tunic, flew into sight, the others bowing to her.

"Your highness, do you know where my father is? Is he alive?" Mel asked, bowing to her small but powerful form.

A murmur of chatter circled through the crowd of Mysenri.

The fierce maiden raised her hand, silencing her companions. "All will be revealed in good time. It is enough for you to know that your mastery of the Abico vault is of the utmost importance." She paused and noticed the expressions of astonishment and confusion on the faces of Mel's friends. "On this occasion, let us speak so that your friends may understand."

"As you wish," Mel said, nodding in deference.

She continued in English. "Melek al Uri, we have been waiting for you for years. Your father, like his father before him, was met by us in much the same way, and, over time, his counsel and actions proved to be priceless on behalf of all who would live in true peace. No Vysard has ever fulfilled his purpose by himself. Please, tell me of these four others who are with you and what role you intend for them in your quest."

"They have been chosen to accompany and assist me. They are each gifted and loyal. They have endangered themselves on my behalf, and I owe them my life, Great One."

"Great One? I have no desire for worldly titles, young sir. My name is Gwyneth, and by that alone am I to be addressed. I seek to lead well and to fight for our clan when necessary. It could have fallen to others to defend our unseen world from interlopers, but it fell to me."

Gwyneth turned her attention to Mel's friends. "Those who would accompany a Gatekeeper of the Vysards must be honorable, as they will encounter the realm of the Mysenri, among many other privileges and responsibilities," she said cryptically. "It is no 'normal' life they will lead."

Gwyneth turned to Mel and stared searchingly into his eyes as though discerning something unsaid. "Your company is not yet complete, is it? Someday others will join you, one of whom you already know," she said with a warm smile.

Mel thought of a girl with curls and a no-nonsense personality sitting by a river, smiling and laughing with him. A girl who had stood up for him when he was an outcast and with whom he shared a boundless love of the creation. His heart filled with a bittersweet longing even as he smiled.

Polly cocked her head in a curious sideways look.

Mel, wide-eyed and eyebrows raised, silently signaled, "*What?*"

Gwyneth barely suppressed a laugh. "I know and trust the One who guided you to your companions. I would like to search their hearts while we share this moment of introduction. You may sit,"

Gwyneth said with a tone of command. Mel again sat in his place beside his friends.

Gwyneth slowly flew to Mihoshi, who sat without blinking or showing any fear and stared back at Gwyneth in amazement.

The flying leader turned to her companions. "A strong shield is on this one." Turning to Mihoshi, she spoke in Japanese. "A star who shines beautifully, bringing the light of His kingdom. Though you and I are already family in the Lord of all created beings, by birth, we were given brothers only. May I consider you my sister?"

Mihoshi's eyes widened with shock. "*Hai*, Gwyneth-sama," she replied, bowing her head and lowering her eyes. "I feel unworthy of this privilege and am greatly humbled."

Rei, who had been listening, smiled subtly.

Gwyneth touched Mihoshi's forehead and continued in English. "Meiji Mihoshi, you are fearless and generous of heart. You have deep wisdom. What a great treasure to your people you will become."

She then came to Rei. Her eyes glowed as she stared deeply at him. "Meiji Rei, you have your father's heart. You have been faithful to fulfill his command, and you will receive what he foresaw for you. You still have a long journey before you, but you will prevail and restore the rightful honor of your family name."

Rei's eyes moistened as she said this. He bowed gently.

She came next to Polly, who, despite the sweltering heat of the jungle night, was shivering. Gwyneth looked deep into her eyes, her own eye color shifting to mimic Polly's emerald irises. The little, flying warrior hovered closer to her than she had to the others. She whispered something in Polly's ear that caused her to weep immediately. She stopped shivering and began to heave with emotion, suddenly overcome with mournful joy. Despite her tears, she whispered something back.

Gwyneth flew next to Garth, who seemed to be melting where he sat. His huge frame had slumped to the ground and was leaning like a beached jellyfish against the rock he had used as his seat. He stared straight ahead, feeling tiny and weak next to the power of this little being.

Gwyneth whispered to her followers something that was unintelligible to the young people, and the entire group of Mysenri laughed. Garth tensed. The little soldiers became alert in response to his movement but continued laughing. Gwyneth spoke to him. "You have a great love of little things, my huge friend. We, small ones, remember those who show this kindness. You befriend the broken, as your heart is that of a healer. We honor you for how you care for other beings with no thought of reward."

Garth's companions glanced at each other as though something obvious had been missed.

Gwyneth giggled, aware of their puzzlement. "You will also be a great leader in the battles yet to come," she continued. "You will lead your men with courage and will take great care to preserve the lives of as many as possible."

Garth looked bewildered. "I dunno how ya knew 'bout me carin' fer the forest creatures back home. With 'em other things ya said, I think ya got me confused with someone else, ma'am. I ain't no leader."

Gwyneth just smiled.

As she turned again toward Mel, her gaze fell on the mechanical arm on the cave floor. She gave a nearly imperceptible sigh and then looked Mel in the eyes. Her expression was a mixture of motherly concern and the somber focus of a veteran apprising a novice. "You will discover that the battle you experienced earlier this night was but your first foray into what is an ongoing global conflict. Similar confrontations have occurred for millennia and will occur again for you and others until your final goal is achieved. We will assist you in your quest in any way that will not endanger our concealment and autonomy. We will be watching. You may go now but beware of mad monks!"

Immediately the Mysenri disappeared like a hundred sparks flying up from a fire.

* * *

From the darkness of the cave's mouth, and without a sound, the team was suddenly surrounded by dozens of bare-chested native men in loincloths, their faces and bodies painted in geometric patterns of black dye. They averaged five feet in height and were dark-skinned and broad-shouldered, with stern expressions. They carried blowguns and bows and arrows.

One of the older men stepped forward and gave an order to Mel and the others in an unfamiliar language. Mel looked at Mihoshi, who shook her head.

Rei noticed their exchange. "I am familiar with many of the local dialects but know only a dozen words in Embera, which is the language and name of this people."

The leader of the Emberas pointed toward the cave's mouth.

"I believe they want us to go with them," Mel observed. "As I understand their body language, they are a bit uneasy around us. Let's be careful not to do anything that might provoke them."

Mel and his companions gathered their belongings and packed them into the wagon. Several of the Emberas approached the horses timidly. Campitor and Candeo submitted willingly to being led with the wagon in tow.

The entire party left the cave and continued through the mountains on a path that Mel was relieved to note was leading toward the destination marked on the map. He and the others walked behind the wagon, surrounded by their escorts.

An hour later, they crossed a ridge and descended into near-total darkness below the jungle canopy. The Emberas found their way along what seemed to the others to be an invisible trail.

Rei tried to engage the Emberas in conversation, but due to his limited vocabulary in their language, he learned little.

"Where they takin' us?" Garth whispered to Rei.

"I am not certain," he replied. "They say that they are our

guides. I believe them since if we were captives, they would have confiscated our weapons. They are quite in awe of Mel and are aware of his abilities with his sword and Sazo projector. They mentioned a 'Jaibaná,' which is a shaman or sage. I presume they are taking us to their spiritual leader, who they will trust to address our presence in their territory."

"Bet they never seen nothin' like us a'fore!"

Rei laughed. "It is true that each of us is unique, but it is unlikely that we are the first outsiders they have seen."

* * *

Mel walked behind Polly, who was still greatly moved by their recent encounter with the Mysenri. He leaned forward and asked softly, "Polly, what did Gwyneth whisper in your ear?"

She began to breathe deeply again, struggling to speak. "She said they still mourn the loss of my father and mother, that they were great friends of her people. My parents asked them to find someone to help me, and they brought my aunt and uncle."

"What did you say to her?"

Her throat constricted, and she coughed slightly. "The only thing there was to say. 'Thank you for saving my life.'"

* * *

Mel had been tracking their progress through the mountains in relation to the map and was exhilarated as they finally reached the marked location and emerged into a broad clearing rimmed with trees that had been grown together tightly enough to keep out the largest jungle animals. Embera guards on platforms above the natural barrier watched the surrounding area, giving the village the appearance of a compound that could not be easily entered or exited. A dozen grass-roofed huts on stilts were arranged in a semicircle around a spacious meeting hut, in front of which burned an enormous community fire. Despite it being the middle of the night when the villagers would normally sleep, every man, woman, and child had gathered to meet the visitors.

The horses and wagon were guided under a grass-roofed awning and hitched to the foundation posts of a hut.

The Embera guides led Mel's party to the vicinity of the community fire, then apprehensively stepped back and joined the spectators. They knew that in the solitude of their remote village, these strange foreigners with strange weapons could harm them if they chose to. Mel could sense their discomfort at the risk their families were facing. The bulk of the villagers kept their distance. A few older women, dressed in colorful flower-patterned wraps, shuffled forward with their heads bowed and placed gourds of liquid and plates of fruit at their feet and then quickly returned to the safety of the outer ring of onlookers.

Mel and Rei exchanged nods that conveyed that they did not consider their group to be in danger, yet they remained alert. Mihoshi was the center of attention for the children, who gestured and walked toward her but were held back by their mothers.

Polly turned to Mihoshi with a smile. "The children seem to think that you're one of them. Or the least intimidating."

Mihoshi smiled back. "The children are the most trusting. If only adults could more often be like them."

The native women began to chatter among themselves and point at Polly's bright red hair. Rei chuckled and turned to Polly. "They are calling you 'Fire Head' or maybe something like 'Raging Wrath' or—"

"That is enough!" Polly interrupted scornfully, her face turning almost as crimson as her hair. "You said you barely understand their dialect."

Rei smiled. "I know only a few words, but body language can speak loudly."

The murmuring among the villagers came to an abrupt halt. Two of their most decorated warriors, who were roughly the same height as Mihoshi, approached Mel and motioned for him to step forward. Mel was nearly a foot taller than they were, but he knew that he dared not underestimate their fighting abilities. Foremost in his mind was the potential peril for his team should he become separated from them. Several other nearby warriors raised their blowguns, pointing them at the rest of the foreigners.

Mel looked at his friends. "It's okay. I'll go and see what they want." He turned and followed the lead warrior. They walked to the edge of the circle of villagers and stopped outside the meeting hut. There they waited until, moments later, a black-hooded, robed monk appeared from inside, a sword hanging from his belt.

Mel grasped the hilt of Vulgladius and began to draw it until a soft voice spoke, "Melamuri, I've been waiting for you."

* * *

The team, who had been watching from a distance, gasped at the sight of the monk but dared not act under the threat of poisoned blowguns. A series of fearful thoughts passed through their minds. Was this the real monk? Had he indeed sent an automaton against Mel earlier in the night? Would Mel have to fight again?

Rei's hand immediately went up in a gesture of peace to calm his startled friends.

Polly stepped towards him. "Rei!" she whispered urgently, "That's him! That's Neco, the Mad Monk! Mel can't fight a rested opponent after this long of a night."

"He has a strength within himself that will be sufficient," Rei responded sternly yet softly to avoid upsetting their captors. "He has surprised me several times already, and I am sure that this test will be no different. Do not worry for our friend. It is out of our hands now."

The monk turned and stepped out of sight. Mel followed him, disappearing into the hut.

CHAPTER 23

THE *NEW DAY*

Rei, Mihoshi, Polly, and Garth were ushered into a small hut and shown hammocks in which to sleep. Entering this shelter came not a moment too soon, as torrential rain began pouring outside minutes later, accompanied by lightning and thunder. The friends could not sleep and sat together on the floor of the hut, imagining flaming swords locked in combat. Each thunderclap that rolled down the jungle valley caused them to flinch.

Their anxiety for Mel's safety, coupled with their unanswered questions about the monk's identity, haunted them. If Mel's opponent overcame him, what chance would the rest of them stand against such a fearsome adversary? Were they merely being kept waiting for their own turn to face this enemy, their weapons allowed to them for the sake of better sport? Polly, exhausted and worried for her friends and herself, buried her head in her hands and began to weep. Mihoshi wrapped an arm around her waist, and Garth rested a hand on her shoulder. He and Rei kept a stern but fatigued watch over the door of the hut. Mihoshi's eyes were closed, and her mouth moved with a silent prayer.

They sat like this for the longest hour of their lives, and then the storm calmed, and the first gleam of dawn filtered through the walls of the hut. As the dwelling grew hot in the morning sun and bugs swarmed them without mercy, the hut door was opened casually, and Mel entered and sat beside them. He closed his eyes and took steady breaths. They stared at him in shock and gathered close around him, eager to hear what had happened.

Polly rubbed her eyes and tried to pretend that she had not

been crying. "Mel! Are you okay?"

Rei looked Mel over and breathed a sigh of relief. "He does not appear to be wounded."

Mel opened his eyes and saw the concern in his friends' faces. He winced with the realization that they had been worried about him the entire time they had been separated. He felt a pang of guilt at not having brought word to them much earlier. "Everything is fine. We are among friends. We should sleep, and I'll explain once we're rested."

* * *

Around noon, Polly woke in her hammock. Garth's hammock was empty. Mel sat nearby and, having just arisen, was putting on his shoes.

Polly tried to wiggle herself out of her hammock and asked, a little frustrated, "How do I get down from here?"

Mel smiled and pointed. "The rope tied to the top of your hammock. Untie it and hold it tightly while easing yourself down."

Polly did not follow all his instructions and fell with a *thud*, waking Rei and Mihoshi.

As the four friends readied for the day, they were startled by the nearby sound of laughing children. Garth entered the hut, bare-chested, wearing a woven hat that looked like a squashed umbrella. He was holding several Embera children in his arms, with one on his back and one more on each leg, many of whom were shouting "*Atubwa! Atubwa!*" Seeing that his friends were awake, he quickly spoke to the children, and they jumped off.

"Hey, lookie here!" he bellowed to his friends and added with a wink, "Up so early?"

Mel glanced at the angle of the sunlight coming through the doorway. "I suppose after being up literally all night, we can call midday 'early,'" he said with a smile.

Garth enthusiastically hugged each of them, picking them up

one by one, except Mihoshi, to whom he gave a gentle embrace.

Polly, surprised by Garth's sudden zeal, brushed off the dust she had acquired from his greeting. "What have you been doing all this time? Playing with the kids?"

"I been learnin' all kindsa stuff today," Garth boasted. "I learnt to shoot a bow 'n arra', how to kill a wild pig with a long, blow-darty thang, and I learnt how to weave this here dandy of a hat. Ain't it great?" Garth finished with a grunt.

Mihoshi took Garth's huge hand in hers and looked at him. "It is good to see you happy this bright day, my friend."

Garth was disarmed by her kindness and shyly drew back, his face crimson. "Yeah, it's the first time I've felt all at ease since we left the lake." He looked at Mel as if asking for rescue from the tender moment. "I reckon I ain't the only one with a story!"

"Yeah, what happened?" Polly asked, her eyes wide.

Mel took a moment to think about his conversation with the monk and then spoke with a subdued voice. "The man you saw step out of the hut startled me at first, and the rest of you, it seems. It turns out that he's a legitimate monk! His name is Brother Joshua, but he goes by Josh. He has lived in these mountains for years now, working with the Emberas, who've been here for centuries. The mark on the map wasn't just a place; it was the way to a friend and the people he lives with. This monk met my father while we were traveling during the early years that I can barely remember. Apparently, I've been to this village before, about ten years ago. Back before the canal, my father needed a place to hide his boat until the next time he would sail on the Atlantic side. Brother Josh helped him find a river inlet, where the boat still is. My father told him that I might be returning this way someday."

Garth tilted his head. "Now, I know your pa was pretty smart, but how in the world could he 'uh figured *that*?"

"I'm not sure, but thankfully, Brother Josh was waiting for us. He had informed the Emberas that they would recognize me as 'the bearer of the Fire Sword.'"

"What if Neco had arrived first?" Rei asked.

"I asked that of Brother Josh. My father had told him that he would be able to discern a spirit of peace upon me. I don't quite understand what that means, but apparently, there were Emberas watching my fight with Neco, and they recognized the difference."

Polly shuddered. "I'm glad *he* never discovered these people."

"What was Brother Josh to do when he saw you?" Rei asked.

"He's to lead us to the boat, hidden along the river further down this valley and not far from the coast. What's next for the five of us will be evident once we're aboard."

Rei tugged on his chin beard. "And when will he do this?"

"Today!" Mel answered enthusiastically. "He said there must be no delay. He suggested we store the wagon in the same location where the boat is hidden."

"Then let's get ready!" Garth shouted.

Garth gathered everyone's belongings in the hut and went out to the wagon, followed by Mel. He placed the belongings in the wagon's bed and checked the horses' harnesses.

"Garth," Mel said with a pained look as he stepped beside him, "when we get to the boat, the horses will have to stay behind."

"What?" Garth snorted. "What's gonna happen to 'em? They need care an' exercise. When we gonna come and get 'em 'gain?"

Mel put a hand on Garth's big shoulder and spoke consolingly. "The Emberas have agreed to care for them. There are some beautiful meadows near where the boat is hidden, where they'll be free to run and graze while we're away."

Garth shook his head. "Well, I don't wanna leave 'em without someone they know. I'm gonna stay too."

Mel smiled. "Brother Josh and I thought you might say that. But you were the first to join me on my journey. It was no accident that our paths crossed. You have to come."

Garth shook his head and furrowed his eyebrows. "I've taken care of Bo... MJ forever. I dunno how I feel 'bout leavin' her here." He walked over to Candeo and petted her cheek. She lowered her head and nuzzled his chest. He could see the brown iris of her now fully healed eye.

Mel petted Candeo's other cheek. "She's got Campitor to keep her company and all these loving Emberas to look after her. She'll be all right. And besides, I need you."

Garth took a step back, amazed and a little suspicious. "You what? A guy with a fire sword needs the help of a lug who cain't say or do nothin' right?"

"Do you remember what Gwyneth told you? You are to be a great leader in battles to come. And you have a healing touch for broken creatures. You never know when we'll come across some of them, now do you?"

"Hold on thar, Mel. All my life, alls I ever heared was how useless I was. Now these words 'bout my worth, I'm still learnin' to make sense of 'em." He turned to Mel, his eyes misty and red with emotion, a grin playing at the corners of his mouth. "If'n ya need me ta come along, then we're burnin' daylight here. It's time ta get a move on."

* * *

Led by Brother Josh with his walking stick in hand and accompanied by what seemed like most of the local Emberas, Mel and the others left the village on foot. Mel walked beside the horses, guiding them and the wagon. They hiked down the valley, passing Embera hous-es spaced regularly along the banks of a steadily widening, rushing creek. An hour later, they reached a cliff with a view of the distant Caribbean coast. A bluish, grey river in the foreground wound for miles out toward the seemingly limitless expanse of the sea.

Making their way down narrow paths to several lower plateaus, they passed sheer rock walls shrouded by hanging vines. As the stream grew, fed by its tributaries, the forceful water fell over preci-pices with a roar. The group continued down the steep path along-side what became a chain of waterfalls. After another hour, they came to the point where the now wide river began its winding path across the nearly flat ground from the base of the mountains to the sea.

As they reached the level ground, Garth was again swarmed by Embera children who climbed on him and clung like moss to a willow tree. They resumed their chanting of his Embera name, "*Atubwa! Atubwa!*" as they rode him down the path along the river's course.

Polly was moved by the affection that Garth showed for the Embera people whom he had known so briefly. "Garth, what does '*Atubwa*' mean?"

He smiled. "Dunno. Just somethin' they been callin' me."

"Yeah, I know, but what does it mean?" she persisted.

"Don't think they got a anglish word fer it."

Brother Josh glanced back at Polly. "It would be translated 'Earth Shaker.'"

Mel raised his eyebrow to Rei, and they both stifled a snicker.

Polly wrinkled her nose. "Earth Shaker, you mean because Garth's so big that the earth shakes when he walks?"

Rei and Mel could not hold back and bent over with laughter.

Garth smiled. "You pipsqueaks are just jealous."

Polly became red in the face, embarrassed on Garth's behalf. "It's funny, but not that funny!"

Mel tried to control himself and barely managed to choke out his words. "Or they call him 'Earth Shaker' because he snores so loud that it shakes the earth, or hadn't you noticed!"

"I had not noticed," Polly replied in a huff, her dignity affronted. "I am a *very* sound sleeper."

Mel and Rei roared with laughter, joined soon after by Mihoshi and then Garth. Polly, a little flushed, finally gave in and laughed with them.

* * *

The path led to the base of a fifty-meter-wide waterfall at the last sudden drop in the river's course. The massive cascade of water drowned out every other sound. Spray in the air was accompanied by a broad rainbow. Here Brother Josh came to a halt. After a moment of searching, he disappeared through a wall of vines behind the base of the waterfall, motioning for them to follow. Campitor and Candeo balked when directed to move closer to the cacophonous torrent but responded to Mel's reassurances and moved steadily forward.

The people and horses scrambled over roots and rocks, trying not to slip on the ubiquitous moss. Passing through the living curtain behind the waterfall, they entered a vine-draped grotto with a wide ledge along the water. At the center, bobbing gently, was a thirty-meter, single-masted sailboat enshrouded in vegetation. The name *Dag Nia* could be seen between the tangles.

Mel marveled that the boat had been completely camouflaged by its environment behind the waterfall and the wall of vines. He removed several vines from the boat's deck and saw that the wood beneath was still in good condition. Here and there were minor scorch marks and superficially burnt panels, but nothing that compromised the integrity of the boat. Mel and the others worked together and removed all the vegetation from the vessel. He was puzzled at the discovery of four rounded depressions in the deck just aft of the mast, two on either side of the cabin top.

Standing on the now cleared boat, Mel felt a tinge of familiarity and closed his eyes, trying to remember what had taken place when he was last aboard.

* * *

Mel and the others worked together to transfer their supplies from the wagon to the *Dag Nia*. Two meters in front of the boat's wheel, four steep steps led down into the vessel's single, spacious cabin, which was unlike any that Mel had ever seen or heard of. There was no galley and no bulkheads to the port side, starboard, or forward. The only cabinets were in the aft bulkhead, on either side of the steps, and it was in these that the friends placed their supplies and belongings. Each cabinet door opened and closed with a hissing sound and a gentle burst of air, which Mel attributed to pressurization. He did not know why this was necessary for the cabinets of a sailing vessel, but based on past experience, he figured he would eventually learn the reason.

He noticed that one of the cabinets was taller than the others and had six notches within it, each of which was shaped like Vulgladius' case. Mel transferred the case from the wagon to the boat.

The boat's hull formed the other walls of the cabin and was smooth with no portholes. Though there appeared to be enough space below the cabin for a lower deck, Mel could find no way to access it. He surmised that the lower compartment was reserved for ballast, though he saw no means of controlling this function. In the cabin, there were six simple rope hammocks dangling side-by-side in sets of two. Between the first and second sets of hammocks, hanging from the center of the ceiling, was a simple rope chair. In front of the chair was a small, built-in, cube-shaped table.

After they finished transferring the supplies, Mel chose a place for the wagon along the grotto's ledge, and he and Garth unhitched the horses, leaving the wagon in its new, temporary home.

Mihoshi and Polly walked back to the path beside the river, where the Emberas had gathered. Mel hitched a tow line from the *Dag Nia* to Campitor and Candeo's harnesses and jumped aboard the vessel. Garth and Rei walked the horses closely along the shore while Mel remained on deck and used the craft's boathook to keep the vessel pushed back from the rocks of the riverbank. In this manner, they pulled the boat out of the grotto and through the waterfall. Mel marveled that the river had sufficient depth along the shore to accommodate the deep draft sailboat and wondered if his father had modified this area of the streambed and perhaps even created the grotto himself. He remembered when his father had built their

Caeli in Cooperton and how he had made complex structures appear to be natural formations.

The craft came to a gentle stop a hundred meters downstream beside the path. Mel, drenched from passing through the waterfall, jumped to shore and unhitched the horses.

Now out from behind the curtain of vines and glistening from the shower of the waterfall, the beautiful *Dag Nia* elicited gasps from everyone present. The entire boat appeared to have been made from dark brown mahogany, with castings of silver and brass that, after years of being buried beneath a living curtain of jungle, showed no corrosion. Aside from the dozen superficial burns, the boat looked like it had just been commissioned for its maiden voyage, with every board and buckle shined to its best.

Rei had never seen a craft like it. It looked like a standard sailboat, with a single mast and a wheel to turn the tiller. But what set it apart was what was missing. There was no sign of a sail, and for rigging, there were only a few pulleys and ropes that went into a hole on the deck.

Knowing that the time of departure was near, the young people hugged Campitor and Candeo around the neck, saying goodbye. As Garth let go of Candeo and stepped back, his face grief-stricken, the horse gently tossed her head in a nodding motion and gave a soft whinny. "It's a'right, MJ, we'll be back in no time 'tall." Garth turned toward the river to hide his face from the others.

"Do not tarry!" Brother Josh urged as he ushered the five friends toward the boat. He continued speaking as the young people pulled themselves away from the horses and bid a reluctant goodbye to the Embera onlookers and climbed aboard the *Dag Nia*. "There is a storm approaching, both physically and spiritually. There is a need for haste and caution. The 'new day' knows the way. She'll get you to your destination. I'll see you when you return!" With that, he pushed the *Dag Nia* away from shore with his walking stick and waved as the river's current carried the boat toward the first bend in the river.

Mel watched as several of the Embera youths approached the horses and gently guided them away from the river and toward a nearby meadow.

The friends on the boat and the Embera families on the riverbank waved goodbye to each other until the boat drifted with the current around the first bend.

Garth's eyes welled with tears as the horses and his group of young admirers and their parents passed from view. Unable to restrain himself any longer, his shoulders heaved with sorrow, and he sat and buried his face in his giant hands and wept. Polly was closely watching her big, softhearted friend and found herself pulled by the same strong emotions. She began to shed her own tears and sat beside Garth, resting a hand on his shoulder.

* * *

Mihoshi glanced across the deck, observing that there was no sail and no typical rigging. "Do we know how to operate this boat?" She looked at Rei in puzzlement, who shrugged his shoulders.

Garth slouched his bulky mass against a side rail, causing the entire boat to roll a few degrees, which startled him out of his bittersweet mood. "Whoa! This makes that biggin' we took from California seem sturdy as an island. Is it always gonna be so... bouncy?"

"Yes," Rei replied. "And I am afraid it gets much worse at times. I hope your stomach is as strong as your arms, Garth."

Garth looked at his stomach and wondered what that had to do with anything.

Rei turned to Mel. "I am unfamiliar with the mechanics of this vessel. With time, I am confident we can learn to navigate her. What do you suppose Brother Josh meant when he said the 'new day' knows the way?"

Mel was walking forward and astern, familiarizing himself with the attributes of the vessel. "*Dag Nia* means *New Day*, in Old Norse. However extraordinary it sounds, there must be something on this boat that helps it navigate. But I haven't found it yet. We'll head out towards the coast and see what happens."

"How are we to do that?" Rei asked. "The boat has no sail. If we drift with the current, it will take a day to reach the sea."

Mel continued looking intently at every square inch of the deck and mast. "It must be here. We cannot spare a day." Mel sat next to the mast and boom, where the sail would be attached on any other sailboat. He placed his hand on the boom and began to hum a tune that had long lain recessed in his memories. It began as a melody and finally emerged as a song.

Suddenly, the mast and boom crackled with energy. A compartment at the base of the mast opened, and the corners of a billowing sail emerged and raced to the ends of the mahogany poles. As the silken material fully unfurled, they could see that it was embossed with a flaming sword. It filled immediately with a northerly wind and the *New Day* lurched forward, throwing several of its passengers momentarily off-balance. Mel stood and took the ship's wheel by instinct.

Garth let out a hearty "Whoowhee!" and raised a hand above his head, waving his straw hat. He turned and faced forward through the fine mist of water that was splashing over the rail.

"Wow, Mel!" Polly exclaimed. "Don't take 'singer' off your list of career possibilities," she said with a wink, eliciting an eye roll from him. She leaned back, putting her hands on the rail to brace herself as she peered up at the sail's image of Vulgladius. Her gaze turned downriver, her spirit exhilarated by the boat's movement.

* * *

Mel asked Rei to take the wheel and, after handing over control, stepped down into the boat's cabin. Polly followed, and they together examined the mysteriously bare room.

They stepped past the first set of hammocks. "Do you think that's how we have to sleep on this boat?" she remarked, pulling at one of the hammocks.

Mel simply shrugged. "There must be a map here somewhere. I checked every compartment when we were loading the gear, and there was no sign of one." He walked along the walls, gliding his hand across them while humming softly beneath his breath. Nothing stirred, nothing opened.

He finally gave up and approached the square table in the center of the cabin. It appeared to be made of wood that had been polished and shined to an unusual brilliance. Mel sat in the suspended seat behind it and put his hands on the table.

Polly was the first to notice a growing luminance. Colors and lines appeared and took the shape of a map on the table, with patterns projected in the air above it. Her eyes widened. "Wow!"

"Extraordinary," Mel observed.

Words in a language unknown to Polly were in a series of colored bands along the map's lower edge. "What do these say?"

Mel studied them intently, his forehead wrinkling. "It's a calendar. Each of these colors is a month. And this strip on the left is a list of years. Let's see what happens when I touch the month marked as 'Janus.'" He touched one of the colored bands, and the patterns and colors flowed into a different form. "Hmm..."

"What? What is it?" Polly questioned.

"This map has a built-in almanac of the ocean currents and weather patterns for every month of the year. And if I am right," he began, touching the sixth colored band and then tapping one small red square among many green squares, "this is today," he said with wonder as a new image formed before them. He touched one more point on the map, and it changed to yet another pattern.

"What's it showing now?" Polly asked breathlessly.

Mel pointed to a raised, dark area near the border of the map. "I'm guessing these are the mountains we just left." He moved his finger to a green dot and chortled. "And here we are right now."

Polly looked bewildered. "Are you saying this map can show the boat's location?"

"Yes, it would seem so," Mel said with a smile.

"I may never cease to be amazed," she said, her jaw agape. "Can this tell us what the weather will be like?"

"Let's see," Mel answered as he manipulated the map. "Here's the weather now and for the next week. When I change it to two weeks or a month from now, the almanac information replaces it."

"So, can it tell us what the weather will be like or not?" Polly asked, her brow furrowed.

"Polly, it apparently can make an educated guess for the next week or so, but no further. It's most likely based on past patterns, and the further out the prediction, the less meaningful it is."

"Huh," Polly responded distractedly, staring in fascination at the image before them. Her eyes widened with a sudden thought. "Can this tell us where you're supposed to go?"

Mel looked at the map, which was moving right before his eyes, the green dot threading its way along a winding path of blue between two dark masses. Manipulating the map for a wider view, two thousand kilometers to the northeast, he noticed a long chain of islands, one of which was glowing with a unique, ruby color. Mel stated soberly, "I'm going home."

* * *

Polly looked at the map and then at Mel's pained expression. "What's wrong?" she asked softly.

"I'm not sure," he stammered, holding back his emotions. "Maybe I don't want to see what's there. I can't remember much, but all the memories I do have are filled with sadness."

"Do you know how to get us there?" she asked.

Mel shook his head, dispelling his emotion. He looked at Polly. "Brother Josh said the boat would know the way."

"Show me again," Polly said, stepping closer to get a better look at the map.

He pointed to the ruby island and, for effect, touched it with the tip of his finger. A barely perceptible hum from the stern of the boat suddenly began, and the vessel changed course by several degrees. Mel looked at Polly with a startled expression. "We need to go topside." They stepped around the table and ran up on deck.

"What happened?" Mel asked of Rei. "Did you lose control?"

"Yes, you could say so," Rei responded. "I was steering us along the river when the wheel began to turn on its own, with a force too strong to resist." They watched as the wheel moved by itself as the boat rounded the next curve of the river.

Mel looked from the wheel to the stern of the boat. "Brother Josh said the boat would know the way. We found a very unusual map, which knows our position and heading. I touched a location on it, and then this happened."

Rei's eyes widened. "May I see this map?"

Mel nodded. "It's not what you might expect."

Rei disappeared into the cabin.

* * *

Rei glanced around the cabin for anything that resembled a map.

Mel took a seat at the central table. "Watch this," he said, placing both hands on the table. The map sprang back to life.

Rei's eyes lit, fascinated. "Three-dimensional? How curious."

Mel manipulated the map to show Central America. He pointed at an area off the west coast of Mexico. "On our way from California to Panama, we ran into a hurricane here. From about now until November is a dangerous time at sea." Mel adjusted the map to focus on the Gulf of Mexico and the Caribbean Sea. He pointed to the easternmost section of the glowing map. "It's as I feared. This dark mass moving towards us must be a storm. Are the Atlantic hurricanes as severe as the ones in the Pacific?"

Rei gazed at the clouds swirling before him. "Their size and strength can be comparable. The forces generated over the warmer water of the Atlantic are longer lasting and more frequent. And more prone to crossing populated areas."

Mel watched soberly as the clouds grew darker. "Brother Josh had good reason to recommend that we hurry."

Rei pointed at the map. "If this green light is our location, we have less than an hour before we reach the open sea and begin to feel the edge of the storm."

Mel called out to Garth and Mihoshi, who stepped into the cabin and stared wide-eyed at the impossible picture projected in the air. "Our destination is my home island of Martinique. Our course requires that we pass through this storm," Mel described while gesturing at the map. "When the main force of it hits us, we need to stay in the cabin until we're through it."

"And the sail? If we are broadsided by a hurricane-force wave, it will capsize the vessel!" Rei exclaimed.

"I think the boat will manage. If it can steer itself, it must be able to adjust or lower the sail as needed. When the time comes, I'll stay topside just in case."

* * *

As the *New Day* neared the sea, the winds strengthened, and Mel took his place on deck to stand watch. He observed with awe as a storm surge swelled the river over its banks and across the flatland closest to the coast. Of its own accord, the boat continued out of the river's mouth and headed northeast into what was fast becoming a tumultuous Gulf of Mexico.

As the *New Day* lurched in the now perilous wind, Mel tried to lower the sail, alternately by singing and by force, but his efforts were to no avail. The sail refused to return to its storage compartment. Black clouds loomed ahead of them like a monstrous wave reaching into the sky, waiting to break upon them.

Below deck, Polly could no longer ignore the feeling that something was terribly amiss and began pacing back and forth. "Mel, are you having any luck?" she called out up the cabin stairs.

"It's not responding," she heard him yell over the wailing wind.

Polly watched incredulously as Mihoshi settled into her hammock and closed her eyes to rest. In an equally inexplicable act, Rei casually took a seat at the map. To Polly, he seemed so fascinated by how the map changed from moment to moment that he had forgotten that their lives were at risk on a storm-tossed boat. Rei touched the map's various features, reading whatever information was not in the Delemnite language and responding with occasional murmurs of surprise or contemplation.

Garth was pale with seasickness. He slumped into a hammock and groaned, holding his stomach. "I don't feel so good!"

On deck, Mel continued to struggle to lower the sail. He watched as it adjusted itself to pull the boat forward through the growing swells. He looked ahead of the vessel to the arms of the storm, which were slowly reaching closer to them. He called down into the cabin, "Rei, what do you see on the map?"

Rei stared intently at the depiction of the surrounding area. "The storm has run amok! The map shows it as nearly pitch black, and if I am not mistaken, there are waterspouts all along our path. One seems to be coming right towards us! Come see this!"

Waves were beginning to wash over the deck. Mel, soaked to the bone, descended the stairs into the cabin. As his feet reached the cabin floor, the hatch behind him snapped shut, and the entire boat began to hum and shudder. Darkness surrounded them, and then a soft glow emanated from the sides and the floor of the cabin. The roar of the storm was immediately silenced, and after a few moments, the rocking motion of the waves ceased entirely.

"What's happening?" Polly exclaimed, panting, as she and the others looked at the now glowing walls and floor. "The storm couldn't be over so quickly. Why did the door lock us in?"

Rei put his hand on Polly's shoulder and said in a pacifying voice, "All seems to be in order. We are safe, and at this point, I will be surprised only if something unique does not happen."

Mihoshi awoke, having sensed the cessation of movement. She listened intently for a moment and glanced in all directions. "We are under the water." She closed her eyes and rolled over to go back to sleep.

Garth arose from his hammock, his nausea calming.

Polly's eyes widened and filled with fear. "What! That's impossible! We're on a sailboat! The only way we can be underwater is if we're sinking!" Polly began to hyperventilate.

Mel looked in wonderment at the glowing surfaces of the cabin. "Of course! That's why we stopped being tossed like a cork in a bathtub. But are we still being propelled? And if so, how?"

"Look forward," Mihoshi said sleepily, her eyes still closed.

The others looked from the alluring glow of the walls to the dim bow. The hull had disappeared into transparency, revealing what looked like a monstrous jellyfish pulling their craft at a speed greater than any vessel could achieve under sail.

Polly looked, was overcome with dizziness, and swooned. Garth caught her and gently placed her in a hammock. Once she was secure, he turned and looked at the creature pulling them, his eyes unblinking and his tongue hanging below his lower lip. "I'll be dawg goned. Taint never seen nothin' like that 'afore."

The creature, upon closer inspection, was not living but was a device that emulated the appearance and movements of a jellyfish. Its blue, translucent wings undulated rhythmically, pulling the *New Day* along its course a hundred meters beneath the storm.

Mel walked to the narrow front of the cabin and rested his hands on the walls, staring forward in fascination. "This must be another of what my father called his 'old' sciences, which he was reticent to reveal to me. It appears to be a projection of a magnetic field, adapted to serve as an underwater sail."

"Except that it is actively pulling us," Rei observed. "Those undulations are how a jellyfish propels itself. I wonder if the map table has more information about this boat."

Polly, who had recovered from her swoon, sat upright and

looked nervously at her friends. She spoke in a deliberate manner to calm herself. "I'm glad that you three gentlemen are taking an interest in the science of this vessel. There are a few questions we need to answer. Such as how long can we stay underwater? What about oxygen and food? I am starving, and it's time I looked over what we've got in our packs."

Garth said, "Hey, that's an idea! I'm starvin' too. Polly, I just love it when ya speaks all librarian like that. And ya sure can cut to the chase. Let's look fer some grub."

Mel looked at Polly. "I'm sure that a boat like this was designed to meet the needs of its passengers. Anyway, I think I'll join you two on your search."

They opened the cabinets and rummaged through their backpacks, finding wrapped cheese, flatbread, and a large bag of dried acai berries. Garth, especially, dug in with zeal.

Rei frowned. "We don't know how long this journey will be, so I believe it is in our best interests to eat judiciously."

Garth slowed his pace, glancing at Polly with a puzzled look.

Polly nodded back consolingly with an "I know" expression. She turned to Rei. "I'm always looking to learn new words. I can take a guess, but what exactly does 'judiciously' mean?"

"With good judgment, conservatively, or sparingly. I apologize for using vocabulary that is not in the common vernacular."

Polly grinned. "Is it uncommon because the west loves its slang and doesn't appreciate words with more than two syllables?"

"It is uncommon because of Jesuits," Rei replied flatly.

"Huh?" Polly responded in confusion.

"My father did not want me and my sister to be educated in the state schools, so he enrolled us at the Jesuit mission. Their standards of education are second to none."

Polly stared at Rei in dazed affinity. "But, what of the religious gap? Wasn't your father concerned that you would convert from Buddhism to Christianity?"

Rei smiled and nodded. "You are correct, Polly, that there are many in Japan who follow the teachings of Siddhartha Gautama and who are at least suspicious of foreigners associated with Christianity. The Buddha is widely revered. He was a saint of sorts. He saw the flaws of Hinduism and hated the caste system with its culture of ignoring the needs of the poor to avoid partaking in their karma. He was once a rich man, who gave his wealth to the poor of his city, and then began his great pursuit of 'enlightenment.' That path led him to renounce the millions of Hindu gods and to seek the truth within himself."

"Did he ever find it?" Polly asked, eyes wide open.

Rei laughed. "I suspect he became tired of trying so hard. If you see the statues of him in his youth, he was emaciated, as he sought to starve himself of every earthly pleasure, even food! But the statues of the Buddha when he was older show him as plump and jolly, making it obvious that he had relaxed. He was a devout, socially conscious man. I personally believe that if he had lived at the time of Jesus, he might well have become one of His disciples.

"My father sent us to be taught by the Jesuits because of what he saw as a problem with both Buddhism and the traditional Shinto. He said there was a basic difference between Christianity and the rest of the many excellent philosophies of this world."

"What was it?" Polly inquired, sensing that she was about to learn a life-changing truth.

Rei nodded patiently at her question. "Well, the Christian scriptures say that Jesus rose from the dead, Polly. No other religion or philosophy has ever claimed that such a thing happened to its founder. If this is true of Jesus, it may be the pivotal fact for evaluating the components of every other faith."

Garth took a huge bite out of one of the fresh guavas they had been given by the Emberas, causing sticky, yellow juice to dribble down his chin. "Ya sure did say a mouthful thar, Rei."

Polly looked at the floor, lost in contemplation of what she had just learned. Rei stretched out in his hammock and closed his eyes.

"We're all seeking the same thing, aren't we? Peace within ourselves?" Polly persisted.

"Yes, Polly," Rei responded, his eyes still closed. "But is that *all* we are seeking?"

* * *

The friends became drowsy after finishing their meal. The hammocks beckoned to them, and they stretched out and allowed their tense bodies to be lulled quickly to sleep. As they slept, the *New Day* continued gliding rapidly along its course, deep beneath the furthest reach of a hurricane.

CHAPTER 24

COMPENDIUM

Polly awoke from a dream of a summer's day in Cayucos. The town's sawmill had been buzzing loudly in the background. Polly had wanted to close the library window so she could stop the incessant noise. She cracked one eye open and was suddenly dragged back into the *New Day*'s cabin. Garth lay on his back, his arms dangling limply over the sides of his hammock. His mouth was open wide, snorting like an angry bull.

Polly nodded in agreement with the Emberas; *Atubwa!*

Mel sat before the map, which was swirling with images. He was reading the text that accompanied the visuals.

"How... how long have I been asleep?" Polly stuttered, waking up slowly.

"About thirty hours," Mel said without looking up.

Polly sat as upright as she could in the hammock. "Thirty hours! That's impossible! I've never slept that long."

"Well, you weren't asleep... exactly."

"Well, what 'exactly' was it, then?" she asked, bristling.

"I'll answer that in a moment, I promise. First, I have to tell you what I've discovered. I woke after a few hours and have learned so much. This device is more than just a map and an almanac. It's also a compendium of the entire history of the people of Delemni. I've been reading from it for just over a day, and what I've discovered is amazing."

"Like what?" she asked skeptically, rubbing her eyes.

"Like the fact that you and the others have been in a state of torpor. It's a suspended rest, like hibernation. The boat emits a resonance that makes this possible for the passengers. Your physical processes were slowed to a near-death state. Look at the others. They breathe just once a minute. And their heartbeat is nearly indiscernible."

"Why is that necessary?" Polly inquired, suddenly feeling even more uncomfortable in the strange vessel.

"Well, in part to address the issues you mentioned before. To preserve our oxygen and food and to help us make a long passage cooped up in this cabin."

Polly squinted with suspicion. "Why didn't the 'resonance' affect you?"

"I'm not sure. Maybe it woke me on purpose, so I would have time to read while alone? These archives have taught me thousands of years of my ancestors' history. They do not, however, reveal the details of the ancient sciences."

Polly's eyes grew large. "*Thousands of years*! I don't even know my great grandfather's first name." Polly looked around the cabin in fearful wonder at the accomplishments of a lost civilization. A sailboat capable of functioning as a submarine. A massive, undulating magnetic field providing propulsion. A three-dimensional map and historical archive. Her friends in a state of hibernation. There was no mistaking that she was on the adventure of a lifetime. "When we first found this map," she continued, "you said this journey was taking you back to your home, in Martinique. Is Atlan—I mean, Delemni, also in the Caribbean?"

"Well," he began and then paused, sensing a drowsiness starting to overtake him. "It isn't anywhere anymore. It *was* in the middle of the Atlantic Ocean."

"And it sunk?" Polly exclaimed. "Islands don't just sink!"

"Occasionally they do, Polly," Mel corrected her softly. "If they are volcanic, they can explode and disintegrate. Delemni was destroyed and vanished overnight."

"What did the Strangers do that destroyed a whole island chain and an entire civilization?" Polly pressed.

Mel yawned. "Please excuse me. They surrendered themselves to the lust for power and wealth and dug too deeply into the Earth's crust. I don't know the details of the science behind what happened, but it was because their hearts had become corrupt." Mel suddenly sat upright, remembering something he had wanted to mention. "Oh, and I found this, which you as a librarian might be at least a little interested in," he said with a wink. From under his rope chair, he withdrew an ancient book of parchments with several Greek words inscribed on its cover and held it out to Polly.

"What! Where did you find that?" Polly gasped.

Mel, exhausted from his marathon study session, could no longer stay awake. He took a deep breath. "Polly, it's not personal. It's the resonance," he said with a smile.

Polly breathed a good-natured sigh as Mel sat back in the rope chair next to the map table and closed his eyes.

* * *

Silence surrounded Mel like a warm blanket. The air was still, with only the occasional sound of a sporadic liquid breath as the gossamer jellyfish pulled them through the water. He opened his eyes and saw Polly sitting at his feet, her eyes moving across the pages of the book like a fisherman hunched over a hole in the ice. "How long have I been out?" he asked.

"About thirty-five hundred years, I guess," Polly replied quickly, startled and irritated at having her reading interrupted. Then, realizing that Mel was awake again, she said, "This book is all about Delemni before its destruction. It was so advanced. They lived in peace. They refined agriculture to the point where no one was hungry. They had advanced waste disposal systems in their cities, hot and cold running water, and created unbelievable forms of transportation. Who wrote this? How come I couldn't read it, but then I could?"

Mel, still groggy from sleep, held up his hand. "Hold on. I just got here. A minute, please."

Polly bit her lip, holding her peace like a seltzer bottle that had just been shaken violently. Ten seconds later, she could not take it any longer. "Why were you so agitated in your sleep?"

"I did have an odd dream. I'd rather not talk about it for now."

She sat for another ten seconds, tapping her foot. "Well!"

Mel picked up the old book while contemplating what he had learned from the compendium. "Much of Delemni's technology was designed to respond to its users individually. With this book, if it recognizes you as a friend of Delemni, and you don't know Greek, it translates for your mind as you read."

Polly scowled with skepticism and started to speak.

Mel shook his head. "Don't ask. You experienced it yourself."

Polly reluctantly nodded in agreement. "I'll take the book's approval as a compliment."

Mel gently laughed. "My ancestors invented all kinds of things that can respond to peoples' thoughts and emotions. I suppose someday I'll learn how it's done."

"Was this brought from Delemni?" Polly asked reverently.

"This book was written after Delemni sank but was created according to the ancient methods. Many great books were written before the islands were destroyed, and a few have been written by the Gatekeepers since then."

"How do the Strangers have so much power when the knowledge has been so carefully guarded?"

"It's the same story that's in the compendium repeatedly. A Vysard with an incomplete Caeli is either defeated by the Strangers, and his knowledge is stolen, or he falls to the lust for power and joins them. I suspect that Neco was one of the latter. My father saw it happening again among the Delemnites in Martinique. He saw the coming crisis, but they wouldn't listen. The Delemnite portion of Martinique perished in much the same way as the original islands."

Polly's curiosity was piqued. "Where is your father's Caeli?"

"We have one in Cooperton, but it's mostly for training me.

I've heard about the Telemai Caeli, but I don't know where it is. If anyone else knows, it's someone who my father trusts. There have been only ten Gatekeepers, each with his helpers, and, in keeping with the training process, the last secrets aren't divulged until the eight vaults are mastered. I'm on the first one."

One of the things that Mel had said did not sound right to Polly, and she did some calculations in her mind. "Only ten? But that would mean each Gatekeeper lived for at least four hundred years!" Polly stared at the floor in bewilderment, shaking her head.

"I couldn't believe it either when I first read it in the compendium. Don't ask me how it can be true, but I found my father's name going back as far as AD 1306. That makes him over six hundred years old."

Polly's mind seemed to go blank. She peered out through the transparent front of the boat at its breathtaking propulsion system. She shook her head. "How did a primitive people from so long ago start developing such inventions?"

Mel smiled knowingly, reminded of his younger self and the questions he had posed to his father and Oscar. "What makes you think they were primitive? No one knows for sure how the pyramids of Egypt were built. Or Stonehenge. The early Delemnites lived for almost a millennium. Think of what one person could learn and accomplish in that time. Our lives are so much more limited, and on top of that, we tend not to do ourselves any favors. Every generation thinks it needs to change what was done by its fathers, so each generation we take two steps forward and three steps back."

Polly's shoulders slumped under the weight of all that she was learning. "What can a little group of friends like us do in comparison to the people of the past? If they couldn't stop the Strangers and couldn't safely bring the wonders of Delemni back to help the world, what chance do we have?"

Mel sighed. "As Gwyneth encouraged us, we can embrace our destiny and give our all to what is ahead."

Polly sat down in her hammock and leaned slowly back, grap-

CHAPTER 25

FEI YU

A rush of salty air poured into the cabin, bringing with it the scents of mango and exotic flowers. The cabin door had opened wide of its own accord. Rei and Mihoshi awoke within a minute of each other. Stretching his arms above his head, Rei gave a wide yawn. He saw Mel sitting at the map table, studying its contents. "*Ohayō gozaimasu*, Mel-san. Did you find what you were looking for?"

"*Hai*, Rei-san. And more," Mel answered. "I'll tell you about it topside." The two young men disappeared out onto the deck. After quietly combing her hair, Mihoshi left the cabin to join them. Garth awoke momentarily to the fresh air and then rolled onto his side in his hammock and went back to sleep.

Polly did not awake. She had been exhausted by her talk with Mel. Her heart had been stirred by his description of the history of his people and the millennia-long heritage of their quest, and she had lain awake in her hammock with her mind racing for what felt like hours before she fell asleep. She had reflected on how her life before had always seemed like a treasure hunt in which she was frantically accumulating bits of information. This had led her to take the job as the Cayucos librarian. Even then, the books had all seemed so incomplete, and what she was looking for had eluded her. Despite the profound sense of intimidation that accompanied the unknowns that now loomed in her future, her conversations with Mel over the past weeks had filled her mind with possibilities. She lay in her hammock like a caterpillar enshrouded in its cocoon, her dreams pervaded by the sense that she was ready to burst forth and take flight.

* * *

The three young people on deck were enjoying a magnificent morning. The deep turquoise of the Caribbean Sea rippled to the horizon, and a soft wind billowed the sail. The *New Day* was conducting itself towards an eighty-kilometer-long island, which lay five kilometers away, filling their view to the east. This island was crowned with a mountainous volcano at its northern end, and it was toward this imposing peak that the prow of the *New Day* was pointed.

Gleaming blue fish leaped out of the water and skimmed across the surface on iridescent, translucently finned wings. Mihoshi giggled in delight. "*Fei yu!*"

Mel watched the aquatic ballet of the colorful fish. "Flying fish," he interpreted. "They're beautiful! I've only ever read about them, but they feel so familiar."

Mel lifted his gaze again to the nearby island, and his heart was struck by a groan of recognition. The smells, the fish, and the volcanic mountain stirred forgotten feelings inside of him. *Home*, he thought to himself with a sigh.

* * *

As they approached to within three kilometers of the island, the boat ceased humming, and the wheel turned lazily with the wind and the swells. The change in the boat's motion stirred Garth and Polly out of their hammocks and onto the deck. Rei took the ship's wheel and maintained their course towards the island.

As they drew closer, they saw the long-burnt remains of what had once been a large and prosperous city. The wood of unpainted buildings showed where tenacious islanders were moving back into the shadow of the volcano and rebuilding what had been lost.

Mel took a deep breath. "Saint-Pierre, Martinique. It has been twelve years since the eruption." Few buildings of the once regal, old-world port were left standing. "It was known as 'the Paris of the Caribbean.'"

Polly looked at the ruined shells of once-grand, multistoried buildings, every flammable portion of their structure burnt away. She wondered about the people who had lived and perished here; children clutching their mothers' legs, lovers holding hands. She was overwhelmed with a deep sense of sorrow.

Garth glanced from the grim city to Mel. "We landin' here?"

Mel shook his head. "No, let's swing around the island. My father's house was on the eastern coast." As they turned north, he looked once more at the city. A painful resolve settled over him. "I suspect that the boat was meant to guide us here so that we would always remember what results from the ways of the Strangers."

* * *

They rounded the northern end of the island and approached a peninsula on the eastern coast. Mel's eyes widened. "This is it!"

As they sailed nearer and began to distinguish details on the shore, Mel experienced pangs of foreboding. The town was gone, wiped away by the rough black sheet of a long-cooled lava flow. The only remaining signs of the settlement were the charred ruins of piers that now stood isolated in the water.

Mel surveyed the harbor and shook his head, then looked southward. Here, the shoreline rose rapidly, and the ocean lapped at the base of magnificent black cliffs. Seeing what sat atop the cliffs caused Mel to gasp and his heart to fill with joyful surprise. There, like the stoic monument of a lost era, sat the Uri castle. It was surrounded by a black and hardened lava flow on three sides. From a distance, it appeared that the castle's perimeter wall had withstood the molten river and that the house within was intact. The only undisturbed approach to the castle lay between its front entrance and the tops of the cliffs.

Sailing as near to the base of the cliffs as they dared, they stood at the railing and stared up at the massive, fortress-like castle above them. Further south, a wide beach ended at the foot of the precipice. Mihoshi silently studied the structure and the shoreline and then closed her eyes for a moment.

Polly let out an exasperated sigh. "The only way in is at the top of a sheer rock cliff! How are we supposed to get up there?" she asked incredulously.

Rei nodded in agreement. "Perhaps we should anchor in the harbor and make our way across the old lava flow."

Mel stared at the shoreline, searching his memories. How many days had he spent on this beach with his parents? Even now, he felt that he could call out their names, and they would suddenly appear from behind one of the boulders on the beach.

Mel pointed to the near end of the beach. "Rei, there's an inlet at the north end of the cove. We'll moor there and go ashore."

Rei directed their vessel to the inlet and drew just shy of a sharp incline of soft sand that led up to the flat expanse of the beach. Mel jumped ashore first and tethered the ship to a boulder, then took off on a playful run down the beach. Garth jumped off and offered to lift the others to the dry sand. Rei politely refused his assistance and sprang from the deck to the beach. Polly gratefully accepted Garth's offer, extending her hand toward him. Garth lifted her over the rail as easily as he would lift a child and gently set her on the dry sand. Polly's breath was taken away, not only by Garth's newfound gallantry but also by the incredible sensitivity of his large, strong hands.

"Thank you, kind sir!" she said and curtsied, pulling the sides of her long green skirt and bowing slightly.

"Twernt nothin', ma'am!" Garth shyly responded.

Garth lifted Mihoshi and placed her carefully on the sand.

Now gathered on the beach, they ran after Mel. He led them directly into a small cave that had at first been hidden from view. They leaned against the sandstone walls to catch their breath. Mel began to hum a childhood melody. The haunting sound of his voice in the darkness of the cave caused Polly to wonder if he was going a little crazy. Moments later, he stopped humming and led them around a blind corner into the daylight. Leaving the cave, Mel's friends marveled that they were now atop the cliff.

"What wizardry is this?" Rei questioned.

Mel smiled. "My father built this lift to take our family to the beach. He always loved walking beside the waves."

"I've heard of similar devices," Rei remarked. "A room called an 'elevator' can ascend and descend inside of a building."

Mel nodded. "Yes, this is like an elevator, but without the cables and gears. This lift operates on magnetics. That's why the ride is silent and feels motionless. Perhaps years from now, this can be introduced into society, but not yet."

"Don't that beat all," Garth marveled. "A movin' cave. I'm guessin' that ain't the last impossible thing we gonna see today."

They looked up at the Uri castle. It stood fifteen meters high, with several towers and a walkway along the top of the wall. Though damaged from the firestorm, it was intact. Black smudges marked where volcanic debris had crashed against the walls.

Mel walked towards the front gate, a flood of unbidden memories filling his mind. He slowed and fell to his knees. The others rushed to his side and saw that he was weeping.

"What is it, Mel?" Polly asked, placing a hand on his shoulder.

Rei looked to his sister, a puzzled look on his face.

"This is where his mother was taken from him," Mihoshi explained. She knelt beside him and bowed her face.

"Oh, here we go, gettin' all mushy," Garth said, coughing to try to keep back his emotions. "I don't even 'member my ma; she left so long 'go. I guess I should go on an' have a good cry too." He knelt beside Mel and mourned with him. Polly knelt and wrapped her arms comfortingly around their shoulders, crying with them.

After several minutes, Mel wiped his sleeve across his emotion-worn face. Mihoshi delicately dabbed her eyes with a silk scarf. Polly let go of Garth, and he blew his nose loudly into a handkerchief. He looked at Polly with big, red eyes.

Everyone noticed Polly's face and burst out laughing.

"What?" Polly asked, frowning and wondering why they were laughing at her expense.

Mihoshi giggled and politely held a silk scarf out to her. After Polly had wiped her face, she understood. "I think we all need a good bath," she said with a smile.

Mel took a deep breath. "Let's take a look around."

They approached the immense, wooden doors that granted access through the castle wall. The double doors were each five meters high and two and a half meters across. Large metal bands crisscrossed their surface and met in the middle at a round, dome-like crest. There was no discernible lock or opening for a key.

"How are we to open this?" Rei asked. "And can we be sure that this residence has not been claimed by new inhabitants in the past twelve years?"

"That would be most unlikely," Mel responded. "There are few men who know its secrets, and they are either dead or no longer dwell in this part of the world."

"Ya sure we shouldn't at least knock?" Garth asked.

Mel turned to Garth with a raised eyebrow. "Knock at my own house?" Mel put both hands on the center crest, whistled a tune, and pushed on the huge doors. They glided open silently and smoothly. Once the friends were within, Mel closed the doors behind them. They crossed the yard and entered the house through a similar, but smaller, set of doors.

Polly's breath was taken away as she peered into the vast interior of the entryway. The high dome of the roof towered overhead, brightly lit by an abundance of windows lining its perimeter. The walls were made of a smooth, white stone in which they saw their reflections as they walked past. The floor was of a smooth marble with colorful ripples flowing through it.

Mel walked quickly to the right and soon came to a wide, stone staircase that led upward. The others followed as close as they could but found it difficult to keep pace with Mel as he broke into a run and rushed up the stairs. Other than their own footfalls, no other sound could be heard within the castle walls. The landing and hall-way at the top of the stairs were sparsely furnished. Polly observed an occasional cobweb and an omnipresent coating of undisturbed dust.

"It's this way," Mel said and pressed on, not looking back.

"What is? What are we looking for?" Polly pleaded.

"I'll know it when I see it."

Finally, Mel came to another pair of large doors and threw them open. He and the others stepped into the chamber, and their eyes went wide in wonder. They were in a massive library, three stories high and a hundred meters long. Above them, a gigantic stained-glass ceiling set with thousands of colors and shapes projected colorful patterns throughout the room.

"Look, Mel-san," Mihoshi remarked, "more flying fish!" She pointed to a section of the ceiling that depicted *fei yu* flying across an ocean surface.

Mel looked at the indicated portion of the ceiling and smiled. Shifting his gaze to the far end of the library, he mumbled "hmmm" and kept pushing forward.

The friends passed a long, bare reading table and three simple, wooden desks with writing, printing, and binding apparatuses upon them. Polly stopped here and looked in all directions at the magnificent, towering collection of books. Her heart pounded within her. She estimated she could spend the rest of her life reading these books and still not finish a tenth of them. She stepped to the nearest shelf and began to peruse several of the titles.

"Polly!" Mel called out without looking. "We're too busy with our adventure to stop and read about someone else's. Keep up!"

Polly ran to catch up with the group.

Mel came to a small, single door at the rear of the library and waited until the others caught up with him. "This was my father's private study," he explained and opened the door.

The familiarity of the room rushed upon Mel. He noticed its many similarities to his father's study in Cooperton, the most notable being the transparent outer wall that provided an excellent view of the ocean beyond.

The room was small in comparison to the library and was warm and inviting. The walls were covered with wood rather than stone. A thick, round Persian rug filled the center of the floor. Several luxurious couches provided seating.

Mel did not see any sign of the type of vaults he was seeking. He sat in his father's chair to think and immediately became lost in a flood of memories. Moments of learning from his early childhood inundated him like the sudden remembrance of countless dreams.

The others wandered around the study, looking in chests and boxes and voraciously reading the titles of the books on the wall.

After several minutes, Mel arose and approached a bookcase on the wall across from the study's entrance. He repeated the pattern of knocks and hummed the tune that he had used to open the Caeli entrance in the back of the closet in his home in Cooperton, and the bookcase slid silently aside, revealing the arched entry of the study's Caeli. Without waiting to note the reaction of his friends, he descended the spiral stairs and stopped at the gnarled door. A flurry of footsteps followed him, and four astonished faces kept as far back on the stairs as they could while still being able to watch his every move.

This door reminded Mel of a further scaled-down replica of the castle's main entrance. He was struck with a sudden, fearful suspicion that he had never learned the tune that opened this portal. Nevertheless, he repeated the knocks and the tune he had used to slide the bookcase aside. Nothing happened. He repeated the tunes that had operated the lift and opened the castle entrance. Nothing happened. He sank to his knees in defeat and leaned his head against the door.

Suddenly, he smelled jasmine, felt the warm rays of the morning sun, and heard a woman's voice singing. The melody infused him with a warmth and affection and sense of safety stronger than any other he had ever felt. Overcome with bittersweet emotion, and with his voice cracking, he repeated the woman's song to the door. It gave way immediately, and he fell forward, catching himself just in time.

The others behind him gasped and watched as Mel rose and entered the dimly lit, close confines of the chamber. They followed cautiously and watched as Mel scrutinized the markings on each of the dozens of small vault doors.

Mel shook his head in disappointment and leaned back against the wall, sliding down to a sitting position. "The Abico isn't here. None of the eight are here."

Polly's face fell. "Is this room his only place like this?"

Mel shrugged. Mihoshi approached and whispered in his ear. "What you're looking for may not be in this castle."

Mel nodded. "That wouldn't surprise me. When I remembered this room, I hoped the castle would be the end of the journey. But the way to it may only begin here."

For the next hour, Mel carefully searched the small chamber of vaults and the entirety of his father's study. Most of the books looked undisturbed. There were no apparent clues to indicate his next step. He grew frustrated at the seeming dead end. He closed the chamber of vaults, slid the bookcase back into position, and stood at the study's entrance to address the others. "Let's go. I thought for sure he would have left me a clue, but I can't find it. Let's get back to the boat."

He abruptly left the study and walked across the main library toward its exit.

Polly sighed. It was torturous to her to be so close to so many historical accounts and treatises on an endless number of fascinating topics and yet not have enough time to even scan the titles. She decided she would take another peek around the library and catch up soon. In keeping with her suspicion that large libraries always kept the best books hidden away, she climbed a staircase and began looking through the books on the top floor.

Mel shouted, "Polly, please hurry. We might miss the outgoing tide." He stood near the central tables of the library and peered at the floors above, trying to see where she had gone. He glimpsed a movement of fabric and saw her leaning against a rail, holding out a large, leather-bound book with a lock on its cover.

"How do I open this?" she yelled to Mel.

Mel crossed his arms and thought to rebuke her but stopped, his face going blank with wonder.

She looked back at him and rolled her eyes at the speech he seemed poised to deliver. She already knew she was out of line. She stepped back from the rail and put the volume back in its place on the shelf. "I'm sorry, Mel," she yelled.

Mel bent over with sudden laughter.

Polly flushed red with indignation and rushed back to the rail. "I don't know what's so funny, Mel! I'm a librarian. Isn't it normal for someone like me to be intrigued by books? Especially books in the personal library of the heir to the throne of Atlantis?"

Mel looked again and laughed more deeply. Rei and Mihoshi looked in the same direction and smiled.

"Some people just cain't see the forests fer the trees, now can they?" Garth said with a smile.

"Et tu, Brute!" Polly fumed at Garth. She stomped down the stairs and rejoined the others, squinting in anger with her hands on her hips. Mel smiled and pointed up at the stained-glass ceiling. Polly followed his gesture and saw the source of their amusement.

Mel explained, "I was looking for a clue; something small or hidden. How was I to know my father had envisioned something a little grander in its subtlety?"

The angle of the sunlight had shifted since they first entered the library, and now a glowing map could be seen in the stained glass. A rendering of the east coast of Martinique showed a small island south of the castle glowing with a distinct golden hue.

* * *

Polly was the last to step out through the front doors of the castle. She carried in her arms a medium-sized leather volume.

Mel noticed the book in her hands and shook his head. "What're you doing, Polly? That's from my father's private library! It's completely unacceptable to take any of his books outside these walls!" He stood, blocking her way forward.

"It's not for me," Polly said unapologetically. "It's for Garth."

Mel sighed with frustration. "I'm supposed to believe that?" Mel leaned close to Polly so only the two of them could hear his next statement. "We both know Garth can't read."

Polly opened the cover of the book and held it up. "Exactly."

Mel saw that the book was *A Basic Primer in Reading* by Sheri Lampou.

"I thought, if we get the chance, we might 'learn him a thang or two.'" She winked, closed the book, and walked confidently past Mel. He nodded in respect. Mortification tugged at his heart as he closed the castle doors behind them.

* * *

An hour later, the *New Day* reached the island. The friends' hearts sank as they saw that the island appeared to be encircled by an impassible reef. Rei steered the boat around the island, looking for a break in the reef or a beach where they could draw near to shore. They traveled at the leisurely pace of the wind blowing softly across the turquoise water.

When Rei finally spotted a break in the reef through which he could steer, he tried to turn the wheel to bring them in closer, but it would not budge. He tried adjusting the sail to catch the wind at a different angle to help propel them landward, but to no avail. The *New Day* slowly coasted to a stop and lowered its anchor to maintain its position.

Mel realized that their further progress was being directed by the *New Day*. But he did not know what the boat meant for them to do. He stared wistfully at the island that he knew held the answers to his quest. The small landmass was a volcanic shell that rose amidst the Caribbean waters like a walled citadel. Its outer cliffs were sheer and apparently impenetrable. A single, broad ribbon of grey water cascaded from atop the cliffs directly into the frothing sea below, across from where the *New Day* had dropped anchor. Waves crashed upon the sharp, hidden face of the reef, which lay below the ocean's surface.

Mel's nightmares of shipwreck and death sprang vividly to his mind. "Rei, I don't like the look of this place. Won't the boat respond at all?"

"The *New Day* has taken control of her course, which seems to be stationary for now, perhaps waiting for a tide or for the morning. We have been well led thus far and should trust who designed the vessel."

Mel looked somberly at the massive back walls towering just two hundred meters away.

Polly followed his stare. "Are we sure this is the right place?"

Rei replied, "This impossible place at the end of the earth is our destination."

Mel nodded. "There's no breach anywhere in the reef except right in front of this waterfall."

The sun's rays began to wane, and the ocean took on a turquoise and crimson aura. Seagulls soared through the air and floated on the water, gorging themselves ahead of the darkness of night. Pelicans skimmed the tops of the waves that feathered across the reef and occasionally swooped above the surf and dove into the sea to catch an unwary fish.

"What did the map table say about this island?" Polly inquired.

Mel shook his head. "I spent the last hour with it, but I can't get it to communicate anything about this place. It's as if the record of this island was erased."

"I think it would be best if we all slept," Rei suggested. "I believe that tomorrow will hold the answers we seek."

Mihoshi, who had been her usual inconspicuous self, said to Mel, "If he is calling, you must go."

Mel blinked. "If who is calling? And to where? I don't understand," Mel said with a face that begged for clarity.

She pointed to the west, where the last golden beams of the sunset were descending like a curtain on the island.

Mel looked to Rei with a pleading stare.

"She perceives things that you or I may miss," Rei said, shrugging his shoulders.

Mel bowed to Mihoshi in a respectful gesture of thanks.

They filed one by one into the boat's cabin and slipped into their hammocks, where the gentle rocking of the boat lulled all but one of them to sleep.

* * *

Mel lay motionless for several hours. His mind replayed what he had learned in his training. Somewhere, there must be a clue to this island. Finally, realizing that he was no closer to falling asleep, he silently rose from his hammock and walked out on the deck.

The salt air of the Caribbean night greeted him with surprising warmth. The moon sprinkled silver across a calmly rolling seascape. The island sat stubborn and grey. The occasional clash of waves on the reef sounded against the steady rumble of the waterfall cascading into the brine.

Mel leaned against the rail closest to the island and stared at the waterfall. There had to be something behind it. The path in the reef led directly to it. Perhaps the channel was not actually wide enough for the boat to safely pass. Mel surveyed the distance to the waterfall. He could safely swim it after daybreak, if needed.

Suddenly, the boat jerked as though something had dislodged the anchor. Startled by the movement, Mel ran to the stern and stared into the water. Somehow, the *New Day* had broken free from her anchorage and was being carried by the current towards the pounding reef to one side of the gap. Mel's heart beat rapidly, his breath quickening. He saw the weighted line dragging behind, skipping across the ocean floor as if it were a coffee can dragged behind a horse. There was a chance it would catch on an outcropping of rock, but if it did not do so soon, they would wreck. The sound of the surf grew louder.

Mel ran to the cabin door and shouted at the top of his lungs, "Wake up! Wake up! We've broken loose and are heading for the reef!" He saw the rapidly approaching whitewater. With no time to wait, Mel ran to the stern and dove into the moonlit sea beside the trailing anchor line.

The water seemed alive, like a wrestler in a frantic match. Mel was instantly pulled to the sandy bottom five meters below, his head thrown against the pliable ocean floor. The saltwater stung his eyes as he grasped anxiously for the anchor line. After several attempts, he finally managed to grab a hold of it, his lungs already aching for air.

He immediately regretted his choice. The violence of the water paled in comparison to the spastic anchor line, which fought him like a raging bull. It took all his strength to hold on to the line. He knew that if he could take the anchor at the end of the line and jam it into a crevice or hook it on a rock, the boat could be saved. Slowly, arm length by arm length, he pulled himself along the line, his muscles burning in pain, his lungs screaming for air. He finally dragged himself to the line's end, praying against all hope that with his dying effort, he could save the boat and his friends upon it.

He held on to the impossibly heavy anchor as it skidded across the ocean floor and watched for a place to lodge it. He spied a ledge on an approaching boulder, and as he scrambled towards it, a surge of the current from behind flung him against the unrelenting stone. His mind reeled, and his hands went limp. As his semiconscious body was pulled into the current flowing past the boulder, he saw the *New Day* floating overhead, silhouetted in the rippling moonlight.

* * *

The roar of water reverberated through the cave. Like a recurring fever dream, it was happening again. He had been in this same cave before. He saw the same rowboat wreckage. His forehead was throbbing in pain. He checked himself and did not see or feel any signs of trauma to his arms or legs. He found a rock nearby and took a seat, reticent to investigate the wreckage yet again.

This must be another dream! he thought to himself. *Why am I here? What do I need to discover?*

He could see the mouth of the cave and the curtain of water flowing from above. He surmised that he was behind the waterfall. A small pool flowed back and forth with the incoming waves. *How can this be a dream?* he questioned. His perceptions and sensations were crystal clear, the pain in his forehead nagging at him that this was real. *How did I get here?*

A sudden, nearby *whoosh* of air and water startled him, sending him flailing off the rock and onto the sand. He turned to the source of the sound. A high wave from outside the cave had burst through a crack in the rock like a whale exhaling after a deep dive. Mel found his startled reflexes strangely comforting as evidence that he was not dead.

He knew that the fate of the *New Day* and his friends upon it had been determined already, for good or for ill, during the moments when the current had carried him to the cave. He turned his attention to exploring his surroundings and was careful to avoid the pile of wreckage that he had seen in his dream.

The cavern sparkled as if a master jeweler had inlaid the walls and ceiling with thousands of precious stones.

Despite the distracting roar of the waterfall, the occasional crescendos of the surf, and the scintillating beauty of the cave's surfaces, Mel's focus was pulled to the dark recesses of the cave's interior. He did not understand why, but he was drawn inward.

He stepped cautiously as the light from the first chamber faded.

Upon passing into total darkness, he felt the ground ahead with an outstretched foot and touched the walls on either side when the passage was narrow enough. Eventually, the sound of the waterfall and the occasional wave-generated geysers fell silent. He continued at a snail's pace for an hour, feeling like he had gone no more than ten meters since the cave had fallen silent. He wondered if, in his fatigue, he had lost track of time.

He began to fear that he had made a serious mistake. "How can I look for something when I can't even see? What's the use of stumbling around in the darkness in this forsaken cave?" He wanted to turn back and do whatever he could to find out whether he had succeeded in lodging the anchor and saving his friends.

But then he remembered his father's letter about the importance of his quest. He remembered that Neco, who had tried to kill him, was just one of many Strangers who would continue in a mad desire for the secrets of Delemni and that there must be a Gatekeeper to stand against them. Gwyneth's reminder to focus on the Abico vault echoed in his mind. He remembered that his friends had risked their lives to help him. Finally, he remembered Mihoshi's words from the previous night. He had to keep going.

Yet, he was tired. He was alone in this dark place he had been directed to, and he was running out of courage. He felt that he could not take one more step by himself. He needed help. He desperately wanted to hear the one whom Mihoshi had sensed was calling to him. Perhaps the only way that would be possible would be if he followed her example of stillness.

He sat and tried to slow his mind and calm his panicking heart. He was focusing on being still, yet everything inside him screamed, "*Do something!*" His feeling of weakness forced itself to the front of his mind. Instead of giving in and losing hope, he faced his weakness with an honest, audible cry. "I can't do this on my own. I give up!" His lungs heaved in anxious gasps. There was no sound but his own heart beating loudly in his chest. No further words seemed useful to voice his plea. He began to moan. His belly tightened with pangs of desperation.

* * *

He felt like he was falling backward, tumbling head over heels through the past. At first, there was the memory of his father's smile and a hug from his mother, followed by a flood of childhood moments. He remembered once he had stumbled and scuffed his knee. When his father had reached to help him, he had refused and ran ahead so no one would see him crying. One night he had snuck to the kitchen and eaten more than his share of a pie. When they asked about it, he lied and blamed it on a hungry mouse. Why hadn't he just told them the truth?

He remembered the many times when he knew he should have come out of his room and participated in the family gatherings, but instead, he had hidden, busying himself with games and books and projects so that he could be alone. How many moments had he given to good things at the wrong time, at the expense of what was better? How much family life had he missed?

He realized how alienated he had been in those moments from everyone who cared for him. He sensed the loss and emptiness of these decisions and began to weep. He sobbed convulsively, regurgitating years of emotional poison that he had harbored and ignored. His guilt and his anger at his own foolishness brought him to the pit of his past and confronted him with the monster that lived within him.

The revelation of his individual acts stung bitterly, but they were not what startled and saddened him the most; it was that the very center of his heart was filled with *self*. He had thought that he was a good person, but he had cared for others only when it was convenient or necessary—never by choice. He had had no proactive compassion for the broken. He had never expressed true thankfulness to the One who made him.

A new resolve welled up within him. Gratitude poured out, mixed with the acknowledgment of his failures and offenses. As his heart raged, he felt cooling waves of forgiveness. Where self-condemnation had been, a cleansing flood now erupted. With each new set of painful revelations, a new surge of healing washed over him. When he felt that his emotions were fully expended, he would sigh with relief like a man gasping for air, only to have the next round of catharsis begin in a deeper place in his soul and drag up more debris.

His emotional reservoir, which he had kept so carefully sealed for so many years, was filled to overflowing with love and, finally, completely burst. He felt like he was flying, like a *fei yu* who had just broken the surface of the water and discovered that an entirely new world existed.

CHAPTER 26

THE ESSENCE

Garth awoke abruptly at the sound of a shout. He saw that Mel's hammock was empty and heard a *splash* from above. Clambering out of his hammock, he woke the others with his grunting, bellowing breaths and his thunderous footsteps out of the cabin. Rei saw the two abandoned hammocks and ran up on deck, followed by Polly. Mihoshi started after them but stopped, staring at the growing brightness of the map table.

Garth searched the deck. Mel was nowhere to be seen. The rising sound of crashing surf caught his attention, and he wheeled around to face the approaching reef.

"Where's Mel?" Rei asked.

"I dunno, maybe swimmin' away from that," Garth said, pointing at the reef.

Rei turned and said, "I'll try the wheel; you two search the water for Mel!" Garth and Polly nodded and began looking out in all directions across the rippling silver ocean.

"Mel! Mel, ya out there?" Garth cried out in a growing panic.

Rei tugged on the unresponsive wheel and tried in vain to adjust the sail. "Look under the surface; he may still be close by!"

Garth looked hurriedly over the side of the boat and, despite not being able to swim, began to work up the courage to jump in and continue the search.

Rei heard the breakers drawing dangerously close and could feel their mist. "We must pull in the anchor and reset it!" Rei bellowed over the growing noise. His glance turned suddenly to the hatch. "Have either of you seen my sister? If we must abandon ship, she needs to be on deck."

Garth and Polly shook their heads. Rei darted into the cabin. Garth and Polly began pulling in the anchor line, which, after a few feet of slack, became suddenly taut. "Rei!" Garth shouted toward the cabin at the top of his lungs. "The anchors snagged on somethin'!" The slack they had drawn up on deck snapped back into the water like a springing snake and pulled tight. The *New Day* lurched to a stop, less than twenty meters from the edge of the reef. Now defying the current, the vessel began to be tossed by the swells. The boat groaned and jerked, slipping closer to the reef as the anchor was jostled in its new position.

"It isn't going to hold!" Polly shouted, her eyes wide with fear.

Rei appeared back on deck. "We all need to get below!"

"We *need* to secure the ship!" Polly implored. "The anchor is slipping!" But he had already disappeared back into the cabin.

Garth put both of his hands on his forehead as his frustration reached its boiling point. "We're gonna crash on the reef, and he wants us hidin' in the cabin? Polly, let's drag 'em both on deck and swim fer it!" He ran down the steps, followed by Polly.

Stepping into the cabin, Garth suddenly stopped and stared at the shape hovering over the map table. There, slowly turning in the air, was a three-dimensional image of the cliffs and the waterfall. The island was transparent, allowing a view into its interior. The channel through the reef ran deep under the waterfall and led to a cave that pierced far into the island.

As soon as Polly's feet touched the cabin floor, the hatch snapped shut behind her. The boat immediately began to descend beneath the surface. The forward wall of the cabin shimmered and became transparent, providing a moonlit view of the reef. Dozens of fish scurried past their hull as the boat navigated in a loop that took it first toward the open ocean. Once the anchor was no longer under tension and had pulled free, the boat's mechanisms drew the anchor line back in. The boat then turned back toward the island and passed into the channel between the walls of the reef. The *New*

Day's unseen helmsman guided her gracefully around jagged edges and past shadowed caves.

"Let's see where this takes us," Rei said as he gazed out at the multicolored reef. An endless parade of fish swirled around them.

* * *

Mel sat with his head hunched between his knees. He rocked in a calming rhythm. His tear-swollen eyes noticed a change of hue through his closed eyelids. Suddenly, a swirling wind arose around him. He felt tiny particles begin to sting the back of his hands.

He opened his eyes and found himself sitting at the base of a towering cliff that curved to form a huge crater, its far side lost in the distance. The wind howled against his ears. He squinted to keep the sand from getting in his eyes. He tried to understand how he had been in a dark cave one minute and the next minute found himself in this massive amphitheater of stone. The rock wall behind him had been smoothed by years of whipping sand.

Turning back to the center of the crater, he was startled to see a hooded man standing just meters away. He could not see his face. His garb reminded him of the robe that Brother Josh wore. "Who are you?" Mel cried out, the roar of the wind smothering his words. The man began walking, and Mel followed.

Despite the din of the raging windstorm, Mel could hear the man speaking to him in a voice that resounded within him more deeply than his ears had ever heard. He could not understand the words but was comforted by their tone of a parent's soothing reassurances to a child who has awakened from a nightmare. He felt he could trust this man, remembering him from his dreams. He knew that he was being led to a life-changing experience.

The surface of the crater floor consisted solely of sand that stretched to the stone walls and for kilometers out of sight toward the far side. There were no living things anywhere to be seen.

They walked across the sand for what seemed like an hour,

and then Mel noticed a small, rectangular, striped tent jutting out of the sand. As they neared it, Mel saw that it was made of either tightly woven fabric or seamlessly stitched hides. From afar, it had appeared rather blandly colored, but the closer he came to it, the more colors he could discern. It was a simple design, with a small flap door and no windows. The nearer he drew to it, the more fiercely the windstorm blew. Mel felt a tingling sensation run down his spine. The hair on the back of his neck began to rise. A mixture of fear and great anticipation filled his heart.

At the door of the tent, the robed man turned and held a small leather pouch out to Mel. He lifted his voice above the din of the windstorm, and Mel heard him for the first time with his ears as well as his mind. "Follow the light of the *New Day*!"

Mel took the pouch and put it in his shirt pocket, reeling at the similarity between the man's statement and the final exhortation he had received from Gwyneth.

"Behold," the robed man continued, "the Essence of Life!" He flung back the flap of the entrance, stepped forward, and stood in the way. Mel tried to look past him but could not see anything beyond his robes. Mel tried several times to pass him, but each time the man shifted his stance and again blocked the entrance.

Mel, bewildered and frustrated, cried out, "What do you want me to do?"

"*Go through me*," was the impression that Mel received. It was another message that was not conveyed by mere language. Mel did not understand what the impression meant, but the same sense that had allowed him to trust the man's reassurances now confirmed to him that he needed to do what the man had said.

Rather than trying again to get around the hooded man, Mel opened his arms and hugged him, burying his head in the soft fabric of his robes. As he did so, he smelled a combination of perfumes and incenses immeasurably deeper and richer than the skill of a human artisan could achieve over innumerable ages. It was the aroma of timelessness itself.

Mel felt dizzy and was enveloped by the most profound and caring fatherly embrace that he had ever experienced. He felt as though he were falling yet was held tight. Mel abandoned himself and completely surrendered to the love that surrounded him.

* * *

The wail of the wind ceased immediately. He was inside the tent. He looked for the man that had led him here, but he was nowhere to be seen. Mel nodded, realizing that he did not need to search for him, as the man's unseen presence remained with him.

The interior of the tent was surprisingly large. From the outside, it had looked small, but inside, it was enormous, lit around the circumference by seven flaming lamps. The floors were covered with a soft, woven rug, dyed deep crimson, with earth-color patterns criss-crossing it like the thorny mesh of a blackberry patch. To Mel, the ceiling seemed impossibly high and appeared to be suspended by an exterior support system, as there were no visible beams or posts. The air of the room was infused with the fragrance of rosebuds and honeysuckle, mingled with a wisp of frankincense and jasmine.

From the floor to the ceiling in the middle of this circular hall, there was a glowing, pulsing presence. It was surrounded by countless swirling particles of light, which reached out like the arms of a living galaxy and moved like a gentle breeze through the room, brushing and fluttering the fabric of the walls. These particles increased in intensity and number the nearer to the pulsing presence at the center.

Mel did not know what else to do, so he began walking toward the presence, his footsteps soundless on the soft floor. There was a slight downward slope as he went. The closer he stepped, the less he could look upon the presence, as its blazing and piercing brilliance intensified as he drew near. It seemed to be breathing.

Finally, Mel passed through the innermost swirling particles of light and found himself standing directly before the presence. Its weight and brightness caused him to fall to his knees and shield his eyes. It emanated a rhythmic, soothing spirit that calmed his anxiety, but still, he dared not look directly at it. He felt like he was caught under the surf again, but with no fear of drowning, and each wave that passed over him filled him with a new surge of life. The waves of this presence filled his lungs with the purest air he had ever breathed. Never had he experienced such an utter lack of need and such freedom. He shook with joy as he felt the final barnacles of darkness get scraped off his soul. He understood now what the man had meant when he referred to the "Essence of Life."

For several minutes Mel simply lay motionless before the Essence. Then he was lifted to his feet, and a gentle touch raised his chin. He lifted his eyes upon that which moments before he had felt so unqualified to look upon. He was astounded at what he saw. Before him was a swirling vortex of shapes and colors, stars and galaxies, people and creatures. Shapes that he could not begin to comprehend moved in a perfect symphony of harmony and grace. He stretched out his arms and walked into the living vortex.

His immediate sensation was a total loss of control. Though tempted to fear, he chose to remain. The embrace was overwhelming and yet invigorating. It weighed on him like the crashing of a waterfall and lifted him like a geyser. He was held in a sacred presence of love and acceptance. Above all, he knew that he was completely forgiven and cleansed.

He began spinning and reaching out, trying to experience every aspect of the magnificent Essence. It was as if every second was his first breath of life. He sensed that there would be no end to these breaths while he dwelt in the Essence. This realization overwhelmed him with joy, and he danced and shouted in celebration, pouring out his love, devotion, and gratitude to the God of Life who was holding him close.

It was then that he saw that the tent was filled with other beings. Some were reveling like him, and some were bowing and trembling. Others were still walking the gentle slope toward the Essence with bewildered looks on their faces. Compassion welled up within him, and he felt impelled to call out. "Don't be afraid! There is only life here!" he shouted.

But those who were still approaching could not see or hear him. He realized that just as it had been up to him to pass through the man and enter the tent and approach the Essence, these others were deciding for themselves how closely they would approach and how tightly they would embrace the source of light. Mel rejoiced, knowing that every person who entered the tent partook in the Essence of Life. He watched with exuberance as the boldest souls drew the nearest to the Essence and surrendered to it, allowing themselves to be engulfed in perfect love.

* * *

The *New Day* continued along the channel through the reef toward the passage beneath the waterfall. The friends in the cabin could hear the crashing water approaching like a relentless stampede. A churning cloud of bubbles lay ahead, obscuring what was beyond. "Hold on!" Rei encouraged the others. "These currents will be strong!"

As they slipped into the frothing mass, the *New Day* listed back and forth, caught between the channel's current and the force of the waterfall. They swung violently in their hammocks for a minute, and then the boat leveled out and ascended to the surface. They saw that they were behind the waterfall and had emerged in the middle of a cavern. The cabin door opened, and the walls immediately became opaque. Polly rushed up the stairs.

The sun was just rising. It shone through the waterfall, filling the cave with crimson, gold, and turquoise light that rippled on the cavern walls. The skeletal remains of former adventurers and their shattered vessels lay strewn on the shore within the cave. Rei jumped off and, with a rope, secured the boat to an outcropping of rock. The others followed him ashore. As they examined this grim tomb of man and vessel, they noticed a fresh set of shoe prints in the sand, leading deeper into the cave.

"Mel's shoes!" Polly shouted with joy over the roar of the waterfall. Rei jumped back onto the boat and emerged moments later, holding two lanterns. He lit them with a box of matches and took the lead, following the tracks. Garth held the other lantern and followed at the back of the group.

Ten minutes later, Rei found Mel lying flat and unconscious.

"Mel!" Polly cried out and knelt beside him. He did not respond to her cry and lay utterly motionless. Rei felt Mel's neck for a pulse. Polly pulled on Rei's sleeve, asking rapidly, "Is he all right? Is he alive?"

"I can feel no pulse, but he is still warm," Rei answered with a puzzled expression. "I see no breath, but he still has color."

"Oh, Mel!" Polly moaned. "Don't die, please don't die. Not like this! We need you!" She bent over him, sobbing.

Garth stood off to the side, feeling somewhat useless. "Well, why don't we make a fire and dry him out a bit?" Not waiting for a response, he turned with his lantern and ran back to the entrance cavern, gathered wood from among the flotsam, and rushed back to the others. Fifteen minutes after they had found Mel deep in the cave, a warming fire was burning near him.

Mihoshi saw Polly's distress and was on the verge of tears for her sake. She knelt beside her and spoke in reverent tones. "He's resting. His life is in the hands of the Essence, the One who knows what is best for him. Don't be afraid, Polly, all is well."

Polly lifted her tear-stained face and frowned, shaking her head. "What are you talking about?" she asked between sobs. "And what... what is the Essence?" She looked pleadingly towards Rei. "Do you know what she means?"

Rei looked with pity at Polly's flow of tears. "It might be difficult for you to understand right now. What is happening to Mel is a mystery even to those who have experienced it. Mihoshi is at peace with this, and I must yield to her discernment."

"What are you guys talking about?" Polly's eyes widened, holding Mel's limp hand. "Can't you see what's happening here? Our friend needs help!"

Rei nodded in agreement. "But the help he needs is far beyond anything that we can do. I agree with my brother Garth; we should keep him comfortable and wait."

Garth beamed with pride. "Gee, thanks, Rei. I ain't never been called summons brother 'afore. I got no close kin at home, and—"

"*Before*, Garth!" Polly blurted out in agitation as she used her hands to scoop together a pile of the passageway's sparse sand. "I have never been called someone's brother *before*!" She gently lifted Mel's head and pushed the sand under, then rested his head on the makeshift pillow. She turned back to Rei. "Wait for what?"

"For him to return, if it is the will of the Essence," Mihoshi answered for her brother. She looked compassionately at Polly for several seconds. "Polly, you believe in God, do you not? You were raised by your aunt and uncle, and when you were young, they taught you to go to church."

Polly did not remember telling this to Mihoshi and began to feel nervous. "Did you talk to Mel about this?"

"No," Mihoshi replied, "but there are many things that do not have to be spoken to be known." She paused as a means of communicating to Polly that her intent was not to attack her. "May I ask you a question?" Mihoshi continued.

Polly reluctantly nodded.

"What exactly did you learn at church?" Mihoshi asked. "A set of rules? A proper way to speak and to pray and to act? Do you think that this is why you were created? So that God could judge how well you performed a set of religious customs? And so He could condemn you if your deeds did not measure up? That ancient lie has been one of the most destructive acts of darkness ever perpetrated against humanity. It results in an extremely poor understanding of God's love. May I continue?"

Polly nodded assent and muttered sarcastically, "I guess I have nothing better to do while I *wait*!"

Mihoshi smiled kindly. "The Essence I spoke of is the Eternal One. He is infinite, yet He allows Himself to be perceived by mortal and limited beings. The spiritual dimension can be accessed only through great humility and trust or, more rarely, through an act of great sacrifice. His ways go far beyond our five senses and require us to submit our wills to His, which is why many never respond, although He calls everyone."

"Calls?" Polly questioned.

"He invites us to know Him and to participate with Him in His plans for this world and for eternity."

"You're talking about God and going to heaven, right?" Polly asked, intrigued by Mihoshi's statements. "I thought if we were good people, then we'd go to heaven."

"That is the other great misconception," Mihoshi replied. "Everyone wants to think of himself as good, but only God is good. And we cannot share in His goodness unless we allow Him to take the throne of our lives. Otherwise, that throne is occupied by self, and we are unprepared for eternity with Him. Though heaven is experienced after death, its holiness confronts us even now. Our time in our flesh could end at any moment. If we refuse to reconcile with the Essence and refuse to live in His presence during this brief lifetime, why would we choose differently when it would mean being with Him for eternity? Our choices for now are our choices for eternity. The moment we yield to His loving call is the moment we begin eternal life!"

Polly did not remember ever posing the exact questions Mihoshi was addressing but nonetheless knew that these were answers she had been yearning for. She felt like she had been picked up and placed at the edge of a canyon, which, until now, she had only ever viewed from a distance. Directly in front of her was the one narrow bridge across, its support structure obscured by fog. Most pressingly, she knew that the moment to decide whether to step out onto the bridge had come. "How could anyone know the things you're talking about?" Polly asked plaintively of Mihoshi, and then looked to Garth for support.

He raised his eyebrows and meekly shrugged. "I dunno. It's all new ta me."

Mihoshi rested her hand on Polly's arm. The only sound in the passage was the crackling of firewood. Mihoshi looked deeply into Polly's eyes. "*Yield.*"

"What?"

Mihoshi took Polly and Rei's hands, closed her eyes, and appeared to be focusing intently.

Polly did not know what to do. She looked to Rei, who was resting his other hand on Mel's forehead and speaking below his breath. Polly's heart ached, and her whole body began to shiver as though she were riding in a buggy on a washboard road.

Garth walked over and took Polly's free hand. "Aw heck, I'm willin' ta give this a go too. What harm could come from it?" He followed Mihoshi and Rei's example and closed his eyes.

After ten minutes of resisting the heaviness that had settled on her, Polly allowed her spirit to relax and her eyes to close. At first, she was aware only of her own breathing. She felt tempted to shake off the whole experience and get practical, but instead, she chose to surrender more to the presence tugging on her. She began to perceive Mihoshi's breath and Rei's soft words over Mel. Garth mumbled a nearly indiscernible phrase that reminded her of a child's bedtime prayer.

She began to let go in her spirit and had a sudden sensation like she was being lifted. Her fear stirred again, and she chose again to yield. Her heart was taken as by a strong wind.

Vivid images sprang to her mind, in which she was emerging from a thick fog and could vaguely see the form of someone dancing. As the clouds evaporated, the look on the person's face chased all her fears away. She reached out and shouted, "Mel!"

At first, the dancing figure of Mel did not seem to hear her, but then as she continued yielding her heart and drawing nearer, he stopped and turned toward her. "Polly, you're here!"

Just then, a log on the fire let out a loud crackle. Polly opened her eyes in surprise and saw Mel sitting upright and staring at her and the others.

"Incredible!" he shouted with a smile. "You won't believe what just happened!"

CHAPTER 27

THE GLOWING DARK

He greeted each of them with a deep hug. Mel's friends recounted their fear upon discovering that he had disappeared from the boat and described their hurried attempts to avoid crashing on the reef. Mel was relieved to learn that his efforts with the anchor had bought them time. They listened with fascination as Mel described waking in the cave and exploring the passageway where they now sat. None of the five of them could explain how Mel had survived the estimated ten minutes underwater from the moment he dove in after the anchor to the moment he woke in the cavern.

He was reserved in his descriptions of his personal reckoning and his encounter with the Essence, summarizing that he sensed he would never be the same.

Mihoshi kept silent and watched Mel intently as he spoke, a curious smile on her face.

Polly was boisterous and boasted of what she had just experienced. In a puzzled tone, she described her strange vision of Mel dancing. "He seemed to be floating as he danced. I've never seen such joy."

Mel smiled and kept his peace. He looked at his friends with misty eyes and thanked them profusely for their concern and their care while he was unconscious.

Rei nodded respectfully to Mel. "Did you gain any insight into what we are to do next?" he asked with expectant eyes.

Mel touched the outside of his shirt pocket, recognizing the bulge of the small leather pouch that the robed man had given to him, and smiled broadly. "Yes, as a matter of fact, I did," he answered at an altogether unrushed pace. "I was given something, along with a hint that it's to be used aboard the *New Day*. I believe we'll then be taken to our next destination."

Rei's eyebrows lifted. "Given? Hinted? By whom? I have seen no other footprints in this cave."

Mel smiled knowingly. "This isn't the kind of gift limited to a physical giver." He stood to his feet and started back down the passageway. "Perhaps I'll explain more later about what happened while I was unconscious, but for now, it's time for us to get underway."

* * *

Rei untied the boat and followed the others belowdecks. Garth sat in his hammock, fidgeting with excitement. "This is great! Whatever's comin' next, I bet it's gonna be a humdinger!"

Polly rolled her eyes at Garth's slang, eliciting a grin from him.

When they were all gathered in the cabin, Mel withdrew the small leather pouch, from which he poured a tiny amount of a fine-grained, sand-like substance onto the map table. Nothing happened.

After a few moments, Polly said, "With everything that was happening, are you certain you heard correctly? Or maybe you need to use more of it?"

"Patience often yields great treasure," Mel answered.

"Of course it does," Polly grumbled under her breath.

The glowing shape of a hand appeared on the flat surface of the map table in front of Mel. He glanced resolutely around at each of his friends and placed his hand on the table.

Polly watched the cabin door, expecting it to shut, but it did not. Her brow furrowed in confusion.

A moment later, four more glowing hands appeared around the edges of the table. The friends glanced at each other in alarm.

Polly balked. "I know what that means, and I'm not okay with it. For one, how does the boat know how many of us are aboard?"

Garth looked at the table askance. "Anybody at's kicked by a mule stays in the cave a' death, I figure." Polly stared at him in disbelief and shook her head.

Mel smiled reassuringly at his friends. "You have nothing to fear. I suspect that we are about to be taken to a secure location. You have all proven yourselves to be friends of Delemni."

Rei grinned with a sudden realization. "It is like the knights of the Round Table raising their swords in a gesture of solidarity."

Mel nodded in affirmation. "Something like that."

Rei and Mihoshi calmly rested their hands on the table, followed by a wincing and hesitant Garth, and finally Polly, who took a deep breath and quickly touched the final space.

The cabin door immediately shut, and the *New Day* began to descend. Mel withdrew his hand, followed by the others. The sides of the cabin glowed dimly and, together with the forward structure, became transparent. The boat dove down for several seconds and then angled slightly forward in a steep descent. The passage grew dark as they sank deep into the foundations of the island. Polly looked fearfully out at the pitch blackness.

"It's all right," Mel said consolingly. "This boat was designed by minds far wiser than ours, and she has never disappointed us yet."

Polly sighed. "Still, I'm not sure I like the idea of diving into a pit in a boat that steers itself."

"Entering the cabin when we were drifting toward the reef was an act of trust, and the ship saved our lives," Rei reminded her.

Polly grimaced. "Garth and I were storming into the cabin to drag you two back on deck so we could all swim for it."

Rei let out a long belly laugh. "That may be the case, but you were guided, nonetheless. And I imagine you're thankful."

Polly stared in wonder at the now shimmering, luminescent colors of the passage walls rushing by them. "Mel, do you have any idea where we're going and what we'll do when we get there?"

Mel's mind raced with ideas and impressions. Finally, he said, "From my lessons, and what I read in the compendium, I suspect we're going to one of the great libraries of my people, most likely the Telemai Caeli."

"Ooh, that's why it's such an inaccessible spot," Polly groaned.

"Indeed," Mel said and turned to his friends. "We would all do well to remember that the knowledge the Caeli contains is much too dangerous for just anyone to access."

"So, you're sayin' if we see any buttons or levers, we should try 'em out?" Garth asked with a wink.

Mel smirked. "It's good to know that someone has been listening," he answered good-naturedly. "Just be careful."

Rei looked closely at the intensifying multicolored light of the passage walls. "At first, I thought we might be in a long-dead lava tube, but now I suspect that this tunnel is not natural."

Just then, the boat ceased its downward momentum, proceeded forward at an even keel for several minutes, and finally rose a short distance. The light from outside grew markedly brighter just before the boat surfaced, and the hull again became opaque. The hatch opened, and an iridescent glow filled the cabin.

They stepped on deck and saw that they were inside of a massive cavern the size of a city. Light emanated from every path and corridor and from the walls of every structure within the Caeli. They saw that the ceiling of the cavern was unsearchably high and hidden from view, except for thousands of bejeweled lights that shone from far above like stars in the night sky. The cavern's perimeter was vast, stretching for many kilometers.

The *New Day* steered itself to a dock carved out of solid marble. "Well, we're here," Mel said in hushed tones. "Let's go find what we've come all this way for."

CHAPTER 28

THE CAELI

As they moored the boat, Mel counted many other docks in the surrounding area. He wondered if the subterranean harbor had once bustled with activity and if it still did on occasion. In the distance was another moored boat, which looked like an older version of the *New Day*.

The group took the main path, which led away from the docks and followed the perimeter of the Caeli. The size of the cavern was accentuated by the antiquity and craftsmanship of its décor. Hundreds of immense columns, sculpted in the images of ancient warriors and Vysards, stood like silent sentinels throughout the expanse, stretching upward into the void that hid the ceiling.

They could see, reaching for kilometers along the walls of the cavern, a row of towering alcoves beyond a perimeter moat, which was filled with what looked like molten silver. Lining the alcove walls were small vaults like those in the chamber below his father's study. Each compartment's front appeared to have been carved from solid onyx and shined as though it had just been polished.

On the near side of the moat, across from each alcove, was a unique symbol, set in a one-meter-diameter golden plate.

"Mel," Rei inquired, "do you understand these symbols?"

Mel looked closely at the nearest one. "It seems vaguely familiar, but I'm not sure. I don't see a way across to any of these alcoves. Let's take a look toward the center."

They turned toward the middle of the cavern and began climbing a long succession of stairs that were two meters wide, two meters deep, and a half meter tall. The stairs had been carved out of solid rock and were highly polished. Etched into them were intricate petroglyphs depicting people going about their daily activities. Some were harvesting, some were preparing for war, and others were celebrating what looked like a national event.

Mel stopped, kneeled, and touched an image of a mother clutching a young child to her chest as she ran through a fiery hailstorm. The floor felt surprisingly warm and smooth.

Mel remained on his knees, and a beautiful bittersweetness overtook him. Mihoshi saw what had caught his attention. She placed a hand on his shoulder. "We are reminded that you have not been alone in your grief."

Mel nodded. "This might even be of me and my mother, for all we know. Either way, it is a day of disaster... and sacrifice."

"Could this be the fall of Delemni?" Polly asked, peering over Mel's shoulder.

"It could be. Or one of the many other disasters that seem to follow my people everywhere." Mel stood. "I could spend days looking at these etchings, but we should keep moving."

They reached the top of the stairs and saw that the path split off in several directions. Low, open structures with smaller collections of compartments were scattered along seemingly innumerable corridors.

"Do you know exactly what you are looking for?" Rei inquired. Like the others in the group, he was beginning to feel persistent hunger pangs but was committed to finding the end of Mel's quest.

"I do. But this Caeli is much larger than I had anticipated; now, I'm not so sure where to look."

"Has any clue spoken of its location within the Caeli? Perhaps there is some way we can begin to narrow our search?" Rei persisted, calmly assessing their daunting task.

Mel recalled the symbol on the Abico vault that had brought about the demise of his tutor, Jora. Mel took a deep breath, calming himself amid the jarring recollection. "There is a symbol for the Abico vault, and it looks like this." He traced the design of the symbol in the air for the others to see.

"Do you know what it represents?" Mihoshi asked.

"The long, slanted 'Y' on the left signifies our will or our choices. The upper two slashes are the first letter in the Akkadian word for 'death.' The lower portion is a symbol of prosperity."

Mel looked soberly at each of his friends, who were all listening attentively. "I must reiterate the need to be extremely careful with these vaults. They are rigged so that anyone who doesn't possess the key to open them will be repelled violently."

"Are you sure you're ready?" Polly asked in concern.

"I won't know until I touch the vault. It's been like this all along. Each lesson helped prepare me to receive the next. There's a painful jolt if you approach a vault prematurely."

"Jora must've felt one, but he kept going?" Polly questioned.

"Maybe his pride drove him to deny the warning."

Mel glanced at each of the paths leading further into the Caeli and saw nothing particularly unique down any of them. He turned to the others. "Why don't we split up and see if that speeds this along? I'll take this path directly ahead, and Rei and Garth, you can go that way, and Mihoshi and Polly, the other way. Just give a shout if you see something like the symbol I showed you. Meet back here in half an hour!" The others nodded in agreement and split off down their designated paths.

Rei and Garth ran beside a stream of molten silver, glancing over scores of compartments full of the untold treasures and unsearchable knowledge of a lost civilization.

Mihoshi and Polly proceeded in the opposite direction at a steady pace, their eyes darting about at the expansive array of vaults and symbols.

Mel saw hundreds of vaults that were not familiar and, out of curiosity, touched one. Not feeling a shock, he opened it slowly. There, in a small round dish, lay a cache of seeds, the word "Tonndiberry" etched into its glass lid. He remembered that it was a variety of fruit that had passed into obsolescence four millennia ago. Closing the vault and stepping back to take a second look at the surrounding symbols, he suddenly caught the aroma of fresh-baked bread and noticed a large doorway standing ajar ten meters down the path.

* * *

Several minutes later, the five friends had reunited after hearing joyful shouting from Mel.

They stepped through the large doorway into a breathtaking banquet hall. The rows of ornate hardwood tables looked sufficient to seat hundreds of people. The walls were hung with paintings and tapestries that depicted Delemni in its full glory. Prominent among them was a massive woven map of the islands of Delemni. Surrounding it were depictions of the lush landscapes and varied climates of the islands, including many undersea biomes. Elsewhere on the walls were images of cities built to sit half in the sea and half on the land. Nearby paintings featured fleets of submarines working deep beneath the ocean's surface, mining mountains on the seafloor. Mel glanced over the images and marveled at how much of the life of Delemni had taken place below sea level.

Mihoshi stopped suddenly in front of a painting of a lavish park interspersed with magnificent fountains. In this setting a wedding was taking place, featuring a husband and wife in ornate clothing, accompanied by a crowd of guests in formal wear.

There were paintings of zoos housing animals that had long since gone extinct. One such image included several colossal reptiles that Polly immediately remembered from the paleontology books in her library. She hesitated before the painting, and her head tilted with incredulity. "Wait a minute. They had dinosaurs in their zoos?"

Mel stepped beside her and looked closely at the image. "It looks like they were employing a great deal of technology to give these animals a comfortable home. Perhaps these were among the last living." They exchanged a somber look, and Mel continued across the banquet hall. As he walked, he said over his shoulder, "A lot depends on who writes the history."

At the far end was an enormous kitchen with shelves that were nearly overflowing with food containers filled to the brim.

As they walked toward the kitchen, Rei laughed. "And I thought that we would need to return to the boat for a meal!"

"I have to apologize for not looking after our needs first," Mel said. "I've been driving us too forcefully. You have all sacrificed so much comfort and safety to help me. When I discovered this chamber, I knew we needed to take a moment before continuing the search. The kitchen is full of foods from all over the world, likely stored here for when the Vysards and their friends visit."

"Indeed," Rei affirmed, in awe at the variety and quantities on the many kitchen shelves. Some of the transparent containers had condensation or frost on the inside surfaces, in accordance with the temperature needs of the food. "There is enough here that, after we find the vault, we could spend a lifetime in the Caeli, discovering new treasures of information with Mel-san's guidance and approval."

Garth rubbed his stomach in agreement. "Man, howdy! I'd be a'right with that. I'm so hungry I could eat a gator."

Polly rolled her eyes. "Have you ever even seen an alligator? I suppose they're all over the hills outside of Cooperton?" she asked with a smirk.

"Fine then, a reg'lar old 'orse."

The others wrinkled their noses in disgust.

Garth smiled and opened his eyes wide. "What're we waitin' fer? I'm starved!"

"*Starving*, you're *starving*," Polly said with a smile. Garth smiled in return, loving the attention.

Unbidden, Mihoshi began taking containers to the table nearest to the kitchen. As she unsealed the first of them, it emitted a hissing sound and a gentle burst of air.

Mel paused. "Does that sound familiar to anyone else?"

Polly's eyes went wide with amazement. "The cabinets on the *New Day*!"

Mel nodded.

Mihoshi continued opening sealed containers and putting their contents on the crystal plates that were already in place on the table. The food in every container was as fresh as the moment it was prepared or picked. There were mangos, watermelons, guavas, nectarines, passion fruit, bananas, blueberries, pears, and figs of several varieties, as well as warm, fluffy pan breads that tasted like they had just been baked and a seemingly endless variety of prepared dishes.

With each newly unsealed container, Mel became increasingly astonished. "There is no way all of this could have been prepared or gathered so recently that it's still this fresh. Somehow, the cabinets on the boat and these containers are sealed and pressurized in a way that preserves the food in perfect condition."

"Amazing!" Polly exclaimed. "That would explain why our provisions stayed as fresh as the day we brought them aboard."

The others nodded in similar amazement as they began taking bites of the highest quality food they had ever tasted.

Polly took five water glasses to an earthen sink in the corner and began to fill them. "If I didn't know we were underneath a volcanic island, about as far down as at the bottom of the ocean, I would've thought someone was expecting us," she joked. She tasted the water and giggled. "It's sweet!"

"Man, what I wouldn't give fer some pork 'n beans 'bout now," Garth said, searching through the food stores.

"Maybe this will do instead," Rei called out. He had found some dried, smoked fish and handed pieces to Mel and Garth.

As Garth bit off a salty chunk, he closed his eyes, savoring it as he chewed. "Mmm mmm mmm! This's some mighty fine jerky!"

As they settled at the table to eat the food they had collected, Mel turned to the others. "I know we weren't out searching for the vault for long but did anyone discover anything?" he asked.

"I did," Mihoshi said. All eyes turned to her. "Though it is not what Mel-san was seeking." From a fold of her kimono, she withdrew a scroll, which was inscribed with Japanese characters, and handed it to Mel.

"This was sitting in the open?" Rei asked in disbelief.

"It was inside of a vault," Mihoshi replied.

"Mihoshi!" Rei answered gruffly. "How could you be so rash after what Mel has told us?"

Mihoshi shrunk back at Rei's rebuke. She bowed her head to Mel, staying in that posture as she spoke. "I have transgressed," she said in a soft, repentant voice. "Please accept my apology. I saw a compartment bearing the Japanese character for 'Empires,' and the vault opened without mishap."

Mel smiled and laid his hand on the top of her head. "You are full of surprises! If you could open the vault safely, then I know that you are worthy to read it. You may do so now if you wish. We'll need to return it before we leave." He handed the scroll back to Mihoshi, who immediately unrolled it and began to read.

Rei sat beside his sister and read the scroll with her. After several minutes, he looked around at the others in excitement. "This is amazing! This scroll appears to have been updated no more than five months ago."

"Hmm," Mel intoned amidst a bite of cinnamon flatbread.

Polly put down a nectarine she was eating. "That reminds me. This place is extremely isolated, yet the few plants I've seen look like they were trimmed this morning. Does someone live here?"

Mel shrugged his shoulders. "If there's technology to perfectly preserve food, I suppose it's also possible that the plants have been treated to maintain their condition indefinitely. I don't think we'll be able to answer these questions while we're sitting here. Let's eat and go back out to look."

Rei nodded in agreement. Garth frowned.

"Will we split up again?" Polly asked.

Mel shook his head. "I've been thinking. Every step of this

quest has been a journey. Nothing has been immediate, close, or easy. I suspect that what we're looking for will be on the other side of the Caeli, furthest from the docks."

* * *

Along their way across the Caeli, they came to a luxurious garden that lay at its center. Mel led them through it, admiring the tremendous variety of plants and the alluring scents of innumerable flowers. A sprawling, five-meter-high trellis of vines with colorful blossoms stood in the middle of the garden.

An array of meticulously trimmed tiny trees dotted the edges of the main walkways. "Bonsai trees!" Rei exclaimed. "Very difficult to cultivate. It takes decades of constant maintenance to train them into miniaturized forms."

"You've seen trees like these before?" Polly asked.

"In my homeland, we have many gardens with bonsai trees, places of quietude where we would go and just listen."

"You listened to the quiet?" Polly asked skeptically.

Rei smiled. "It can speak volumes to the heart and mind."

Polly was outwardly incredulous, but in her thoughts and feelings, she knew that Rei was speaking the truth. She was sensing the blessing of peace for herself as they strolled through the garden. It had been a long time since any of them had experienced such peace. They reached the other side of the garden and gave a collective sigh as they left it behind and continued onward.

* * *

As they neared the far side of the Caeli, Mel stepped a few meters ahead of the others, walking faster in expectation, eager to see if his suspicion would prove correct.

As he passed the edge of a bubbling, silver lake, he glimpsed something out of the corner of his eye that brought him to an immediate halt. Where Mel stood at the shore, inlaid in a one-meter-tall golden placard among many other symbols, was the symbol of the Abico vault.

Across the lake were two columns, the first hundred meters of which were sculpted in the shapes of ancient Hebrew warriors, their surfaces covered with vaults. Above the sculpted warriors, the columns were smooth and round, disappearing up into the unguessable heights of the Caeli's ceiling.

The others caught up to Mel. Mihoshi stepped next to him and saw the Abico symbol. "Your goal is near."

Mel scratched his head as he looked across the lake at the towering columns. "It's most likely at the top of one of those warriors, across a lake of molten silver. I understand that this shouldn't be easy, but why does it have to be so challenging?"

Mihoshi spoke softly. "Things of great worth are often acquired through great challenge."

Polly, feeling anxious for Mel, rolled her eyes at Mihoshi's proverb. Garth saw her expression and stifled a chuckle.

Polly glanced at the sheer vertical walls on the left and right sides of the lake and then at the expanse of bubbling liquid. "Now, let's figure out how to get across."

* * *

Rei jogged the path for a kilometer in either direction and found no routes that led toward the other side of the lake. Polly searched along the shore, looking for a boat. Garth wandered off, hoping to find scraps of metal or anything that would be useful for constructing their own boat.

After an hour of searching, the five of them had discovered nothing to help them get across. Mel put his hand to his forehead, thinking deeply. He went over in his mind everything that had led him to this point.

Mihoshi sat still with her eyes closed as though listening to an inaudible voice. Suddenly she stood and walked to the base of the placard. She bent and looked closely at it, then called to Mel.

Mel hurried to her. "What is it? What did you find?"

She pointed at the placard's base. "There is an inscription here. Can you read it?"

Mel leaned close and scrutinized the inscription, which was written in Sumerian. "Yes! Yes, I can. It reads,

> *Through raging sea and death's door*
> *The narrow gate shall go*
> *To the one whose world is inside out*
> *The narrow path shall flow*
> *A touch of sand from holy grout*
> *The narrow door will glow*
> *And light the broken heart into*
> *Secrets yet untold."*

Polly squinted with skepticism. "Um, how does an inscription in another language rhyme when translated to English?"

Mel chuckled. "That's exactly the kind of thing my father would do, just to give it another layer of design. He likely anticipated that I'd be reading it aloud to others."

"What are we to learn from the inscription?" Mihoshi asked.

Mel pondered it for a moment. "This Caeli can only be accessed by the sea, and the door to it is through that raging waterfall, a 'door of death.' This cavern is a world inside out. Who could have imagined that a place like this exists? As for the path, I don't know what it's referring to. And the rest is a mystery."

Mihoshi's eyes grew wide. "Sand from holy grout, Mel-san! Is there more of the substance that was sprinkled on the compendium?"

Mel nodded and took the small bag from his pocket. He called loudly for the others. As soon as they were all standing together on the shore, Mel took a pinch from the bag and sprinkled it on the edge of the silver liquid.

Immediately, the entire surface of the lake began to boil intensely. They backed away and waited, watching as the liquid frothed and became iridescent. Finally, the activity subsided, and a narrow, ivory-colored path emerged from beneath the surface, leading to the opposite shore.

"Wow!" Polly exclaimed.

"I should go first," Mel cautioned.

He stepped onto the ivory path and felt that it was solid, then walked to the halfway point and motioned for the others to follow.

As they stepped cautiously onto the narrow path, the boiling liquid's intensity again began to escalate. When they were ten meters from the shore, Rei motioned for them to stop and saw that while they were standing still, the boiling did not continue to increase. As they resumed moving forward, the activity of the liquid again worsened. Finally, as the molten silver began splashing onto the edges of the path near their feet, they stopped. Polly squealed with fear and clung to Garth. Mel motioned his friends back. "I'm sorry; the four of you need to stay on the shore. It seems that I'm meant to cross alone." The others reluctantly turned and hurried back. The moment they were again standing on the shore, the lake reverted to a gently simmering silver.

"Call out if anything occurs!" Polly shouted to Mel, who was nearing the far side of the lake.

CHAPTER 29

THE ABICO VAULT

"What now?" Polly asked as they sat on the shore and watched Mel move further into the distance.

"We stay until he returns," Rei replied. "At least one of us, perhaps while the others explore."

"I will stay and alert you when he returns," Mihoshi informed the others. Her expression as she stared vigilantly across the lake betrayed an additional motive for staying behind.

Polly stood. "I volunteer to explore. But I sure don't want to go alone. I can't help but feel that we're being watched."

Garth nodded. "This place gives me the heebie-jeebies."

Rei laughed. "Perhaps it is the sentinels," he suggested, motioning at the towering columns throughout the Caeli. "Speaking of which, there are three nearby that caught my eye." He peered toward a trio of columns that were each as wide as a wagon and elaborately portrayed three samurai standing back-to-back in battle-ready posture. "We won't be far," he reassured Mihoshi. They exchanged nods, and he and Polly and Garth set off toward the columns.

Mihoshi patiently watched Mel. After a moment, she closed her eyes and bowed her head and began to speak under her breath.

* * *

Mel continued across the narrow ivory path and reached the far side of the lake. As he stepped onto the cobblestone shore, the lake hissed and sputtered again, and the path submerged. Though star-

tled by this, he quickly shook off his consternation, sensing that he
had better keep his nerve for whatever challenges lay ahead.

He approached the two warrior-shaped columns and saw that
there was an inscription in Hebrew at the base of each, one on the
left column and one on the right:

THE LIGHT APPEARS ∞ THE PAST IS BLACK
FORWARD ONLY ∞ NEVER BACK

Mel gulped at the riddle's implication of a point of no return.
He glanced at where the ivory path had been and saw Mihoshi on
the shore, her head bowed. He knew that he was not alone.

Refocusing on the columns, he wondered where to begin. Some
of the symbols on the compartments looked familiar, while a great
many others did not. The Abico vault was nowhere in sight. His
throat constricted as he fought the first pangs of panic, and then
he remembered the bag of sand that had helped him thus far and
pulled it from his pocket. He discovered that there was little left,
and if he used it, there would not be any remaining to again raise
the ivory path for his return after opening the vault.

He wanted to cry out for Mihoshi's advice but restrained himself. He knew this was his choice to make. He had not come this
far to fail. Finally, he had reached the crux of his quest. There was
no giving up. He committed himself to the task and poured out the
rest of the grains of sand in equal portions at the bases of the two
columns. He stepped back and waited. After the longest several
seconds of his life, a vault began to glow nearly eighty meters above
him on the column to the left. He groaned inwardly.

Walking around the base of the column, he saw that there were
no stairs or ladders. The only way to reach the vault would be by
somehow climbing the sculpted surface of the column, which at first
glance appeared impossible. He slumped to the ground and buried
his head in his hands.

Then he remembered his father's encouraging voice, echoing

through his countless lessons. He saw his father's smile as he had waved goodbye as he left on the journey from which he had never returned. And Mel remembered the all-encompassing embrace of the Essence, a flicker of which he had continued to feel in his heart ever since the vision. He leaned back and opened his eyes to look out again at the breathtaking Caeli. He knew it was already his responsibility to safeguard this.

While surveying the immensity of the cavern, his gaze turned upward, and the handles of the vaults above him caught his eye. Most of the handles were smooth and thin, but several were thick and angular and appeared to form a path leading towards his objective. When he had first examined the columns, all the handles had looked the same. He guessed that these had changed when he had sprinkled out the remaining sand. He fixed his gaze upon the glowing vault and set his foot on the first knob while grasping the handle above him.

He began to climb. Compartment by compartment, he ascended, moving sometimes in a straight path and at other times diagonally, depending on the route provided by the handles.

He understood now why his father had insisted that they practice rock climbing on the cliffs below their home in Cooperton. He recalled how at first, he had slipped and fallen off into the soft sand. But gradually, his hands had grown stronger, and his sense of balance and decision-making had become more acute. He had learned to skip some of the easier handholds and to reach for those that were more ambitious. He had learned to focus on the goal, rather than on his circumstances, and had come to understand that accomplishing an objective would often require him to take tremendous risks.

When he had started climbing the Cooperton cliffs, he had practiced for months before attempting routes over ten meters high. On several occasions, the sand had not been nearly as soft as he would have liked. He had become so enamored with the challenge of the cliffs that he had often snuck out and climbed by himself. Several times he had gone out at night and practiced in the dark to refine his "feel" for the climb.

As he followed the path of the vault handles, he came to a point where he was on the opposite side of the column from where he had started, with no acceptable hold in sight. It was then, for the first time, that he looked down.

He suppressed a surge of panic as he perceived that he was now fifty meters up. The ground looked far away and as solid as steel. He dared not give in to his anxiety. Scanning the surface of the column, he realized that he had strayed above the route of ideal handles and needed to undo his last several moves, come down two meters, and traverse before resuming the ascent.

* * *

The three samurai-shaped columns had proven to be much larger and further away than they had seemed at first. Rei, Polly, and Garth had nearly traveled the intervening kilometer when they observed that the entire Caeli was beginning to grow noticeably darker. The light emanating from the floor and the walls was fading as if in imitation of the natural day and night cycle. They decided to turn back and find the lake before it became too dark to see.

Rei led them at a jog. "This artificial day and night must be what allows the plants to thrive as if they were on the surface."

"That's great for the plants!" Polly exclaimed. "But what about Mel? Do you think he'll be able to find his way in the dark?"

"Mel's got eyes like a cat's at night," Garth chimed in. "He'll be just fine."

In a manner that reminded them of the dwindling twilight after sunset, the fading light of the Caeli gave their surroundings a grey, ghostlike appearance. When they saw that the darkness was rapidly encroaching, they pushed themselves to a running pace.

* * *

They arrived at the lake and found Mihoshi on her knees, rocking back and forth.

"Has something happened?" Polly gasped.

Mihoshi opened her eyes and saw the near darkness enveloping them. "Oh my!"

"Where's Mel?" Polly asked insistently.

Mihoshi peered at the columns on the far shore, which were now shrouded in a thin, grey light. "Mel is climbing the column on the left. He went out of sight a half hour ago and had ascended one-third of the warrior. The vault is glowing, approximately eighty meters up," she said, pointing at the column.

Rei recognized the danger of Mel's situation and shook his head in dismay. "We must intercede," he said hurriedly.

Polly's anxiety flared at Rei's uncharacteristic expression of concern. "He wouldn't have started climbing unless he knew he could finish no matter what, right?"

"I doubt that he anticipated this circumstance."

"Well, what do you want to do to help him?"

"There is no more recourse available to us now than when he went on alone. Perhaps we will be shown an unforeseen means of assistance, and then we will act. In any situation, whether we know what to do or can do nothing, we should pray." Rei took Polly's hand and pulled her gently next to Mihoshi, and the three of them sat. "We need to appeal to God to protect our friend and give him supernatural abilities to find his way to a safe place."

Polly wrinkled her face in frustration. "I thought prayers were for things we hoped for or about things that will happen after we die, not for what we need right now! This is a *real* problem, and we need to *do* something!" Polly implored in alarm, beginning to panic.

"Polly," Rei said, "the Presence you experienced in the cave and who preserved Mel's life is not limited by our circumstances or our abilities. Our friend is not alone. If you wish, you may join us in requesting the help of the One who is with him on the column."

As Polly watched, Rei and Mihoshi began to appeal audibly to God, who they addressed as "Father" and spoke to as though He were sitting with them. They asked that He comfort and strengthen Mel and send angels to guide him.

Garth, who had little experience with prayer, sat quietly with his head bowed, secretly watching Polly's response.

After a minute of listening to the calm and deliberate prayers of Rei and Mihoshi, Polly bowed her head and closed her eyes.

* * *

Mel sensed the light beginning to dim and feared that he was experiencing impaired vision due to fatigue. When he realized that the Caeli was indeed growing dark, he reached deep within himself for every vestige of strength and calmness that he could summon. He found that he was dipping his bucket into an empty well. He knew the only way he would avoid panic would be to place his hope in the Essence that had faithfully guided him thus far. He chose to surrender to his fate.

Splayed across the surface of the sculpted column, he imagined himself to be a gecko on a granite wall. *Only a gecko could crawl out of this mess*, he thought to himself with a smile. His eyesight was no longer useful in what had become pitch blackness, but he could feel his way. There was no sign of the glowing Abico vault, but he knew that it must still be tens of meters above him.

He was struck with the sudden thought that if, along his route, he happened upon a vault that he was not ready to open, the simple act of using its handle for the climb could result in a painful shock or even in him being repelled while far above the ground. He dismissed this concern, knowing that his father would not have put such vaults along the route to the Abico. Remembering when he had strayed off the route just minutes before, he felt thankful that he had been spared from what might have occurred.

He resumed climbing. Each time he reached out, blindly flailing at the slick wall in the now total darkness, he miraculously found a vault handle that provided a tiny handhold or ledge to grasp. After a while, he could not tell if he was making more progress upwards or sideways. All he knew was that he could not allow himself to stop.

Inch by inch, he felt the route ahead, while in his mind's eye, he envisioned the cliffs back home during the blindness of a night climb and remembered the reassurance of his father's voice calling him onward from atop the precipice.

After what felt like hours, he finally reached up and discovered a wide ledge and was startled out of his dreamlike state. He pulled himself onto what he guessed must be the top of the sculpted section of the column.

Even as he lay safely on the hard, flat surface of the ledge, which in his state of exhaustion felt as comfortable as a feather bed, he was dismayed that he had somehow passed the Abico vault without realizing it. Had he diverged from the intended route? Had the vault ceased glowing? He had not been able to see any of the symbols on the vaults in the dark. He did not look forward to the struggle of climbing back down to find it, open it, and then return safely to the ground. He sighed, and his dismay was overwhelmed by a sense of relief at having reached a deep ledge where he could rest and perhaps even sleep. He surmised that the Caeli was on a twenty-four-hour light cycle and decided he would resume his search in the daylight. He closed his eyes and immediately fell asleep.

* * *

Mel woke as the light returned to the Caeli. His first glance down the side of the column confirmed that the ledge was indeed above the sculpted section. He realized that during his ascent, he had circled the column at least once, as he remembered climbing across the opposite side, and now he was on the front, above the face of the warrior. In the distance, the familiar corridors across the silver lake glowed with an increasing tangerine hue. He looked closely at the far shore and saw his friends sleeping.

Turning his attention again to the column, he stared in disbelief at the thirty meters of compartments below him, which appeared smooth and devoid of any usable holds. He scratched his head and tried to remember what the last meters had been like as he had climbed in the dark. The surface had been smooth, but he had always found holds, however infinitesimal, to use to pull himself forward.

At times, during that last leg of the climb, he had drifted dangerously close to unconsciousness. In each desperate moment, he had surrendered his fear and thought back to the lessons that had been drilled into his very fabric. Years before, when he had returned to his Cooperton home exhausted after his first few night climbs, he had pleaded with his father to explain why he had to work so hard at something he would probably never use. Each time, his father had calmly answered, "Every lesson we learn forms our character. You never know when aspects of your training will be called upon. It's not just about the lessons themselves; it's the building of your character that matters most." Those nights, Mel had drifted to sleep reliving every nook and cranny from the hours of climbing.

Seeing no means of safe descent, Mel wondered if he was meant to take a different route down and followed the ledge around the side of the column. Everywhere he looked, he saw the same thirty meters of smooth surface below him.

At the side opposite the lake, his attention was drawn unexpectedly away. Below him, fifty meters back from the bases of the two columns, was a seventy-meter-high onyx wall, its surface as smooth as glass. Lifting his gaze to look past the wall, he gasped in surprise. Beyond it, the Caeli opened into a second cavern, which had not been visible from the shores of the silver lake, and which stretched for what looked like kilometers, extending beyond his sight. The columns of this cavern took the forms of tall natural structures of many types: trees, entwined vines, kelp, flocks of birds soaring upward in a spiral, waterfalls, geysers seemingly frozen in mid burst, stalactites and stalagmites, tall crystal clusters, and at what seemed to be the center of the cavern, a massive column sculpted in the shape of a volcano in full eruption that Mel interpreted as a reminder of the fate of Delemni and a warning to the Vysards to fulfill their purpose.

Between these columns was a living forest of colossal redwood, Shorea, and eucalyptus trees, much grander than any that Mel had seen or heard of in the outside world, many of which stretched hundreds of meters upward into the shrouded recesses of the Caeli's ceiling. At ground level, around the bases of the columns and the trunks of the trees, was a labyrinthine series of structures interspersed with gardens and waterfalls and linked by orderly, well-kept paths. The dirt and cobblestone paths of this region gave it a much more organic and lived-in appearance in comparison to the marble of the Caeli's archives. Mel thought he caught a glimpse of firelight far off, but when he looked directly at it, it seemed to disappear. As he peered into the distance, trying to pinpoint the source of the light, he was startled by a shouting of his name from the far shore of the silver lake.

He hurried along the ledge and looked across the lake to see Polly staring at him. "Mel," she yelled again, relief and joy evident in her voice as it reverberated several times, "did you get it?"

Mel thought for a moment, *Get it? Get what?* And then his task came flooding back to him. With it came a sinking feeling as he looked again at the smooth surface below him. Mel knew that Polly was waiting expectantly for his answer, and he did not want to disappoint her. "Not yet, Polly," he shouted back. "I'm still working on it. I've got to look around some more. I'll be back." He turned and followed the ledge around to the opposite side so that Polly could no longer see him.

* * *

Mihoshi woke at the sound of Polly's voice. "Did he make it?" she asked with a hint of anxiety. "I am so sorry that I fell asleep. I just couldn't keep my eyes open."

"He's at the top of the warrior. He said he was still looking for the vault and went around to the other side. I want to think that he's past the worst, but I'm not so sure."

"Why is that?" Rei asked as he stretched his arms.

"He still has to try the vault. And climbing down, well, he must be tired, and it's at least as challenging as an ascent."

Rei lifted his spyglass and peered across the distance. "Perhaps we are too far away to discern the details, but the surface of the warrior does not appear to offer any features to hold on to, especially not near the top. We must ask him how he accomplished this climb when he returns."

"How ya s'pose he gonna do that?" Garth asked, scratching his head. "If he climbed over the side, he'd have nothin' to hold onta, and'd go an' get hisself killt."

Mihoshi saw the pained expression on Polly's face and rested a comforting hand on her arm. "Do not look with your eyes only."

Polly looked at Mihoshi with a blank expression. "If I hadn't spent some of the strangest weeks of my life with you and your brother, I'd say you were both a little loony."

Mihoshi smiled. "Begin by looking. We see that Mel has gone to a place where we are not permitted, along a route that appears to no longer exist. The fact that he has reached such a place should increase our confidence that he will return. Faith is built on what has been observed, including the 'impossible.' Only upon that foundation do we make the 'loony' assertion that yet another impossible thing can occur," she said with a wink.

Polly's frown relaxed. "I get it. We *have* been through plenty of impossible things recently."

Mihoshi nodded. "And remember, he is not alone."

Polly returned her gaze to the ledge atop the towering, sculpted warrior where Mel had walked out of view.

* * *

Mel double-checked the surface below the ledge on the sides and back of the column. It was the same as the side facing the lake.

There were no handholds for at least thirty meters below him. He wished he had thought to bring rope. He could have tied it around the column and rappelled down to the vault and then lowered himself to the ground.

Staring again at the beauty of the second cavern, he leaned against the column in defeat and slowly slid to a sitting position. As he slid, he noticed an irregularity. The place that his back was resting against was slightly recessed, while the rest of the column above the ledge had the perfectly round surface of a cylinder.

He examined the almost imperceptibly concave surface. The stone was off-white and devoid of markings. He put his hands on the surface and slid them across. At first, he felt nothing, but then he noticed a distinct warmth at certain places on the stone. He traced the warm points and found that they formed a circle.

He excitedly withdrew the small bag of sand, desperately hoping that he had not actually used it all. To his dismay, there was none. He shook out his pockets, hoping to find a particle that may have dribbled out of the bag, but found only fabric lint.

His shoulders slumped. A moment later, he remembered the gift of music and hummed each tune that had proven useful along his journey. When nothing happened, he sang several more tunes, but to no avail.

Having exhausted all the keys that he had learned during his adventures, he closed his eyes and allowed his mind to drift back to the tent in the desert. His heart yearned to be enveloped again by the Essence, and for a moment, he felt as if he had never left it. His heart was lifted once more by the complete love and acceptance of the Being who had formed everything in existence.

He opened his eyes, expecting to be inside the tent, but was back on the ledge. He was pleased to note that the concave section of the column's surface had receded and was now sliding aside, revealing a hollowed-out space inside the column, lit by luminescent stone.

Once the door had slid fully aside, Mel stepped into the perfectly round room. On the far side, several meters from him, was the top of a staircase. He crossed to it and began to descend. The gradual spiral stairs followed the inside contours of the sculpted warrior. To Mel's relief, this inside surface was lined with internal hatches to the same compartments that he had seen from the outside.

As he passed dozens of vaults embossed with different symbols, some familiar and some unknown, he was reminded of the spiral staircase that led down to the chamber of the vaults in his father's small Caeli in Cooperton, which he and Jora had descended on the day he had first sought the Abico vault.

After descending thirty meters below the staircase entrance, he came to a compartment that bore the familiar Abico symbol. Finally, he was standing before the lost vault! This was the door that he was supposed to have opened more than a month before in Cooperton. This was the twin of the compartment that had exploded and shattered Jora. This was the single objective that had brought him across thousands of miles and two oceans.

He stared at the symbol that had become associated with so much loss, grief, and struggle. He hesitated to try the handle, unsure of himself now that he faced it. He knew that the symbol represented submitting one's will and finding abundant life, but he did not know if he understood its implications. Nor did he know what the vault would hold. Apprehension filled his heart.

The memory of Jora's demise passed through him like a freezing wave. He relived the moment when Jora aimed a Sazo at him, took hold of the Abico vault's door, and was destroyed by it.

Mel's mind raced, and his heart pounded audibly. Am I ready to open this door? Have I learned the lesson? Am I in harmony with this vault? What if I'm not, and I get blown to pieces inside this column? What will my friends do? Will they even know what happened to me? What would become of them?

He tossed these thoughts back and forth until he realized that he was taking much too long to make this decision. He calmed his thoughts, took a deep breath, and committed himself.

Reaching out, he cautiously touched the compartment's handle and tried to sense any adverse signals. Other than the tingling he felt all over his body because of hyperventilation, he could sense no danger. He closed his eyes, held his breath, and slowly turned the handle. A seemingly endless moment later, the rotation was complete. As he pulled the door open, a severe vibration coursed through his entire body, causing him to shudder uncontrollably. He wondered if this was what being hit by lightning felt like. A burst of warm air gushed from the door's seals with a loud POP! Stunned and paralyzed, Mel fell back uncontrollably, expecting the fatal shockwave to follow. He hoped it would be over quickly.

* * *

Hours passed, and the four adventurers on the shore grew hungry. Against Polly and Mihoshi's protests, Rei and Garth began walking back toward the banquet hall, followed reluctantly by the girls. On the way, they all agreed to retrieve food and eat at the shore, where they could have a meal ready for Mel when he returned.

They were surprised to find the door of the banquet hall ajar.

"Who was the last to leave this room?" Rei asked quickly, in hushed tones. Each of them tried to remember.

"I think it was me," Polly whispered timidly.

"Did you close the door?" he asked in a firm whisper.

"I... I can't remember," she stammered in a low voice.

"I will go first," Rei declared as he stepped in front. Garth stepped to the back of the group, glancing at the nearby corridors.

They walked slowly and silently into the banquet hall.

Their mouths fell agape at the sight of an older, overweight, balding man in colorful clothes rifling through the cabinets in the kitchen and muttering under his breath. He suddenly turned and, with a frowning and distraught demeanor, roared, "I can't find it!" The man was small of stature and stout, with red hair and round, rosy cheeks. The wrinkles on his face divulged that he often smiled, though a furrow between his eyes revealed great grief as well. He was dressed in a simple cream-colored shirt with billowing sleeves and a pair of vertically striped red and blue pants that were similarly loose-fitting. His nose was slightly redder and more swollen than his cheeks, which sat below pale, sky-blue eyes that were topped with bushy, red eyebrows.

He stood still, as surprised to see the four young people as they were to see him. His eyes darted back and forth, trying to size up these unfamiliar persons. He looked as if he were about to speak when Polly blurted out, "Land's sakes! Who are you?"

The man flinched. Rei subtly motioned Polly to speak more quietly and cautiously. Garth instinctively stepped forward and assumed a defensive posture in front of Polly and Mihoshi.

"I thwore," the man said, his agitation now joined by fear as he more clearly saw the massive Garth.

Rei looked calmly at the man. "My name is Meiji Rei. Is your name Thwore?" he questioned gently.

The stout man's eyes narrowed, and he grunted in anger while quickly pointing his arm towards the young men. He made two small, jerking motions, and Rei and Garth collapsed to the ground.

Polly let out an earsplitting shriek, startling the man once more. He pointed his arm at her but did not make the sudden motion that had felled the young men. He backed up, keeping a cautious eye on the two young women.

Polly and Mihoshi were appalled. Rei and Garth lay motionless at their feet, though they did not appear to be wounded. Mihoshi knelt and felt their necks for a pulse. A moment later, she breathed a sigh of relief and nodded reassuringly to Polly.

Polly's surprise and dismay gave way to anger as she turned and stared at the stout man.

He began to shake, unnerved by the distress he saw on Polly's face. "I thwore, I thwore..." he groaned.

Polly looked at him with a fiery glare. "No one hurts my friends. We have been through too much already. Mel will learn of this sooner or later, and you won't find him so easy to stop. Hand over that Sazo!" Polly shouted as she walked toward the man with her fists clenched.

"Polly!" Mihoshi shouted in warning, but to no avail.

The man let out a squeal and pointed at Polly, screaming, "I thwore, I thwore!" Polly collapsed and fell next to Rei and Garth.

Mihoshi, seeing the volatile nature of this man, considered her actions carefully. She bowed and said softly, "I am Meiji Mihoshi, the daughter of Meiji Chiba, a prince of the Japanese island of Kyushu. The four of us are on a quest with the son of Telemai of Uri, and we mean you no harm."

He looked at Mihoshi with a tortured, pleading look in his eyes. "*I thwore*," he whined sadly.

CHAPTER 30

BACK WOODS

All was dark and silent. Then the dust-obscured light of luminescent stone and the hiss of a depressurizing vault filtered back into
his consciousness. The dust cleared, the hissing diminished, and
Mel found himself lying on the spiral staircase. He cautiously wig-
gled his fingers and then his toes to check if he was still intact. Carefully examining his skin, he was relieved to find no wounds of any
kind. Finally, confident that he was free of serious injury, he rolled
over into a kneeling position and pushed himself to his feet.

In front of him was an open vault door. Aching all over, he hobbled to the vault and cautiously peered within. Inside was a small
scroll cinched shut with a tied leather strap, and next to it, a small
leather pouch. He carefully reached inside and took them.

He saw that the scroll was made of the same fine cloth as the
scrolls from the Caeli at home in Cooperton. The leather strap,
which was tied around the scroll, looked as if it were brand new and
had never been undone.

The pouch felt so light that he wondered if there was anything
in it. He shook it and felt only slight movement within. He carefully undid its strap and reached inside. It seemed to be empty. He
cupped his hand and turned the small bag upside down and shook
it. A few dozen small seeds fell out onto his palm. He looked inside
and saw nothing more. He carefully placed the seeds back into the
bag and tied it shut.

He looked at the scroll in his hand. He decided to wait to open
it until he was reunited with his friends. Tucking it and the small
pouch into his shirt pocket and buttoning it shut, he ascended back

up the spiral staircase.

The door he had used to enter the interior of the column had shut itself. Mel let out a sigh. He tried to open it, but neither pushing nor pulling nor singing brought the desired result. Half an hour later, he turned away from the door and descended the spiral staircase, hoping that it would lead to an exit lower down.

He reached the lowest row of vaults at the base of the column. There was no sign of an exit, nor had there been during his descent. He observed that the vaults themselves were much too narrow to use as exits were he to choose one and manage to open both its interior and exterior door. The spiral staircase continued downward, the wall below consisting of smooth, featureless stone. Having no other choice, Mel took a deep breath and continued descending. Some twenty meters lower, the staircase ended, and a long, straight passageway proceeded for what looked like a half kilometer. He guessed that this passage would lead away from the direction of the lake. "*The light appears—forward only*, indeed!" he said to himself.

Following the passage to the far end, he reached a thick, stone door that stood ajar, a brightness like daylight shining in around its open edges. Mel slowly pushed on the door, and it swung outward without a sound as if its hinges had just been oiled. He saw that it was nearly a meter thick and likely weighed several tons.

Mel stepped out into a garden world, which reminded him of the backwoods near Cooperton. Colossal, bark-clothed redwood trees stretched upward hundreds of meters, seeming to brush the ceiling of the Caeli. Throughout the forest was an apparently endless array of buildings, which looked to Mel like workshops, storehouses, and homes.

Mel recognized this inner land of the Caeli as the same that he had viewed from the heights of the column earlier that morning. Thinking again of his friends, he turned to see if there was a path back to the lake, but there was only the smooth, seventy-meter-high onyx wall and the tops of the two warriors visible beyond. If there were a way out of this forest, it would likely be by means of another tunnel like the one he had just passed through. Though this inner land was clearly meant to be isolated, he was sure that the designer of this lush kingdom would have created a direct route to and from the archives.

Mel started down a dirt path, which led slightly uphill and parallel to the outer wall of the forest, watching for doorways in the wall's foreboding surface as he went.

After several hundred meters, he crested a hill and came to a small, thatched-roof cottage with smoke rising from its three round-rock chimneys. His heart raced. Who could be living here? Only one person came immediately to mind. He climbed the several stone steps onto the cottage's front porch. There was no door but simply an opening with a threshold of polished green jade.

Mel tested his voice under his breath and then softly said, "Hello?" through the opening. When no response came, he ventured slowly into the cottage, watching carefully for any sign of danger. The house was furnished with a simple elegance. It was clear of clutter, the center of the main room having only two handmade chairs and a massive burl table in front of the fireplace, where several logs were smoldering lazily. The floors were made of polished hardwood, partly covered by an ornate, colorful rug under the table and chairs.

By a flickering light that came from an adjacent room, Mel caught sight of a moving shadow. A subtle, hummed melody, which seemed vaguely familiar to Mel, began wafting through the cottage. He crept slowly towards the source of the sound. Peering around the corner into the other room, he saw an older man with silver hair tied back in a ponytail fussing over several boiling pots suspended over a fire in an open hearth against the far wall. A hole in the ceiling above funneled the smoke away.

"Excuse me," Mel said quietly so as not to frighten the man. There was no reply. "Excuse me!" Mel called out as he stepped fully into the room, keeping his right hand and its Sazo hidden behind his back, set and ready to stun if necessary.

The man whirled around much more quickly than Mel would have expected from someone of his advanced age. His look of surprise swiftly shifted to joyful recognition. He stared with deep, probing eyes that simultaneously warmed Mel's heart and paralyzed him where he stood. Then he raised his hand towards Mel.

Mel stood still, his disciplined muscles refusing to flinch in fear or to make any threatening motions. If the man took any sudden actions, he was ready to activate his Sazo and spring out of the way.

The man studied Mel for several seconds, emitting several different intonations of "hmmm." With his hand still outstretched toward Mel, he said, "Come here, come here, Melamuri!" while gesturing towards himself. "Let me get a better look at you. Amazing! You *so* resemble your father." He circled his arms around Mel's neck and embraced his taut and wary frame.

"Take a seat and tell me of that old Vysard," the man said while leading Mel towards the kitchen table. "Does he fare well? How was your trip here? Is your current quest fulfilled?" The questions came tumbling out with barely a breath in between.

"If I may, sir," Mel requested as they took seats across from each other, "who are you? And what is this place?" Mel decided to refrain from any mention of his father's disappearance until he knew more about his host.

"Oh yes, yes! How rude of me. I'm sorry; I rarely get to speak to others and tend to get carried away. And how could I expect you to possibly remember an old coot like me? Why, it's been over twelve years since you left. But you did have a sharp mind. Even as a young boy, you could always remember the most difficult of equations and unravel the most convoluted matrixes. Tell me, how has your father been? Is he with you?"

Mel's forehead wrinkled. "Sir, my questions, if you please," he reiterated while discreetly disarming his Sazo and resting his hands on the table.

The older man stopped and crooked his head as if he did not understand and then caught his breath. "I suppose I hoped you would remember me, after all. 'Uncle Tothar' I was called for those few brief years. In any case, welcome to my home, where you may stay anytime you wish. For the sake of a proper introduction, I am Tothar, the son of Thar of Uri, and please forgive me, but I am in the midst of helping my much more talented brother prepare dinner." He rose and returned to tending the boiling pots, where he looked back and forth between Mel and his task as he continued speaking. "It is fortuitous that he insists on preparing several meals' worth at a time. If you wish to join us, there will be plenty. I am more of a librarian than a chef. I steward the books of Toleth Mar, which is the name given to the archives of this Grand Telemai Caeli of the Martinique Isles. I helped your father build this place. I was on duty during the eruptions of Mount Peleé in 1902. The ground shook even here. Very few survived," he said, looking at Mel with sad, knowing eyes. "After the first eruption, we knew we had to move the last of the ancient records from his castle to the archives here. My family was never with the insurrection. We all sided with Telemai. Of course, then the whole sordid rebellion repeated itself seven days later, and Mount Peleé got the final word. My brother and I were spared along with your household and some others, and off you went."

Mel shook his head, his eyes betraying a lack of understanding.

"You don't remember it?" Tothar asked, looking puzzled.

"Not for lack of help or lack of trying. When I was eight years old, there was a boating incident." Mel rubbed the knot that had remained on the back of his skull since his household had first arrived at the Cooperton coast.

"Another? After you barely survived escaping Martinique when you were four?"

Mel heaved a sigh. "Maybe sailing isn't for me. Let's not talk about what happened at the gap in the reef just before I got here."

Tothar's eyes narrowed with curiosity, and he grinned at Mel's self-effacement. "And yet here you are. Saved by Telemai at least once, but guarded by someone greater than him, ultimately. For what it's worth, I would not expect even severe memory loss to persist for long in anyone of his lineage. I am not aware of any Gate-keeper who has had such extraordinary recall."

Mel smiled at Tothar's reassurances. "I'd assumed he'd told his friends about my accident, but he was always concerned about me not being seen as 'different.'"

Tothar's eyes opened wide with recollection. "My, did Oscar and I, and others, have conversations with him over whether it was worthwhile to keep our peoples' history hidden during a child's early years. Telemai has always so highly valued innocence."

Mel stared solemnly at Tothar and saw the eyes of a friend of his family. A friend who deserved to know.

"He's gone," Mel said abruptly, swallowing hard from the difficulty of the admission. "He disappeared several months before I was to open the Abico vault. He wasn't there to keep Jora from destroying it and from destroying himself."

Tothar drew in a long, slow breath and seemed to stare into the distance. He gulped and then returned his attention to Mel. "I would never wish to hear of anyone who attempted to open a vault prematurely, though I am not surprised that Jora did such a thing. He was a worry from a young age, though your father held out hope that he could be redeemed and trained into a disciplined Vysard. Is Oscar with you?"

Mel shook his head. "He went to look for my dad."

"You found a way here alone?" Tothar asked incredulously.

"Me and four good friends I made along the way."

Tothar nodded with acknowledgment and raised an eyebrow. "You said he's gone... disappeared? He must be on some mission. Your father is not the kind of man who would forsake his son on the cusp of opening the Abico. Someone must have been in dire peril for him to leave at such a crucial stage of your training."

"He left all the clues I'd need to find the replica of the vault," Mel spoke in defense of his father. "So, it wasn't like I didn't have his help. But there were some unforeseen mishaps that—"

Their conversation was interrupted by a loud voice from outside. "Trethpatherth! Tothar, we have trethpatherth!"

Mel followed Tothar to the main room, where they watched the front entrance.

The cottage suddenly filled with bustle and noise as a stout man burst into the room, towing the unconscious forms of Rei and Polly on what looked like a hovering rug. Garth followed them in, his eyes groggy. Mihoshi entered last, her head bowed.

Mel saw the flustered, red-faced man and again discreetly readied his Sazo. He quickly glanced at the humble and demure Mihoshi, who would not look him in the eye. "Mihoshi, what happened? What did he do to them?"

Tothar sighed. Mel, keeping an eye on the newly arrived stout man, coiled, ready to attack or defend. Tothar quickly stepped in front of Mel and held out his hands consolingly to the stout man.

"Kenthar! There's no need to worry! These are our guests. This is Melamuri, Telemai's son, and his friends. Now take a seat, and when you're ready, you can tell me what happened." He guided Kenthar, with the hovering rug in tow, to the kitchen and to a seat at the table, rubbing his back to calm his hyperventilation. Mel and the others gathered nearby. Kenthar looked ashamed and hung his head. Tothar turned to Mel. "This is my brother Kenthar. He didn't mean any..."

Kenthar began to sob. "I thought they were trethpathing, and then it thounded like they were making fun of me, Toth!" He pointed at the still unconscious Rei. "He made fun of the way I talk, and... and..." Kenthar straightened and spoke indignantly. "They, they thoudn't have been thneaking around in the archiveth. And... and I lothed it! I can't find it anywhere!"

Tothar put a comforting arm around his brother and turned to Mel. "Kenthar has a generous heart, but he startles easily and can become quite hostile when people don't understand him."

Tothar patted his brother on the shoulder and walked over to Rei and Polly and gently but precisely squeezed a spot between their shoulders. They woke immediately and looked around in surprise at the room they found themselves in. They were startled and pleased to see Mel standing nearby.

Rei jumped to his feet and looked to Mel. "Are we in danger?"

"It's all right," Mel answered calmly. "Everyone, please meet our hosts, Tothar and Kenthar, the stewards of this Caeli."

Rei and Mihoshi bowed. Garth and Polly nodded. They kept an eye on their surroundings and Kenthar, who remained seated.

Kenthar looked at Garth warily. "He didn't thay thunned, Toth. Everyone who geth thunned thayth that way."

Tothar looked at drowsy Garth and slapped him across the face. "Well done, son! You've just confounded four thousand years of science. Melamuri, where did you get this young bull?"

Garth rubbed his cheek. "Man, that was some howdy! If that's how ya thank folks, I'm sure glad I ain't on yer bad side."

"I must apologize, but it should help the stun to wear off. The more of a surprise, the better." Tothar turned and addressed all five of the young people. "You may have noticed that my brother Kenthar has a small speech impediment. He sometimes feels slighted when people ask him to repeat what he said, or worse, when *they* try to repeat what he said, and it involves an 's' sound. It doesn't help our conversations that I have hearing loss and often have to ask him to repeat himself. We've gotten used to each other's weaknesses, but it's different with newcomers, and as you can probably tell, we don't get too many of them around here."

Rei remembered the moment when he had repeated what he had thought was Kenthar's name. "I am sorry, Kenthar. What was it that you swore?"

Kenthar smiled, then crinkled his forehead again. "I thwore to Tothar that I would be right back with the ingredienth to make my pie. But... but they were gone. I loth'd them!" He hung his head.

"My brother goes at his own pace with some things," Tothar explained, "but he's the finest chef in the Caribbean and takes great care with all of his ingredients." He turned to Kenthar. "I'm sure we can find something to replace them. Use your imagination, Kenny.

You'll come up with something."

Kenthar slouched forward with his head between his forearms and both hands on his balding pate, thinking.

Tothar turned to Rei and Polly. "I'm sorry for any inconvenience my brother has caused you. The pain in your head will subside in due time. Come join us for dinner. Food will quicken the healing."

Rei bowed, acknowledging the apology while still massaging the back of his neck.

Mihoshi looked at Mel. "Did you find what you were looking for?" she asked.

Mel beamed. "Yes, I did! For a moment, I wasn't sure if I was ready, but it turned out all right." He pulled out the scroll and the leather pouch and placed them on the table.

Polly looked closely at the objects. "Well, what is it? What does it say? What's in the bag?" she barraged him.

"Seeds of some kind."

"What does the scroll say?" Polly asked anxiously.

"I don't know yet," Mel replied shyly. "I haven't opened it."

Polly leaned back, folded her arms, and tapped her foot on the floor. "Well, go ahead! What are you waiting for? You just came six thousand kilometers through hurricanes and disease-infested jungles, not to mention Mr. 'I'd love to kill you all,' to get to that scroll. Now, what do you say we find out why we've gone through all of this?" Polly's voice was beginning to rise.

Mel nodded in assent and slowly unrolled the scroll. Tothar watched from across the table with a quizzical smile on his face. Mel turned to allow the firelight, the brightest source of illumination in the room, to shine on the scroll. As he began to read, his radiant expression turned to puzzlement and then to a frown. He scratched the back of his head. "Brumble Berry Serendipity. There's a list of common herbs, a few spices, and cooking instructions." He looked at each of his friends, who were equally at a loss. He turned to Tothar and was about to ask him a question when Mihoshi put a hand on his arm.

"Your leather bag is gone," she said.

"What?" Mel roared, whirling to see the vacant spot on the table where he had placed the pouch.

Kenthar came bounding back from a mixing bowl by the stove with the bag in his hand. "I did it! I finithed the pie, Toth! I uthed my imaginathin!"

CHAPTER 31

BRUMBLE BERRY SERENDIPITY

"No!" Mel gasped. "Do you realize how far I came to get those?" He turned to Tothar with a tormented look and then slumped into his chair, placing the scroll on the table in defeat.

"I'm thorry," Kenthar whined, defensively wrapping his pudgy arms around his belly. "He thaid to improvithe. And they were perfect!" He put the bag next to the scroll and whispered something into Tothar's ear.

Tothar bent over with a deep belly laugh, rose to gasp for air, and then folded over again in fits of uncontrollable guffaws.

The five weary travelers looked back and forth at each other, wondering if they had not stumbled upon the Caeli's insane asylum. Kenthar erupted in laughter, joining in synchronous harmony with his brother.

"I don't find this to be a particularly humorous incident, Tothar," Rei said sternly.

Between gasps of air and raucous fits, Tothar tried to respond but finally gave up and simply nodded amidst his laughter. He finally gasped, "This is what all good Vysards must go through. That hard-fought scroll," he said, pointing to the opened parchment on the table, "is the recipe for Brumble Berry Serendipity. It's one of our most delicious pies and is the reward for a lesson well learned."

Kenthar smiled broadly. "Brumble Berry Therindipity!"

Mel shook his head in disbelief at the apparent madness of the moment. "Could you please explain? Losing part of my lesson to an 'imaginative' chef's pie does not strike me as especially funny!"

"In truth, ith a humble pie," Kenthar mumbled. He and Tothar bent over again in spasmodic laughter.

Tothar finally composed himself and sat upright. "I apologize. We mean you no disrespect. Soon you will understand."

Mel hung his head. "The scroll doesn't make any sense, and the seeds are gone."

"The *berries* are not gone, Mel. Those were dried Brumble Berries, and speaking of serendipity, moments before you read the scroll, my bumbling but innocent brother saw the bag of berries, assumed them to be ours, and started following the recipe from memory! The berries are the essential ingredient of the pie, which is the proof of your success. You will soon enjoy the fruit of your labor," he said with a cryptic smile.

"The contents of the Abico were all about me eating a pie? How does that prepare me to open the Piaculum vault?"

"You are assuming that it is like the Abico. Some vaults are accessed after great struggle and growth, others after merely enjoying the contents of the previous vault. The pie might seem like a simple reward, but you will find that there is much more to it than that. Whether the rewards of a vault seem great or small, they are secondary to what it took to gain them. The lesson is in the learning, not for the reward's sake, but for the discipline it took to qualify for the reward. The real reward is the formation of your character. If this is maintained, it will last forever."

"You are reminding me of my father," Mel remarked.

Tothar laughed. "I'll take that as a compliment."

Mel shook his head despondently. "It would have been so much simpler if he had been there, and Jora hadn't..." he said, trailing off. He unconsciously reached to his side and felt the scar of the wound he had received at the moment of Jora's demise. He reflected on the years of teasing and mistreatment that he had suffered at Jora's hands. Despite the pain that Jora had inflicted, Mel had chosen again and again to forgive his tutor and to value him as a member of the Uri household. Jora had been the closest thing that he had had to a big brother while he was growing up. The memory of Jora's fate provoked more pity than anger in Mel. He preferred to believe that Jora would have one day experienced his own purifying personal reckoning and would have had his own encounter with the Essence. Mel sighed at the thought of all that had been lost that day, and of the trouble that could have been avoided if his father had been home.

"Don't despise difficulty that comes by no fault of your own," Tothar counseled gently. "We learn deeply during desperate circumstances that try us to our foundations and confront us with our intrinsic ineptitudes. *Humility*, the heart of the Abico lesson, involves recognizing our limitations and accepting help. We can't delve into deeper truths, nor should we assume great responsibilities, without it. After humility must come patience, the ability to wait for guidance, inspiration, or wisdom that transcends our own. Patience gives us the strength of character to complete what most others would abandon, as they cannot tolerate the slow process of a work done well. Anything worth doing is worth taking the time to do well, and time is the crucible that refines patience. Much patience and humility are required to open the Abico vault, and you have done it! Congratulations!"

"Yes, thank you," Mel answered, trying not to sound dispirited.

Tothar smiled understandingly. "Think of what you've gained! These four good friends! You've begun to learn that you are a part of a greater plan and begun to surrender to that power and intelligence that is greater than your own and taken your first steps into 'The Rest.'"

"The what?" Garth muttered.

"'The Rest' comes from ceasing to trust your own talents and instead choosing to rely on *the* higher power."

"Don't got nothin' 'gainst y'all," Garth said, "but I'm gonna need some'en to boil this down fer me when yer done."

"I got ya covered," Polly answered, elbowing him playfully.

"Now, as to the matter at hand," Tothar continued, "the pie

needn't be only for you. You could not have gotten here without your friends, and you may share it with them. That is, you *will* share it with them if you wish to enjoy their company for very long." Tothar smirked, trying not to laugh.

"Now we're talkin'," Garth said, rubbing his hands together.

"Is there something about the pie that you're not telling me?" Mel asked suspiciously.

Tothar smiled like he had a great, wonderful secret that he would never divulge.

Kenthar grinned. "For one thing, it taketh great pathenth and humility to make it. I remember the firth time I tried; I think I threw the pie againth the wall in fruthtrathon."

"Well," Polly exclaimed, "I can't wait to taste this 'humble pie.' How long 'till we eat?"

Tothar giggled. "It's the wait *after* that'll surprise you!"

"Why do I suspect that it's going to make us sick or something?" Polly asked.

"Quite the opposite. By your permission, we'll eat some with you if you're at all concerned. I haven't had Brumble Berry Serendipity in a great many years." He and Kenthar broke out in new howls of uncontrollable laughter.

The young people looked at each other and rolled their eyes.

Rei whispered in Mel's ear. "Could it be that they have dwelt in the Caeli for too long?"

"I don't know," Mel whispered back. "They seem to be in their right minds, despite being secluded here for years. There must be a secret about these berries. Though, at this rate, I doubt they'll ever divulge it. Knowing who has arranged all of this, we can trust it'll be good for us."

Five more chairs were brought in, and they enjoyed a delicious dinner. Garth expressed his enthusiasm for sampling as many of Kenthar's kitchen treats as the chef would permit, and Kenthar, in turn, was delighted to have someone to share his talents with.

Midway through dinner, as the aroma of a berry pie baking in the oven began to fill the room, Tothar gestured to Mel and took him aside into his study. He sat down in a leather chair before a blazing fireplace. His amused expression subsided, and he looked solemnly at the young man and began to talk in a way that reminded Mel of one of his father's or Oscar's long stories.

After twenty minutes, Mel, followed by Tothar, returned to where his friends were busily eating the lavish meal. He looked like he had seen a ghost. Just then, Kenthar smiled and delivered the pie to the table.

Mihoshi sat upright with curiosity and watched Mel and the others over the rim of her cup of green tea.

Polly immediately froze with concern. "Mel, what's wrong?"

Garth, between gulps of a juicy sweet potato, managed, "Ya' better hurry on up, Mel, or there won't be no mo' grub. I caint wait ta' taste summa that pie!" He served himself one of the already cut slices of Brumble Berry Serendipity and separated a portion with his fork, preparing to take his first bite.

"Not yet!" Mel blurted loudly. Everyone except Garth stopped eating. Garth set the portion of pie aside like a child forced to relinquish one treat too many and moved on to other food.

Rei politely rested his utensils. "What is the matter, Mel-san?"

"I need to explain something before we eat dessert." Mel looked at each of his friends in turn. "As you know, the rewards of the Caeli are not about intellect alone. Does anyone want to guess how long it took for my father to gain both the knowledge and wisdom he needed to serve as the Gatekeeper?"

Polly answered quickly. "Probably decades?"

Mel tilted his head sympathetically and grimaced. "Centuries."

Garth almost choked. "Whaaa?"

Mel looked at Polly. "Remember when we spoke of how old my father might be?"

Polly shook her head. "Yes, but it had to be a metaphor or something. How could anyone live six hundred years?"

Tothar leaned back, grinning and watching the young friends.

"A medda what?" Garth asked Polly while chewing.

Mel held up his hand. "Please, there's more to explain. The Abico reward, this pie, is the first step toward me becoming the leader of the Vysards." He hesitated, his eyes widening at an intimidating thought that he was reluctant to voice.

Polly squinted. "Where are you going with this, Mel?"

He winced and said, almost in a whisper, "As it was with my father, my responsibility means I must live longer than most."

"What's he sayin'?" Garth asked huffily between bites of food.

Mel breathed deeply and gathered his courage. "The ancient Delemnites cultivated a berry that provides a unique nutrient that extends a person's lifespan by hundreds of years. It was decided that only the one who was to be the Gatekeeper, and his closest companions, would partake of the Abico reward."

Realization dawned on Polly, and she pushed back from the table. "The pie is why he lived so long?" she asked in alarm.

Mihoshi set down her cup of green tea and closed her eyes.

"Yes," Mel continued, "and you should each think about what this could mean for your life from this point on. No one knows exactly how long each person will live if they eat this, but it'll be many times longer than a normal lifespan." Mel sighed with relief. "I wanted you to know, so you can choose whether to eat the pie."

Polly looked at Tothar. "The Brumble Berry? Really?"

Tothar chuckled. "Now grown only in this Caeli! And that only once in a hundred years," he said with pride.

Rei put his hand to his goateed chin while staring at the pie. "What a curious and unexpected question is raised by such a simple thing. This is quite a revelation, Mel-san. What will it mean for our journey together?"

"I don't know all that it implies just yet, but I know that the five of us have been guided into some extraordinary encounters over the last weeks. It seems that we are meant to be in this struggle together. If any of you choose not to partake, I will understand, and no one will fault you."

Garth continued to eat dinner. The others sat in silence and, one by one, turned and looked searchingly at Tothar.

The older man nodded his head and smiled bittersweetly. "I remember when Telemai presented me and my brother and a few others with this very decision. The life it brings is a great blessing and a solemn responsibility. There is nothing like it. It is an experience of 'more' in many ways. More joys, more sorrows. More meetings and partings. It can begin to feel endless, but there is yet a mortal horizon. Some who we knew and who assisted Telemai for a time chose not to partake of the Abico reward. They took that path with honor, as it was solely their decision to make. Though, I do still miss those who chose thusly."

Tothar and the young people, each of them on the verge of tears, were interrupted by a loud belch as Garth smacked his lips and patted his tummy. "Mmm, mmmm! Y'all 'll be glad to 'ear 'at that pie is yummy!"

CHAPTER 32

WESTERN BOUND

Dinner was followed by Brumble Berry Serendipity for dessert for everyone except Garth, who had already finished his slice. Each of the four others ate the pie very slowly at first but soon found themselves struggling not to gobble it down.

There was one piece of pie left over, which Kenthar carefully wrapped in an airtight container and set before Mel. "Thith ith for later for only thomeone very thpethal," he said with a wink.

Mel thought for a moment on this and smiled.

After dessert, they moved their chairs to the burl table in the main room, where they sat and had warm chocolate drinks and told Tothar of their adventures. After a great many questions were answered on both sides, Mel's friends retired to bed one by one.

After the last of the team was resting quietly in the soft, feather beds, which Kenthar had prepared, Tothar approached the rapidly tiring Mel. He presented an envelope with a red wax seal that had been impressed by a crest bearing the design of a flaming sword. Tothar bowed low. "I believe this is for you."

Mel sat upright, and his heart leaped as he recognized the seal from his father's signet ring. He had often watched his father carefully heat wax and drip it onto envelopes addressed to people across the world. Before it could cool and harden, he would take off his ring and press its emblem into the center of the wax.

"Where did you get this?" Mel asked expectantly of Tothar. "And why didn't you give this to me earlier?"

"A few weeks ago, someone dropped this off in Fort-de-France at a bakery storefront that my brother operates during tourist season. To answer your second question, there was a note attached to it, which requested that I wait until I knew it was the right time."

"Was it my father who dropped it off?" Mel asked quickly.

"Kenthar was not in at the time. He found it the next day, where it had been slid under the door. Perhaps the letter will explain." Tothar stepped into the kitchen, leaving Mel alone.

Mel looked at the yellowed parchment envelope, which bore the stains and stiffness of an earlier exposure to saltwater. His heart beat rapidly, and his fingers hesitated to open it.

Mel experienced mixed emotions as he carefully peeled back the wax seal so as not to break it and withdrew the letter.

Mel, my son,

I have heard of your difficulties at our home. I was deeply saddened to learn of the loss of Jora and am terribly sorry that such tragedy and unnecessary hardship have befallen you.

By now, you have opened the Abico vault and partaken of your reward. I am so proud of you, my son. This took great courage to accomplish. This is the first step in a gauntlet of trials that grow steadily more severe. They will usher you into your place as a vessel of the truth.

And an even stronger vessel you will now be, as it is the painstakingly cultivated qualities of the Brumble Berry that confer upon the leaders of the Delemnite Vysards their extraordinary longevity. Even now, processes within your body are taking place that will enable you to live at least five hundred years. If you have shared your reward with the companions that have helped you on your journey, they now also share that much more deeply in your responsibilities. Their lives will also be extended, though perhaps not as greatly as yours. May their loyalty thus far prove to have been just the beginnings of many grand and necessary adventures to come.

There are some somber facts that I must mention. First, if the berry or the pie made from it falls into the wrong hands and is eaten by one who has chosen the path of the Strangers, for him it will have no effect. Second, should anyone who has eaten the berry choose to become a Stranger some day after, he will lose his reward and will age at the normal rate from that point on. But enough caveats, this is a time for celebration!

I was greatly blessed to have had Oscar, Tothar, Kenthar, and Armando at my side to help me with my challenges, along with a few other close friends whom you have yet to meet or who are no longer with us. Years after I became Gatekeeper, there was one other who joined our company and partook of the Abico reward. She was your mother, Ella. You owe her your life in more than one way. Her loss is one of the very few touches of sadness that accompany my enjoyment of my own Abico reward, though I know that when my time on this Earth has passed, I will see her again.

Now to look forward! Your next vault is the Piaculum. You must get home and open it within three months of the day that Jora met his fate. I wish I could tell you that the challenges before you will decrease upon your discovery of the Piaculum's contents, but that is not the case.

And I must warn you: there is grave danger in the world right now. I cannot describe it in detail in this letter. Just be on your guard. A new and yet ever old darkness has been unleashed on this world, which seeks to dominate. And it is uniquely interested in you, my son.

I must conclude this letter as I am on an urgent mission, which, for all our sakes, I cannot fail. Please use haste in completing your next goal, as the fate and safety of many rest upon its mastery.

I hope to see you soon. I love you with all my heart.

Telemai

"He's alive!" Mel said, stunned. "Or he was a few weeks ago."

Tothar poked his head around the corner. "Ah-ha! Telemai has not been called home just yet! It would be so unlike him to pass away without first notifying us obliquely," he said with a wink and disappeared back into the kitchen.

Mel reread the letter and found comfort in imagining his father saying the words. But he was perplexed by its cryptic message. What was this new evil that was uniquely interested in him? Had his father learned of the existence of Neco? Were there other, greater foes already pursuing him?

He felt emotionally exhausted by the many revelations in the letter. His desire was to get some rest and go home, yet his mind raced at the need to be back in Cooperton within a few weeks to open the next vault. He wondered if the contents of the Piaculum vault would lead him on a journey as bizarre as the one to find the Abico. With thoughts of caves and robed monks brandishing swords, Mel found his bed and slipped into a fitful sleep.

* * *

The day erupted with a shout. "Ith time to get up!" Kenthar bellowed as he threw open the curtains.

Mel slowly dragged himself to a sitting position and squinted against the profusion of light. "So soon?"

"Yeth, you thleeply head," Kenthar said giddily. "There ith a freth plate of blueberry pancaketh and a bathket of tropical fruit waiting for you. Come on, leth eat!" Kenthar playfully herded Mel to the main room, where the others were already enjoying brunch at the meticulously set burl table.

"Morning," Mel forced himself to say as he was being pushed into his chair. He looked at his friends through barely focused eyes. "Have you been awake long?"

"We've been up for hours," Polly interjected before anyone else could speak, "and have been on a tour of amazing gardens." Polly continued without taking a breath. "Did you know that they grow almost all their food hydroponically? And that they get here an entirely different way than we—"

Mel held up his hand. "Polly, I didn't sleep too well, and it's quite early for a full volume conversation."

"Early? It's after eleven in the morning! The day is half done!"

Rei watched sympathetically as Mel winced at Polly's barrage. He leaned close and spoke softly. "What are we to do next?"

Mel looked at his friend, with whom he had already shared · many dangers and joys. His heart was moved by Rei's loyalty and that of the others. Exhausted and still grappling with the enormity of what he had learned the night before, he dared not try to tell them just yet of his father's letter and its warnings. But he saw on their faces a need for some form of resolution to their shared odyssey. "We're going home," Mel said quietly.

"When?" Polly asked, still at full volume.

"Right after breakfast...err, brunch."

"That soon?" she whined. "There's so much to learn here, so much to see, so much to *read*! We can't leave right away, Mel. Aren't you curious to at least see the entire library?"

"I am, but I still need to return to Cooperton within three months of my birthday, which leaves us only a few weeks. If it's any consolation, I believe we'll have plenty of time to return someday and enjoy as much of this Caeli as we like."

Tothar let out a short, giddy laugh. Mel tried to stare at him sternly but broke into a grin.

"I'll go and prepare the boat," Rei offered.

"It's already done!" Tothar announced. "While you slept, we stocked the *New Day* with enough provisions to get you back home fatter than when you left. We inspected the boat's mechanisms and found them in perfect condition."

Mel was struck by a sudden curiosity. "We saw another boat at the end of the docks. Is it yours?"

Tothar smiled. "That is the *New Dawn*, the boat your father inherited from his father. Kenthar and I do indeed get here by other means, but Telemai left it for our use in case of emergency."

"What kind of emergency?"

"The kind that is too familiar in our peoples' history."

Mel nodded with understanding. "Does anyone who is not among my father's friends know that this Caeli is here?"

"I imagine not, or we would've been invaded by the Strangers long ago. But there will always be those who will wonder what gold or jewels might be hidden in some unknown cranny of an island."

Tothar stood from the table. "May you all return someday soon and put our library to good use."

"Thank you, Tothar," Mel replied with a respectful nod. "I appreciate all that you've done for us."

"You are most welcome. Now go ahead and finish your meal."

* * *

363

Mel paused as he unmoored the *New Day*, and gazed at the *New Dawn* in its distant dock. He wondered why his father had rarely spoken of his own father or of his own early years as a Vysard apprentice. What adventures had he and his friends shared aboard the older vessel? What perils had it delivered them from? What of the man who had built it, who Mel felt that he did not know? Mel wondered if one day he would build his own boat and retire the *New Day* for emergency use.

These thoughts stirred in Mel a sense of the passing of the mantle of generations and infused in him a further resolve to responsibly steward all that was being entrusted to him.

The young travelers together stepped onto the deck of the *New Day* and turned and exchanged waves of goodbye with Tothar and Kenthar, who stood on the shore.

The friends descended into the cabin. After stowing the last of their gear, they sat in their hammocks, except for Mel. He took a seat at the map table and selected the river on the north coast of Panama as their destination. The boat drew back from the docks and spun its prow away from the Caeli. The hatch shut itself, and as the craft began to submerge, its walls became transparent, and a blue glow filled the cabin. They watched in awe as the boat descended into the darkening cave. Several moments later, it proceeded at an even keel. It soon entered the ascending tunnel, and, after what seemed like a fraction of the time it had taken to descend, the glow of the outside world approached.

Remaining submerged, the boat passed through the turbulent current of the waterfall and entered the channel that led out through the reef. Mel looked in wonder at the rainbow display of corals, fish, and sinuous sea creatures. He delighted at the sight of a two-meter-long leatherback turtle, noting its distinctive five dorsal ridges and dark, star-speckled hide. The placid marine reptile seemed to make eye contact with him as the *New Day* glided past.

"I think I prefer this means of passing the reef," Mel said with a grin.

"I bet," Garth answered. "You ain't much better at swimmin' than I am," he added with a wink.

The boat proceeded out into the open ocean, where it dove ninety meters deeper and deployed its underwater propulsion system.

Moments later, as the boat glided through deep water, a dark shape loomed ahead. As they drew nearer, they discerned that it was a humpback whale and were relieved as the propulsion system guided the boat safely around the colossal creature. As they passed, it let out a low cry, which sounded like a massive door creaking on its hinges. Garth stumbled backward into his hammock, eliciting quickly suppressed smiles from Rei and Mihoshi.

"Whale song!" Mel marveled. "It thinks we're another whale."

"Why am I not surprised that you understand it?" Polly asked.

Mel laughed. "I wish I could! It was just an educated guess."

Polly stared at the whale with a mixture of fear and amazement. "Could we stop here for a while and just watch?"

Mel furrowed his brow and looked compassionately at her. "I honestly wish that we could, but we still have a long journey ahead and a limited amount of time. If we go to sleep now, the boat should wake us just before we reach the Panama coast."

Polly nodded and returned to her hammock, glancing one last time out at the now featureless, bluish-green water of the sea. Soon, all five of the young people were in a deep sleep, which would last them for the next several days.

* * *

The light in the cabin increased slowly until the door opened and fresh air and sunlight flooded in, waking Mel and his friends.

They stepped out on deck to see the morning rays of the sun piercing the eastern sky like the prongs of a golden crown. A hundred meters to the south was land as far as the eye could see. Mel recognized the mouth of the river from which they had sailed less than two weeks before.

Suddenly, the mast raised the sail on its own, and the boat leaped forward on a course toward the river.

Two hours later, the *New Day* rounded the last bend in the river, and the friends saw the familiar waterfall in front of the vine grotto where the boat had been stored for nearly twelve years. As they guided the boat to a stop at the riverbank, two horses came running as though they had been called, their manes and tails flowing freely as they galloped down the path. Several Embera keepers were running hurriedly after them.

Polly and Garth recognized the horses and together began to cry. "Campi... Candi," Polly sobbed. She and Garth jumped to shore and ran to the horses, throwing their arms around their necks. The horses whinnied and nuzzled them with joy.

Rei smiled at his sister and put his arm around her. "We will be home soon."

"What will we do, brother? Go back to town and continue to live in hiding?"

Rei was taken aback by her questioning of their obvious duty. "What else did you have in mind, little one?"

Mihoshi looked at him with conviction through narrowed eyes. "I suggest that we be open to where the wind may blow us."

Rei planted his feet and thrust his shoulders back. He looked sternly at his sister. "We were told to wait for word from our father. We cannot disobey; it would dishonor him to do so. We have already risked much by accompanying Mel-san."

Mihoshi approached him and gently put a hand on his chest. "Be open," she said calmly and stepped ashore. At her soft words, his shoulders slumped, and his hand rose to tug at his goatee.

* * *

After exchanging greetings with their Embera friends on shore, they explained via gestures and Rei's limited knowledge of the Embera language that they had no time to visit Brother Josh in the village and needed to depart on the boat as soon as possible.

Mel and Garth led Campitor and Candeo into the grotto and retrieved the wagon.

While examining the boat for the best place to secure the wagon, Mel noted that the four rounded depressions in the *New Day*'s deck just aft of the mast, which had before puzzled him, matched the distances between the wagon's four wheels. He nodded knowingly at his father's foresight.

Mel, Garth, Rei, and several Embera men lifted the wagon onto the deck of the *New Day* and slid it into position over the cabin top behind the mast. Mel saw that there were several centimeters of clearance between the highest point of the wagon and the boom of the mast. As he and the others prepared to tie the wagon down, they were startled by the sudden emergence of metal hooks from panels beside the depressions, which pivoted and retracted, cinching the wheels tightly to the deck.

"Ooh," Garth exclaimed, "I hope we can get it loose 'gain when we wanna."

"It's all right," Mel responded, "we've got you to sing to it."

Garth raised an eyebrow and feigned a glare at his friend.

Rei gleaned from the Emberas that Brother Josh had paid for a special gift to be given to Mel and his friends. Moments later, their smiling hosts brought forth a generous supply of tightly bundled hay and burlap bags of grain to feed the horses on their return voyage, which they helped the young people to stow in the *New Day*'s cabin. Mel thanked them profusely with a few Embera words of gratitude recommended by Rei.

The friends did not enjoy the prospect of transporting horses on the open deck of a sailboat or of having to travel at surface speeds, but they knew that they had no choice. It was decided that they would hitch Campitor and Candeo just forward of the mast, where the deck had the most open space and where the horses' considerable weight would be as close as possible to the vessel's designed center of buoyancy.

Candeo was the first to be brought aboard, and as all four of her hooves rested on the boat, Polly shrieked and jumped across the deck, knocking into Garth. Candeo shuffled uncomfortably, and the others stared at Polly. Her eyes were wide with fright, and she pointed to the place where she had been standing. They turned at her direction, and their mouths fell open in amazement.

"You gotta be kiddin' me," Garth remarked in shock.

The section of the deck just starboard and aft of the wheel, where Polly had been standing, was glowing. The luminance was the shape of a rectangle, oriented longwise from bow to stern, and was slightly wider and longer than a large horse, with enough room at the forward end for a person holding a halter.

"Wonders never cease," Mel observed in stunned awe.

"Where does that go?" Polly asked, still frightened.

Mel smiled with a sudden realization and giggled. "The lower deck, of course."

"What 'lower deck' would that be?" Rei asked skeptically.

"The one I thought was just for ballast," Mel replied. He looked at the others, whose expressions were a mixture of incredulity and surprise. "I'll go with Candeo."

Garth shook his head. "Nuh-uh, Mel, this one's fer me an' MJ," he said, stepping forward and reaching out his hand to take the halter. "If anyone's gonna get locked in the hold with 'er..."

Mel smiled kindheartedly at his friend's concern. "I don't think we have anything to fear, and I agree that you are the perfect person to guide 'Bob' to a place that might frighten her at first," he said and handed the halter to Garth.

Garth's eyes welled up with emotion, and he turned and patted Candeo reassuringly. He led her carefully to the indicated place and caught his breath as the section of the deck began to slowly descend. "'Nother el'vator," he said with a grunt as he and his horse descended out of sight.

* * *

Garth held the halter in one hand and put his other arm around Candeo's neck as the section of the deck where they were standing gently descended three and a half meters down a glowing shaft into a similarly illuminated hold. The hold's walls were comprised of the boat's hull, the space wider at the top than at the bottom. The hold was long enough to fit two large horses, one in front of the other and wide enough to allow a person to pass the horses on either side. A gentle breeze of intermittent strength flowed through the hold, from silent and hidden fans at the forward end to similar fans aftward. The deck was composed of a firm rubber grating, able to allow stable waste to be automatically washed away down a shallow channel below.

There were two sets of pre-positioned equipment for feeding and accommodating the horses, the primary item of each being a padded canvas sling, the port sides of which were already fastened to the two-and-a-half-meter-high ceiling. The equipment also included mangers and water troughs at the forward end of each sling, affixed to the wall on either side at shoulder height. A cabinet of brushes and farrier tools was attached to the portside wall between the two sets of equipment. A two-level saddle rack was mounted to the floor a meter shy of the forward end of the hold.

Garth took a deep breath and gently led a hesitant Candeo to the forward set of equipment. As soon as they stepped off the deck lift, it silently rose back into position. Garth talked to Candeo calmly and patted her head, then reached for the canvas sling and brought it under her, attaching the other side to the ceiling so that it was snug for her but not tight. A sudden sound of rushing water caused him to jump, and he turned to see the water trough automatically fill. "Yep," he said, recognizing yet another inexplicable wonder. A moment later, he squinted at the water, then leaned close and sniffed it, and finally scooped some in his palm and tasted it. His eyes opened wide with pleasant surprise. "Them 'orses gonna have it better 'an us," he said aloud.

Just then, a panel of the ceiling at the forward end of the hold began to lower. A section of the floor of the *New Day*'s cabin descended into view and came to rest just beyond the saddle rack. Mel stepped off the cabin lift, and it rose back into place. He stared in wonder at the hold and its accommodations for the horses.

"Little did we know we could have taken them with us to the Caeli," Mel commented. "Though I think it's better that they were able to run and play and graze."

"Ya know how to get outta here?" Garth asked.

Mel glanced forward and aftward. "I imagine it has something to do with those." He pointed to two brightly glowing spots in the middle of the walls at the two ends of the hold.

Minutes later, Campitor courageously cooperated with being brought into the hold, though his neck was stiff with alarm. Once secured in place near Candeo, he relaxed and drank from his trough. Polly and Mihoshi volunteered to bring the horses' first food down to them, and soon Campitor and Candeo were happily chewing on hay and oats.

The young people again stepped ashore, and the few Embera children from the families who were able to gather on short notice once more climbed onto Garth and joyfully repeated his nickname "Atubwa!" Their parents soon rounded them up, and Mel and his friends climbed aboard the *New Day* and exchanged waves of sad farewell with the Emberas until the boat sailed out of sight back down the river toward the sea.

* * *

Mel decided it would be best for the *New Day* to maintain the appearance of a normal sailboat until they reached the Pacific Ocean. After several minutes of studying the map table, he learned how to set an above-water travel destination and indicated the Atlantic entrance of the Panama Canal. The boat took them there smoothly, where it shifted back to manual control. Rei insisted on taking the wheel, and they began the slow, eighty-kilometer journey through the canal.

Resting in the still waters of the first lock, they could hardly believe that just weeks before, they had been in the same region fleeing for their lives from Neco. The peaceful calm of the tropical air was broken occasionally by the distant screech of a blue parrot or by the sight of a bird of paradise drifting slowly through the trees, its long red and green feathers rippling gracefully behind it.

* * *

Two days later, they passed through the final lock and continued south along the deep blue waters of the Pacific Ocean channel. Mel glanced in every direction to make sure they were not being watched. The friends used the deck lift to bring the horses up and hitched them forward of the mast for grooming in the fresh air and sunlight.

Mel turned to Rei. "So! Back to Panama City?"

Mihoshi stopped her grooming of Candeo and stared intently at her brother, awaiting his response. Rei caught her glare and stepped next to Mel, putting his arm around his shoulder and facing them both away from his sister. He spoke softly so Mihoshi could not overhear him. He and Mel conversed in low tones for several minutes. Then Mel said aloud, "Well, we're going to the city and should be there in less than an hour."

Mihoshi's face fell. She turned and continued grooming Candeo. Her arms moved mechanically as she stared off toward the cloud-soaked mountains.

CHAPTER 33

THE HONOO KATANA

They sailed south toward Panama City, the gentle waves of the inlet slapping softly against the boat's side. A group of seals swam alongside and splashed and played tag in the boat's wake.

Estrangement hung in the air between Rei and his sister. To distract herself from thinking about their impending return to their double lives, Mihoshi continued grooming the horses. Rei checked his bags and wrote in a small, leather-bound notebook. Mel sat over the compendium, checking details and making plans for their trip back to Cooperton.

Rei guided the boat to a pier, where Mel leaped off and tied it to a mooring. Rei was preparing to jump to the pier when a large, red-faced harborworker with a handlebar mustache gestured for him to halt. "Hold on thar, sonny. Whar do ya think you're 'eaded?"

Rei closed his eyes and composed himself. He was reminded of why Mihoshi was so reluctant to return to the city. "I am returning to my home, sir."

He cast a disdainful eye on Rei. "We got other piers for yer kind. You don't belong 'ere."

Garth, overhearing this, stepped off the boat and walked boldly up to the overweight ruffian, who wore a tight-fitting, striped shirt that revealed several tattoos and an ample belly behind his belt. Garth was a head taller, though they were roughly equal in weight. He stood toe to toe with him and stared in his face.

"Look," the harborworker stated loudly but without conviction, "we don't want no trouble 'ere. We got rules, and I'm paid ta enforce 'em. So I'm gonna say it one last time." He produced a large hardwood club from his side and started slapping it against his palm. "Either that yella boy stays put, or you'll get back on your boat an' move on. Now, you white folk can go about your business, but he's got to stay on board."

Garth's eyes narrowed, and his muscles tensed at the insult to his friend. He looked like he was about to unleash his wrath on the perspiring man. "Don't be callin' him *yella boy*! Where he comes from, he's sumtin' like a prince, ya stupid swab. You should be bowin', not slingin' 'em ig-nor-ant slurs."

Mel stepped forward and put his hand on Garth's arm. "Let me talk to him for a moment." The harborworker stopped slapping his baton and straightened with overconfidence at being confronted by the much smaller young man.

Garth left the two of them to talk in low tones and walked back to the boat. He stood by Rei, his chest still tense with anger.

Rei looked at Garth and smiled. "Not so long ago, you were using those same 'slurs.'"

Garth hung his head. "Seems a lotta folks got the same disease. They're all tore up with ignance at people they don't wanna figger out. When I first met ya and yer sister, I didn't know what tu think. I ain't never had seen nobody like you 'afore. After travelin' and makin' friends, well I... I..." He began to get choked up.

Rei put a hand on his shoulder. "It's all right, I understand."

Garth straightened himself and cleared his throat. "No! Nothin' 'bout it's all right. I was stupid and scared, and so's this whole darn place. We oughta just march in there and put some learnin' on this stupid town."

"And if we were to make a show of violence, would that change the town's mindset regarding the potential danger of Asians?"

"Now see, thar ya go again! You and yer ideas. Most folk couldn't think that good if they tried. You're always lookin' further on down the road and gettin' things right without havin' to learn from gettin' 'em wrong." Garth's chin sank to his chest. "Lord, I'm so sorry 'bout treatin' you like I did."

"I know, Garth, I know."

Just then, Mel returned to his friends. "Okay, let's head into town. Rei, if you would lead the way?"

Rei nodded respectfully to Mel.

Mel turned to Mihoshi and Polly, who stood on the deck of the *New Day*. "It would be best if you two remained here until we're sure it's safe." Polly stared blankly and let out a small sigh. Mihoshi nodded in silent agreement.

The wary harborworker continued his route to another pier.

"What'd ya say to the thug?" Garth whispered to Mel.

"Just a little something in his favorite language," Mel answered with a wink, jiggling the small bag full of gems that he kept in his shirt pocket.

Rei glanced back at the boat and saw his sister peeking around Candeo's neck, tears in her eyes. When she saw her brother's glance, she ducked out of sight, wiping her tears with her forearm.

The young men left the pier and walked quickly through the city, from which, a few weeks before, they had narrowly escaped with their lives.

* * *

In the *New Day*'s cabin, Polly was gathering supplies for dinner when she was startled to find Mihoshi standing beside her, holding out her hands in an offer to help. "Oh!" Polly exclaimed. "Mihoshi, I didn't know you were there."

"I'm sorry, I did not mean to frighten you," Mihoshi answered sensitively while helping Polly arrange the supplies. "I'm distracted in my thoughts."

"What's wrong?"

Mihoshi's brow furrowed. "I never expected to see this day."

"What day is that?"

"The day my brother and I would walk different paths."

Polly stared at her in blank puzzlement.

"I'm going with Mel," Mihoshi explained.

Polly coughed in surprise. "Going with Mel? Does he know?"

"I believe he needs my support."

Polly smiled. "You don't think he, of all people, could take care of himself?" she asked with a hint of sarcasm.

"Gwyneth spoke to each of us as though we are meant to stay together. And now we are bonded by the Abico reward. His apprenticeship will not wait until our father sends word."

"You're willing to risk never seeing your brother again?"

"I will see him again, and Mel-san's training *will* continue."

"Suit yourself. But I don't think people are gonna treat you a whole lot better in America than they did here. At least here you have a family."

"But I *will* have family, Polly."

Though still unsure of Mihoshi's hidden meanings, Polly shrugged and smiled at her friend. "Well, whatever happens, I'm glad we don't have to say goodbye just yet. And I'm grateful for your help. When the boys get back, they'll be starving."

* * *

As they walked the hot, dusty streets of Panama City on their way toward Rei's house, hundreds of sets of eyes either looked away or stared suspiciously at the three weary travelers. Rei's face became blank, and he stared at the pavement as he walked.

"Well now," Garth muttered lowly to his two friends, "ain't we the center of attention? I'd rather take my chances in the jungle, where all ya gotta worry 'bout is hungry animals."

Rei smiled despite his somber mood.

They rounded the corner of The Lost Lagoon and came face to face with the burnt remains of Rei's home. Rei halted in his tracks, and his eyes narrowed in anger. Garth's mouth fell open in surprise. Rei clenched his fists and scanned the faces of the scattered townspeople, searching for anyone who looked familiar. Mel sensed his growing wrath and stepped forward, putting a calming hand on his shoulder. "I'm sorry," Mel said. "This was my fault. If I hadn't accepted your offer to accompany me..."

"No," Rei stated firmly, taking deep breaths to calm himself. "I understood the dangers. This was meant to happen." Rei gave an ironic smile. "It would seem that for some weeks, my sister and I have been destined to move on. Even if I had decided that we should stay, this is reason enough to go."

"Rei, how's your pa gonna write ya now, with nowhere to send the letter?" Garth asked, scratching his chin.

"Two days ago, I considered how I might receive notification from him if I were not here. Despite this destruction, those plans need not change. It will require only a simple arrangement with a friend at the post office to forward whatever I might receive." Rei patted his shirt pocket, indicating its contents. "I have already written my request, which we must deliver before returning to the boat."

They stepped into the remains of the living room. Rei stared in shock at what had been the entrance to the tunnel. The portion of the tunnel directly under the house had been deliberately demolished, leaving only a sunken trench in the ground. Rei's face went pale, and he stared across the city in the direction of his other home in the Chinese Quarter.

"Well, if they found the tunnel, they prolly followed—" Garth began before Mel placed a hand on his arm, shaking his head "no." Garth looked away in embarrassment. Rei took off, running toward the far neighborhood.

* * *

They discovered that Rei's Japanese home had met the same fate. A fragile skeleton of burnt beams was all that remained. Another trench in the ground indicated that this end of the tunnel had also been demolished. Rei stared in agony at the tragic remains. "My home! The artwork and books! They were prized in my family for generations!" Rei ran forward and began rifling through the charred interior for anything that had survived the flames. Mel and Garth joined the search, carefully avoiding any contact with the brittle weight-bearing beams that appeared ready to topple the remains of the upper story onto their heads.

Rei stopped suddenly. "Thank you for your help, but what was kept in this house now survives only in my memories."

Mel looked at his friend with compassion. "I am so sorry."

Rei bowed in agreement. He took one last forlorn glance at the ruins of the home that he had treasured, and then his expression shifted to grim resolve, and he turned and rushed to what had been the dining room. "Do not let grief overtake you. There is one last place the fire could not have reached." Rei shoved aside the burnt remains of a low table. Kicking away the debris of a destroyed rug, he uncovered a blackened hatch. Mel and Garth exchanged surprised glances. The edges of the hatch crumbled in Rei's hands. "If we lift it together, it should remain intact."

Mel and Garth rushed to him, and the three of them carefully lifted the burnt trap door. Beneath it was a descending stairway.

Rei led the others down the musty stairs. At the bottom was a massive door made of polished metal and inscribed with *Kanji* lettering. The door had no lock nor latch nor any visible means of being opened.

"What's that say?" Garth inquired.

"Miyamoto Musashi's Key."

"What's that 'sposed ta mean?"

"Do you remember what I told you of my nation's most famous samurai, Miyamoto Musashi? He was the greatest sword maker in Japan. Among the many methods he developed, there was one that he employed to craft just two blades. No one has yet been able to duplicate it. Many have tried, including my father, who very nearly discovered the formula in his youth."

Garth looked at the solid metal door and tapped it with his

knuckles. "This thang's solid thick. How you 'spose we gonna get in there, with no handles or nothin' to pull it open?"

"Why do you assume it must be *pulled* open?"

"Ain't that what they do in banks an' stuff? How else would it work? Anyhow, what's so awful 'portant 'bout what's in thar that it gotta be locked up like this?"

"Aside from the technology that Mel's ancestors developed, the items behind this door are among the wonders of this world."

"You ain't just pullin' my leg, are ya?"

"I'll let you be the judge of that." Rei carefully untied his pony-tail and loosened the braids. From the hair at the back of his head, he slowly withdrew a razor-thin piece of metal that flexed in his fingers.

"That's some hidin' spot fer a key." Garth stepped back to see what Rei would do with the odd little piece of metal.

Rei lifted it up and eyed it. "I never thought I would be doing this. I had thought that my father would return and that the honor would be his." He took the thin strip of metal and deftly slipped it into a virtually invisible slot on the door. He slid it along the slot to the left and then to the right and then inserted it into two smaller slots on either side, making the *Kanji* symbol for fire.

The door silently opened inward, revealing a single table in the middle of a round room. Upon it were two swords resting on blocks of gold partly covered by silk cloth. The swords glowed through their ivory sheaths as if the blades were illuminated by an inner light. The longer sword glowed blue, and the shorter glowed red. Against the wall opposite the door were a bow and a quiver of arrows and a chest that appeared ancient.

"These are the most priceless treasures of the Meiji family," Rei said proudly. "The greatest is the Honoo Katana, the blade that glows blue."

Garth simply stared in awe.

The three friends reverently entered the dimly lit, noiseless chamber. Rei walked slowly, almost ceremonially, to the alabaster-handled swords while replacing the key in his hair, reweaving his braids, and tying off his ponytail. He withdrew three plain, burlap knapsacks from beneath the table, two of which were large. He wrapped the silk cloth on the table around his hands and swiftly covered the swords and placed them in a large knapsack, which he then slung over his shoulders. He put the gold blocks into the small bag and handed it to Garth to carry. He stowed the bow and quiver of arrows in the other large bag and handed it to Mel. Finally, Rei opened the old chest and withdrew a fourth bag, which was already filled, and handed it to Garth. Rei nodded in thanks to the others and headed for the door.

As he approached the exit, he heard two sets of footsteps crunching on the charred remains of the floor above. The three of them stood back against the wall to one side of the door.

"I'm tellin' you," a voice sounded from atop the stairs, "'em's the same guys we saw a few weeks back. The boss wanted 'em *real* bad. 'Specially that little, white kid. That bigin' don't matter, we can take him out, and the China man. But the boss needs the kid, named Mal or Mel or sumtin', ta give a talkin' to."

Mel glanced at his two equally incredulous friends.

"He can't be daid," the man continued, "so be careful with your guns. I don't want the boss sendin' my wife a basket with my haid in it."

Mel tensed for a fight. Rei reached into the knapsack on his back, drew the Honoo Katana from its scabbard, and started toward the stairs, holding the glowing, blue blade at the ready. Mel held him back and whispered, "Wait."

As the sounds above them grew closer, one of the men suddenly cried out. "Hey! Looks like we got some stairs goin' to the basement. I'll check it out."

Another voice replied from farther away. "A'right. The two 'a us is gonna take a look 'round the neighborhood and make sure we ain't missed 'em a'ready."

Rei glanced through the door and saw the flickering light of a recently lit lantern. Dusty boots descended the stairs, followed by dirty cotton trousers and a hand brandishing a rusted, Civil War five-shot revolver. Rei ducked back out of sight.

The friends stood against the wall, ready to strike. Just as the man was fully within the room, Mel grabbed his gun-wielding hand and threw him to the floor with a thud, sending the revolver skidding across the room. Rei grasped the man's glass lantern out of the air, inches above the hard floor. The man grunted as he landed. Mel silenced him with a grasp to his throat. "Why are you here?" Mel demanded as he released his hold enough to allow him to speak.

The man coughed to catch his breath. "Hey there! I don't mean ya no harm. I'ze just snoopin' 'round this old burnt house."

"Oh, so you're *not* here to capture me and kill my friends?" Mel said, sneering. Rei put his sword to the frightened man's neck.

"Look!" the man said. "I just do what I'm told."

"And what *were* you told?"

"We is to be on the lookout for some Chinese guy, a big brute, and a smaller white guy, who might come snoopin' back here some-day. We was promised good money if'n we'd bring 'em to the boss."

"Who told you the name 'Mel'?"

The man was sweating profusely and staring at the gleaming blue edge of Rei's sword. "The boss. I don't got no grudge 'gainst you. I'ze just told ta bring you back ta talk to the boss."

"But you could kill the others. Is that what the boss said?"

The man's eyes darted back and forth in reluctance. "Yeah."

"And where can I find this 'boss' of yours?"

"I don't know! I swear! He comes and goes. We never know when he's gonna show up. He always finds us!"

"What's his name? Or does that come and go as well?"

"The boss's name? We ain't allowed to use it no more. He'd kill me if I told ya."

Rei held the blade closer to the man's throat.

The man clenched his teeth and squinted in fear. "All right! All right, I'll tell you. His name is..." The man's eyes froze with fright, and he went suddenly still. His breath slowly let out the word "Neeecooo." The man relaxed and did not breathe again.

Garth jumped back. "What was *that*? We didn't do nothin'."

"Neco?" Rei asked. "How could that be?"

"I have a suspicion about what caused it," Mel whispered to Garth, fraught with concern. "The only people who could do something like that are the—"

"Danny!" a man yelled from atop the stairs, "ya find anythin'?"

"Nup. Nothin's heh," Mel responded in Danny's exact voice and accent. "I'm gonna 'ead back to the other 'ouse in a minute an' keep an eye on it."

"We'll be thar soon, still checkin' the streets 'round here."

Garth looked at Mel, amazed at his imitation of the dead man. "How didya do that?"

"It's just a trick I learned." Mel turned to Rei. "We'll talk more about Neco later. Let's wait till the other two are out of sight and then head back to the boat. We'll drop off your letter on the way."

Mel climbed to the top of the stairs and peered out. A moment later, he signaled to the others, and they scrambled up the stairs. As a group, they slipped out into the city, their burlap bags strung over their shoulders.

* * *

In the *New Day*'s cabin, the two young women were preparing dinner at a portable stove, which had been provided by Tothar. Polly was putting vegetables and portions of rice into the flaming wok, which Mihoshi was handling with skill.

Outside, two men silently crept from the pier onto the prow of the boat, batons at their sides and machetes in their hands. One of the men looked at the other and pointed toward the cabin. The second man nodded.

Polly was chopping carrots with a butcher knife, and Mihoshi was continuing to mix the ingredients in the wok when Polly was startled by the sound of the horses whinnying simultaneously and stomping their feet. She whirled around, her knife at the ready. Mihoshi turned calmly, breathing a sigh of relief. A sound like two sacks of potatoes being hit by a train came from on the deck, followed by two loud splashes in the water beside the boat. Echoes of painful cries and frantic swimming drew away from the boat toward another nearby pier.

Polly rushed to the deck, followed by Mihoshi. They laughed as they saw the two thugs desperately swimming away.

"Did you know they were aboard?" Polly asked incredulously.

"The boat dipped under their weight and swayed with a different rhythm," Mihoshi explained.

The horses were still breathing heavily from the excitement. The two young women patted them and embraced their necks, proud of their guardians.

Realizing that the thugs might return, Mihoshi glanced across the harbor in every direction. "Polly, if I may ask you to finish dinner, I believe it would be wise for me to stand guard."

"Of course," Polly replied and disappeared into the cabin.

Mihoshi took one more look around and then ducked into the cabin to retrieve her bow and arrows. She crouched at the top of the stairs and surveyed the surrounding area in the growing darkness of the evening.

* * *

Mel, Rei, and Garth came running. Mel stopped and untied the boat while the others jumped aboard. He finished his task and leaped after them, and the boat began to drift away from the pier. "Garth," Mel said swiftly, "can you please take Candeo below?"

Garth unhitched Candeo and led her to the deck lift.

Mihoshi rose from her crouched position and ran to her brother. "What has happened? Why are we leaving?"

"Panama City made a decision of its own," Rei replied. "We

found our homes destroyed and men seeking to kill us."

Mihoshi gasped.

Rei continued, "It would seem that you have the gift of prophecy, my sister," he said with an affectionate smile.

Mihoshi embraced him. "Rei," she said with tears in her eyes.

Rei wiped his eyes and returned his sister's embrace.

"There is something that I must confess," Mihoshi said in shame. "If you had found the city unchanged from how we knew it, we would still have been parted. I had resolved that I would go with Mel-san. I was afraid you were gone forever."

Rei stared into her eyes. "I suspected as much, and I do not blame you. You know it would not have been forever."

Polly had heard the voices on deck and now appeared from inside the cabin. "We had some guests while you guys were gone," she said with a frown. She put a hand on Campitor's shoulder. "Thankfully, Campi and Candi took care of them, but next time how about one of you gentlemen stays with us?"

Mel grimaced in embarrassment. "I'm so sorry, Polly. I had thought this town's hostility would have died out with Neco, but his fate was not as clear as we assumed."

"What do you mean? He's not dead?" Polly asked fearfully.

"I'd guess that he sent those men to capture you to get to us."

Polly glanced nervously at the slowly receding city.

Mel turned to Rei. "I suggest we set sail in earnest before they regroup. Once the horses are below, we can submerge."

Rei nodded, gave his sister a kiss on the cheek, and stepped quickly to the boat's wheel. Mel ran to the mast and sang the song to release the sail. A moment later, the sail emerged and filled with wind, and the *New Day* began moving swiftly away from the harbor.

"My sister," Rei said, "I also have something to confess."

Mihoshi looked at him with curiosity.

"Two days ago, before we entered the canal, I decided that I also would go with Mel-san. We made our expedition into the city only so I could have our letters forwarded to Cooperton and retrieve a few items from our homes, the most important, of course, being the Honoo Katana, the Nasu-no-Yoichi Bow, and the contents of the Wafuku Chest."

Mihoshi looked at the four bags that the young men had deposited next to the entrance of the cabin and then glared at her brother. "Why did you not tell me of your decision?"

"For your whole life, you have been devoted to me," Rei explained, "and have abided my authority. I recognized an opportunity to see what you would do when you believed me to be wrong. I did not enjoy the experiment, but from it, I have gained the certainty that my sister will make the right decisions in the days when I will not be there for her. I can rest, knowing that you will never be alone but will always have someone who is much wiser than your brother, or any man, to guide you."

"I cannot say that I would have chosen this test," Mihoshi responded, "but I am honored to hear that you were proud of my conduct." Her formal demeanor fell away, and she ran to Rei and gave him another hug. "And may I soon find my chance to test you in return," she said with a wink.

Rei laughed. "It would be justice." He again kissed her cheek.

"Hey, guys!" Polly shouted. "I see a whole bunch of lanterns heading toward the harbor." Mel followed her gaze and saw the approaching mob. The *New Day* had moved several hundred meters offshore when gunshots rang out. Everyone scrambled for cover except Mel, who readied his Sazo.

Garth ducked his head out of the cabin. "We's outta range," he cried out, watching the bullets splash harmlessly into the water twenty meters away. "What in the world's this Neco guy got 'gainst us anyways?" Garth emerged up the stairs, and the others stood up from behind the cabin top.

Mel stared intently toward the harbor with a worried expression, searching for one specific person. "It's not 'us,' Garth. It's just me." Rei handed his spyglass to Mel, who continued to watch the mob closely.

"Well, he had some bees in his britches 'bout Rei too!"

"Only because he appeared to be my contact in this town. And we can be sure that Neco isn't the kind of man to be satisfied with burning down buildings or with letting his prey get away. You were wondering what happened to the man who died beneath Rei's house? He was under a 'Mortis Trance.' My father told me that it's part of an ancient curse that is put on a person and lies dormant within him until it's triggered by a breach of confidence."

"A breach 'a what?"

"Confidence," Polly repeated. "It's like keeping a secret."

Mel nodded to Polly in thanks. "The person submits to a powerful hypnotic spell and swears never to reveal certain information. It remains binding until the 'boss' is removed from his position of authority. When the oath of secrecy is broken, the curse is fulfilled. Few people know how to perform such a curse."

"Like who?" Garth asked hesitantly.

"I don't know their names or how many of them there are, but I know where they came from. The only persons who practice the black art of the Mortis Trance are the Strangers. They can come from any of the tribes of Delemni. To one degree or another, they're all related to me."

CHAPTER 34

SOBRANTE'S POINT

As Garth started leading Campitor to the hold, the others watched as the lights of the lanterns streamed onto a barge, slowly crossed to the westward side of the channel, and proceeded at the speed of riders on horseback along a coastal road in tandem with the *New Day*. Mel asked Rei to keep the boat just beyond the range of their pursuers' firearms and to match their speed while he continued watching for Neco.

"How long can they keep following us?" Polly asked Rei, who was steering the boat and watching their pursuers' movements.

"They are driven by an evil force. They fear for their lives if they fail. They will press forward as if the future of their families rested on their success. But we need not worry; we will be able to easily leave them behind soon enough."

After overhearing Rei speak to Polly, Mel took a deep breath. "I'm going to give them their success." As his friends stared at him, dumbfounded, he pointed ahead of them along the coast. "That small, flat peninsula should serve the purpose. If we pull into the cove a half kilometer beyond it, we should be just far enough ahead of them for me to have time to climb up and meet them near there."

Polly shook her head in disbelief. "There are at least a dozen lights! Are you planning to take them all on?"

"No, just one of them. If I confront him, I may be able to arrange for the others to be set free."

"Do you think that Neco is with them?" Polly asked.

"If not, he's somewhere nearby."

Rei glanced over the steep coastal terrain, assessing its strategic potential. "How shall we assist you to reach Neco without us having to first confront the others? Will we draw the gang away while you take Neco aside, like what happened in the mountains?"

"*We* are not going to confront them at all. The cove where we're headed is surrounded by steep cliffs, too dangerous for any of you to climb. Besides, my plan is not to fight them; they're just innocent dupes who are tracking their boss's enemy. I will not have their blood on my conscience."

Polly turned to Mel, her neck veins protruding. "You're going to let them capture you? Are you *crazy*? They're no threat to us. In a minute, they won't even be able to see us! They're bound to give up sooner or later."

"Polly, Rei was right. Those men and their families will most likely die if they fail this mission. I'm going to meet with their 'boss' and see if anything can placate him. And I must go alone."

Garth emerged on deck, incredulous at what he had heard on his way up from the cabin lift. He turned to Mel and stood tall in the starlight. "We done come too far with ya to sit back and let ya face this by yerself."

Mel looked up at his big-muscled and big-hearted friend and said compassionately, "I will not put any of you in danger needlessly, and as we learned from our confrontation in the mountains, if it comes to a fight, I can't guarantee I can protect myself, let alone the rest of you as well."

Rei looked to Mihoshi, who was sitting with her eyes shut.

Mel walked to the case that housed Vulgladius and touched it lightly. The lid opened, and he looked at the dormant sword encased in its simple leather scabbard. He was amazed at the incredible power that rested in such a simple guise. He took the sheathed sword and strapped it to his back to allow for an unhindered climb up the cliff.

Rei adjusted the sail for a faster speed and changed their course to head for the cove that Mel had indicated. Polly stomped towards Rei, where he stood at the ship's wheel. "How can you let him do this? It's absurd, and he's going to get himself killed!"

Rei looked back at her with a resolute gaze. "Mel must do what he has been called to do. He is not ours to control."

Polly slouched to the deck in defeat. Mihoshi rose, sat beside her, and put a comforting arm around her.

Mel stared at the approaching shoreline. "After I'm ashore, sail out of range and drop the anchor. If I'm not back on the beach by dawn, sail to the next town and report me missing." He glanced at Rei, who nodded in agreement.

* * *

As they reached the inner edge of the sandy cove, Mel slipped over the side and swam the short distance to shore. There he swiftly climbed the steep granite cliff. He found the climb much easier than the path he had taken to reach the Abico vault. Though there was little light, the stars illuminated Mel's route, and he quickly ascended to the dirt road above.

After running a half kilometer back toward the city, he found an ideal stretch of road near the small peninsula, with tall cliffs on the land side and a steep drop to the tidal rocks below. He chose this first location hoping it would prevent his pursuers from surrounding him and gaining command of the encounter. He planned to do everything in his power to avoid killing the hapless men and needed to determine if they would be receptive to his plan before the intended meeting with Neco took place on the peninsula.

One minute later, the thundering of two dozen galloping horses and a glow of lights approached along the winding coastal road. The first man, carrying a lantern, rounded the corner and saw Mel standing cross-armed in the middle of the road.

"Whoa!" the man yelled as he slid his horse to a stop. The frenzied pack of riders behind him narrowly avoided colliding and pushing one another over the cliff in their frantic efforts to halt.

"What ya doin' here, boy?"

"I'm here to meet your boss," Mel replied.

The man dismounted and prepared to take out his gun as he barked orders to the others behind him. "Be careful not to plug this kid. And don't be accident'ly puttin' one in my back either."

He turned to Mel and sneered. "Look, sonny, we ain't got no boss, and I cain't figger why anyone'd be lookin' fer a little pip squeak like you anyways."

"Then why have you been racing along the coast? Taking your horses out for exercise?"

"What's with you, kid? You oughta have the sense to know you're in a tight spot. We'z two dozen killers runnin' from the law, and we ain't in the mood to let a little kid get in our way."

Mel smiled in the lamplight. "You're two dozen poor canal workers and shopkeepers frantically chasing someone you don't know. Someone who wants to save your lives."

The men laughed together, mocking Mel.

"My name is Mel. Your 'boss' has requested to see me and would doubtless appreciate being informed that I'm here."

"Heavens, Joe, that's him!" said a man behind him, who had a shaved head and scars across his face.

"Shaddup, Fred. Now, listen, kid. We was told to chase some powerful hombre and bring him to justice. You don't look too powerful, and ya ain't old 'nough to count as no outlaw. How do we know you're the Mel we're lookin' fer? If'n we go back with some kid, and he ain't the one, we're in a heap 'a trouble."

Mel reached behind his neck and drew Vulgladius, which instantly ignited in a flaming swirl of energy.

Joe leaped back. "Watch out, boys! Looks just like the one Necaaaah...." He grabbed his neck and fell to his knees. Fred and several others ran to Joe's side but could only watch helplessly as he slumped to the ground and remained utterly still.

Mel looked at the now very frightened group of men and sheathed Vulgladius. "I'll wager that the 'boss' put each of you under hypnosis at one point and called it 'training' that you needed if you were going to work for him. What he actually did was put each of you under a potent and deadly curse. You and your families are in mortal danger. If you do as I tell you, I may be able to help you escape from him."

They looked at Mel and then at the lifeless body of Joe. With a nod from Fred, the men put away their firearms. "What... what should we do?" Fred stammered. "We're just folks who saw a chance to make some money. Didn't think there'd be no harm in it. And certainly didn't 'spect we'd be joinin' forces with some devil."

Mel sighed in relief. "Send word back to your boss that you found me and have me surrounded and that I'm willing to meet."

"That's all? But we was told ta bring ya back."

"I doubt that Neco actually planned on you bringing me back."

The men cringed at the mention of their boss's name.

"He's waiting for word of a fight," Mel continued. "When he hears it, he'll come and face me himself. That is, if he isn't already on his way." Mel pointed at the nearby peninsula. "I'll wait there, so it looks like you have me trapped."

Fred nodded to the others, jumped on his horse, and galloped back towards Panama City.

Mel started walking. The men stepped aside and watched him with somber eyes, few of them daring to hope. Several minutes later, Mel reached the fifty-meter-wide, flat-topped peninsula. It was bordered on three sides by vertical cliffs that fell one hundred meters into the crashing ocean below. A cliffside updraft filled the air with a light, salty mist. The men followed and waited nervously on the adjoining stretch of road, taking up positions to feign having Mel trapped.

Mel addressed the men. "In case Neco returns first, it would be best if you kept your firearms aimed at me." They complied, and Mel walked to a position near the end of the peninsula and again drew Vulgladius.

* * *

An hour before dawn, Fred returned on a new horse, breathing laboriously and holding his side in pain. "He's on his way," he gasped, dismounting and handing his horse's reigns to one of his companions. "He said the meetin' will be just the two 'a ya, and y'all won't be usin' nothin' that shoots. Sounds like he wants it to be mano a mano."

"What about the rest of you?" Mel asked.

Fred looked worriedly at his companions and spoke loudly enough for them to hear. "We're to wait 'round the corner down the road durin' the meetin'."

Mel nodded. "I'll see you after we come to an understanding."

"I'm 'spose ta keep a close eye on ya till he shows up." Fred reluctantly drew his pistol and pointed it at Mel. He did his best to counter the anxiety that was causing his gun hand to shake and his eyes to dart to and fro. He knew that he would need to be composed for his boss's arrival. "They call this place Sobrante's Point," Fred explained, his voice cracking as he forced himself to talk to calm his nerves. "It's Spanish for 'excess.' Course, it'll be diff'ernt now with tuh canal, but fer years folks've dumped cargo on the beach over there, stuff they don't needta carry all way 'round the Cape and 'ave it taken by road to the 'lantic side."

"A fitting name. May this place be used again tonight to leave a burden behind," Mel responded.

Fred smiled with understanding. "Amen to that." His expression changed to puzzlement. "Why you doin' this, anyways? We was all figgerin' ya'd just keep sailin'."

Mel looked him in the eye. "I'm a child of my father. He wouldn't want innocent men to die because of me, not when I could give them a chance."

Fred shook his head in disbelief. "This is too much. If I don't die tonight, I might just let the Missus take me back to church."

Mel laughed. He took a seat cross-legged on the ground and breathed deeply to maintain his calm and build his focus. He gently rested Vulgladius on the ground beside him, where it remained inactive. Gulls coasted gracefully on the wind, which flowed along the cliff walls. Seals and otters barked playfully on the rocks offshore. Suddenly, the sounds of the animals' pre-dawn feeding ceased, the gulls turned north, and the seals and otters disappeared off their rocks into the water. Sensing an impending arrival, Mel lifted Vulgladius and again stood, taking up a feigned defensive posture against Fred.

The sound of heavy hooves echoed along the coast as a giant coal-black horse galloped around a bend in the road, spitting and bucking, and skidded to a stop at the neck of the small peninsula. A hooded figure dismounted from the steed amidst an encompassing swirl of his dark cloak, his face hidden by the shadows of his garments. With a dismissive wave, he gestured for the men to withdraw down the road. He approached to within twenty meters and, with a nod, dismissed Fred. Fred walked hurriedly away until he was out of the man's field of view and then ran full speed to join his companions on the road. From his position near the end of the peninsula, Mel could see around the bend in the road to where the men stood staring fixedly in his direction.

Mel wondered if Neco had somehow survived Campitor's charge or if this were another Stranger who had adopted the same name. Mel tried to gain a glimpse of the face within the cloak as the man drew his own flaming sword and stepped closer.

The hooded man stretched out an artificial hand. "You have stolen something that has long been owed to *us*," he hissed in a deep, raspy voice, beckoning for Mel to hand over an item.

"Neco," Mel said in solemn recognition. "I didn't know you until several weeks ago, yet you speak as though we have a feud."

"You have *never* known us!" Neco bellowed rebelliously. "You knew someone close to us. And you killed him so you could steal his reward. We have come to take it back!"

Mel reflected on his adventures over the past months. He had had many close encounters with people who had tried to kill him. A few of his attackers had died, but he had not taken anything from them. He looked at Neco. "If you explain further, I might know if I can help you."

Neco roared in anger. Flinging back his hood, he revealed his terribly scarred and disfigured face, which was covered in recent burn marks. Deep, stitched scars ran up his cheek and across his left eye. His right ear was missing. He sneered, revealing several gaps in his teeth.

"If you can *help* us?" he said in a mocking, whining tone. "Don't give us that condescending dribble, you little worm. You stole our life," Neco said, pointing a black, accusing finger at Mel. "You destroyed our destiny, you pathetic slug."

Mel was in stunned disbelief. He could not visually recognize the man, but the tone and the words were all too familiar. "*Jora?*"

"*No!*" he shouted. "He is *dead*! You killed him! You and your father rigged that vault to explode. You *knew* he was better than you and more deserving of a Vysard's discipleship, so you sabotaged his rightful destiny and rid yourself of him."

Mel decided against provoking Jora by correcting his claims.

"He died that day, and we were born," Jora continued. "While you have been traipsing around the world with your new friends, *we* have been working. Others found us, who were not deceived by your father's lies. They recognized the worth that we possess. They have not abandoned us, as those who called themselves our 'family' so lightly did.

"We have been welcomed by great men, some who escaped the holocaust of Mount Peleé, and some who have hidden since the fall of Delemni itself! They have continued our discipleship. Great knowledge was buried for centuries by spineless egg-suckers like Telemai, but, despite his cowardice, the secrets of true power have been discovered!"

Mel looked at his old tutor with pity. Outwardly, he was barely recognizable through his grotesque disfigurement, and inwardly, his contempt and bitterness had only grown. Mel felt tempted to despair and to resign Jora to his condition but instead chose to hope that he might finally be able to address the root of Jora's consuming anger if he could keep him talking.

"What caused you to stray from your first discipleship, Jora?"

"*Neco!*" he raged. "You will never again call us by that enslaved name! We'll tell you what caused it—it was your father and you, his putrescent son. Telemai knew that your superior was curious, that he had a thousand questions, yet few were ever answered. Your superior was deemed too inquisitive and was 'graciously' reassigned to serve as a helper for you, the new protégé. A helper! Ha! He was a prisoner, forced to help you learn all the years of training that he had worked so hard to accomplish. He was shackled with you and would never again have access to a Caeli, except when it would be to help you with your lessons. After all that time, still Telemai refused to again train him. And what was accomplished? You are the epitome of failure, and your father knew it. Telemai knew you would never rival your superior's achievements unless they were exploited for your training. Though he knew that your superior was better than you, still he banned his progress to enable yours, you *despicable* little *puke!*"

"I was a young child with no memories," Mel pleaded. "I knew nothing of your history except what you told me, and I only ever hoped for your good!"

Jora sneered. "Oh, the poor baby lost his memories," he said, finishing with a hiss. "Your superior's greatest achievement was near before you reached Cooperton. But Telemai plucked you from the sea."

Mel's jaw went slack, "Your *achievement?*"

"It was no accident that befell you during the storm. It was not the boom of the mast that struck you. Your superior had hoped that if you were gone, Telemai would turn again to him."

Mel felt anger welling up at the revelation that Jora had attempted to murder him and that his many years of struggle with his memories were due to the man who now stood before him as a monstrosity. Still, Mel knew that he could not let the evil that had befallen him turn his own heart dark. Forcing back his anger and pain, he chose to speak with compassion. "My father loved you, Jora. He would have done anything to help you succeed."

"Lies! Deceit and poison! That's all that an Uri knows to speak. Your father is the master of lies. He deceived the elders in Martinique and created a hidden Caeli, accessible only to himself, his family, and his closest friends. He blinded you to believe that your superior was a willing tutor, that he enjoyed pandering to a worthless snot. I bet he even told you that your mother *died*! Didn't he?"

At those words, the searing flame of Vulgladius crackled and flared red, echoing the passion Mel felt within. "What are you saying? My mother is *alive*?"

Jora recognized with a devious grin that his words had inflamed Mel's anger. "Oh, we don't know if you could call it 'alive.' Being the slave of the Warlord of Mauritania isn't much of a life."

"No!" Mel shouted, beginning to panic. "She died saving me!"

"Oh! Was that the story they told you, parasite? The fact that they never knew for sure is one of your superior's proudest accomplishments. He had made a deal with local flesh merchants who mingled in with the mob. While your father was away, seeking to save himself from the mountain, your superior let the merchants within the walls. When they found your mother near your unconscious body, they carried her away to a new fate washing the mud off the horses of a Chief with twenty wives, in a land five thousand kilometers away."

"They found her body. There is a grave."

Jora laughed smugly. "It is the grave of another woman whose body was brought by the flesh traders, burned so badly that no one could tell the difference. Do you remember that it was your superior who brought you home while the firestorm still raged?"

Mel felt overwhelmingly confused and vulnerable. Tears of anger and despair flooded his face. "But why would you save someone that you hated?"

"He had hoped that Telemai would be grateful and reinstate

him. But no! He was rewarded with a prison sentence!" Jora spit, and the heat from his flaming sword caused it to sizzle and evaporate in midair. "Enough talk! Now, give us what you stole from us!" he shouted while swinging his sword from side to side.

Mel remained motionless, struggling to control his emotions.

"*Give it to us!*" Jora roared.

"What?" Mel cried in exasperation. "*What* do you *want?*"

"How stupid can you be? Why do you think we drove you back toward the hidden Caeli? Why do you think we allowed you to complete your task?" He cocked his scarred neck and yelled, "Give us the contents of the Abico vault!"

Mel stared at him in amazement and then began to laugh with incredulity.

"Do you mock us?" Jora asked bitterly. "We will not be denied!" He held his sword high as if to strike.

A leather pouch with a small scroll protruding from it fell at his feet. "What's this?" Jora hissed.

"The reward for your effort, for all the lies you've told, all the men you've killed. Tell me if it's worth the misery you sowed."

Jora reached out greedily, seething with malevolent delight as he picked up the leather pouch. "We knew you were a little coward, that you wouldn't dare stand up to us. We have always been your better in every discipline of combat. Now you will live the rest of your useless life knowing that you equipped your enemies with the tool that will secure your destruction."

Mel stared with pity and disgust at the wreck of a man before him. "'Brumble Berry Serendipity.' I'm sorry, but all the berries were used to make a pie. Even if they hadn't been used, the reward wouldn't mean anything to you, as you clearly chose long ago that it wouldn't."

"What are you babbling about, you flea-infested rodent?" Jora asked as he withdrew the small scroll.

"'*I ate the pie, that was the prize,*'" Mel replied, quoting an old riddle that Jora, himself, had taught him years before. "I'm afraid you just don't get it, Jora."

"What?" Jora snapped in frustration as he futilely tried to shake out the contents of the empty bag.

"I'm afraid that what was required to open the vault and to enjoy the reward was something you do not understand."

Jora, with one hand holding his sword, was trying to open the scroll with his free hand, but the paper recoiled on itself. Finally, he gripped one end with his lips and rolled the scroll out. It burst into flames, its burning fragments temporarily blinding him.

He leaped back, screaming, "Liar! It was a trick!" He began slashing his sword madly in all directions while backing up, and unwittingly ignited patches of brush as he went. Flaming pieces of scroll fell to the ground and drifted on the wind, further igniting the vegetation across the peninsula. Jora's horse, spooked by the flames, bolted back down the road toward the city.

Mel was distracted by the flames beginning to spread around them and was caught off guard by a sudden advance and flurry of attacks from Jora. A desperate swing caught Vulgladius and flung it far from Mel, where it skidded to a stop amid a rapidly expanding patch of brush fire mere meters from the cliff's edge. Mel saw where Vulgladius lay, and ran toward it, patting out flames that licked at his clothing.

Jora wiped the last of the ashes from his eyes and saw Mel's helpless state. With a cold expression, he loped his mutilated, though agile, frame toward the defenseless young man.

Mel extinguished a swath of fire as he slid to his knees and reclaimed Vulgladius, finding its hilt to be as cold as a river rock.

Mel, still on his knees, turned toward Jora just in time to fend off a blazingly powerful blow. Sparks flew in every direction. Jora hacked incessantly as Mel, on his knees, parried to one side or the other to prevent Jora's sword from severing his head.

Mel regained his footing as the onslaught continued. With Jora's initial advantage now negated, the opponents met each other with deliberation, employing the fullness of their lethal skill. The rushing and whirling of their footwork during the frenzied struggle stamped out the nearby flames.

From down the road, Fred gaped at the burning peninsula and its now mortally locked combatants. He watched in utter awe as the furiously crackling and resounding swords met like two undeniable forces being repeatedly unleashed against each other, only to be frustrated at every turn.

Mel feigned left, Jora's blade barely missing his shoulder. He darted past Jora and slashed at his back. The slash, which should have inflicted a serious wound, neither pierced the cloak nor singed its fabric. Mel backed away carefully, wonder and puzzlement writ across his face.

Jora, who was beginning to tire, paused his attack to comment on the phenomenon. "A little innovation from our new friends! We will have bruises in the morning, but nothing more. The fabric is impervious to the magnetic blade and the fire of our swords. You cannot defeat us!" Jora shouted and renewed his attack.

Mel began to wonder how he could outmatch someone who was part mechanical and whose cloak was impenetrable to his sword. He decided that his only hope was to strike at Jora's head, which was no longer covered by his robe. He attacked Jora repeatedly, swinging from many different angles, but to no avail. He soon became fatigued from the exertion. With his last bit of strength, he swung with all his might, catching Jora on the shoulder with a blow that would have killed him if he had not been wearing his protective cloak. Mel was utterly spent and sank to the ground, Vulgladius falling from his exhausted hands.

Jora, in triumph, gloated over the bent form of Mel. "A final lesson for the pupil. We shall teach you of the usurper's death and of the rise of the true sons of Delemni." He lifted his sword for the final blow.

Mel looked at the ground and prayed for a quick release. There was a sudden sound like several bees darting through the air in quick succession. He looked up and saw three arrowheads protruding from the front of Jora's robe where they had passed through his body, followed an instant later by a glowing, blue blade that emerged from his chest. Blood flowed into the cloak's fabric. The blue sword was quickly withdrawn.

Jora hissed as he started to turn to see his assassin. Weakness suddenly overwhelmed him. He dropped his sword, stumbled toward the precipice of the peninsula, and toppled headlong over the edge, falling a hundred meters into the raging surf that buffeted the base of the cliff.

Mel looked up at Rei, who was cleaning his katana with a piece of silk. Mihoshi approached across the still-smoldering landscape, the open flame beginning to flicker out as it consumed the last of the low brush on the peninsula. Rei sheathed his blade, and Mihoshi hung her bow over her shoulder.

"Where did you..." Mel trailed off in exhaustion and disbelief as his friends ran to him and hugged him. Mihoshi clung to his shoulder and began to weep. Mel looked, awestruck, at his brave and faithful companions who had sacrificed and risked much for him, and he felt unworthy of their loyalty. Shedding his own tears and still on his knees, he bowed slowly and respectfully to Rei and Mihoshi, who each responded in kind. "I am thankful to you, my friends. And thankful to the One who brought us together."

Mihoshi looked at him with surprise through her tears. "It is you who has given a gift tonight and who is owed thanks. A gift to the men whose lives have been changed. You are correct that this gift was prepared by the One who is greater than any samurai or kyudoka or Delemnite."

Rei spoke softly, "You followed your calling, and we followed ours. We have each walked the path set before us. Besides, we had to get off the *New Day* to escape Polly's incessant nagging that we 'Do something!'"

"But his cloak?" Mel asked in puzzlement. "It was magnetically shielded. Even Vulgladius couldn't pierce it."

"Not all blades and arrowheads are created equal. I *told* you that these were special weapons."

"Non-magnetic steel, crafted hundreds of years ago?" Mel asked in incredulity.

"One of many unique qualities that Musashi and Nasu-no-Yoichi were able to instill in their weapons," Rei answered with a secretive smile.

"Mel-san," Mihoshi said softly while wiping away her tears, "let us make haste and bring this great news to Polly and Garth."

Mel nodded and stood to his feet, finding that his strength was beginning to return. He sheathed Vulgladius and walked to the edge of the peninsula, where he peered over the cliff in search of Jora's body. Below he saw only tumultuous water and waves bursting against the coastal rocks.

Mel turned and walked to where Jora's sword had fallen to the ground and now lay dormant. "You never know when you'll need another one of these," he said, tucking the sword into his shoulder straps alongside Vulgladius.

Suddenly, gunshots rang out from fifty meters away on the coastal road. The three young people instinctively ducked and looked toward the sounds. The entire party of men from Panama City was mounted and riding back along the road toward home, some waving their hats in celebration and others firing their rifles and pistols into the air. The men looked in Mel's direction with smiles and grateful nods until they disappeared down the road. Fred lingered longer than the others, keeping his agitated horse as still as possible as he looked toward Mel and held his hand in the air in thanks. As Mel returned his gesture, he saw that Fred was leading another horse. Draped over its saddle, and held tightly in place by a tarpaulin, was a body. Mel knew that it was Joe, who had died earlier that night. The gift had come at a price. Tempted to dwell on whether the cost could have been avoided, Mel was suddenly reminded of Mihoshi's words aboard the *Musashi* weeks before. *Many lives have been lost, and many will be saved.*

Fred turned away and was the last man to disappear around the bend in the road.

As the three friends walked back toward the cove where the boat was anchored, the morning sun crested the hills, and a new day dawned.

CHAPTER 35

THE JOURNEY HOME

The five friends were reunited aboard the boat in a flurry of hugs and tears and began a peaceful voyage north. The wind carried them quickly away from the tropical coastline to where the *New Day* could dive into deep water. Mel set Point Conception on the California coast as their destination, far enough from their first stop at Cayucos to allow for an inconspicuous, above-water arrival. The boat submerged, and they were underway.

For a week, the friends intermittently slept for long periods, visited, and took the cabin lift down to care for the horses, who were often asleep in their padded slings for days at a time.

Polly and Garth plied Mel with questions about what had happened at Sobrante's Point, but other than recounting the basic course of events, he kept what he had learned to himself. He was astonished by the revelation that his mother might still be alive and was haunted by the thought of her living in torment.

They finally surfaced at Point Conception at an early morning hour and began making their way up the final stretch of coastline. As the friends gathered on the deck to fish and enjoy the fresh air, Mel sat near the prow and slumped into a depressed mood. He avoided conversation and simply stared ahead, lost in thought.

After two hours, Mihoshi quietly came and sat next to him. "You are almost home," she said.

He found it comforting to sit next to someone who cared. After a moment, he realized that she was not going to continue speaking, though he knew that she never started a conversation without a goal in mind. "Home," he replied simply, weighing the meaning of the word.

"Perhaps your father has returned."

Mel felt encouraged by that hopeful thought but feared disappointment. "I don't know where I belong, Mihoshi," he admitted, finally finding the courage to share his emotions. "The more I learn about my past, the more I fear what I have yet to discover. I was born on an island I can barely remember and tutored by a man who betrayed me and hurt everyone I ever loved."

Mihoshi reflected for a moment. "Everyone?"

Mel caught himself and shook his head to clear his mind. "No, not everyone. He didn't hurt you... guys," he finished awkwardly.

"There's something else, isn't there?" she asked with pleading eyes, her hand touching his.

He looked at her vulnerable, sensitive expression. "I can't talk about it. It's too... confusing."

"Something was told to you on that peninsula in Panama. Something that you pray is true, and yet fear that it is."

Mel glanced around as if looking for someone who was feeding Mihoshi information. He wondered how much of the conversation between Jora and himself she had overheard. "Have I been talking in my sleep?"

"No more than usual."

"About what happened on the peninsula?"

"I know only what you have already mentioned," she answered with respect. "I do not try to overhear or learn secrets, and I refuse to listen to gossip. I believe that personal matters should only be shared by permission," she said and turned her face away.

"Or when you persist with questions?" Mel asked and immediately regretted his impertinence.

Mihoshi did not respond. And after a long moment of silence, she rose to leave. Mel put his hand on her red silk sleeve. She stopped and looked at him through misty eyes.

"I'm sorry, Mihoshi, for my rudeness," Mel said at last. "Jora told me that my mother might still be alive."

Mihoshi's eyebrows lifted, and she again sat. "This should be good news."

"It would be more so if it weren't for the kind of life that he sold her into."

"Her life as described by one who hated you? One who was trying to kill you?"

"Yes."

"And you are afraid to believe it?"

"I could not bear to think of her being a slave to some warlord in Africa."

"She is a child of Delemni?" Mihoshi asked.

"Well, I'm not sure. My father didn't talk much about her lineage, only about his love for her and her love for me."

Mihoshi thought for a moment and then handed Mel a small wooden puzzle that she had been holding. It was a set of five interconnected wooden rings.

"What's this?"

"A Matsumoto Maze."

"And what do I do with it?"

"Solve the puzzle."

"Why?"

She looked at him expectantly.

He carefully examined and shifted the assortment of interconnected circles and, within minutes, held them up, each ring separated from the others. "Now what?"

Mihoshi had tears in her eyes. "During the time that we were with him, my father could not solve it. He never gave up, and when we return, he will try again."

Mel related to Mihoshi's compassion for her father. He gently and quickly reconstructed the puzzle and handed it back. "What does it mean?" he asked, sensing more behind her words.

Mihoshi kneeled, took Mel's hands, and looked firmly into his eyes. "If a puzzle that takes many years to solve can be unwound by you within minutes, why would you think that your mother would remain anyone's slave for long?" Mihoshi stood and walked to the others, who were fishing off the stern.

Mel smiled and joined them just as Polly hooked a large fish.

* * *

An hour later, they sighted Polly's hometown of Cayucos and Rei directed the boat toward the town's small harbor. It was decided that Polly and Garth would go ashore and visit Polly's aunt and uncle while the others would stay on board. As soon as the boat was moored, Polly and Garth jumped off and ran several blocks to her uncle's house.

Polly spotted her auntie Rose in the backyard, beating the dust out of rugs draped over a clothesline. "Looks like they'll domesticate the old squaw out of you yet!" Polly said jovially to her aunt.

Rose turned and saw Polly. She let out a loud cry as she ran and hugged her niece. "No one's ever gonna tame this old squaw, youngin'. Welcome home! What have you been doin' for the last couple of months? We 'bout gave you up for dead!"

At that moment, Garth appeared around the corner of the house and stopped next to Polly, his face pale with nervousness. He took off his hat and held it in his left hand while extending his right for a handshake. "Howdy, ma'am. You must be Rose."

Rose shook his hand and then looked at Polly. "What have we brought home?" she asked in mock disapproval.

Polly blushed. "Aw, Rose, it ain't what you think. This is Garth. He's a good friend of mine. We've been spending a lot of time traveling with a group of friends for these past two months or so, and..." She paused, noticing a grin on her aunt's face. "Well, you had to be there to understand."

Rose's eyes scanned the large young man and winked. "The older ya get, the more ya understand without havin' to be there."

Garth flushed red in embarrassment and fidgeted with his hat.

"Oh my! I'm sorry, Polly," Rose continued. "I forgot my manners. Would you two like to come in and get a bite to eat?"

Garth perked up. "Yes'um, I'm starved!" he answered eagerly.

The two women entered the house, followed by Garth, who ducked his head as he passed through the low doorframe.

They found Polly's uncle Cheveyo inside and received another warm welcome. Polly and Garth talked with Rose and Cheveyo for the rest of the day about their adventures, leaving out any mention of floating wagons, flaming swords, or libraries under the ocean. When dusk began to fall, Polly and Garth reluctantly informed their hosts that their friends were waiting for them at the harbor to continue their travels north. They said their goodbyes and made their way back toward the *New Day*.

Rose and Cheveyo stood on their front porch and watched the two young people disappear into the town. "How long do ya think she'll be gone this time?" Rose asked her husband.

"As long as it takes."

"Takes for what?"

"Takes for her to do what's she's got to do. Travelin', settlin' down someplace, who knows? She'll send word, I reckon."

"How long is it gonna take you to fix our roof?" Rose asked, punching him in the arm.

He laughed, walked to the end of the porch, and picked up a ladder. "As long as it takes."

* * *

Early the next morning, the *New Day* arrived at the South Fork harbor, where Mel was informed of a private pier that Armando Lucia had built a kilometer further up the coast to facilitate the shipment of horses and supplies closer to his hacienda.

Rei steered the vessel to the new destination, and Mel sprang to the pier and secured the boat. "The landlord of this ranch will be eager to see Campitor and Candeo. This place used to be their home," he explained to Polly, Rei, and Mihoshi. He leaped back onto the boat, and he and the others carefully brought the horses up from the hold and walked them to the shore.

Campitor and Candeo raised their heads, caught the familiar scents of the hacienda, and stirred with excitement. Mel put a hand on each of their necks and then took their halters and led them and the others to the old Mission-style gate of the hacienda. He pulled on a lever that rang a bell, announcing their arrival.

Armando opened the gate and flung his arms wide in a warm welcome. "Bienvenidos, señores, y señoritas! Mi casa es su casa."

Mel smiled and nodded in thanks and turned to his friends. "Everyone, allow me to introduce Señor Armando Lucia, one of my father's *oldest* friends." He turned to Armando, and they exchanged knowing grins. "Señor Lucia, you know Garth. Please meet Polly Logan, Meiji Rei, and Meiji Mihoshi."

Armando slapped Garth on the back and then bowed politely to the newcomers, a gesture that they returned in kind. "It is always a pleasure to meet new friends of the Uri family."

Polly followed her bow with a curtsy. "It's good to meet you too, Señor Lucia. As a former librarian I think I've fallen in with just the right gang," she said.

Armando laughed. "Yes, I think you will like the work, Miss Logan," he said warmly.

"The honor is ours, Señor Lucia," Rei said in turn. "My sister and I look forward to assisting the Uri family for many years to come."

Armando smiled. He recognized the familiar attire and bearing that bespoke Rei and Mihoshi's heritage, and his expression filled with somber respect. "I feared I would never see another samurai after they were officially disbanded forty years ago. I have fought beside them and have never seen their equal."

Rei's eyes filled with bittersweet tears and his mouth quivered as he fought to maintain his composure. "Should you ever wish to speak of these warriors and share accounts of these battles, my sister and I would treasure hearing of them."

Armando nodded and bowed again, this time in the manner of the samurai.

Armando wrapped an arm around Mel's shoulder and continued in Spanish, "I have been anticipating your return. I see that you have been greatly blessed with exceptional companions. Did everything go well?"

Mel relaxed in the presence of this man who shared an incomprehensibly vast history with his family and who had been a true friend as he and Garth had begun the journey. "Yes, but not without our share of trouble," Mel replied, also in Spanish.

"Is that not the way of life? Great goals often take great effort. You are welcome to rest here as long as you wish," Armando said as he turned his attention to Campitor and Candeo, "though I do not think it is rest that they seek." The horses bowed their heads in respect to their former keeper as he patted their necks.

"That is a gracious offer, though I'm afraid we must keep moving," Mel explained reluctantly.

Armando's face fell. "Will you stay for lunch and give them some time to run?"

Mel nodded.

"Then we shall not keep them any longer from their favorite pastures!" Armando declared enthusiastically. He signaled to two stable hands, who hurried forward and led the horses around the back of the house.

"Have you had any word from my father recently?" Mel asked as casually as he could manage.

"Not for many months, but he may still be traveling, and he does not always return home from the south. He will be most proud to hear of his son's success."

Garth sighed. "Sayin' anythin' 'bout eatin' in all that Spanish?"

Armando laughed.

Mel smiled at his giant, perpetually hungry friend. "Yes, we're staying for lunch."

Armando's wife, Consuelo, and his four beautiful daughters

emerged from the hacienda and greeted Mel and his friends with cries of joy and a frenzy of hugs. They ushered their guests toward the house.

"You know, I didn't do this huggin' thang growin' up," Garth explained to Mel, "but I guess I could get used ta it."

Polly cast a scornful eye at Garth as he allowed himself to be escorted arm in arm into the house by two of Armando's lovely daughters. Rei appeared beside her and presented his arm, which she gladly took and confidently followed the others into the house.

* * *

Everyone took a seat in the Lucia family's expansive living room, which had a dark-stained wood ceiling with three wrought-iron chandeliers and white stucco walls with arched-top windows looking out over the vast horse stables. Armando stepped to the front of the room and addressed them in English. "The horses look wonderful. Was anyone in particular responsible for the care of these marvels of nature?"

"Garth and Mihoshi took care of them for the most part, sir," Polly explained. "Except for the couple weeks that we—ow!" she cried as Mel gently and subtly kicked her shin. She caught his gaze and then restarted. "Garth and Mihoshi were, sir."

Armando turned to Garth and Mihoshi. "Anyone who can care for such prized animals would be more than welcome to live with us here and help care for our horses and would, of course, receive generous compensation. Consider it an open invitation."

Mihoshi nodded respectfully. Garth stared, awestruck at this fortunate turn of events.

Armando saw Garth's shocked expression and felt a pang of compassion. "Ah, there is something I must do!" He stepped behind Garth's chair and rested his hands on the brute's shoulders. "I have long known of the Malingo family of Cooperton." Garth swallowed hard and tensed in his chair. Armando continued, "Your surname means 'of ill will,' but I do not believe that it suits you. So, allow me to suggest a new name. I, at least, will now address you as Garth Embellecedor, 'one who makes another beautiful or hand-some.'" Armando returned to the front of the room.

Garth did not know what to say or feel. He had never been praised by his father. The closest he had ever come to receiving a compliment had been on the occasions when his father had re-frained from hitting him as a reward for a hard day's work. Garth sat stunned by Armando's magnanimous gesture.

Polly noticed the way that Armando's daughters beamed at Garth's newfound favor. "Señor Lucia, sir, that is very generous of you. The five of us have some *really* important things to do still, which I'm sure Garth and Mihoshi will want to be a part of."

Garth finally spoke. "Thank you, sir, fer your kind words. I'd be honored to help out and learn all 'bout smithin' and horses. We's gonna keep movin' for now, but I'll think on it, fer sure."

"Of course. It is entirely up to you." Armando glanced around at the rest of the group. "You are all welcome any time to stay at our hacienda for as long as you wish. As for today, we will be having lunch, and then we will set you off in a manner befitting our most esteemed guests."

* * *

Polly and Mihoshi joined Consuelo and her daughters as they pre-pared the meal. Garth and Rei ventured out to explore the grounds of the ranch. Armando walked with Mel to the back pasture, where Campitor and Candeo were running freely, nudging playfully, and rearing in celebration of their spacious surroundings.

Mel noticed a small group of horses that he had not seen during his first visit. "It looks like you have four new horses, beautiful ones at that."

Armando led him to the group and stroked one's muzzle. "These, my young friend, are prized Arabian horses. I have seen none finer. They have just arrived from the nation of Mauritania."

The word "Mauritania" hit Mel like a hammer. His thoughts and feelings scattered in a hundred directions, and he barely heard Armando as he continued speaking.

"They are not nearly as strong or as fast as your Campitor and Mons Candeo," Armando continued, "but you and your friends will find that their stamina is second to none."

Mel nearly missed this last statement. "What did you say?"

Armando smiled with the joy of one who is unveiling a wonderful surprise. "These magnificent horses are a gift to you from an anonymous donor. Come and see the notes I received with them." They stepped in through a side door of the house, and Armando pulled two letters from a desk, handing one to Mel. "You can imagine my surprise when they arrived with just these two notes and a year's worth of boarding fees. One was addressed to me and the other to you. My note simply instructed me to care for them until you came to claim them. And here you are, just as expected! Again, you will be taking some of the world's finest horses away from me," he said with a wink.

Mel turned the folded piece of paper over and saw his name written in unfamiliar handwriting. He lifted the note to his nose and sniffed. His heart froze.

He unfolded the note, which contained only two lines:

> *These are the Best because their spirits are unbroken*
> *They always have been and always will be Free*

Mel stained the note with his tears as he continued smelling the faint wisp of jasmine.

* * *

After a lavish lunch, Mel led his friends to the back pasture and introduced them to the new steeds. Now in possession of more horses than they could hope to transport aboard the *New Day*, it was decided that they would continue to Cooperton via wagon and horseback. With the help of Armando and several stablehands, Mel and his companions lifted the wagon onto the pier. The young adventurers transferred their supplies and belongings from the *New Day* to the bed of the wagon, and Mel again sealed Vulgladius in its case and secured it in the compartment where he had first discovered it. He arranged with Armando for the boat to be kept at a hidden mooring in a cave near the hacienda.

It was decided that Mel and Garth would ride in the wagon, while Polly, Rei, and Mihoshi would each take one of the Arabian horses, and Rei would lead the fourth by its halter.

They spent two hours with their new horses and were amazed at how compliant such wild-looking steeds could be. Armando watched as the young people saddled and rode their new mounts. "When they first arrived, I saw that these horses had been extremely well trained by someone with a strong and loving hand," he explained. "Better mounts you will never find."

Mihoshi rode towards Mel, who sat astride Campitor. "Who do we have to thank for these gifts, Mel-san?"

"Someone who knows how to solve puzzles." He handed her the note and watched as her face filled with poignant emotion.

"And who is the fourth horse for?" Mihoshi managed as she handed the note back and wiped her tears with a silk handkerchief.

"Our company is not yet complete," Mel said with a sly smile. "I hope to introduce all of you to her after we get to Cooperton."

Mihoshi's face went blank, and she sat strangely still in her saddle for a moment. "I wish that you had told me of 'her' before. I look forward to making this new acquaintance," she said politely and then urged her horse across the pasture for further exercises. Mel watched her with a puzzled expression while placing the note back in his pocket. He flicked Campitor's reigns and took him over a series of jumps.

In the mid-afternoon, they all changed into new clothes. Rei and Mihoshi donned the royal silk robes that they had retrieved from the Wafuku Chest, and Mel, Garth, and Polly were generously arrayed in the finest Spanish apparel Armando and Consuelo could provide. They expressed their indebted thanks to Armando and bid him and his family farewell, waving till they were out of sight along the coast road. They urged their horses into a canter, hoping to reach the Uri farm before sunset.

* * *

As they neared Cooperton, they saw Bobby Simcox throwing dirt clods at the butcher's hogs. The mischief-maker looked at the passing entourage, dressed in their shiny silk capes and elaborate Spanish clothing, and stared in incomprehension.

The townspeople on the road did not recognize Mel or Garth. Some whispered that the five strangers were a foreign delegation from Sacramento, in town to explore the beauty of the California coast. With such fine horses, they had to be rich. They were so well-dressed! And who were the two Asians in the group? With silk clothes like that, they had to be royalty or close to it.

They reached a point where the road divided along two routes. One way followed the coast, and the other turned inland toward the center of town. Without hesitation, Mel conducted the wagon down the inland road. Garth tilted his head with confusion. "The other road goes right to yer farm. We need somethin' from town?"

Mel smiled. "I want to see if someone in town is home."

"Dunno who yer meanin', but there's a man in town I sure hope ain't home."

* * *

They passed the shack that had been Garth's home and saw his dad lying on the porch swing, dead drunk. His old bloodhound looked at them and then drooped his floppy ears and fell back asleep. Garth stared straight ahead as though he did not recognize the house.

Continuing toward town, Mel slowed their pace as they approached the Thurman farm. He slumped in his seat, seeing that, once again, the family's two wagons were not there. Mari's flower garden appeared well-tended, but the homestead was motionless and quiet. Mel flicked the reins, and the horses resumed their previous pace. Garth glanced over at his crestfallen friend with the knowing grin of someone who had just figured out a great secret. Mel sighed.

Minutes later, the cavalcade of young travelers trotted regally through the center of town, causing every eye to turn and stare at the strange, silent parade. Only one pair of eyes opened joyfully as Mel approached. He caught Mari's gaze and returned her smile. She blushed, and both of their smiles stayed long after they had passed from each other's view.

They brought their horses to a halt at the front gate of the Uri farm, where Mel had lived for eight of his sixteen years. Everything looked exactly as Mel remembered it from the moment of his departure on his quest. There was no indication that anyone was home. Mel hesitated, his mind flooded by memories of so many meetings and partings at that very spot. After a moment, he smiled gently and reached out and unlatched the gate.

The dirt of the path looked like it had been disturbed recently, with several sets of footprints going back and forth from the road. Mel wondered if either his father or Oscar, or both, were home. His chest tightened with anxiety as he and the others stopped in front of the porch steps and dismounted and hitched the horses to the railing.

Mel led Polly, Rei, and Mihoshi forward while Garth stayed to watch the horses. As Mel climbed the steps, the third step creaked, as it always had. It reminded him of how he had been able to tell who was coming home by the sound of the creak. His father's step had been quick and purposeful, Oscar's had been longer and louder, while Jora had been annoyed by the sound and had often skipped the third step.

Mel found it strange that he was finally returning home yet felt like an intruder on his own family's property. Flushed red with embarrassment, he knocked on the front door. Polly looked at him sideways with a perplexed expression. When no one answered, Mel opened the door slowly, calling out, "Hello? Dad? Oscar? Anyone home?"

He led the others into the house. Not one piece of furniture had been moved, and not one book was out of place. It was as if the house had been frozen in time since the day he had set off on his adventure. He turned and looked at his friends and was struck again by how much had transpired since that departure.

Looking carefully through each of the bedrooms, he could not tell for sure if anyone was currently living there. The floors had been swept, and the windows had been washed, but otherwise, there was no sign of recent habitation.

Mel stepped back out the front door and suggested that Garth take the horses to the nearby fenced-in pasture where they could graze and run. He stepped back inside and invited the three others to take seats in the living room.

"Perhaps your father or Oscar was in town and did not see us?" Rei suggested.

"Or they could've gone up the coast for supplies," Polly offered with a shrug.

After several minutes of speculation, Mel sank back in his chair with weariness. Garth stepped in through the front door, a questioning expression on his face. Mel shook his head.

Garth rubbed his belly. "Well, if there ain't nobody here, there ain't gonna be nothin' 'cept some canned food, I reckon. I don't know 'bout y'all, but I'm thinkin' 'bout gettin' together an ol' fashion fish fry. If you got any poles 'round here, or just some line an' hooks, I'm thinkin' 'a scroungin' up some bait 'n shimmyin' on down to the water ta catch some rock cod or sumpen."

Mel had a sudden thought and sprang to his feet. "Fish! Of

course! Why didn't I think of that?"

Garth rubbed his hands together and smiled. "Now we're talkin'! Sounds like I got least one helper."

To their surprise, Mel darted out of the room and into the hall closet and did not reappear. They looked at each other with quizzical expressions and then hurried after him. They caught up to him just as he opened the Caeli entrance at the back of the closet. He ushered the others inside and then followed, closing the door behind them. He led them along the passage and down the stairwell. As they made their way down through the Caeli, they passed dozens of doors, each bearing a different symbol.

Finally, they came to the bottom level and approached a huge doorway. Mel stopped and turned to his companions. "This room can be a little dizzying at first. If you lose your balance, just look at the floor, or hold onto someone."

His heart pounding in anticipation, Mel opened the door, and they walked slowly into the expansive room. Mel's friends looked in awe through the massive transparent dome at the underwater world, lit by the many hues of the sunset. The light streamed in through a kelp forest, casting odd shadows. The wiggling orb of the sun was narrowly visible through the marine vegetation and the dark, turquoise water. The young people locked arms and subconsciously swayed back and forth with the rhythmic movement of the sea.

At the far end of the room, silhouetted among the shadows, Mel saw the figure of a tall, slender man. He turned at the sound of the newcomers' footsteps. "Perfect!" a voice rang out. "Mel! Come here. There's something I want to show you!"

EPILOGUE

The air was warm and humid. Dragonflies danced as a soft breeze stirred the lazy willows bordering the Thurman family farm.

Mel's hands shook with the jitters as he neared the farmhouse. On his back was a knapsack full of a picnic basket and a blanket. Approaching the front yard, he stepped onto the Thurman's cobblestone entry path and heard a beautiful, hummed melody, which made him smile.

He found Mari sitting in her small, flower-enshrouded garden with her back towards the road, happily humming and busily making herself a crown from a variety of flowers. He let himself through the gate, closing it firmly to elicit the sound of the small bells that hung on its inner side.

"Hey, Mel," she said without turning to look. "I was hoping you'd visit." She continued her melody, a smile tugging at the corners of her mouth.

Mel flushed red. "How did you know it was me?"

Mari laughed and turned towards him. "You're the only one who knows the trick with that gate's latch and can shut it on the first try." She finished the crown of flowers and placed it on her head. She straightened it and tried to look up at the portion above her eyes. "What do you think of this one? I wanted to use something more than the ones I make with daisies."

"This one is beautiful," Mel said, staring at her.

She looked at him searchingly, not sure if he meant what she thought he meant.

Mel felt suddenly vulnerable. "I, um, ah...," he stuttered and then took a deep breath. "I was wondering if you would like to go to the cliff and have a little picnic? I know it's been a while since we spent any time together. There's... there's something I want to talk to you about." He suppressed a grimace, expecting her to laugh him all the way off the Thurman farm.

She jumped up and brushed pieces of flowers off her dress. "I thought you'd never ask. Yes, I will go with you on this perfectly wonderful day for a picnic. We can talk about what's on your mind," she said knowingly and approvingly, "and I hope you'll share a few stories of what you've been up to these past months."

Mel smiled as she said 'yes,' then stared in intimidation at the thought of recounting his journey. He suddenly felt again the wonder and terror of all that he had experienced. Finally, he realized he should say something. "I've certainly had a few memorable moments since I last saw you. I look forward to telling you all the details, in time."

They turned and left the garden and walked side by side, occasionally brushing against each other as the dirt road dipped. Choosing to save mentions of lost civilizations and enemies and danger for later in their conversation, Mel began by describing his journey as one that his father had sent him on to further his studies and to reconnect with their old home in Martinique. For the moment, he highlighted the friends he had made and the places he had visited.

They left the road and followed a trail that led to the top of a cliff. Mel took the blanket from his knapsack and spread it out. They both sat and looked out over the Cooperton Valley and the Pacific Ocean beyond.

"I just love this place!" Mari said as she waved two dandelion clusters in sweeping motions until all the seeds were dispersed. "I am starving. What did you bring?"

"Well," Mel said while withdrawing the picnic basket from his knapsack, "Oscar made fried chicken. And we have some potato salad and a jar of fresh lemonade."

Mari watched excitedly as Mel opened the picnic basket and brought out two paper-wrapped ceramic dishes and a tall glass jar with a metal lid. He paused with his hand on the basket, seemingly lost in thought, and then brought out one last item, a tightly wrapped ceramic bowl. "And lastly, a slice of Brumble Berry Serendipity," he said as he presented the bowl to her. "I've already had my portion, and I want this one to be for you."

"Oh," Mari intoned with intrigue as she unwrapped the paper. "It's a pie!"

"Yes, it's a very special pie! But before you eat any of it, I need to explain some things."

Mari placed the pie beside the other items and leaned back, folding her arms and looking at him with amused skepticism. "What, pray tell, is necessary to say about a piece of pie?"

Mel's expression shifted to a good-natured, teasing grin. "For one thing, it's dessert, so you should eat it last."

"Uh-huh, very funny," Mari said, unconvinced. "And?"

"You might be surprised," Mel said nervously, his face going blank as he stared off at nothing. He knew that the next few minutes would be the most formative moment of their relationship and that what he was going to share had the potential to irreparably separate them. He chose to take courage and to trust in the honesty that Mari deserved from him.

He considered where to start. "It'll get into a lot more of the details of my journey. It has something to do with where I come from and who I really am. After I tell you, I promise we'll talk about what I've got on my mind."

"All right, have it your way," Mari said with a knowing smile. "If you're not careful, I'm going to nickname you Mysterious Mel."

Mel laughed. A suspiciously bright and concentrated swarm of dragonflies danced above their heads as he began to tell the tale of an ancient island nation that sank into the sea.

CHARACTERS
(IN ORDER OF APPEARANCE)

Melvin Uri: (Mel) (Melek 'al Uri) (Melamuri) A Vysard apprentice

Telemai Uri: (Telly) The father of Mel

Oscar Bottoms: A medical doctor and old friend of Telemai

Jora Blacksworth: Mel's tutor

Jed Malingo: The town drunk and father of Garth

Marigold Thurman: (Mari) A young girl who befriends Mel

Billy & Bobby Simcox: Troublemaking twin brothers

Garth Malingo: The town bully and son of Jed

Bob: (Mons Candeo—Latin—Mountain Jewel) (MJ) (Candi) A female horse who helps Mel on his journey

Armando Lucia: A ranch owner and old friend of Telemai

Campitor: (Latin—Warhorse) (Campi) A fierce male horse who helps Mel on his journey

Polly Logan: Librarian with a fiery personality

Jorge Ascensión: Captain of the ARA *Patagonia*

Neco: One of the "Strangers" who seeks the knowledge in the Caeli

Meiji Rei: (Rei) Samurai and son of sword maker Meiji Chiba

Meiji Mihoshi: (Mihoshi) Kyūdōka and daughter of Meiji Chiba

The Mysenri: Tiny fairy-like people who live discreetly throughout the world

Gwyneth: Tribal leader of the North & Central American Mysenri

Emberas: A tribe of natives who help Mel on his journey

Brother Josh: A monk and friend of the Emberas

Kenthar: Master chef and son of Thar of Uri

Tothar: Keeper of the Toleth Mar archives and son of Thar of Uri

Fred: A man helped by Mel

422

GLOSSARY

Caeli (Pronounced: KAI-lee): Latin—skies, heavens, the vault of heaven
A library containing a broad range of historical records, including the ancient documents of Delemni

Delemni: A destroyed and sunken island chain off the coast of Great Britain, now known as Atlantis

Gatekeeper: The leader and trainer of the Vysards

Kendo: Kendo (剣道 kendō, lit. "sword way," "sword path," or "Way of the Sword") is a traditional Japanese martial art that descended from swordsmanship (kenjutsu) and uses bamboo swords (shinai) and protective armor (bōgu)

Kyudo: Kyūdō (弓道) is the Japanese martial art of archery. Experts in kyūdō are referred to as kyūdōka (弓道). Kyūdō is based on kyū-jutsu ("art of archery"), which originated with the samurai class of feudal Japan

The *New Day*: (*Dag Nia*) The boat that Telly used to escape from Martinique with his son and two friends

S.M.R.: Sonic-Magnetic-Resonance: A force that allows magnetic sources to interact with each other for multiple uses

SAZO: Latin Acronym: Saevio Arma Zelus Oppugno—The Unquenchable War Flame — A weapon that uses magnetic pulses and liquid hydrogen orbs to project temporary force fields or to achieve a variety of effects against an enemy

Strangers: Said to inhabit the land of "Xenos," these impetuous survivors of the destruction of Delemni are the enemies of the Vysards

Uri: An island in the Delemni chain where Mel's ancestors dwelt

Vulgladius: A two-edged sword composed of a magnetic force field with a burning plasmatic core

Vysard: A person who undergoes training and a series of tests and becomes a practitioner and steward of the sciences of Delemni

Xenos: The "homeland" of the enemies of the Vysards—a metaphor for spiritual and ideological estrangement

THE PIACULUM
(THE SACRIFICE)

THE ODYSSEY OF MELAMURI: BOOK TWO

PROLOGUE

16th of December, 1707

The soft white crown of Mount Fuji glimmered in the moonlight like a diamond setting. Though mystically peaceful on the surface, the mountain was a beehive of activity within.

Hundreds of workers bustled about in hidden caverns, digging, hauling, hustling to the orders barked at them by their taskmasters. Dim light reflected off the cavern walls from the lake of lava stirring beneath them. The masters were rushed in their pursuit, driving the workers to exhaustion.

The master Vulcanist reviewed his notes and surveyed the quality of magma being harvested from the depths of the pit. Wearing an anxious frown, he knew their time was running short.

"How much longer until the quota?" he shouted down the pit.

A weak reply echoed back, "At least three hours!"

"Three? The mountain has just one! Faster!" he yelled angrily.

The taskmasters redoubled their efforts. Soon the earth began to rumble with boiling jolts.

The slaves who had been in captivity here for the past two years began to panic. They fled frantically towards the steep path that led out of the center of the mountain. There were too many to stop, and their overseers soon dropped their tools of subjugation and ran with them.

The groan of the mountain swelled as it gathered its strength. A pyroclastic explosion blew out one side of the ice and snow-encrusted cone and vented catastrophic quantities of ash across eastern Japan.

Two months and over five thousand dead later, the mountain finally calmed.

THE DEEP DESERT
Mauritania, 1913

The hot desert winds whirled relentlessly. The team leaders scanned their surroundings with darting, fearful looks. They had heard of Pazuzu, the wind demon of the desert, and did not wish to learn if the rumors were true. It was said that when he appeared, death and destruction always followed.

The burning arms of the sun pushed all those beneath it into the meager and overcrowded shade of scattered shelters.

Sweat streamed down the back of the Berber guide as he led a small caravan of exhausted and ragged slaves to their new post at the open-pit copper mine. At the coast, six days before, the slaves had been unloaded like cattle from a ship, then tied together and hiked at a merciless pace until they reached the mine at Akjoujt.

The slaves had heard of Pazuzu as well and clung tightly to one another. Sixteen at last count, they had lost four during the journey. Arriving now just before sunset, they were thirsty and sunburned. The Akjoujt locals averted their eyes from the haunted stares of the thirteen men and three women. The locals had witnessed such arrivals for many years, and their hearts had become callous to the needs of the endless flow of enslaved laborers.

When they reached the village square, the guide stopped to talk to the mining agent. One of the newly captured slaves crawled to a wall and clung to its shade. Just a few degrees cooler felt like a spring breeze. A robed figure stepped in front of him and reached down, offering a tin cup full of water. Kindness was rare in this part of the world, and since the slave's capture four weeks earlier, he had been so mistreated that he did not trust anyone. He withdrew along the wall though he desperately craved the life-giving liquid.

"Don't be afraid. I won't hurt you," a hooded voice whispered.

The slave reached out and took the cup, which felt inexplicably cold to the touch in the desert heat. He held it to his parched lips and quickly drank the soothing water. He closed his eyes and bowed his head in gratitude.

Just then, he was jerked to his feet and pushed from behind towards a large, distant, tin-clad building.

He glanced around in search of his robed benefactor, but the hooded figure had vanished. He noticed that an impression of the cup remained in the shaded dirt beside the wall.

On the way to the tin building, a gale-force wind rose from the desert. Wagons were toppled. The guide released his caravan's rope, and the slaves, now unbound to each other, dispersed. Both the slaver and the enslaved shielded their eyes from the stinging sandstorm as they fled for shelter. A shed full of mining explosives was set ablaze. A rapid series of detonations obliterated the structure in a billowing fiery plume, leaving a crater in its place. The slaves saw a lone, robed figure approach down the windswept road, who beckoned to them to follow.

Some refused, shaking in fear and covering their eyes. Others looked at each other and stepped into the maelstrom, considering death to be preferable to a lifetime of slavery.

The man who had received the tin cup of water rose from behind a fallen wagon, followed the strange, robed person into the storm, and disappeared.

ABOUT THE AUTHORS

Bruce Muller uses his imagination to explore the places that exist beyond this dimension. Readers will journey into the wild and the wonderful and there discover the inherent truths that define us all. He has worked as a musician, teacher, and college professor. He has studied journalism, world history, and theology. Above all, he loves to meet with imaginary friends and ask, "Where are we going today?"

* * *

Abraham Sherman has one foot each in film and fiction. He is a screenwriter, author, and Mars colonization enthusiast. His interests include biology, gardening, culture commentary, and theology. The imaginative fiction of Edgar Rice Burroughs inspired Abraham to become a writer. At age fifteen, he began an award-winning independent screenplay adaptation of Burroughs' novel *A Princess of Mars*. Abraham writes about stories for the page and screen at The John Carter Files (thejohncarterfiles.com) and on his author page (facebook.com/writerabrahamsherman).

CPSIA information can be obtained
at www.ICGtesting.com
Printed in the USA
BVHW030751091122
651113BV00007B/4